**BEST PRACTICE
PUBLICATIONS**

# The Change
# Champion's Fieldguide

## *Strategies and Tools for Leading*
## *Change in Your Organization*

**Editors**
**Dave Ulrich • Louis Carter**
**Marshall Goldsmith • Jim Bolt**
**Norm Smallwood**

Foreword by Dr. W. Warner Burke

**Published by Best Practice Publications**

Copyright © 2003, Best Practice Publications, LLC
Published by
Best Practice Publications, LLC
New York, New York
Boston, MA
www.bestpracticepublications.com
www.bestpracticeboard.com

ISBN: 0-9740388-0-6

Library of Congress Cataloguing-in-Publication Data

The Change Champion's Fieldguide : strategies and tools for leading
change in your organization / editors David Ulrich. . . [et al.] ;
Foreword by W. Warner Burke
    p.  cm.
  ISBN: 0-9740388-0-6 (pbk.)
  1. Organizational change. 2. Leadership. I. Ulrich, David.
  HD58.8.C4535 2003
658.4′06--dc21                                 2003010088

Significant discounts on volume quantities of Best Practice Publications books are available to practitioners, associations, corporations, and other organizations. For details and discount information, contact the special sales division at specialsales@bestpracticeboard.com.

No patent liability is assumed with respect to the use of the information contained herein. Although every precaution has been taken in the preparation of this book, the publisher and contributors assume no responsibility for errors or omissions. Neither is any liability assumed for damages resulting from the use of information contained herein.

This publication contains the opinions, ideas, and practical advice of its contributors. It is intended to provide informative and practical information on the subject matter of change and organization development.

The contributors and publisher specifically disclaim any responsibility for any liability, loss of risk, personal or otherwise, which is incurred as a consequence, directly or indirectly, of the use and application of any of the contents in this book.

Cover Design by Kelly Gordon of Akins Design.
Interior Design by BookMasters, Inc.

# CONTENTS

# ACKNOWLEDGMENTS

## BEST PRACTICE PUBLICATIONS TEAM

*Louis Carter*, founder and CEO
*Michal Samuel*, research associate

### PRE-PRESS AND DESIGN
*Kristen Butler*, BookMasters, project director
*Kelly Gordon*, graphic designer

### CONSULTANTS
*Warner Burke*, professor, Department of OD and Leadership, Teachers College, Columbia University and author, *Organization Development: A Process of Learning and Changing*

*Phil Harkins,* CEO of Linkage, Inc. and a world renown expert on leadership

*Dr. John Sullivan*, professor of human resources and head of the Human Resource Management Program at San Francisco State University

*David Ulrich*, ranked by *Business Week* as No. 1 management educator and guru

*Norm Smallwood*, co-author of *Results Based Leadership* and *Why the Bottom Line Isn't!*

*Marshall Goldsmith*, ranked by *Forbes* as one of the top five coaches, and by the *Wall Street Journal* as one of the "top ten" management educators

*Bill Hawkins*, consultant, Alliance for Strategic Leadership and contributor to the Organization of the Future.

*Kathleen Dannemiller*, co-founder of Whole-Scale Change

*Daniel Moss Carter*, leading corporate benefits and retirement planning expert

*Jerry Sternin*, founder of applied positive deviance

### SPONSORING ORGANIZATION
The Institute for Management Studies (IMS)
(see page 316 for more information on IMS)

## CONTRIBUTORS
*Kathleen Dannemiller*, co-founder and partner emeritus, Dannemiller, Tyson & Associates (DTA)
*Lorri Johnson*, partner DTA
*Mary Eggers*, partner, DTA
*Marshall Goldsmith*, co-founder, A4SL
*Howard Morgan*, senior consultant, A4SL
*Marc Effron*, global practice leader for Hewitt Associates Leadership Practice
*Jerry Sternin*, visiting scholar, Tufts University
*Erica Glasser*
*Ralph Jacobson*, president and CEO, Synthesis Consulting
*Jim Bolt*, founder and CEO, Executive Development Associates
*Ron Meeks*, CDR International
*Steve Terrell*, president, Aspire Consulting, Inc.
*David Cooperrider*, co-founder, Center for Business as an Agent of World Benefit and Appreciative Inquiry Consulting
*David Bright*, Case Western Reserve University
*George Land*, president and founder, Leadership 2000
*Greg Zlevor*, president, Westwood International
*Lawrence Susskind*, MIT/Harvard, CEO, Consensus Building Institute
*Judith Katz*, executive vice president, The Kaleel Jamison Consulting Group, Inc.
*Steve Barnett*, Cultural Analysis Group, Global Business Network
*Scott Ventrella*, president, Positive Dynamics and Fordham University School of Business
*Bill Hawkins*, senior consultant, A4SL
*Lori Riordan*, conference board/independent consultant
*Jodi Knox*, president, Action Dialogue Associates
*Ryan Mathews*, futurist and CEO, Black Monk Consulting, LLC
*Stu Noble*, founder and president, 3D Learning
*William Rothwell*, professor, Penn State University
*David Ulrich*, founding partner and thought leader, Results Based Leadership
*Norm Smallwood*, founding partner and president, Results Based Leadership
*Richard Lynch*, partner, Results Based Leadership
*Jim Dowling*, partner, Results Based Leadership
*Ivy Ross*, VP of Design and Development, Mattel
*Dave Kuehler*, director of Project Platypus, Mattel
*Larry Peters*, professor, Neely School of Business, Texas Christian University
*Joseph Grenny*, president, VitalSmarts, Inc.
*Deborah Rozman*, president, Quantum Intech, a division of the Institute for HeartMath
*Doc Childre*, founder, Institute of HeartMath
*Dr. John Sullivan*, professor and director, San Francisco State University Human Resources Management Program

# WHO SHOULD READ THIS BOOK?

*Only in growth, reform, and change, paradoxically enough, is true security to be found.*

—Anne Morrow Lindbergh

This fieldguide is for all change champions who are learning about, seeking to, or who are in the midst of leading social or organizational change. It is dedicated to the disenfranchised, the wrongly accused, those who are not receiving the care and understanding they need, those who need to deliver more to their stakeholders or shareholders, those seeking to innovate, those seeking to improve their mergers and/or partnerships with corporations or individual contributors, and all those who seek truth and integrity in all that they do.

If you are reading this book, you may be a leader, practitioner, student, or consultant within any size of organization, small to large. You most likely perform, or are learning to implement, a performance management initiative, merger, or acquisition, leadership development program, change management program, innovation and product development program, recruitment and retention, organization development, organizational learning, customer service enhancement initiative, ethics and integrity program, diversity intervention, sales development initiative, or any other program that enhances the success of your organization and helps you and your organization to meet your strategic goals and objectives.

Within a corporation, association, or organization, you should read this book if you are the chief executive officer, chief learning officer, chief information officer, chief knowledge officer, or chief operating officer. Within other parts of the organization, you should read this book if you are the vice president or director of learning and development, organizational learning, performance management, training and development, diversity, or human resources. You should also read this book if you are a line manager, head of customer service, director of a division, or anyone throughout any ranks of your organization. As long as you are someone who is willing to see and do something about your vision—as a champion of change.

Whether you are a student of change, trainer, facilitator, practitioner, lawyer, doctor, religious leader, public defender, or consultant from a consultancy or association, you will find hope in this book during the most challenging times.

As you champion change, you will most likely take on one or more of the following "change agent roles," that Fritz Steele describes in his book, *Consulting for Organizational Change*[1] that deserve mention.

*Student*–The change champion's primary role is to "learn." Learning or being a "student" can be an uncomfortable position for someone cast in the role of "expert."

*Teacher*–A major function of the change agent is teaching communication and other social/organizational and behavioral science theories and practical applications to clients who might not understand group dynamics and processes.

*Detective*–The change champion must engage in a detection or assessment process in which he or she gathers data.

*Barbarian*–One of the most challenging roles of the change champion is a violator of dysfunctional (and often unspoken) rules and norms of the group. For example, many groups develop taboos about openly discussing such issues as salaries and inadequate performance. As a Barbarian, you may need to violate many group rules.

*Clock*–There may be times when your most important role is that of a timekeeper or clock for the client system to watch. Your presence in the system at different time periods seems to initiate the client's thinking about the actions to which they have agreed. Many people might think of this role as project manager—or others might view this role within training and facilitation.

*Talisman*–A talisman is a good luck charm or symbol of success. Your presence may be the factor of legitimacy and security. Your presence allows clients to feel a comfort level when experimenting in areas they might not act without your support.

*Advocate*–This role is one of a "subjective value clarifier," in the system rather than an "objective observer." There are certain fundamental values and relationships inherent in the practice of championing change. Values such as respect for the individual, collaboration, and non-exploitive relationships are espoused. The change champion's values are not hidden; instead they are openly and honestly advocated in order to be effective in creating a functional system.

---

[1]Steele, Fritz. Consulting for Organizational Change. Boston: University of Massachusetts Press, 1981.

*Ritual Pig*–There might be some circumstances when the primary function of the change champion is to serve as a threat that needs to be "killed off." Being killed off might take the form of being fired, challenged, or resisted in order for the system to develop enough sense of solidarity and strength to be able to begin difficult changes. In this circumstance the change champion acts as a "container" for the group's shock, anger, denial, or blame. This phenomenon is very much like the process of "killing the messenger." Being aware that you might be in this role is half the battle—and can enable you to be more effective in championing change. View this role as an opportunity for organizational learning.

# ABOUT THIS BOOK

The purpose of this fieldguide is to provide you with all of the necessary elements to implement a best practice change or leadership development initiative within your organization or social system. Contributors in this book are widely recognized as among the best in organization change and leadership development. They provide invaluable lessons in succeeding during crisis or growth modes and economies. As change champions, they share many similar attributes including openness to learning and collaboration, humility, innovation and creativity, integrity, a high regard for people's needs and perspectives, and a passion for change.

Within the forthcoming chapters, you will learn:

- Key elements of leading successful and results-driven change
- Tools, models, instruments, and strategies for leading change
- Trends and research on innovation, change, and leadership
- Critical success factors *and* critical failure factors
- How to design, implement, and evaluate change and leadership initiatives

The reference to a circle as well as the non-linear elements within the circle at the top of each page and the circular metaphor on the cover design refers back to such religious theories found in many texts including the Kabbalah, New Testament, Old Testament, Koran, Dhammapada, Bhagavad Gita, and Tao Te Ching as well as other scientific theories such as Newton's Laws of Physics and Peter Senge and the Society for Organizational Learning's popularization of systems thinking. The graphical elements describe how when you exhibit force on a system, there will be a reaction and consequence of your action. Another way of understanding this circular theory is that you only get what you give—and you must learn to study the reactions and consequences of each action to completely understand how and where to lead change.

# HOW TO USE THIS BOOK

## APPLICATIONS ON THE JOB

This fieldguide contains successful tools, instruments, case studies, and models that you can immediately apply for initiating and leading change within your organization. Think of yourself as an artist and this book as your palate; you have many best practices to choose from to implement a highly successful and results-driven initiative. Most of the elements in this book may be modified to fit your organization and its stakeholders' unique needs.

## TAKING FULL ADVANTAGE OF THIS BOOK

1. Read over the summary section to get a feel for the specific elements within each chapter. Ask yourself the specific questions outlined in the introduction of this book including:
   - What is my organizational culture and context?
   - What kind of organizational system am I leading change within?
   - How can I implement a program that best meets the needs of all stakeholders involved?
   - What do I want to change? Why am I motivated to change this area?

   And lastly consider a question posed by Kathie Dannemiller, "What moves people from *despair* to *hope*?" This will help ground you in the realities of your work and global environment, choose which chapters that are the most helpful for you, and help you move toward your passion to lead change.

2. Once you have determined your specific needs, design your own table of contents of chapters that fit your needs. For example, if you are designing a leadership development intervention, consider the chapters within the fundamentals of change section. These fundamentals might serve exemplary competencies for your program such as Ventrella's ethics and integrity chapter. Next, you might want to examine elements of Dannemiller's Whole Scale Change™ chapter as a way of understanding how to enable organizational, individual, and team trust and shared vision. On this same note, perhaps you should learn from Cooperrider on how to build appreciative capacity in organizations. Then, gain an understanding of winning the approval of your senior managers through Bolt or Rozman's chapter on how to gain the commitment of the top brass in your organization. Rozman and Bolt's approaches to working with the top of the organization and leading change balance each other nicely. Perhaps you might run into a roadblock at that point, and not be able to gain the commitment for which you were hoping. Not everyone is showing up. People are getting angry. If that happens, it is probably time for you to read the last chapter of the book. This chapter prepares you for developing a strong business case for increasing your budget and measuring the results of your program. Or, maybe you should consider the very process of innovation by Land—this might give you some hope about the very process of change and transformation itself. Now, to give you some serious grounding, it is sage advice to begin reading over other chapters outlined by Ulrich, Sullivan, Rothwell, Smallwood, Goldsmith, Susskind, and Lynch. These chapters will provide key information on developing first-rate, highly results-driven leadership programs. Go back to other chapters as you run into roadblocks. I would especially consider reading Rozman, Land, Sullivan, Noble, Susskind, and Ross as you meet these roadblocks. Don't leave anything out, though—there are golden nuggets of wisdom throughout the entire book!

3. Go back and choose specific chapters to read over carefully. Work with your design team or other managers, fellow employees, and/or senior executives whom you chose for your change team. Determine why the elements in the chapter are applicable to your organization's unique system(s) and its culture. What initiatives and change leadership techniques best fit your organization's goals and objectives? Why are some elements working better than others? What is it about your organization's system that is making it challenging or successful to implement these specific elements? Think critically about your stakeholders—as well as how and why the elements within the chapter are working or not working. And, lastly think about your own motivations for change and what is driving you to lead change and why. Knowing why you are leading change will give you the peace of mind and clarity to help lead a clear path for others.

# INTRODUCTION BY THE EDITORS

*David Ulrich, Louis Carter, Norm Smallwood, Jim Bolt, Marshall Goldsmith*

> *Corporations must create an environment where one's true identity and gifts are celebrated. People will rally around what they feel passionate about and what holds meaning for them. Creativity exists in everyone; when it is not surfacing, it is usually being suppressed by judgment. Failure to innovate is often a result of an organization that is paralyzed by fear. It is afraid to let passion out of the bottle.*
>
> —Ivy Ross, SVP of Design and Development,
> Mattel (excerpt taken from Chapter 19)

We have brought you twenty-two chapters of "best practice" or successful practices strategies, ideas, tools, approaches, and cases from some of the most respected authors and practitioners in change management and leadership development today. Because the topic of leadership and change is so broad, the content is divided into three sections:

1. Transformational and Large Scale Change
2. Fundamentals of Leading Change
3. Transformational Leadership and Sustaining Results

In the Foreword, Dr. W. Warner Burke describes the book as a dynamic, non-linear ride. This structure is necessary given today's dynamic, non-linear world. Murray Hiebert, author of *Powerful Professionals* and *The Encyclopedia of Leadership* (McGraw-Hill, 2002) has a fascinating perspective on the diversity of approach and content in the book.

Murray argues that an apt metaphor for the book and leadership development today is alchemy. Alchemists get a bad rap because most of us only remember their role in trying to turn base metals into gold—although the metaphor still works if you think about turning managers into leaders. However, alchemists also played an important role as healers and were often very effective in "curing" sicknesses such as leprosy. The problem with alchemy and the state of leadership development today is similar. Successful outcomes depend as much on the practitioner as the methods used. When the alchemist failed, he usually blamed the patient for not having enough faith. Similarly when a change intervention fails, we often blame senior leaders for their lack of commitment. For alchemists and for change agents, this is sometimes true and sometimes just an excuse.

Eventually alchemy evolved into chemistry, a science that could demonstrate repeatable results. In leadership and in change management, we do not yet have much in the way of repeatable results and continue to attempt the wrong kind of intervention for the situation. For example, Six Sigma practices are probably not appropriate outside of a manufacturing environment no matter how much discipline the process might create in a research lab. Likely there are Six Sigma people who would like to argue this point—and that is the point. We do not agree about very much, if anything. This does not mean that we should be trying to discover "the truth or the one best way." This approach has already been tried and found wanting. The real questions are about what works and under what conditions. This question moved alchemy to chemistry and seems to be the next step in the evolution of our field.

This book contains a series of diverse examples that have worked. Your job as a reader is to be a chemist, not an alchemist. You must determine which approaches suit your unique situation.

Now, as a chemist, allow yourself to take a Taoist journey. In Chinese, "Tao" refers to the way of the universe and suggests the wondrous journey of the mind that is willing to see. Read critically and with an open, Taoist mind:

- What is our context today?
- What do I want to accomplish? Why?
- What area am I most passionate about leading change in? Why?
- What are the issues(s) and concerns we are challenged with?
- Are we asking the right questions?
- Who are the right stakeholders?
- What approaches have worked in the past before? Why?
- What approaches have failed in the past before? Why?

*In the perfect world of a nice neat change journey, one would start with strategic direction and move clockwise around the star—but rarely is any part of life perfect and certainly not in the world of organizational change!*

*We "meet the client wherever they are" and begin our work from a systems perspective from that point forward.*

—Kathleen Dannemiller, co-founder
of Whole Scale™ Change (excerpt taken from Chapter 1)

As the editors of this book, our collective backgrounds represent the same diversity that is found in the book. We have different interests, clients, and approaches. We have each experienced successes and failures while hoping only for success. The failures were almost always failures to make correct assumptions about the fit between type of intervention, organizational system, and situation. It is these failures that help us learn; they make us humble and open our minds to different approaches. We have a commitment to moving this field in a positive direction. This fieldguide presents you with an array of choices for how to approach many complex situations. You will find many ideas that you can adapt to your own situation and needs. And, when you do lead change, lead with the same passion, humility, creativity, and commitment to stakeholders, customers, and excellence that have been exhibited by the change champions contributing to this book. And, as Ivy Ross says, don't ever be "afraid to let the passion out of the bottle!"

# SUMMARY OF CHAPTERS

| Chapter | Title | Authors | Main Ideas | Key Factors |
|---|---|---|---|---|
| **Part I** | Transformational and Large Scale Change | | | |
| 1 | *Restore Hope During Times of Mistrust* | Dannemiller, Johnson, and Eggers | Tried and true experiences, models, and tools for organization change, utilizing a systems-thinking framework and behavioral change model. | *Take-away key learnings that will help you to catalyze the process of trust-building and total organizational change:*<br>✔ Listening carefully for THE truth rather than YOUR own truth<br>✔ Creating organizational purpose and strategic direction<br>✔ Leading with your heart<br>✔ Thinking systemically and acting with an understanding of the whole organizational system. |
| 2 | *Changing Leadership Behavior: Impact of Co-Workers and Coaches* | Goldsmith, Morgan, and Effron | Practical approach for coaches interested in getting personal leadership behavior change. Most important variable is increasing frequency of leader interaction with co-workers. | *Through research-based approaches, you will learn the benefits of follow-on coaching and development as a transformational strategy:*<br>✔ Coaching by telephone works almost as well as in person<br>✔ External or internal coaches make positive differences in leadership development and change programs<br>✔ Training can make a highly significant positive behavioral change when combined with follow-up coaching. |

| 3 | *Practice Positive Deviance for Extraordinary Social and Organizational Change* | Sternin | In every community, there are certain individuals whose special practices enable them to find a better solution to problems than neighbors who have access to same resources-applied to community change interventions. | *Learn to apply community and social change to your organization*:<br>✔ Learn the actual six-step process to implement positive deviance in your organization<br>✔ Be provided with benchmark examples of where positive deviance has resulted in positive cultural or behavioral change |
| 4 | *Do Leader's Have Tools and a Common Language to Work Together for Sustainable Change?* | Jacobsen | Shift emphasis from developing individual leader skills to developing shared organization leadership deliverables by providing a common language, common process, and the tools to accomplish them. | *Take-away tools for creating common lexicon and shared understanding*:<br>✔ Practical and applicable leadership tools<br>✔ Case study examples of how to implement the toolbox approach in your company<br>✔ The "science" of leadership as a reputable, measurable, and improvable process |
| 5 | *Rapid-Cycle Design of Executive Development Strategy and Programs* | Bolt, Meeks, and Terrell | Method to engage line leaders in the design of executive development strategies and programs to enhance the business value of the designs and increase commitment. | *Benefit from practical and applicable tools to engage the highest ranks in your organization*:<br>✔ Web-based leadership development surveys<br>✔ Executive interview questions<br>✔ Examples of typical Rapid Cycle Design(tm) Programs<br>✔ Critical success factors to consider for your initiative |

| 9 | *Diversity and Inclusion: Leverage Differences for Bottom-Line Success* | Katz | Organizations that leverage their workforce diversity and create an inclusive culture will see positive changes resulting in higher performance. | *Among the many elements for implementing and sustaining a 43p3.5culture of diversity and inclusion, you will learn:*<br>✔ The eleven behaviors for inclusion<br>✔ Implementing a diverse workforce in a changing workforce and changing business environment<br>✔ Individual diversity competencies for managers, senior executives, and all associates |
|---|---|---|---|---|
| 10 | *Understand and Apply Sociology, Anthropology, and Other Disciplines to Development and Change* | Barnett | Current practices in market research are insufficient. New solutions include ethnographic methods, outsourcing emerging digital and information technologies, providing real-time insightful data, the ability to use that data to differentiate brands and to develop and retain customer loyalty. | *Be challenged with several new options for planning for the future including:*<br>✔ Scenario planning<br>✔ Customized consumer panels<br>✔ Emerging technologies and outsourcing<br>✔ A new model for consumer research company future options |
| 11 | *Raise the Bar from Corporate Compliance to Total Organization Integrity* | Ventrella | An organizational framework and mindset for creating corporate identities of the highest ethical standards. Step-by-step approach for building a "culture of integrity." | *Be able to implement immediate ethics and corporate integrity tools and models such as:*<br>✔ Total organizational integrity<br>✔ Individual integrity models<br>✔ The Three-Point Ethical Dilemma Checklist |

| | | | | |
|---|---|---|---|---|
| 12 | *Be a Skilled Manager-Not a Manager of Corporate "Tenure"* | Hawkins and Riordan | Few managers are developed on much besides technical job skills resulting in an executive failure rate at between one-third to one-half. | *Take-away several skills-based learnings including*:<br>✔ An understanding of the need to develop competencies through skill-building experiences<br>✔ The need for mentors<br>✔ The case for new challenges on the job and outside resources |
| 13 | *Lead Dialogue Processes to Build Commitment and Reach Shared Understanding* | Knox | Moderating dialogue processes get whole-hearted action for an initiative where people are energized and behind a plan that builds commitment and generates action. | *Learn several fundamentals of the dialogue process including:*<br>✔ How to build shared understanding<br>✔ The differences between dialogue and discussion<br>✔ Examination of key strategic issues within your organization<br>✔ Values and outcomes of dialoguing |
| 14 | *Be a Trendsetter: The Future of Branding, Marketing, and Organizational Complexity* | Matthews | It will require deviant thinking to take advantage of changing market conditions and a different approach to corporate organization to maximize future opportunities. Branding and marketing will have to be reinvented. | *Take-away practical, real-life examples of deviant thinking, futuring, and branding:*<br>✔ What and who are some examples of "fringe dwellers"<br>✔ The "Realm of the Cool"<br>✔ How to become a "deviant brander"<br>✔ Building the better corporate brand<br>✔ The perils and potentials of trendsetting |

| 15 | *Understand Adult Learning and Development* | Noble | Well-designed simulations surface symbolic "maps" of multi-dimensional organizational realities and therefore a great way to enhance leadership development and skill building. | *Apply leading views and models in adult learning theory and development including:* ✔ Learning needs assessment ✔ Cognitive Experiential Self-Theory ✔ Multiple and emotional intelligence theories ✔ Learning as a social act ✔ Actual group simulation exercises |
|---|---|---|---|---|
| 16 | *Go Beyond Replacing Executives: Thoughts on Managing Work and Values* | Rothwell | Succession planning must evolve into how work can be accomplished and points to values modeling and competency modeling as drivers for future succession and work management efforts. | *Critically reflect and apply new methods of executive replacement by learning several key features:* ✔ Terrorism's effect on succession planning ✔ A step-by-step STAR model approach to the process of succession management ✔ Traditional problems with succession management ✔ Checklist for alternative approaches for getting work done |
| **Part III** | Transformational Leadership and Sustaining Results | | | |
| 17 | *Developing Leaders Who Build Market Value: The Right Results the Right Way* | Ulrich and Smallwood | The purpose of leadership development is to build leaders who know how to increase organization capability that delivers current and future earnings consistent with firm values. | *Learn results-based leadership tools and tactics including:* ✔ How leaders build intangible value ✔ The leadership development process for business impact ✔ Ideas for conducting a case for change ✔ Measurement tools |

| | | | | |
|---|---|---|---|---|
| 18 | *Put "Actionable Results" into Leadership Development* | Dowling and Lynch | Use technology tools with Action Learning to enable individual and organizational learning that delivers desired results. | *Apply tools and models for generating desired results:*<br>🗸 Best Practice case study examples<br>🗸 Individual, team, and organizational learning models at 3M<br>🗸 Learning evaluation levels<br>🗸 Action Learning Center Model |
| 19 | *Keep Good Company: New Ways to a Sustainable, Blue Chip Creative Culture* | Ross and Kuehler | First-hand account of how the Girls Division at Mattel successfully reinvented how the world's number one toy company innovates by creating a product development process called Project Platypus. Platypus brings out human potential through the synthesis of collaborative experiences resulting in new business opportunities. | *Benefit from knowledge of key tools for creating a creative culture that produces revenue/profitability:*<br>🗸 The thirteen ways to a sustainable culture<br>🗸 The importance of trust and collaboration<br>🗸 Key elements of design<br>🗸 The power of storytelling, intuitive leadership, and other creative product development strategies |
| 20 | *Does Your Organization Have Crucial Conversations and Transformational Moments that Lead to Organization Change?* | Peters and Grenny | Organization change comes about only when we hold the kind of conversations that speaks to our dysfunction as individuals or teams. When people see the "integrity gap" between what they espouse and what they do, they have an opportunity to make new choices about moving forward in a more effective way. | *Gain an understanding of how to apply crucial conversation tools through:*<br>🗸 A real-life case study of a CEO's crucial conversation<br>🗸 Specific barriers to crucial conversations<br>🗸 Transformational questions |

| | | | | |
|---|---|---|---|---|
| 21 | *Manage Organizational Emotional and Business Chaos for Exceptional Business Performance Results* | Rozman and Childre | Coherence is an alignment of energies that facilitates the higher organizational intelligence capacities of the human brain. Coherence in individuals and between teams cuts through decision-making and business processes that are complex and time consuming. | *Through proven research and results, learn to create coherence and improved performance out of chaos in your organization through:*<br>✔ Emotional alignment tools<br>✔ The Stress Affect<br>✔ Getting "in sync" for critical business decisions<br>✔ The "freeze-frame" technique |
| 22 | *You Can't Be a Champion . . . Unless You Keep Score* | Sullivan | HR professionals must understand that the world of business has lost its tolerance for decisions made without facts and for programs that don't produce measurable results. | *Learn why and how to measure change and development in your organization:*<br>✔ Nine reasons to measure results<br>✔ Eight steps in developing metrics<br>✔ The five different categories of business impact<br>✔ Examples of business impacts and how to measure them<br>✔ How to build a business case for increasing the budget<br>✔ Top decision factors for approving projects |

# FOREWORD

*Dr. W. Warner Burke*

You may recall that we used to live in a linear world. Things could be planned in an orderly fashion and even implemented in an orderly fashion. We knew what to expect from our leaders. Harry Truman was clear and direct. John F. Kennedy said we were going to the moon—and we did. Richard Nixon was another matter, but we won't go there. From Nixon forward, things were not as clear (with the possible exception of Ronald Reagan).

Today we seem to live in a nonlinear world. And as Louis Carter puts it, we are attempting to lead in a "crisis economy." We once again need leaders who are clear and direct and have understandable and agreed-upon goals—but these kinds of leaders are hard to find in a chaotic, nonlinear world. Moreover, we used to live in a world of leadership research that was fairly simple and easy to understand. By the 1950s, trait theory had begun to lose credibility and independent studies showed that there were really only two functions of leadership—a task function and a people function. Blake and Mouton took these results and created the Managerial Grid, a model positing that there was one best way to lead and manage, and that was to place equal and full emphasis on both functions. Using the same two functions—task and people—for their model, Hersey and Blanchard disagreed with the Grid thinking and stated that leadership was situational; it all depended on the maturity level of followers. Fred Fiedler also used the two functions for describing leaders but went further with the situational dimension and developed a more complex framework that was helpful for understanding in more depth the nature of a leader's situation. Three aspects for Fiedler were key: (1) the position power of the leader, (2) the quality of leader-follower relations, and (3) the degree of structure regarding the task. However, to claim in today's world that leaders are either task oriented or people oriented is a huge over-simplification and even trite. In other words, theories and models of leadership based on the original two functions, while perhaps viable for their time—the 1960s—are not sufficiently complex and this kind of thinking even seems a bit quaint today. Instead of task orientation, we might want to consider how much a potential leader has the desire to make a difference. And instead of people orientation we might want to know the degree to which a potential leader has a healthy curiosity about people.

However, this is not to say that we are much smarter about leadership today. In spite of the stated goals and purposes, most leadership development efforts and programs today are more about socialization than about growing and developing leaders. In their superb summary of what we know (and don't know) about leadership, Hogan, Curphy, and Hogan (1994) raise such questions (a) as to why more than half of all leaders fail (circumstances, insufficient skills, and abilities—too abrasive and arrogant, for example—and a lack of vision), (b) how should leaders be evaluated (by team, group, i.e., follower-performance, and by others' ratings including but not limited to the boss), and (c) why do we continue to select flawed leaders? With respect to this last question that Hogan and his colleagues raise, one of the reasons is that we continue to hold on to beliefs about traits; we seem to have implicit "theories" about what a leader should be and look like. In other words, we need to stop paying so much attention to irrelevant facets of personality. Being friendly, courteous, and kind helps a young lad to become an Eagle Scout but has little if anything to do with leadership. Being tall, dark, and handsome worked for Clark Gable in Hollywood, but was he a leader? John Wayne was certainly tall, and he could lead his horse to water, but he couldn't make his steed drink.

So, we are back to the earlier point: Leadership is more complex than what we may have been led to believe. Moreover, most of the research on leadership has been conducted with supervisors and middle managers rather than with executives, and most of those studied were not leaders. Thus, we do not know a great deal about *executive* leadership; that is, those senior people in organizations who "call the shots."

There have been contributions, however. A fine one is the book by Stephen Zaccaro (2001). He has covered four primary models/theories of executive leadership: (1) conceptual complexity theories, (2) behavioral complexity theories, (3) strategic decision-making models, and (4) visionary and inspirational models.

*Conceptual complexity* theories, e.g., stratified systems theory by Elliott Jaques and his colleagues (e.g., Jaques, 1986) concern executives' capacities to monitor and deal with their rapidly changing environments, both external to and internal to their organizations. These capacities mean that executives must possess and apply a higher order of cognitive abilities and skills (knowing how to think and decide) that match the degree of complexity in their environments. So conceptual complexity is about information processing—the amount, diversity, and rate of change regarding information and putting into understandable language what all of the buzzing confusion means for organizational members and the organization's future.

*Behavioral complexity* theories concern the levels of social demand on executives and their abilities to manage multiple organizational roles. Behavioral complexity theories also concern boundary management, especially between the organization as a whole and its board of directors/trustees and between the executives' subordinates and supervisors. Finally, these theories concern the executives' abilities to manage conflicting values and demands from a variety of constituents and stakeholders. An executive who is highly able in these domains would likely rate equally highly on Goleman's (1998) five components of emotional intelligence—self-awareness, self-regulation, motivation, empathy, and social skill.

*Strategic decision-making* models concern organizational and environmental co-alignment, similar to the previous complexity theories, but these models are more about *how* executives make strategic decisions. The decision making process is typically in three steps: (1) environmental scanning, (2) interpretation and making sense of the scanned data, and then (3) making strategic choices and determining how the leadership role (involving others, communicating, and structuring the implementation phase) will be accomplished. Wortman's (1982) five major strategic management functions of the executive exemplify this kind of model. The five functions are:

1. Analyze problems and opportunities
2. Formulate appropriate solutions and responses
3. Implement solutions and responses
4. Interpret policies and operations
5. Evaluate the effectiveness of policies and operations

*Visionary and inspirational* models have more to do with characteristics of the leader as a person such as cognitive abilities, self-confidence, socialized power motive, risk propensity, and social skills (Goleman's emotional intelligence components would be illustrative as well). Of course, being visionary and having inspirational motivation are key for this model of executive leadership. These executives concern themselves with leader development and training, selection and assessment, and follower empowerment and performance. Examples of these models are transformational leadership (Bass, 1985; Tichy and Devanna, 1986) charismatic leadership (Conger and Kanungo, 1987; House, 1977) and credibility (Kouzes and Posner, 1987).

These four theories and models should not be viewed as mutually exclusive. They overlap and the ideal executive leader would be imbued with all four. Leadership is about managing complexity and, after all, creating and communicating a vision is only the beginning.

Just for a moment, though, suppose we had to boil it down to only two factors like the two functions from the 1950s—task and people. What might they be? My choices would be self-awareness (there is growing research now that this quality relates strongly with performance), and a deep desire to make a difference. An effective leader of change is, after all, a highly motivated and energetic individual.

And as this book demonstrates, effective leadership is more than two factors irrespective of how important any two may be. To illustrate the diversity of thinking and examples of leadership and change as well as the complexity that leaders deal with in today's world, chapters in this book range from succession management; the importance of integrity, innovation, branding, and marketing; coaching; trust; building consensus; "positive deviance;" market research and scenario planning; getting buy-in; commitment; and ownership; to building market value. In other words, if you want to know more comprehensively what is meant by leadership complexity, then simply read this book. And be clear that you are in for a dynamic nonlinear ride!

# REFERENCES

Bass, B.M. (1985) *Leadership and Performance Beyond Expectations.* New York: Free Press.

Conger, J.A. and R.N. Kanungo (1987) "Toward a Behavioral Theory of Charismatic Leadership in Organizational Settings." *Academy of Management Review,* 12, 637–647.

Goleman, D. (1998) What Makes a Leader? *Harvard Business Review,* November–December, 92–102.

Hogan, R., G.S. Curphy, and J. Hogan (1994) "What We Know About Leadership." *American Psychologist,* 52 (2), 130–139.

House, R.J. (1977) "A 1976 Theory of Charismatic Leadership." In J.G. Hunt and L.Larson (Eds.), *Leadership: The Cutting Edge* (pp. 189–204). Carbondale: Southern Illinois University Press.

Jaques, E. (1986) "The Development of Intellectual Capability: A Discussion of Stratified Systems Theory." *Journal of Applied Behavioral Science,* 22, 361–384.

Kouzes, J.M. and B.Z. Posner (1987) *The Leadership Challenge: How to Get Extraordinary Things Done in Organizations.* San Francisco: Jossey-Bass.

Tichy, N. and M.A. Devanna (1986) *Transformational Leadership.* New York: John Wiley & Sons.

Wortman, M.S. (1982) "Strategic Management and Changing Leader-Follower Roles." *Journal of Applied Behavioral Science,* 18, 371–383.

Zaccaro, S.J. (2001) *The Nature of Executive Leadership: A Conceptual and Empirical Analysis of Success.* Washington, DC: American Psychological Association.

# PART I

---

# TRANSFORMATIONAL AND LARGE SCALE CHANGE

# CHAPTER 1

# RESTORING HOPE DURING TIMES OF MISTRUST

*Kathleen Dannemiller, Mary Eggers, and Lorri Johnson*

## ABSTRACT

*Widely recognized as the founder of the Whole-Scale™ change process, Kathleen Dannemiller and her partners, Mary Eggers and Lorri Johnson, teach us through tried and true experiences, models, and tools of societal and organizational change, that hope can be restored even during the most "untrusting" of times in our nation's and world's history.*

This chapter includes key elements such as Richard Beckhard's change model, the five key ingredients of HOPE, the STAR model, Whole-Scale™ change in action, systems thinking examples, and other golden nuggets of wisdom from one of the foremost women pioneers in the history of change.

## SUMMARY

When faced with a crisis that threatened everything they stood for, 600 people from across the country, representing all functions and levels of this organization, came together to share their concerns and hopes for the future. As they listened to each other, participants quickly recognized how important it was to set aside their own agendas around "back home" issues and come together for the greater cause. By telling their stories and sharing their diverse perspectives through the four-day meeting, it was obvious that their fellow brothers and sisters shared many of the same concerns they were dealing with "back home."

Their sense of urgency was heightened as a panel of speakers painted a picture of the external factors (social, political, and economic) that threaten to dismantle what this organization has worked so hard for over seventy years to preserve. Futurists shared their ideas about what was on the horizon, *e.g.,* trends, demographics, etc., and how the organization might be impacted. The cynicism and skepticism that prevailed when the meeting started began to dissipate. Rather than blaming and pointing fingers, the discussion quickly turned to, "How do we combine our energy and resources to deal with our challenges? What are our priorities and what should we be focusing on right now?"

The group then turned its attention to discussing and enriching the proposed strategy for moving the organization forward. There was a buzz in the room as participants passionately debated the priorities for the organization and worked to consensus to give their input to the proposed mission, vision, values, and strategic goals such as growing the organization's membership and increasing its visibility.

The leadership team along with volunteers chosen by their peers worked late into the night to revise the strategy incorporating the wisdom of the larger group in such a way that everyone felt heard and proud that they were able to influence the future of the organization. The re-write team presented their work the following morning and everyone rose to their feet in support of the new strategy and to show their appreciation.

The next step was to begin identifying the actions that must be taken in support of the newly agreed-upon strategy. For each goal, participants looked into the future and brainstormed vivid images of what was happening, what they were seeing and hearing that told them they were making progress and moving the organization in the right direction. Next, hundreds of ideas for actions to move them toward the future they yearned for were generated at the tables and participants had an opportunity to vote for the ideas they felt should be implemented first. Laptop computers at each table enabled the data gathering in such a way that the results could be seen in "real time." The entire room was quickly able to get a read on the direction the group should be taking and what individual and collective roles were in moving the strategy forward.

When asked to brainstorm ways for taking the strategy "back home" and getting traction at the local level, participants again generated ideas in "real time" for sustaining the momentum that had been created. Excitement in the room was palpable as everyone watched the growing list on the huge monitor above the stage.

At the end of the day, the evaluations reflected the hope and renewed energy of the crowd: "We have a new awareness of what we must do to stay alive," "I am excited that so many people from such diverse backgrounds and environment can come together and unite around our common threats," "I have new friends in [this organization] and we are now a working/cohesive unit . . . we must continue to focus, focus, focus," and finally, "We've planned the work, now we must work the plan—keep hope alive!!!"

## INTRODUCTION

For the past 20 years we have been part of the development of "whole system" change processes that we call "Whole-Scale™.." A mystery that we identified as we uncovered and tested these processes was based on our discoveries that the processes always worked at a predictable point during an event, that they continued to work after an event, and spread even further in an organization after an event had ended. We identified the reason for these outcomes as evidence of a true paradigm shift both in individuals and in the organization as a whole. We called this shift "magic," because it always felt like magic. How did that happen? In addition to this predictable feeling of magic, there was another predictable outcome from all of our Whole-Scale™ work—what will always emerge is a true sense of hope. *I think I can. We know we can. Watch our dust!*

In 2001, we began to realize that there was an expanding feeling of massive distrust around the world: skepticism and mistrust of world leaders in Afghanistan, Palestine, Israel, and the United States; skepticism, despair and mistrust of numerous companies in the stock market as we experienced devastating personal financial losses and dwindling retirement savings; mistrust of organizational leaders from companies, WorldCom and Enron among others, who lied to us and to their employees and investors; skepticism, fear, and mistrust of our own organizational leaders; skepticism of and disbelief in our local and national and government leaders. It was the beginning of an epidemic of mistrust.

As this worldwide epidemic escalated in this country, we were struck by the continuing power of whole system results, unleashed by the Whole-Scale™ processes we know how to use. Simultaneous to the widespread distrust, when people were called together in a Whole-Scale™ change process, the outcomes were empowerment and hope for their individual and collective futures. We found ourselves asking the question "What moves people from *despair* to *hope?*" What is the difference between a mob gathering that lets loose their individual and group frustration versus the outcomes from a gathering of the same kind of people when they are exposed to, and involved in, "Whole-Scale™" processes?

## WHOLE-SCALE™ IN ACTION

This difference was clearly evident at the gathering of 600 people described in the opening story. This group was driven by common values and beliefs, represented the entire United States geographically, and were led by a leader who had the courage to bring all of them together for four days. His purpose was to build a common database and connect people with each other as a microcosm of the whole system and to agree on actions that could allow the organization and its members to survive. There was an audible buzz and a growing surge of energy in the room as participants began shifting from the old paradigms they entered with to a new shared vision of the future for the organization and their individual and collective roles in getting there.

# THE SECRETS TO UNLEASHING HOPE

We believe that isolation is the unfortunate key to creating distrust, and we believe that connecting people around what's happening and what they collectively yearn to do in response to changes in the world as they know them will unleash hope: "I'm not alone. I'm not the only one who wants change. I am not the only one who yearns for collective action. And oh, by the way—our leaders even care about the things we care about and are willing to have us 'put their money where our mouth is'."

As we have worked over the past couple of decades with whole system change, using our increasingly robust Whole-Scale™ change processes, we have experienced predictable success in helping all kinds of organizations and communities reach wholeness. We have seen them become "one-brain" (all seeing the same facts inside and outside the organization) and "one-heart" (combining and celebrating our joint yearnings for the future of the organization). When these results have been achieved, the feelings that are loose in a meeting or ballroom bring to mind the story of *The Little Engine That Could:* "I think I can, we think we can, we *know* we can!" Hope and empowerment will predictably run loose in the room. The consultant(s) can literally *feel* it, as do the participants. The dictionary definition of hope is " . . . hope is never a static or passive thing. It is dynamic, active, directive and life sustaining." Hope is what you experience when you start to believe we *can* achieve what we all yearn to achieve.

# KEY INGREDIENTS

So what are the key ingredients in Whole-Scale™ that lead to hope—individual and collective hope?

*Purpose is first.* We are always asking what is our purpose and the answer is not always an easy one. To say that our purpose is to create an organization that ensures shareholder dividends stay high is quite frankly not a very ennobling purpose. It isn't one that will capture your heart, and therefore, it won't capture your energy and commitment either. Ennobling purpose—it's our fundamental reason for being. Whether it's this meeting or this organization or this change effort, it considers all stakeholders' hopes and aspirations. Purpose identifies stakeholders' needs and connects the organization with what the stakeholders really desire from the organization, phrased in terms of deeply held wants and needs. In framing the conversation to develop purpose, we often ask "How will be the world be different because we've done this?"

*Heart comes next.* It's essential to have leaders like the one described above, who are courageous enough to speak from their heart and to listen when others do the same. A leader who deeply believes in the wisdom that exists in each and every member of the organization, and who believes enough to risk tapping that wisdom, can help move the organization forward. A leader must know he or she doesn't have all the answers.

*The willingness to listen is third.* A leader must be willing to really listen and to listen from a place of deep knowing that what the other person is saying is truth, not *the* truth but rather *their* truth, *their* wisdom. Combining all of the individual truths and wisdoms creates the collective wisdom of the whole. We invite people to listen to see the world through the eyes of the speaker, not because it's right or wrong, good or bad, but rather because it's his or her view. When we truly take in the view of others we shift in profound ways.

*Next is the power of the microcosm.* It's our way of ensuring that we take into consideration the rich diversity that makes up our world, be it an organization or a community. If you want to shift the whole system at one time, creating what Malcolm Gladwell calls a "tipping point," you must be able to think the way the whole system thinks. Using microcosms, real subsets of the larger group that represent all the "voices" of the organization, in the overall change process is the one feature of the Whole-Scale™ approach that allows you—and the organization—to think and see "whole system."

*The fifth is the power to think and act in whole systems.* Microcosms help us stay systems-focused. The value of staying systems-focused is best demonstrated by the following example from Russell Ackoff. In 1981 Ackoff gave a speech to a group of high level Ford executives. The speech was designed to encourage them to leave the old industrial paradigm as they approached change in their industry. We think it's still one of the best pragmatic descriptions of why we need to think "whole" if we are to be successful in the future. Ackoff said:

> "Let me try to give you a feeling of why that (Systems Thinking) is so, by giving you an example rather than trying to give you a generalized proof. I would like you to go through the following thought experiment. I read in the New York Times the other day that there are 142 makes of automobiles available in the United States. So let's get one of each and bring them into a large garage—142 cars.
>
> We'll hire ourselves a good group of first rate automotive engineers and first ask them to do the following: Inspect those 142 cars, test them, do any damn thing you want to, but come

out and tell us which one has the best carburetor. So they run a series of tests, and they come out and say the Buick has got the best carburetor. So we make a note: Buick carburetor.

Then you say fine, now we would like you to do the same thing on transmissions. So they test the transmissions, and they come out and say the Mercedes has the best transmission. We make a note: Mercedes transmission.

You say okay, take the distributor, and they run through, and they come out and say the Dodge has got the best distributor.

Then one by one, we take every part until we have every part required for an automobile, and we have identified the best part available. Now when that is done, we tell them to now take those parts off those cars and assemble them, because then we ought to get the best possible automobile.

But, do you get it? You don't even get an automobile. And for a very obvious reason.

Because it turns out that the parts don't fit, and that's what systems thinking is all about.

It says that the performance of the whole is not the addition of the performance of the parts, but it is a consequence of the relationship between the performance of the parts. It is how performance relates, not how it occurs independently of the other parts. That is what systems thinking is about.

So, synthesis is a different way of thinking and looking for explanations. It tries to find it by looking at wholes, the larger whole, of which things are a part, rather than by taking things apart."

The last sentence in the above quote illustrates one of several key beliefs that Whole-Scale™ rests upon. You do not analyze and break down issues into smaller problems to be solved. The magnitude of wasted energy such a breakdown causes equals what a mechanic would require to re-work the separate parts from the 142 cars into a functional automobile.

Now let's put it all together and look at two models that guide how we design conversations and interventions. At the core of our work is a change model inspired by Dick Beckhard that we use to design conversations small and large. The formula, $D \times V \times F < R$, says that if an organization wants to bring about system-wide change, it will need to work with a critical mass of the organization to uncover and combine the people's *Dissatisfaction* (D) with the current situation. The next step will be to uncover and combine the yearnings for the organization they truly want to become—their combined *Vision* of the future (V). If real, sustainable, change is going to take place, the third design element needs to be *First* steps (F). First steps are a series of tasks that everyone in the organization believes are the right ones

Equation for Change

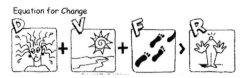

**Figure 1**

needed to achieve their vision. Simple algebra suggests that if the D, the V, or F is missing, the product will be zero and the effort will not be able to overcome the *Resistance* (R) to change. Using DVF as a design model creates a paradigm shift in the organization. The process of collectively uncovering and combining the three elements creates a positive shift in how individuals view the potential of the organization. People can no longer continue doing things the old way. A shift has occurred and change has begun.

We work in organizations and communities. Hope is alive when members of these organizations and communities have a real say in the workings of the organizations. In Whole-Scale™ that means having a real say in creating a sustainable future.

The second model that guides our thinking and actions is the Star of Success. As we work with this model in organizations, we are constantly creating space for people to have a voice in the "operations" of the business. Whole-Scale™ change is grounded in the elegant synthesis of more than 100 years of systems theory (as articulated by Fritjof Capra, *Web of Life* and Meg Wheatley, *Leadership and the New Science*). The Whole-Scale™ version of systems theory is the Star of Success, and it provides a framework for looking at an organization or a community.

We believe (and our experience confirms our belief) that for an organization or community to bring about significant, lasting change, it must make each star point "twinkle" at the same time—not an easy thing to do in a world that thinks more about the pieces of something rather than the whole. Potential clients often call us in because they are having trouble with the "resources" star point: too little money/too many people, too much technology/too few that know how to use it. They think that by focusing just on this, their troubles will be solved. So they downsize or move people around ("form"),( often doing this in a vacuum without a whole system perspective.( They lack a clear understanding of where they're going ("strategic direction"), what their work is, and how it gets done ("functions").

The Star of Success Model

**Figure 2**

Unfortunately, the last thing they often think about is how to keep people informed ("shared information"), the glue that holds everything together in the first place!

In the perfect world of a nice, neat change journey, one would start with strategic direction and move clockwise around the star, but rarely is any part of life perfect, and certainly not in the world of organizational change! We "meet the client wherever they are" and begin our work from a systems perspective from that point forward.

If we are called in to facilitate an organizational redesign initiative, for example, we start by asking questions to confirm or deny placement of a strategy that is passionately agreed upon by all the leaders and that has been shared in a meaningful way with the members of the organization. If we're called in to help leaders develop the strategy, we ask questions to confirm or deny the capacity in the organization to carry out the strategy. Regardless of where the work starts, the most critical process that we use is conversation, whether it's a conversation to create an ennobling purpose or a conversation to redesign the payroll process. *"Meaningful conversations depend on our willingness to forget about neat thoughts, clear categories, narrow roles,"* says Margaret Wheatley in her new book *Turning To One Another.* As we move around the star involving members of the organization—giving them a real voice—it's often not a *neat* process or conversation–instead it's a *real* conversation about things that really matter in the hearts and minds of the members of the organization.

## CONCLUSION

Albert Camus said years ago, "In the depth of winter I finally learned that there was in me an invincible summer" (*Healing Words*, p82, by Caren Goldman). We believe everyone in our nation and around the world is looking for and perhaps praying for this "invincible summer," the essence of hope restored. This hope is not just that we would find it individually, but rather that we as a people of the world would find our way to a collective "invincible summer."

This will not be easy, but rarely has anything really worth doing been easy. It takes incredible courage to have hope in the face of skepticism in the world around us. When the clouds part and the conversations begin, we can see our yearnings again. When we believe that achieving our dreams is actually within our grasp—this is hope restored. Hope is essential to life.

# CHAPTER 2

# CHANGE LEADERSHIP BEHAVIOR: THE IMPACT OF CO-WORKERS AND THE IMPACT OF COACHES

## A Review of Research Results in Five Major Organizations

*Marshall Goldsmith, Howard Morgan, and Marc Effron*

## INTRODUCTION

Five very different organizations set out with similar goals—to determine the desired behaviors for leaders in their organization and then to help leaders increase their effectiveness by better aligning actual leadership behavior with these desired behaviors. Each of the organizations developed a custom leadership profile that was specifically designed to meet their requirements. Each developed a 360° feedback process that included behaviors that were consistent with the leadership profile. Leaders in all five organizations received feedback that was reviewed with a consultant (either internal or external). Leaders were encouraged to identify one to three key areas for improvement, discuss these areas with their co-workers, follow up with co-workers on an ongoing basis and then use a custom-designed mini-survey to measure if they had become more effective over time (as evaluated by their co-workers).

Each of the five organizations used a somewhat different approach to achieving the same goals. All were extremely successful! The purpose of this article is to review their approaches and their levels of success in order to understand better the most important factors in helping leaders achieve a positive, long-term change in effectiveness (as evaluated by their co-workers).

## THE FIVE ORGANIZATIONS AND THEIR APPROACHES

The five organizations included in this article are very different. Each is in different industries and faces different competitive pressures. Each is one of the leading organizations in its industry. Three of the five companies used a targeted approach to this leadership process. In these cases 75 to 250 high-potential managers were involved in the study. Since each manager received feedback from an average of six co-workers, 450 to 1,500 co-workers (in each company) were respondents in the research. In the remaining two companies, a minimum of 1,500 managers were trained and received feedback, while over 9,000 co-worker respondents were in the database.

Each of the organizations had varying degrees of international representation. One was almost exclusively American; one was 50 percent US and 50 percent international. The other three had representation varying between these two. The results for leaders inside and outside the US were very similar.

As discussed earlier, leaders received 360° feedback in each of the five organizations. Every leader was asked to follow up with his/her co-workers. In each case, leaders chose one to three areas for improvement. They then received mini-survey feedback (from three to fifteen months later) to measure perceived improvement on both their selected areas for improvement and on their overall change in effectiveness as a leader.

The five organizations and their approaches to changing leadership behavior, are listed here.

A) An aerospace/defense contractor. Approximately 1,500 executives and managers (starting with the CEO and his team) received training for two and one-half days. Each person reviewed his/her 360° feedback with an outside consultant (all in person). Each received at least three "reminder notes" to help ensure that they would follow up with their co-workers.

B) A pharmaceutical/health care organization. Approximately 2,000 executives and managers (starting with the CEO and his team) received training for one and one-half days. Each person reviewed his/her 360° feedback with an outside consultant (almost all by phone). Each received at least three "reminder notes" to help ensure that they would follow up with their co-workers.

C) A telecommunications company. Approximately 175 executives and high-potential leaders (including the CEO and his team) received training for one day. Each leader was given a personal external coach (a coach from outside the company). Coaches were instructed to have one-on-one sessions with their clients on an ongoing basis.

D) A financial services organization. Approximately 150 high-potential leaders received training for one day. Each leader received a personal internal coach (a coach from inside the company). Coaches had one-on-one sessions with their clients on an ongoing basis (either in-person or by phone).

E) A high-tech manufacturing company. Approximately 75 high-potential leaders received coaching for one year from an external coach. This was not connected to any training program. Coaches had one-on-one sessions with their clients on an ongoing basis (either in-person or by phone).

# FIVE KEY LEARNINGS

*In all cases the most important variable in predicting increased leadership effectiveness was the leader's interaction with co-workers.*

All five organizations measured the frequency of the leader's interaction with co-workers and compared this measure to the perceived increase in leadership effectiveness. Company C used a "percentage improvement" scale to measure increased effectiveness. The other four companies used a "-3 to +3" scale. The results were very similar in all cases. Leaders who discussed their selected areas for improvement with their co-workers and followed up with these co-workers on a regular basis showed dramatic improvement. Leaders who did not have ongoing dialogues with their co-workers showed much less improvement. This was true whether the leader had an external coach, internal coach, or no coach.

Leaders who were seen as having frequent or periodic interaction (concerning input on areas for improvement) were always seen increasing in effectiveness far more than leaders who had little or no interaction with co-workers.

The following tables indicate the impact of co-worker follow up on leadership effectiveness by comparing Company A and Company D. While these companies are in very different industries, used different approaches to change participant behaviors, and had different participants, their results are almost identical! Leadership involves a relationship. The most important factors in improving this relationship are clearly neither the coach nor the training methodology. They are the leader and the co-worker.

*Feedback or coaching by telephone works about as well as feedback or coaching in person.*

A common belief is that feedback or coaching is a very personal activity and that it is much more effective if done in person (as opposed to by phone). Research conducted by these five organizations does not support this belief. Scores for increased effectiveness in the organization that conducted almost all feedback by telephone were almost identical to those of the organization that conducted all feedback in person.

The organization that used all external coaches made sure that each coach had at least two one-on-one meetings with his/her client. Some coaches met with clients regularly in person, while some had almost all interactions by telephone. There was no clear indication that either method of coaching was superior to the other.

One client did a customer satisfaction study comparing client satisfaction with 360° feedback by telephone vs. feedback in person. Clients were equally satisfied with either process. While this type of "happiness measure" is not as valid as long-term measures, it shows that even the short-term experience of feedback by telephone is as positive as the experience of feedback in person.

*Either internal or external coaches can make a positive difference.*

In Company E only external coaches were used. In Company D only internal coaches were used. Both approaches produced very positive, long-term results in increasing leadership effectiveness. The three major variables in determining whether to use an internal or external coach seemed to be time, credibility, and confidentiality.

In Company D internal coaches were given the time to do the job. This was treated as an important part of their responsibility, not an "add on" to do "if they got around to it". They were trained in the coaching process and viewed as highly credible by their internal clients. (In fact, their internal clients said they preferred them to external coaches.) Each internal coach worked with a leader in a different part of the business. They assured their clients that this process was for high-potential development, not evaluation.

In many organizations, internal coaches just do not have the time to interact with a meaningful sample of leaders on an ongoing basis. In some cases they may not seem as credible to executives. In other cases they may appear to be in a conflict-of-interest position in terms of their role as a coach and their role as an evaluator. If these perceptions exist, then external coaches may be preferable.

Internal coaches were seen as having the advantage of knowing the business and understanding the key players. External coaches were seen as having the advantage of an outside perspective and objectivity. Neither choice seemed to be better or worse in an absolute sense. The appropriate answer appears to depend upon the needs of the client and the organization.

*Training, when coupled with ongoing follow-up can make a huge positive difference.*

Companies A and B provided training on how to involve co-workers in follow up and continuous improvement. Leaders also received ongoing reminder notes, suggesting that they should follow up. With today's new technology, very sophisticated follow-up systems are available to help ensure that follow up occurs. As a general rule, the more the company follows up with the leader, the more the leader follows up with the co-workers, and the more effective the leader becomes.

One reason that coaching is so effective is that it helps inspire leaders to follow up with their people. For example, Company "C" found a strong correlation between the number of times that the coach followed-up and the perceived improvement in the effectiveness of the leader. These results are consistent with those companies who had a follow-up system in place.

Follow up with leaders does not have to be a costly tool. Internal coaches can make follow-up telephone calls. Computerized systems can send reminder notes. Almost any follow up is better than none. One of the great weaknesses in most training and development programs is the insufficient attention to follow up. Many companies spend millions of dollars for the "program of the year" and almost nothing on the follow up that can ensure that the program actually gets executed!

*Frequency of interaction with co-workers and coaches seems to be more important than duration of interaction.*

In all five companies the frequency of interaction seemed to be a major variable. All companies noted that frequency of interaction with co-workers was a key driver of success. As was mentioned earlier, Company C also mentioned that frequency of interaction with coaches made a positive difference.

Historically, a great deal of leadership development has focused on the importance of an event. This event could be a training program, a motivational speech or and executive off-site meeting. The experience of these five companies indicates that real leadership development is a process.

A good analogy might be working out. The historical approach to leadership development would be to have leaders sit in a room and watch demonstrations on how to exercise. The company would then wonder why everyone was not in shape a year later! Arnold Schwarzenegger wisely said, "Nobody ever got muscles by watching me work out." The key to getting in shape is not in understanding the theory of working out. It is in engaging in the process of working out!

The personal trainer example seems very applicable to the role of executive coach. The role of the personal trainer is to remind the trainee to do what he/she knows should be done. Most personal trainers spend far less time on theory than they do on execution. The same seems to be true for leadership development. Many leaders know what to do. They have all read the same books and listened to the same "gurus" giving the same speeches. Their challenge is not in understanding the practice of leadership; it is in practicing their understanding of leadership.

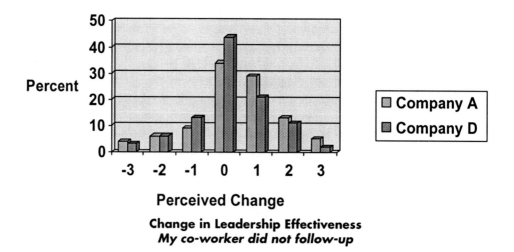

**Change in Leadership Effectiveness**
*My co-worker did not follow-up*

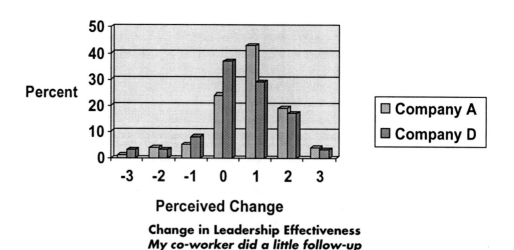

**Change in Leadership Effectiveness**
*My co-worker did a little follow-up*

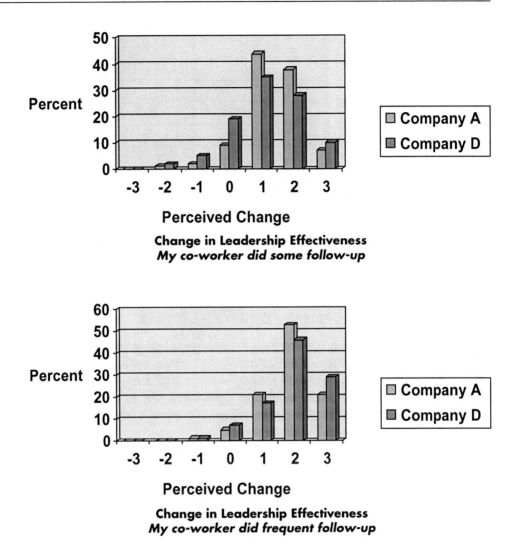

**Change in Leadership Effectiveness**
*My co-worker did some follow-up*

**Change in Leadership Effectiveness**
*My co-worker did frequent follow-up*

One lesson is clear from the four companies in our study that included training programs. If leaders go to a leadership development program, and do not follow up with their people, they might as well stay home. While there is some evidence that coaching without follow up can produce some positive change in leadership behavior (from Company E), there is no evidence that training without follow up can produce positive change in leadership behavior that is any greater than random chance.

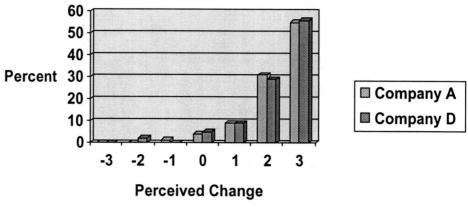

**Change in Leadership Effectiveness**
*My co-worker did consistent or periodic follow-up*

## IMPLICATIONS FOR LEADERSHIP DEVELOPMENT

This study was not conducted involving a few graduate students at a university. This was a review of the leadership development efforts of five major corporations. It involved thousands of leaders and over 20,000 co-worker respondents. The findings are clear and encouraging. Companies can do a great job of helping leaders achieve a positive, long-term, measurable change in behavior without spending unneeded amounts of time or money!

Leaders can clearly benefit from coaching, but it does not have to be done by external coaches. Company D has shown that internal coaches can produce the same positive results as external coaches. In fact, in Company D, internal trainers conduct the train-the-coaches sessions for internal coaches. Company D is now in the process of documenting how line-manager internal coaches can produce the same positive results as internal coaches within the human resources division.

Coaching can be a great complement to training. Companies C and D both showed how either internal or external coaches can help make training "come to life" though frequent coaching interactions.

Coaching can work as a stand-alone process, even when it is not combined with training. Company E produced fantastic results by having leaders receive coaching that was completely disconnected from any training.

Leaders who do not have coaches can learn to be coached from their co-workers. The key to changing behavior is to learn to learn from those around us, and then to modify our behavior based upon their suggestions. Companies A and B used a highly streamlined and efficient process of focused training and reminder notes to help leaders achieve a positive, long-term change in effectiveness without either internal or external coaches. Feedback discussions by telephone were shown to work as well as feedback discussions in person (and at a much lower cost)! By using new computerized follow-up systems and telephone coaching, companies can provide outstanding support to a larger numbers of leaders in a cost-effective manner.

The key learning from these five companies is that leadership is about the relationship of the leader with his/her co-workers, not about the relationship of the leader with a coach or trainer. If the organization can teach the leader to reach out to co-workers, to listen and learn and to focus on continuous development, both the leader and the organization will benefit. This process does not have to take a lot of time or money. It does, however, require a lot of commitment and follow-up.

# CHAPTER 3

# PRACTICE POSITIVE DEVIANCE FOR EXTRAORDINARY SOCIAL AND ORGANIZATIONAL CHANGE

*Jerry Sternin*

## ABSTRACT

*In his own words, Jerry Sternin, widely known as "the father of applied Positive Deviance," explains the story of how an acute crisis led him to the practice of Positive Deviance (PD). He tells how he was propelled, over a twelve-year period to develop and amplify the approach which has enabled communities of more than 2.2 million people in Vietnam to sustain the reduction of childhood malnutrition and has been replicated in 24 other countries around the world.*

*The chapter includes a step-by step approach to positive deviance, a formula for positive deviance, exceptional stories of change within societies, and a "how-to" and "what-to-do" approach to positive deviance that could be applied within organizations, institutions, or your own society.*

## SUMMARY

Positive Deviance (PD) is based on the belief that in every community there are certain individuals/entities whose **special practices or strategies** enable them to find a better solution to a pervasive problem than their neighbors who have **access to exactly the same resources.** We call these individuals "positive deviants". The PD design provides a tool to enable the community to discover the positive deviants' uncommon, but demonstrably successful strategies. The community then analyzes those strategies retaining only those that are accessible to all its members. Finally, the community designs an intervention, enabling all its members to access and **practice** the newly discovered PD strategies.

## INTRODUCTION

Nasirudin, the great Sufi mystic, appears in different guises in different stories. In one story, he is an acknowledged smuggler. Every evening when Nasirudin arrives at the customs house, the inspectors feverishly search the contents of his donkey baskets to discover what he is smuggling. But, each day their efforts go unrewarded. No matter how thoroughly they inspect, they find nothing but straw.

The years go by and Nasirudin grows richer and richer. The customs officials vainly continue their daily search, more out of habit than hope of actually discovering the source of his wealth. Finally, Nasirudin, now an old mans, retires from his smuggling trade. One day he happens to meet the customs chief, who has now retired as well. "Tell me, Nasirudin," pleads his former adversary, "now that you have nothing to hide, and me nothing to find, what was it that you were smuggling all those years?" Nasirudin looks the customs chief in the eye, shrugs his shoulders, and replies, "Donkeys, of course!"

In December of 1990, the confluence of a remarkable set of opportunities and potentially disastrous challenges compelled me to find the "donkeys" among the straw or risk professional ruin.

## POSITIVE DEVIANCE DEFINED

> *"It's easier to ACT your way into a new way of THINKING, than to THINK your way into a new way of ACTING"*

"IS POSITIVE DEVIANCE JUST 'BENCHMARKING' AND 'BEST PRACTICES' IN DISGUISE?" is a question I often hear when talking with people at corporations.

The simple answer is "no". Best practices and benchmarking build off a proven success formula. There is nothing wrong with that except that onlookers often view the circumstances that foster the success as quite different from their own. The examples of highly successful development models that have not made it past the pilot phase, or have failed during attempts to reach scale, are all too numerous.

Given sufficient time, funding, technical expertise and control over inputs, it doesn't take a rocket scientist to create a successful prototype, be it a community development model, a car, or an efficient production team. Building on best practices and customizing the prototype to meet the particular needs, climate and culture of the intended beneficiary/client virtually assures its success.

Try replicating the model, however and in more cases than not, you are greeted with cries of "Not invented here;" "We're not them;" "Our cultural, religious, socioeconomic climate is radically different from theirs;" or "It just won't work here"

Why all the resistance? Because you are attempting to impose a model whose best-practice status was conceived and nurtured within the context of a foreign, carefully constructed, and controlled best-case scenario. The very kernel of its success, its sensitivity to the idiosyncratic climate and culture of the intended beneficiary/ client, renders it sterile in less hospitable soil. I think that communities and corporations alike mirror the body's immune defense response to what is perceived as the threat of foreign matter.

Building upon a best-case scenario may ensure the *success of the prototype,* but usually spells the death knell for efforts at replication or scale. PD begins, therefore, with a "worst-case scenario." It identifies those individuals who should be the least likely to succeed, but somehow or other have managed to do just that!

By choosing those least advantaged, who have no access to special resources, but yet have succeeded against all odds, PD guarantees the accessibility of their successful strategies. If they can do it, anyone can. And because the selection of the PDs comes from within a given community, PD ensures that "it is invented here;" "They are us, so if they can do it so can we;" and most convincingly, "It **can** work here, because it **does!**"

## POSITIVE DEVIANCE PROCESS

1. **DEFINE** the problem and what the outcome of a successful program to address it would look like. (This is usually stated in terms of behavior or a state of being.)

**Example:**
Define Problem: Poor children are malnourished (a state), or employees do not participate in company community projects (a behavior).
Define Successful Program Outcome: Poor children would be well nourished or employees would participate in community projects.

2. **DETERMINE** if there are individuals with the community who already exhibit the desired behavior (*i.e,.* identify the presence of Positive Deviants).

**Example:**
There are already today poor families in the community who have well-nourished children or there are employees outside of the Corporate Responsibility office, who actively participate in corporate community projects.

3. **DISCOVER** their uncommon practices or strategies that enable the Positive Deviants to succeed when their neighbors do not.

**Example:**
Poor families with well-nourished children add shrimps, crabs, and greens to their children's diet and feed them four times a day rather than twice. Or, employees who participate in community projects, tutor students online from their desks. They choose weekend projects which are targeted for families and enable them to participate while spending quality time with their wives and kids.

4. **DESIGN** an intervention enabling others in the community to access and *practice* the PD behaviors.

**Example:**
Bring mothers of malnourished children together to cook and feed the identified PD foods to their children. Require all moms to actually **bring** a handful of the new PD foods (shrimps, crabs, greens) everyday, thus creating a new habit.

Create a roster of volunteer activities which can be done online from the employee's desk. Hold an online volunteer workshop for all employees. Encourage employees to volunteer by providing an extra one-half hour at lunchtime for those who volunteer for office-based community activities.

## BACKGROUND: DESPERATE TIMES LEAD TO DESPERATE ACTIONS

In 1990, the US Save the Children (USSC) received an unprecedented invitation from the Government of Vietnam to create a program that would enable poor villages to solve the all-pervasive problem of childhood malnutrition. What was unprecedented about the invitation was that at that time the US government had a full embargo against Vietnam and had no diplomatic presence in the country.

Save the Children asked me if I would leave my post as director of their Philippines program and go to Hanoi to open the Vietnam program. Although, (or was it *because?*) the challenge was so formidable, I eagerly accepted, and in December of 1990, I left for Hanoi along with my wife, Monique, and son, Sam, to become the thirteenth, fourteenth, and fifteenth American residents in that city. The challenges facing me as country director were overwhelming and had a programmatic as well as political nature.

## THE CHALLENGE

In 1990, between sixty and seventy percent of all Vietnamese children under the age of 5 suffered from some degree of malnutrition. It was clear to the government that traditional supplemental feeding programs (implemented by indigenous and international development organizations) provided temporary solutions at best and were dramatically unsustainable. Although there were significant gains in children's nutritional status during the period of program implementation, they were all but lost after the programs ended.

The reasons for the failure were not difficult to discern: a) villagers were passive program beneficiaries who were neither encouraged nor required to change any of the underlying behaviors/practices which led to their children's malnutrition; b) the nutritional gains which were realized during the program's implementation were completely based on *external* food resources which were no longer accessible to villagers after the implementing agency departed; and c) the major focus of the program was on providing additional food, with little or no attention paid to improving the all-important child caring, and health-seeking behaviors associated with good nutritional status. In short, "they came, they fed, they left" and nothing had changed.

On the political front, many officials were not at all happy to have Save the Children; an American non-governmental organization (NGO) working in Vietnam at the very time the US government was actively trying to punish the country through its embargo. The depths of those feelings were made clear to me at a meeting with a friend from the Ministry of Foreign Affairs. Mr. X had been very supportive of Save the Children from our very first meeting and could be counted on to pull no punches. "There are many officials who do not want you in this country," he warned during my first month in country. "You have six months to demonstrate impact, or I'm afraid my ministry will be unable to extend your visa."

Six months! It usually takes a year to just *begin* to set-up an office in a new country. Staff has to be identified and trained, office space found, potential development partners identified, meetings held with potential program communities, etc. But here we were with six months to actually demonstrate program impact. I was clearly stunned by the enormity of the challenge, and only minimally reassured by my recollection of the fact that the Chinese character for the word *crisis* is made up of two ideograms, *danger* over *opportunity*.

The Government of Vietnam did not, and never would have, the resources to address the problem of ongoing malnutrition in 10,000 villagers. A strategy had to be identified to enable the villagers themselves to sustainably solve the problem. The focus clearly had to be preventive as well as curative. Given our six-month deadline, as well as my concern for sustainability, I knew that this couldn't be "business as usual." A radical new approach would have to be developed: the solution to community malnutrition would have to be based on resources already available within the community. It was the search for such a strategy that led me to Positive Deviance (PD).

Although the PD concept had been around for many years, it had been used primarily as a research tool to answer questions such as "What enables some malnourished children (the positive deviants) to be rehabilitated more quickly than others receiving the same treatment in the same medical facility." The research identified the factors that led the positive deviants to better outcomes than other members of their cohort. However, it stopped at that and didn't use that knowledge to actually build a program.

The PD idea intrigued me. If it were true that some individuals in a community were better able to solve problems than others with access to exactly the same resources, could we use that simple truth to build a sustainable national nutrition program? With less than five months left until our visa renewal deadline, I was more than eager to test the hypothesis.

## TESTING THE HYPOTHESIS

After discussions with Hanoi-based officials, my wife, Monique, our Vietnamese counterpart, Mrs. Hien, and I identified Quong Xuong District in Than Hoa Province, some four hours south of Hanoi, to test the PD approach. We were eager to choose a location close enough to the capitol so that if successful, the pilot site could be easily reached by government officials and other visitors, thus facilitating program replication.

In late January 1991, with only 14 weeks left until "impact,-or-no-visa" time, our gang of three rented a black 1970 Russian Volga and made the first of what was to be hundreds of visits from Hanoi to Quang Xuong, 120 kilometers south on Highway number 1.

Over the next week we met with members of the People's Committee, Women's Union, and Provincial Health Cadre to discuss the proposed project. We emphasized our commitment to collaborating with villagers to identify solutions to the problem of malnutrition from within the communities. The independent and proud Vietnamese officials, all of whom had suffered greatly during the "American War," warmed to the idea that solutions would be Vietnamese rather than foreign and that the project would not cause dependency. They were also, however; clearly skeptical that it would work.

The deputy chairman of the province asked how much money and what kind of material inputs the project would provide. I explained that in order to create a sustainable model most of the inputs would have to come from the villagers themselves. We would, of course, provide some material input, but would focus attention on training and developing the capacity of the villagers to address their own problems. The deputy chairman, (responsible for development of an extremely resource-poor province), reluctantly gave the go-ahead to the "rich American NGO" which promised nothing more than "capacity building" and "self reliance" instead of medical equipment or supplemental food, the stuff of "real assistance" in his estimation.

Next, we conducted a sample nutritional baseline survey in four villages proposed by the local leaders as potential pilot sites. The good news was that the villages definitely needed help and provided a most appropriate choice for the first PD trail.

The bad news was that between sixty and seventy percent of the children under the age of three were malnourished!

Immediately after the survey, we met with the People's Committee, Women's Union and Farmer's Union members and leaders to discuss the proposed project. Villagers shared their beliefs about the causes of malnutrition as well as their aspirations for future improvements. We explained the PD approach and how it might help the community realize its objectives.

Fortunately the villages had previously had supplementary food programs initiated by an international development agency. Their experience provided an excellent backdrop against which to explain and contrast the Positive Deviance approach:

**SC:**        Have you ever had a Supplementary Feeding Program here before?

**Villagers:**    Yes

**SC:**        What was the result of the program?

**Villagers:**    Our children got healthier and put on weight.

**SC:**        What happened after the program was over?

**Villagers:**    Our children became malnourished again.

**SC:**        Why?

**Villagers:**    Because the (agency name) project was over and there was no one to give us those foods (supplemental oil, milk powder, wheat, high protein biscuits, etc) which made our children better.

**SC:**        Well, what would you like to see different in the future then?

**Villagers:**    We want to see our children get better, and stay better.

**SC:**        Do you think it would be better if you could do that on your own, rather than be dependent on outside help?

**Villagers:**    Of course, but how is that possible, we are a poor village?

With more faith at this point than proof, I crossed my fingers behind my back and explained that PD could help them address the problem of malnutrition through the identification of **solutions, which already existed within their community.** They would require some initial help with those children who were **already malnourished,** but PD would show them how to **independently sustain** their children's improved nutritional status once they had been rehabilitated. In order to do so, however, the village would have to assume major responsibility for the program.

The first step towards community assumption of program responsibility was the creation of village health committees (VHCs), comprised of members from the Women's and Farmer's Union, People's Committee, and village health cadre. Next, the VHC chose health volunteers (HVs) from among those women in the community willing to serve in that capacity

# COMMUNITY OWNERSHIP OF THE SOLUTION: DISCOVERING THE POSITIVE DEVIANTS

The newly selected health volunteers were taught to weigh children and chart their nutritional status by placing a dot on a simple card with two axes, one for age, and the other for weight. Although some children had been previously weighed during the sample nutritional baseline survey, the GMP held in late February 1991 was the first universal weighing of all children under three in the communities. After the children had been weighed, we met with the health volunteers to review the findings. Consistent with findings from the sample survey, sixty to seventy percent of the children suffered from some degree of malnutrition.

We asked the volunteers to study their lists to see if any of the **well-nourished** children came from **very poor families.** Volunteers reviewed their lists and noted "Co, co vay chao rat ngheo nhunhg khong suy dinh duong." (Yes, yes there are some children from **very poor families** who **are well nourished!**) "Do you mean," we asked, "that it's possible **today** for a **very poor child** in this village **to be well-nourished?**" "Co!" came the reply, "it is!"

*It is important to stop the narrative here to note how important it was that it was the health volunteers who identified the positive deviants .As a result; from the very onset of the program the community felt ownership for discovering the solution to their own problem.*

*As the Positive Deviance Approach became refined over the next years, the importance of" the "aha," the self-discovery that a solution was already present within the community, took on every increasing importance. As we will later see, the discovery step became a central component of the PD design.*

Having established the possibility of being well nourished despite poverty, the group explored the implication of the discovery. If some very poor families in the village had well-nourished children, it was probably possible for their poor neighbors to do so as well. This realization set the stage for what would become the Positive Deviance Inquiry, the process that would identify how some very poor families were able to adequately nourish their children, while their neighbors of the same economic status, were not.

The newly selected HVs and SC staff held several focus group discussions in each of the program villages. Meeting informally with mothers, grandmothers and community health providers, they discussed the **conventional** behaviors, beliefs regarding feeding, caring, and health-seeking practices in the community.

It is important to note that positive deviants, are only deviant within the context of their **divergence from the norm,** (in this case, the traditional feeding, caring and health-seeking behaviors practiced by the majority of the community). We needed then to first identify those prevalent practices and behaviors before discovering what the positive deviants were doing differently.

One of the distinctive characteristics of the PD approach is that it helps people learn by use of contrast. Trying to identify PD behaviors, without looking at how they contrast with the norm, would be a much less powerful behavioral-change motivator.

## POSITIVE DEVIANCE INQUIRY

In early March 1991, the moment of truth was at hand. We had identified those poor families who had well nourished children. Now the challenge was to see if we could actually identify some uncommon strategies or behaviors that would account for their kids' superior nutritional status.

Choosing six of the poorest families with well-nourished kids, Mrs. Hien, (our SC counterpart), several health volunteers, a few village leaders and I divided into teams and went to see if this PD hypothesis would actually work. Over a two-day period we visited the six households, asked questions, and most importantly, observed how moms and other family members fed and cared for their PD kids.

Pay dirt! We met back together after visiting the positive deviance homes and were ecstatic. Each team had discovered that in every instance of a poor family with a well-nourished child, the mother (or caretaker) was collecting tiny shrimps and crabs (the size of one joint of one finger) from the rice paddies and adding these to the child's diet along with the greens from sweet potato tops. Although readily available and free for the taking, the conventional wisdom held these foods to be inappropriate, or even dangerous, for young children.

Along with the addition of the shrimps/crabs and greens, we discovered other positive deviant practices involving frequency and method of feeding and quality of care and health-seeking behaviors. For example, most families fed their children only twice a day. Because these children under three years old had small stomachs, they could only eat a small percent of the available rice at each sitting. The PD families, however, were feeding their kids four or even five times a day. Therefore, using exactly the same amount of rice, spread out over an additional two or three meals, the PD kids were getting twice the calories as their neighbors who had access to exactly the same resource!

This first working experience with PD was invaluable to me in beginning to develop a conceptual framework. Although the approach has undergone many iterations and refinements over the past 12 years, the definition of a positive deviant emerging from these first 6 household visits has remained remarkably constant over the past 12 years: *A positive deviant is one whose special practices or behaviors enables him to outperform or find a better solution to a problem than his neighbor who has access to the same resources.*

## Designing The Intervention

Within the context of those first villages we had discovered what it took for a poor family to have a well-nourished child. The challenge now was to design an intervention that would enable the villagers to actually access and **practice** those demonstrably successful behaviors.

Our first objective was to rehabilitate the malnourished kids, who only required the provision of sufficient additional nutritious food. The real challenge, however, was to enable the parents to **sustain** their kids enhanced nutritional status at home after rehabilitation.

To address the issue of sustainability, the program would have to avoid the pitfalls the villagers had previously experienced with the supplemental feeding programs. It would require an intervention that would provide parents an opportunity to practice the new behaviors needed to sustain their child's enhanced nutritional status at home **after** rehabilitation.

The newly identified and **demonstrably successful** PD behaviors provided the answer to the challenge. The addition of a small handful of shrimps/crabs and greens, in combination with increased frequency of feeding and other uncommon caring practices, was clearly sufficient to keep a child well nourished in the pilot communities. Moreover, as we had learned during the Positive Deviance Inquiry, these foods and practices were accessible even to the poorest families in the village Getting parents and caretakers of malnourished children to adopt these new foods and practices was another question!

Given the program objectives, and very mindful of the approaching visa deadline, we wasted little time in designing, with our community partners, a Nutrition Education and Rehabilitation Program (NERP) which incorporated the lessons learned from the Positive Deviance Inquiry. For two weeks every month, mothers/caretakers brought their malnourished children to a neighbor's house for a few hours every day. Together with the health volunteers, they prepared and fed a nutritious, **supplemental** meal to their children. The mothers/caretakers practiced cooking new recipes with the health volunteers and also learned and applied basic health and childcare practices. The sessions provided an opportunity to practice the other successful behaviors identified during the Positive Deviance Inquiry.

Great! We could get moms to practice these new behaviors during the monthly two-week NERP sessions. But I was plagued by how to ensure that they continue those practices at home **after** the sessions. I had seen so many examples of failed programs that relied on **teaching** people what to do, as though that knowledge would necessarily change their behavior.

If we were going to meet the government's request to create a model that would enable villagers to address their own nutrition problems, we had to be certain that the newly discovered, demonstrably successful behaviors be practiced and internalized rather than perfunctorily performed during the Nutrition Sessions. Although it would be another ten years before I came across the phrase, I was struggling with an intuitive awareness that *it's easier to act your way into a new way of thinking, than to think your way into a new way of acting.*

It was the concern for the sustainability of behavioral change that led to the mandatory "daily contribution" component of the nutrition sessions. Every day, each mother/caretaker was required to bring a handful of shrimps/crabs and greens as the price of admission to the sessions.

Although, I didn't know it at the time, the daily contribution established the precedent for another of the critical PD principles: *Once the PD behaviors have been discovered, an intervention must be designed which gives others in the community the opportunity to access and **practice** the new behavior.* (In this case, going out to the rice paddies every day and collecting the small shrimps and crabs.) This focus on practice rather than knowledge has proven to be the successful key element in the PD approach that brings about lasting behavioral change across a range of issues.

All children were weighed on the first and last day of the nutrition session. Their mothers/caretakers and health volunteers anxiously awaited the hands of the scale to come to rest a few hundred grams higher than at the previous weighing. After the two-week session was over, the mothers/caretakers returned home to continue practicing their newly acquired feeding, caring and health-seeking behaviors. (Having gone out to the rice paddies every day for two weeks to get shrimps and crabs and encouraged by the visible changes these brought about in their children, it was quite natural for the mothers/caretakers to continue the new habit for the rest of the month.) Those children who reached normal nutritional status during the nutrition sessions "graduated" and those who remained malnourished were signed up for the next session to be held the following month.

## DISCERNING AND DISSEMINATING

### *Keeping Score and Scoring Another 6-Month Visa*

By June of 1991 just over six hundred children had participated in the first four two-week nutrition sessions. On the last day of Session 4, we anxiously awaited for the final results of the weighing. The very encouraging trend of the first three sessions continued, and a total of 183 kids, (more than 30 percent) had been rehabilitated. It's difficult to say who was more excited: the moms of the newly rehabilitated kids; the health volunteers who saw themselves as an integral part of that success; the district health personnel (who scrupulously monitored our every move and reported back to the higher officials); or our Save the Children team who had just received a reprieve and another six-month visa.

By the end of the first year of the program more than 1,000 children were enrolled in the nutrition sessions and more than 90 percent of them had "graduated."

The swift and visible improvement in the health status of the kids who participated in the nutrition session was to have a dramatic impact on the nutritional status of children born into program communities in the future.

As families witnessed first hand, the extraordinary improvement in their children's and their neighbors' children's health status, brought about through the adoption of the new Positive Deviance feeding, caring and health seeking behaviors, these practices became the new conventional wisdom. When babies were born in the community, families would continue to practice the newly adopted behaviors that had been so successful with their older children.

An external evaluation of the program in 1994 by a consultant from Harvard School of Public Health found that "younger siblings, not yet born at the time of the nutrition program implementation, [were] benefiting from the same levels of enhanced nutritional status" [as their older siblings].

In December 1992 I decided that the model had proven its efficacy and it was time to demonstrate that the success could be replicated elsewhere as well. We expanded to an additional 10 villages, bringing the total number to 14. It took just over a year to realize the same dramatic results in the new villages as in the original four pilot villages.

It is important to note that although the new villages were adjacent to the original ones, and the resource base was almost identical, we insisted that the Positive Deviance Inquiry be carried out in each new village. By now it was clear to me that the **process** of self-discovery was every bit as important as the actual uncovered behaviors. This focus on self-discovery would continue over the next decade to be a key element of the PD approach and one that separates it from many other expert-driven approaches.

Although working on issues of program quality was a major priority, I also spent a lot of time making sure that people in the development community, (other non-governmental organizations, UN agencies, and the Vietnamese Health and Foreign Affairs Ministries) knew about the success of the program. I met with various groups and made many presentations, always focusing on the success achieved by the Vietnamese villagers and health volunteers in solving their own problem. The latter was not only true, it was also extremely important to emphasize in the context of the extremely proud Vietnamese social and political milieu.

Because the program site was only 4 hours from Hanoi, dozens of delegations came to visit, and soon there were numerous requests for help in accessing the model to use in other parts of the country. In keeping with the essence of the PD approach, I was committed to ensuring that people learned by doing.

Enter serendipity. During the time our Save the Children team was struggling to create an intervention that would enable interested parties to access and practice the PD approach, I brought the UNICEF representative, Steve Woodhouse, to the field to visit one of the pilot nutrition program communities.

It was a rainy day, and we sat together in a dark, thatched roofed hut with a group of local moms whose kids had participated in the nutrition program. The moms were animatedly explaining to Steve, how **they** had rehabilitated their children, and how it was possible for any poor family to have a well-nourished child if they only did things the right way. After an hour or so, we thanked the women and left the hut. Steve, standing in the pouring rain, said, "That was amazing, I've never learned so much so quickly. It was really a . . . a . . . a 'Living University.'" A name and a concept were born.

The Living University was comprised of the 14 program villages, which provided a "social laboratory" for the study of the nutrition model at different phases of implementation. Groups wishing to replicate the model came to Than Hoa to learn the conceptual framework as well as to make field visits to the 14 program villages for first hand observation and hands-on participation in different program components.

Upon graduation, Living University participants returned home to implement the PD Nutrition Program in a single site, which they then used as their own "Mini-Living University" for further program expansion in adjacent areas. Using this strategy an estimated 50,000 children had been rehabilitated through the efforts of more than 400 Living University graduates who have replicated the program in 250 communities with a population of over 2.2 million.

Because the PD Nutrition Program is based on the successful behaviors of individuals within the **socio-cultural context** of **each** program community, it is always, by definition, "culturally appropriate." This unique feature of Positive Deviance has led to a replication of the nutrition program by 20 national and international NGOs in some 25 countries in Africa, Asia, Latin America, and the Middle East.

## Same Paradigm, New Applications

After the success of PD in the field of nutrition, I was eager to try out the approach in other sectors. As the PD conceptual framework continued to take form, I realized that it should work to address any problem requiring social or behavioral change **if** there were some individuals (the positive deviants) who **already exhibited the desired behavior.** Rather like a mathematical formula: $bc > db = eb = (PD)$

where bc = Behavioral Change, db = Desired Behavior, eb = Exhibiting Behavior (already) = appropriate to use PD.

The next opportunity to test out the hypothesis came when I left Vietnam in 1996 to take over the Save the Children Director position in Egypt. We had been there for little over a few months when the Egyptian Female Genital Mutilation (FGM) Task Force, working through CEDPA, an American INGO, contacted Monique. They wondered if PD could be used to help them in their work, advocating for the elimination of female circumcision (labeled Female Genital Mutilation by the task force).

Female circumcision constitutes an enormous challenge for those who advocate against the practice. It goes back more than 3,000 years to Pharaonic times and is practiced by an estimated ninety to ninety-five percent of all women. How does one begin to attempt to change a practice so deeply ingrained into the very fabric of Egyptian culture for three millennia?

As you might imagine, the local NGOs advocating against the practice were quite demoralized. Their focus, typical of most traditional development perspectives, was on the problem. PD provided a dramatically different worldview. Rather than dwelling on the enormity of trying to end a custom practiced by ninety to ninety-five percent of the female population, PD turned the proposition on its head: How is it possible today for the families of the 300,000-500,000 women who are not circumcised to withstand the enormous social and religious pressures to undergo the procedure?

Working with Monique several of the collaborating local NGOs began to identify the first few positive deviants. In this case, the deviant was not the uncircumcised girl or woman, but rather the parent who had decided against the procedure, the sheik or Coptic priest who spoke out against the practice, or the husband who knowingly married an uncircumcised woman.

It was an extremely difficult and sensitive process, but gradually the first few positive deviants helped identify others, who helped identify still others. The Positive Deviance Inquiry was directed at discovering the precise factors that led to the decision to abandon the millennia-old tradition as well as the strategies enabling the positive deviants to actually act on that decision.

The PD approach provided the local NGOs with a crack in the wall of silence surrounding FGM and an entry to begin a dialogue that had previously been strictly taboo. Once the process began, the community equilibrium was disturbed, unleashing a series of powerful and unanticipated outcomes.

A circumcised teen-age girl emboldened by the breach in the taboo, gathered together a group of girls from her village circumcised the same year as she. She had them relive the fear and trauma they experienced, and asked them if they wanted the same to happen to their younger sisters. Circumcised daughters began talking to their mothers about their trauma and sense of betrayal at the time of their circumcision. A

PD father who had circumcised his oldest daughter but refused to do so with his other daughters, poignantly recalled, "Ever since the day I had my eldest daughter circumcised, she has been lost to me. She will no longer look me in the eye. I will not do the same with my other girls."

Some of the positive deviants were not only willing to give testimony, but also eager to assume a more active role in advocating against the practice. Through the positive deviants' testimony which revealed the reasons they did not circumcise their daughters, or in other cases, why they disagreed with the practice, local NGO staff and community members were able to design more effective, demonstrably successful ways of combating the practice in their communities.

Last month, Monique received e-mail from her former colleagues in Egypt sharing some great news with her: "There have been no reported circumcisions in the first four pilot villages in the past year." Although this represents an infinitesimal percent of the Egyptian population, it proves that change is possible and that the identification of positive deviants can be leveraged to bring it about. For those local NGOs working on the problem the experience has been profoundly empowering. They have expanded the approach to other villages and instead of going through the motions, while doubting the potential for change, they now know it is possible.

## From Condoms to Corporations—PD Amplified

After Monique's Egyptian experience, I had my next opportunity to try PD in the context of HIV/AIDS risk reduction. An international NGO working with commercial sex workers in the North of Vietnam was eager to apply PD to help in their work. The vast majority of commercial sex workers (CSW) are unable to negotiate with their clients to use condoms. In the context of their high exposure to HIV/AIDS this constitutes a life threatening risk.

Working with the local partners of the INGO, I met with a group of CSWs who had been trained and employed as peer educators to advocate for condom use among their sister workers. They acknowledged that they knew for sure there were a few CSWs who could always negotiate to get their clients to use condoms. These women charged the same amount of money, were the same age, worked in the same establishments, but yet were obviously doing something different from the majority.

Using the PD Inquiry, the peer educators identified and then interviewed the positive deviant CSWs to discover their uncommon strategies. They returned to the room where we were holding our workshop, genuinely excited by their discoveries. It seemed that the only difference between those CSWs who could and couldn't get their clients to use condoms, was merely having the right negotiation strategy. The right words were the only resource that stood between success and failure.

One of the CSWs reporting on her PD Inquiry said, "I can't believe how simple it is. We usually plead with our clients to use condoms because our children would be helpless if anything happened to us. She (the PD) turns it around and says, 'I know you are a good and honorable man, and I'm not worried about you. But I have so many clients every day that I may have a disease. Please don't risk your health and your family's good name for a moment's pleasure. Put on a condom and then we don't have to worry about you catching a bad disease from me."

The PD negotiation strategies were analyzed by the CSWs and by their partner NGO and then a plan was implemented to enable the wider CSW community to access and practice the newly discovered strategies. We began by having the CSWs role-play the successful PD dialogue for getting clients to use condoms. They next practiced the successful lines used to convince drunken clients, old clients, young clients, and foreign and local clients to use condoms.

The CSWs then set up a schedule for group support meetings where they will continue practicing successful negotiating strategies and share new ones. In addition, the local NGO realized that their former strategy of **telling** CSWs to use condoms or risk getting HIV/AIDS was much less effective then designing a program that would enable them to **practice how** to get their clients to comply. The CSW pilot is also informing similar programs in Burma and is being networked elsewhere as well.

Here again, the success of the PD approach in bringing about behavioral change was based on creating an intervention to enable people to **practice,** rather than learn about the successful, uncommon strategies. This last example is also illustrative of the importance of enabling the very people whose behavior has to change to be the ones to discover the solutions already present in the community.

In addition to the HIV/AIDS, female circumcision, and nutrition applications which I've described, the PD approach is now being used to look at other problems requiring social or behavioral change as diverse as asthma management, obesity, education performance, malaria, anemia, and street children.

# FROM PD PRACTITIONER TO "AMPLIFIER"

In June of 2001, after 16 years overseas with Save the Children, Monique and I decided the time was right to return to the US to try to take PD to another level. My years as a PD practitioner had been among the most exciting in my life, but I wanted to figure out a way to make PD accessible to a wider audience of development workers, social entrepreneurs and particularly those individuals responsible for setting policy.

Because of the demonstrated success of PD in countries throughout the developing world, and in a growing number of sectors, I was able to get a grant from the Ford Foundation to amplify the positive deviance approach in the US and internationally. The grant, funded through Tufts University where Monique and I are visiting scholars, has provided an excellent launching pad for a whole new spectrum of PD activities.

Among the most exciting has been the foray into the corporate world. In 1998 I had made a presentation at the State of the World Forum in San Francisco. Unbeknownst to me, in the audience was a women named Barbara Waugh whose title at HP

"Worldwide Change Manager" pretty well describes her mandate. Barbara got really turned on by the idea of PD and created a PD initiative within HP, trying to amplify the work of those special individuals in the company who make uncommon contributions beyond their job responsibilities, but who have access to no special resources. I have had the opportunity, at Barb's invitation, to run PD workshops at HP. Barb has authored several books where she has written extensively on her PD experience The network continues to grow.

As my interest in the use of PD in the corporate world grew, I was able to find ways to reach a wider audience. During 2000 and 2001, my keynote addresses at corporate responsibility conferences at Warwick University in England and Boston College's Center for Corporate Responsibility in Miami seemed to evoke real interest from a whole new set of players. My focus at these workshops was to orient corporate participants to the use of PD not only as a means of maximizing their returns on investments in community projects, but also as an internal tool to enhance corporate productivity.

The head of corporate responsibility at a large US corporation lamented that the only people who lived the corporate good community *citizenship* mandate were the people working within his department. A PD exercise revealed that that was not completely true. A few PD outliers within other branches of the company were heavily involved in community activities. What enabled these positive deviants, working within the same work time and family responsibility constraints, to tutor students and take active roles in other company-sponsored community activities, when their workplace neighbors did not?

The exercise PD Inquiry revealed that the PDs addressed the time constraint issue by tutoring students online, thus saving the hour round trip to the local high school. The need to spend time with their wives and kids on weekends was cited by the majority of employees as a prime reason preventing their participation in community activities. The PDs with the same concern chose corporate community activities that were specifically targeted for families, thus enabling them to have quality time with their families at the same time they participated in activities that benefited the community.

Other examples of corporate problems got workshop participants thinking out of the box and identifying solutions that already existed within the corporation. The shift from focus on the problem and its causes to discovering existing solutions and building on what was going right was empowering for many of the participants.

# CONCLUSION

The more I talk to people about PD, the more I am convinced of its power and utility. There is an exquisite simplicity about the approach that makes it intuitively accessible to most people. Simply stated: Identify what is going right within the community and build on it. A typical reply to my description of the PD approach is, "Oh yeah, I often try to do that in my work, but never really had a name for it."

The PD approach provides a conceptual framework and a specific design for what many leaders and innovators intuitively do. However, providing the name and concept is very important. It's like the 40 words that Eskimos are reported to have for snow. The expanded vocabulary actually enables them to see qualities of snow that those of us without the vocabulary can't. Similarly having the PD concept, vocabulary and design enables us to more effectively harness its power

I hope that the case studies and PD design described in this chapter are sufficient to get you to consider how you can use the approach in your own work. The possible applications are as broad as the number of problems that require some kind of social or behavioral change.

Solutions don't have to be complicated and externally identified to work. The answer does exist at this very moment. PD provides a demonstrably successful approach to solving problems while valuing the wisdom that already exists within your community. In that sense; it is an unusually empowering and respectful approach. Look no further than your own community, and when faced with a seemingly insoluble problem—think donkeys.

# CHAPTER 4

# HAVE THE COMMON TOOLS AND LANGUAGE TO WORK TOGETHER FOR POSITIVE CHANGE

*Ralph Jacobson*

## ABSTRACT

*The majority of leadership development activities fail to significantly improve organization performance. This article reveals that it may be highly beneficial to shift the emphasis from developing individual leaders' skills to developing shared organization leadership deliverables, by providing a common leadership language, a common leadership process, and the tools to accomplish them. It describes a number of best practice tools for leadership development and the outcomes of a leadership development approach that was implemented in a Fortune 100 financial services organization and in a mid-sized construction company. The approach taken in these two companies is applicable to a broad range of organization challenges and cultures.*

## INTRODUCTION

### Context

It is clear that the costs of weak leadership are high. Witness the latest spate of leader malfeasance, which is costing the affected organizations, their shareholders, and the national economy billions of dollars. Many corporations exist in industries so highly competitive that a single misstep risks their very survival. It is also clear that the leaders in those organizations destined to thrive in the long term have learned how to leverage their human, financial, and technical resources to greatest advantage.

If you are looking to improve the performance of your organization's leaders, you will find no shortage of advice. Type the word *leadership* in Amazon.com's search engine, and 11,835 book titles appear. Billions of dollars are spent every year in thousands of attempts to find the holy grail of leadership development. And yet, in most organizations there appears to be less and less correspondence between what we know leaders should do and what leaders actually do. The reasons are three-fold:

First, much of the training that purports to develop leaders could more appropriately be considered management training. Management training focuses on such subjects as dealing with difficult people, providing one-on-one job coaching, conducting performance appraisals, and comprehending finance for non-financial managers. Management training typically addresses immediate needs for enhancing managers' interactions between their peers, upper managers, and individual employees.

But the practice of leadership is significantly more complex. Leadership requires anticipating future events and building organizational environments to encourage collaboration between stakeholders who must forego their immediate self-interests to gain long-term organizational benefit.

Second, most leadership development approaches focus on assessing the leadership competencies of individual leaders and providing specific training to moderate their weaknesses. Although some individual leaders are interested in determining how to utilize their strengths and moderate their weaknesses, others are not. And some leaders are capable of making significant change. Others are not. Thus, leadership development is often confined to developing the skills of individual leaders, who must strive to learn in situations where they are isolated from their peers.

Third, most leadership development approaches assume that individual leaders are responsible for the success of business units. Such approaches are based on the notion that organizational health and achievement are best attained when individual leaders work independently to achieve organizational goals. But the complexities of modern organizations require that human, financial, and intellectual assets be fluidly combined and applied. Individual leaders working independently cannot provide sufficient power to sustain long-term organizational health. Therefore, it is critical that leaders learn how to lead together. To do this, leaders need a common understanding of the deliverables expected of them in their leadership roles and how they must work together to create them. Collaborative leadership is tied to the use of a common language and common processes and to the establishment of mutual accountabilities for performance.

## *Approach*

The Leader's Toolbox approach, rather than focusing on individual leadership capabilities, provides a common understanding of what all leaders must do. It defines what the organization must improve, not what individual leaders must improve. After working through the Toolbox together, leaders focus on a shared agenda for organizational improvement, instead of individual development plans.

A comparison of the traditional competency approach and the Leader's Toolbox approach appears in Figure 1. A comparison of the traditional training approach and the Leader's Toolbox approach appears in Table 1. We do not suggest that one approach is better than the other, but rather that some combination of approaches will more significantly accelerate leader performance.

# THE LEADER'S MAP™ AS A TOOL

The Leader's Map is the foundation for the Leader's Toolbox. It

- defines what leaders can be expected to deliver to their organizations: direction, competence, and implementation. The degree of leadership in an organization can be evaluated and improved by measuring these three deliverables.
- defines and creates the five universally experienced leadership challenges leaders encounter in delivering direction, competence and implementation.
- provides a universal leadership language and demonstrates the major steps in the leadership process.

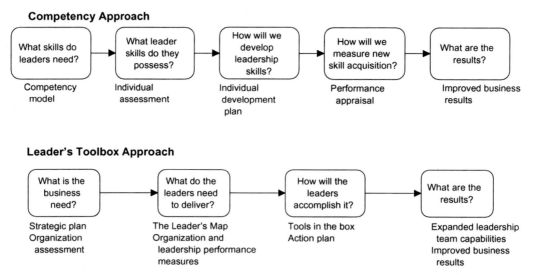

**Figure 1. A comparison of the competency approach and the Leader's Toolbox approach**

*Source:* Leading for a Change: How to Master the Five Challenges Faced by Every Leader by Ralph Jacobson

**Table 1. A comparison of the traditional training approach and the Leader's Toolbox approach**

| Traditional approach | Leader's Toolbox Approach | Rationale |
|---|---|---|
| Defines set of leadership competencies | Define the deliverables of shared leadership and the processes used to create them | Rather than perceive leadership as a set of skills, view it as a process. Processes can be defined, learned, measured and improved. |
| Assess each leader's skills | Measure the level of organizational leadership | Create a common ground for action, and avoid individual assessments that cause shame and fear |
| Improve individual leader's skills/competencies | Focus on common language and tools and total leadership team competence | Build a foundation for work in overcoming common leadership challenges. Build a climate for team learning and action. |
| Each leader focuses on his or her objectives | Create opportunities for leaders to work together to resolve complex organizational issues | Focus on the development needs of the organization. Encourage leaders to work together and experiment in aproductive manner. Free individuals from a sense of being judged. In the long term, promotes faster paced individual leadership growth. |
| Objectives are defined as meeting financial targets and/or accomplishing specific tasks | In addition to meeting standard business objectives, seek progress in meeting broad leadership objectives | Encourage leaders to pay attention to both short term and long-term business performance. |

## When to Use the Leader's Map

The Leader's Map provides a path to help you develop an agenda and implement change. Use this tool when you

- want leaders to work together to lead change.
- want to determine where to put forth your leadership efforts.
- prepare for a major organizational challenge.
- diagnose situations that may not be going as planned.
- establish a leadership agenda.
- develop colleagues into better leaders.

# The Leader s Map "

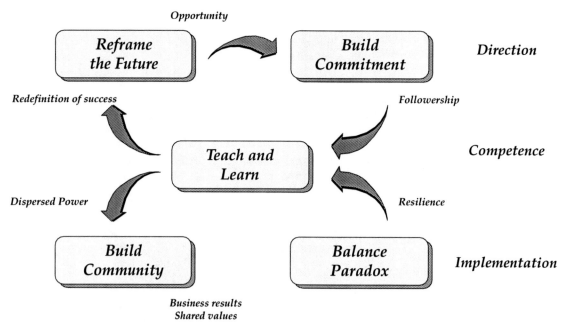

Figure 2.    The Leader's Map

## Table 2.  Overview of the Leadership Challenges

| Challenge | Purpose |
| --- | --- |
| Reframe the Future | Establish a strategy that repositions the company to take advantage of its strengths, redefine relationships with key partners, revolutionize how the product is produced or delivered to customers, and create new products and services. |
| Build Commitment | Develop a critical mass of supporters who understand the strategy and will do what is necessary to achieve it. |
| Teach and Learn | Develop the leadership skills needed to move the organization forward. Build competence in people throughout the organization. Establish learning processes that encourage undertaking new challenges now and into the future. |
| Build Community | Create the infrastructure that enables people to work together effectively and accomplish the expected results. |
| Balance Paradox | Build in the mechanisms to manage the conflicts that naturally occur when reality collides with expectations. |

## How to Use the Leader's Map

To use the Leader's Map, follow these steps:

### Step 1. Gather the leaders or form the appropriate group

1. Determine the purpose for meeting together.
2. Determine who the appropriate people are.
3. Tell those assembled that the purpose of this exercise is not to evaluate the capabilities or contributions of each individual, but to assess the overall effectiveness of the contribution made by the whole group of leaders.
4. Provide an overview of the Leader's Map to the group.

### Step 2. Determine where you are on the Leader's Map

You can now use the Leader's Map to measure the strengths and weaknesses of your organization's leadership group as a whole. You can decide not only to assess your group's strengths and weaknesses, but also to determine which of the five challenges is the most critical. You can use three methods to determine where your group is functioning on the Leader's Map™: opinion, dialog, and survey:

- **Opinion**. Ask the members of the group first to describe the activities and outcomes for each of the five challenges and then to reach consensus what they believe their leadership agenda should be.
- **Dialogue.** Ask the members of the group to determine the most important issues that must be addressed by the organization. The group should focus on defining the broad-based issues that are fundamental to the long-term success of the organization. Ask them to avoid focusing on short-term issues. The senior leader of the group creates an atmosphere for open and honest communication.
- **Survey.** Appendix A of *Leading for a Change: How to Master the Five Challenges Faced by Every Leader* contains a survey and a scoring key to use in evaluating organization leadership and how leaders are meeting the five challenges. The members of the group can limit who takes the survey to their own group or they can expand the survey to other organizational members.

### Step 3. Develop the leadership agenda

Establish the leadership agenda based on the findings of your evaluation. The leadership tools that will be of special interest to you appear in Table 3.

**Table 3. Example Leader's Toolbox Tools**

| Challenge | Example of Tools |
|---|---|
| Reframe the Future | • External relationship map |
| | • Scenario planning |
| | • S curve |
| | • Appreciative inquiry |
| Build Commitment | • Commitment wheel |
| | • Stakeholder analysis |
| | • Stories |
| Teach and Learn | • Core organization competencies |
| | • Type I and type II learning |
| | • After action review |
| | • Situational leadership |
| Build Community | • Team formation and functioning tools |
| | • Alternate leadership structures for different kinds of leadership work |
| | • Internal contracting |
| | • Seeing organization processes |
| Balance Paradox | • Polarity map |
| | • Organization, role, and individual paradoxes |
| | • Conflict management approaches |

# LEADERSHIP TOOLS

Once the leaders understand and accept the challenges described in the Leader's Map as their leadership work, they can begin to use the appropriate tools to address them. These tools, which are based on the wisdom of the best organizational thinkers, are presented in such a manner that their theoretical foundations are transparent to the users. An individual leader, a small or large group, can use the tools. The tools offer leaders and their followers sets of options for addressing each challenge. As leaders from different parts of the organization come together to address organizational issues, they will be more productive whenever they use the same tools and the same terminology to address them.

*The External Relationship Map:* Based on the work of Michael Porter, this tool provides a current and future state analysis of suppliers, customers, competitors and substitutions to determine how the organization will achieve long-term strategic advantage.

*Scenario Planning:* Based in part on the work of Peter Schwartz and Kees van der Heijden, this tool develops sets of alternate futures to help organization leaders rehearse how they will deal with future unpredictable uncertainties.

*S curve:* Based on the work of George Land, this tool determines where the organization is positioned in its ability to grow given its current products and services. It helps anticipate the internal organization dynamics that are likely to occur when a new direction is implemented.

*Appreciative Inquiry:* A methodology, based on the work of Cooperrider and Srivastva, provides a worldview that focuses on the positive to determine what is possible and desired. The approach is particularly useful in determining a new vision and building the support to implement it.

*Commitment wheel:* Leaders determine their purpose, the roles they expect others to play, the structural and cultural alignment and how they will build relationships with critical stakeholders. The result is clarity of the major steps leaders need to undertake to ensure that followers support a new initiative.

*Stakeholder Analysis:* Before communicating with critical stakeholders, this tool encourages leaders to first understand what is important to each stakeholder, be clear about what they want those stakeholders to contribute, and determine how to fashion messages so that they positively resonate with the needs of the various audiences.

*Stories:* Stories are useful in fashioning and communicating strategy, shaping organization culture, and learning from the past. This tool provides the format and architecture of a story to increase their impact.

*Core Organization Competencies:* Based on the work of Prahalad and Hamel, organization competencies are the unique skills possessed by the organization that allow it to create superior products and services. This tool helps leaders define those competencies so they can be successfully created and maintained.

*Type I and Type II learning:* The obstacle to new learning as defined by Chris Argyris is the inability to overcome two kinds of fear of failure: The fear of undertaking a new experience and not succeeding and the fear of failing because new skills have not been learned. This tool helps people in new learning situations develop an appreciation for the underlying obstacles that often prevent the acquisition of new knowledge.

*After Action Review:* Developed by the United States Army, this tool provides a very structured debriefing process after an event has occurred to fully understand what has happened. This provides the learning to improve future organization, team, and individual performance.

*Situational leadership:* Developed by Hersey and Blanchard, this tool describes the leadership and coaching style behaviors to help new learners in different situations succeed.

*Team productivity model:* Developed by Ralph Jacobson, this tool helps teams define the tasks that must be completed during the form, storm, norm and perform stages of their development. By consciously building their productive capability, teams are more likely to perform faster and more efficiently.

*Alternate leadership structures:* The nature of leadership work varies widely. Reliance on the traditional organization chart as the primary means of establishing authority can hinder success. Alternative structures such as matrixes, hub and spoke, dialogue, and teams provide organization agility to deal with different leadership situations.

*Internal Contracting:* Often people from various parts of the organization have to work collaboratively. This tool results in a contract that defines what each party will deliver and ensures their commitment to do so.

Seeing organization processes: Rather than see the organization as a set of department or functions, this tool encourages people to see the underlying processes that are required to create and deliver products and services to customers. This encourages people to work together more collaboratively and helps define the work to be accomplished.

*Polarity Map™:* Based on the work of Barry Johnson, this process helps people determine whether they are dealing with problems or paradoxes. It provides the framework to effectively manage and balance paradoxes.

*Organization, role and individual paradoxes:* Paradoxes can be experienced at all three of these levels.

Conflict management approaches: This tool, based on the work of Killman and Quinn, provides leadership strategies for those who are in the midst of conflicting demands from various stakeholders.

## Example Tool: The Four Cs (Communication + Commitment + Consequences = Contract)

Projects often require people from different departments or functions to work together. Coordinating work across the organization can be difficult when people have different agendas and perspectives around what is important. Use this tool to:

- determine the specific work and timetable to accomplished cross-functional/department projects.
- determine how the parties will work together.
- establish the communications process.

## Step 1: Communicate

*Before meeting* with an individual leader, ask yourself the following questions:

- What is the important background/context of the situation? What do I need the other person/department to do?
- How will the output of their work be measured? When do I need it to be accomplished? Why?
- Why is the completion of this work important? To me? The organization?
- What is the best way to communicate my expectations?

*During your meeting,* ask yourself the following questions:

- What additional information do I need in order to understand what this leader should be delivering? Are there better ways of getting my expectations met?
- What concerns do I have about this leader delivering what I expect?

## Step 2: Commitment

- What will each of us do?
- Do we agree? If we don't agree, what will I do? How will we communicate the progress we have made?

## Step 3: Consequences

Before the close of the commitment conversation determine the answers to the following questions:

- What will happen if either of us fails to meet our commitments to one another?
- In the event one of us is unhappy with the other's performance, how will we communicate our concerns?

If a commitment is not met, ask the following questions:

- What is the business result of our inability to meet established commitments?
- What can we learn from this experience that will help us work together in the future?
- How has this transaction impacted our working relationship? What do we need to do about this?

# CASE STUDY #1: IMPLEMENTATION OF THE LEADER'S TOOLBOX AT A FORTUNE 100 FINANCIAL SERVICES ORGANIZATION

## Impetus for action

In the spring of 1999, the senior leaders of a *Fortune* 100 financial services organization foresaw changes in the marketplace that would require the company to institute major innovation. The organization had a long history of making significant investments in leadership development efforts. In addition, for many years the company had linked a percentage of merit pay to the acquisition of a core set of leadership competencies.

The company's leaders would be required to focus their efforts beyond the boundaries of their traditional functional silos or business units. They had to work together with internal and external partners to create organizational environments where high levels of performance could be achieved and sustained. They had to focus well beyond their usual one-on-one interactions and the management of their own groups. They had to use broad, deep skills in strategy building and scenario planning. They had to engage stakeholders who had competing interests and agendas. They had to deal with complexities that would not yield to traditional problem-solving approaches.

A design team was assembled and charged with creating a new leadership development approach, one that would build on the organization's current leadership competency model and further enhance its leadership culture. The design team was given the following criteria to use in evaluating the quality of their effort:

- Incorporate the ideas of well-known organization thinkers.
- Provide well-rounded tools to help leaders focus on the whole spectrum of their leadership responsibilities.
- Apply what is learned to impact business results.
- Ensure that individual leaders grow and find value in their development effort and that the organization achieves long-term sustainability
- Provide opportunities for leaders to become actively involved in developing their colleagues and facilitate meaningful communication networks across the organization.

## Implementation

The design team chose to use the Leader's Toolbox because it easily accommodated a broad range of leader responsibilities. It provided processes to guide short-term thinkers a better understanding and process for the strategic aspects of their responsibilities. The language used in the Toolbox was easily understood. Further, the examples amply demonstrated that the process of leadership could be learned, measured, and improved.

The design team reviewed the tools described in *Leading for a Change: How to Master the Five Challenges Faced by Every Leader.* They selected the following five tools for their initial development effort.

The design team planned and implemented a two-day, action-learning session, during which participants worked in small groups to address a wide variety of leadership challenges to an organizational business case. Participants then applied the tools to a personal business case (*e.g.,* a current leadership situation).

To reinforce the learning from the group activities, the design team provided 30 minutes of individual coaching one-week and four weeks following the program. In these coaching sessions, participants further refined their leadership issues, and they developed plans and strategies for appropriately using the tools in their situations. The coaches used an evaluation template to determine if participants were using the tools correctly and whether improvements to future training sessions should be made. During the second coaching session, the coaches asked participating leaders if the tools had been useful.

## Results

The initial feedback from the coaching sessions indicated that participating leaders improved the quality of their decisions and their abilities to engage greater numbers of colleagues. When participants from different parts and levels of the organization worked together, they reported that they experienced greater understanding, increased performance, and more incentives for applying the tools. Several participants noted that when

**Table 4. Example leadership tools and their purpose**

| Tools | Based on the work of | Purpose |
|---|---|---|
| External Relationship Map | Michael Porter | Assess business threats and opportunities |
| Scenario Planning | Integration of numerous authors | Develop alternate strategies |
| Stakeholder Analysis | Ralph Jacobson | Build engagement with diverse stakeholders |
| Core Organization Competence | Gary Hamel & C.K. Prahalad | Determine, measure, and implement organization skills necessary to achieve market dominance |
| Polarity Map | Barry Johnson | Balance Paradox |

their traditional leadership approaches had proved to be ineffective, the tools offered workable alternatives. Most disheartening to the design team, however, was their observation that although participants found the tools quite useful, most, in the stress of completing day-to-day tasks and meeting deadlines, had retreated to their traditional ways.

The following insights were derived from this experience:

- Unless new leadership is called for in the environment, participants will revert to short-term thinking and familiar leadership behaviors, regardless of the quality of the development activity. Therefore, in the context of the daily operating environment, senior leaders should expect participating leaders to balance short-term task goals with long-term strategic leadership goals.
- For participants to risk functioning in new, perhaps higher, organizational levels, it is generally necessary to blur the boundary between learning and pursuing a strategic business objective. Rather than offering a generic training program throughout the company, it is cost effective to offer development experiences only where there is a strategic need and the presence of senior leadership to provide support.
- Future leadership development efforts should be modularized to meet specific situations. Workout sessions and coaching should be designed to deepen the learning and improve business results.
- When several levels of leaders understand the tools, greater engagement and more thorough understanding will result. Therefore, the definition of leadership development must shift from focusing on the organization's top levels to reaching deep within the organization.

These insights suggest the need to spend as much time considering how participants will improve organizational performance after the development experience as designing the development experience itself.

Several months after the first phase of the Leader's Toolbox, the organization undertook an exhaustive study to evaluate every one of its leadership development programs. It identified the leadership competencies needed to move the business forward and found ways to evaluate current development offerings. It instituted new, more effective ways to equip leaders for greater diversity and reflective thinking. The team measured the effectiveness of current training/tools by using the

- assessment data from participants (and trainers where applicable).
- frequency and degree to which training and tools were accessed within the various divisions of the organization.

- leadership strengths and weaknesses as indicated by established organizational measurements.
- data from interviews with leadership at all levels to determine what competencies leaders need to meet current and future organizational goals.

One conclusion from the study was that the Leader's Toolbox filled a critical gap in the company's training curricula; that is, it encouraged greater strategic thinking on the part of middle management. Most surprising was the finding that the Leader's Toolbox encouraged collaborative behaviors and a greater sense of community among leaders. Dialogue about the various tools encouraged a process of accepting differing perspectives equally.

## NEXT PHASE OF IMPLEMENTATION

It is highly unlikely that the Leader's Toolbox approach will be declared a major corporate initiative in which everyone above a certain grade level must participate in two days of training. Delivery of the Leader's Toolbox will remain innovative, fresh, and flexible enough to fit a wide range of business issues and contexts. Clearly, there is a need to develop the leadership skills of a broad range of people, who will then be aware of broad market issues and strategic options. For example, leaders at all levels will understand the organizational context so that when midcourse corrections become necessary, their buy-in will already have been developed. Leaders will find it easier to lead cross-functional collaborations during periods of innovation and change.

Thus the Leader's Toolbox will more likely be implemented where

- there is a strategic need.
- building leadership to achieve better organizational performance is highly valued.
- several levels of leaders are expected to use the tools.
- leaders are encouraged to test their new leadership behaviors and evaluate the results.

It is possible to provide advanced reading and coaching to senior leaders on the use of the appropriate tools and offer the opportunity to identify the leadership issues to be addressed. Then senior leaders, in the presence of the coach, would plan to use the tools with large and small groups of critical stakeholders. They would facilitate sessions in which to address the identified issues. Performance measures of their leadership behaviors would include the quality of the session, the ideas and the sense of community that emerged, and the impact of subsequent leadership initiatives.

## Summary of Learning from the *Fortune* 100 Financial Services Organization's Initiative

The Leader's Toolbox supports the belief that leadership can be taught and that the organization will gain from investing in leadership development. When senior leaders want their people to change, they must be the first to model the new behaviors. If senior leaders do not demand change and do not model new behaviors, leaders at other organizational levels will remain focused on achieving short-term results. The problem with not using skilled leadership behaviors typically becomes obvious when it is too late and the business is forced to address significant issues that should have been dealt with earlier.

## CASE STUDY #2 IMPLEMENTATION OF THE LEADER'S TOOLBOX AT HARRIS COMPANIES

### Impetus for Action

Since 1947, the Harris Companies have designed, built, installed, and maintained piping, plumbing, heating, ventilation, and air conditioning systems for industrial and commercial customers. The organization, which is one of the largest and most successful mechanical contractors in the upper Midwest, has experienced exponential growth. Its dedication to quality service and timely delivery, its commitment to developing long-term relationships with customers, and the continuously upgraded technical capabilities of its employees have made the organization a viable force in the marketplace. The Harris Companies organization consists of a number of completely autonomous profit centers with separate profit-and-loss accountabilities. Project managers/leaders are free to contract with internal or external vendors.

When the boom in the building industry recently weakened, the demand for Harris's services also weakened. Primary contractors appeared to be less interested in quality of service and more interested in low cost. The value of Harris's brand eroded in a tough market. The demand for lower costs took an internal toll on morale as project leaders began to treat their peers (with whom they could subcontract) less than professionally. Rather than choose internal partners, project managers began to choose outside subcontractors.

The weak external demand and the dwindling use of internal partners had a significant impact on revenues. Long-standing corporate strategies and structures no longer worked their motivational magic. The CEO recognized the need to help people several levels deep in the organization to see the broader business issues and to develop more comprehensive responses to fewer and more demanding customers. As the rules of the marketplace changed, so should the company. Leaders throughout the organization needed to become more strategically focused, their internal relationships needed to improve, and their work processes needed to be refined. None of this would happen without strong leadership throughout the organization.

## Implementation

Rather than focus on developing the competencies of individual leaders, the CEO decided to build a common platform for supporting new leadership behaviors. He encouraged people to complete their current projects and then begin to focus on the long-term prosperity of the organization. He wanted leaders who could lead the performance of their profit centers and the performance of the corporation as a whole. The Leader's Toolbox offered the Harris Companies an opportunity to deal with its leadership issues.

A leadership survey was administered to all employees to measure the current quality of organizational leadership. The survey did not assess the strengths and weaknesses of individual leaders. Rather, it assessed the delivery of the five leadership challenges of the Leader's Map. Survey results indicated the organization was indeed experiencing difficulty with two of the challenges: Build Community and Balance Paradox. The tools presented in a follow-up two-day workshop focused leaders' attention on the need to address these two leadership challenges. To demonstrate his commitment to change, the president, who had been given individual instruction, presented four of the ten tools to his colleagues in the workshop. As in Finance International, participating leaders were provided with individual coaching one week and four weeks after the program.

## Results

The Harris Companies' leaders understood that unless their use of the tools became an integral part of their on-going work, their investment of time and money in training would yield little or no return. Following the workshop and the coaching sessions, the design team reviewed ways to incorporate the tools within the existing leadership processes of the organization.

In preparation for their strategic planning responsibilities the profit-center leaders were asked to use The External Relationship Map to describe their business as it is today and as they would like it to evolve in the future. They developed better means to assess their market environments and gained greater understanding of how their leadership behaviors impacted business performance. In almost all cases, the profit-center leaders gained valuable insights and greater understanding of ways to improve their businesses. The quality of their discussions at strategic planning sessions increased. They identified new opportunities to expand the business. The Harris Companies will use the External Relationship Map in evaluating future business ventures.

The Stakeholder Analysis tool helped Harris's leaders plan their approaches to peers. They became much more accomplished at selling ideas to one another. Further, they empathized more with one another. Conflict with environmental stakeholders—suppliers and customers—diminished, allowing Harris's leaders to focus on the needs of their customers and the business as a whole.

The three roles leaders play was used in discussions about career development and performance appraisal. This tool has proved particularly useful for making the role transition from individual contributor/supervisor to manager/leader. The feedback from participants suggested that they more easily understood why it was so difficult to exhibit the behaviors required of their new leadership responsibilities.

The CEO presented the Four Cs tool to project managers, who agreed to use it in all internal meetings associated with interdivisional projects, such as planning sessions and progress reviews. The Four Cs tool has been particularly successful in kick-off meetings and problem resolving sessions. It has significantly enhanced communications, reduced conflict, and reduced waste.

## *Learning from the Harris Implementation*

The impact of the Leader's Toolbox on business performance was far greater than that of Harris's previous leadership development efforts because the participants, from the very beginning, were expected to incorporate new learning in their work. The elimination of many issues during planning sessions and the reduction of internal conflicts encouraged greater collaborations between contractors and customers. The Harris Companies today operates at a higher professional plane than most of its competitors.

## SUMMARY OF THE LEADER'S TOOLBOX APPROACH

Leadership tools are a proven means to improve organizational performance. The learning and skill building primarily occur when leaders use the tools to accomplish important leadership and organization work. Through the use of the tools common terminology and shared leadership processes emerge, allowing participant leaders to impact organizational performance in a positive manner.

Unfortunately, the leaders of most organizations have not received training to accomplish the following five challenges:

- Reframe the future
- Develop commitment
- Teach and learn
- Build community
- Balance paradox

Furthermore, most leaders' frames of reference differ when they discuss how to accomplish their leadership work. In addition, most leaders struggle to define their agenda. The Leader's Toolbox will provide these leaders with a common terminology and sound processes.

The two examples of the Leader's Toolbox presented in this chapter demonstrate that the approach can be applied to a wide range of situations. When a common language and effective processes are applied to improving business performance, informed leaders can directly impact business performance.

In the design phase, it is critical to anticipate the leadership behaviors that should be exhibited and how to shape the environment to elicit them. Rather than rolling out a general training program to all employees, we recommend using the Leader's Toolbox to enhance leader responses to specific business needs.

# BIBLIOGRAPHY

Argyris, Chris, and Donald A. Schön, *Organizational Learning: A Theory of Action Perspective*. Reading, MA: Addison-Wesley, 1978.

Blanchard, Kenneth, Donald Carew, and Eunice Parisi-Carew, *The One Minute Manager Builds High Performing Teams*. New York: William Morrow and Company, 1990.

Cooperrider, D.L, and D. Whitney, *Appreciative Inquiry: Collaborating for Change*. San Francisco: Barrett- Koehler Communications, 1999.

Hamel, Gary, and C.K. Prahalad, *Competing for the Future*. Cambridge, MA: Harvard Business School Press, 1994

Jacobson, Ralph, *Leading for a Change: How to Master the Five Challenges Faced by Every Leader*, Woburn, MA: Butterworth Heinemann, 2000.

Johnson, Barry, *Polarity Management: Identifying and Managing Unresolvable Problems*. Amherst, MA: HRD Press, Inc., 1996.

Land, George, and Beth Jarman. *Breakpoint and Beyond: Mastering the Future Today.* City: HarperBusiness, 1992.

Porter, Michael. *Competitive Advantage.* New York: The Free Press, 1985.

Quinn, Robert. *Beyond Rational Management: Mastering the Paradoxes and Competing Demands of High Performance.* San Francisco: Jossey-Bass, Inc., 1988.

Schwartz, Peter. *The Art of the Long View: Planning the Future in an Uncertain World.* New York: Doubleday, 1991.

Sullivan, Gordon, and Michael Harper. *Hope Is not a Method.* City: Random House, 1996.

Van Der Heijden, Kees. *Scenarios: The Art of Strategic Conversation.* West Sussex, England: John Wiley and Sons Ltd., 1997.

## CHAPTER 5

# DEVELOP YOUR TOP EXECUTIVES THROUGH A PARTICIPATIVE "RAPID-CYCLE" DESIGN PROCESS

*Steve Terrell, Ron Meeks, Jim Bolt*

## SOUND BYTE

Rapid-Cycle Design®[1] (RCD) is a method of engaging line leaders in needs assessment and design of executive and leadership development programs that not only significantly increases senior line leaders' understanding, acceptance, and support of the solution by actively involving them in the process, but also cuts the time to market in half. Engaging line leaders in the general design of executive development strategies and programs enhances the business value of the designs, and increases the level of ownership and commitment to both the programs and to executive development in general.

## INTRODUCTION

> Our business is changing rapidly and more decisively than ever before, and we need to quickly have something in place to redefine our expectations of leaders during this time, and to provide specific ways of preparing them to lead differently . . . can we have this in one month?
>
> *Director, Executive Leadership Development*

This type of expectation of executive development resources from the top leaders is becoming more the norm than the exception. In response to this more frequent request by clients, we created a new approach to assessment and design of executive and leadership development strategies and programs, Rapid-Cycle Design®.

---

[1]Rapid Cycle Design® is a registered trademark of Executive Development Associates.

**Table 1. Comparison of the Traditional Approach vs. Rapid-Cycle Design®
Process**

| Traditional Approach | Rapid-Cycle Design® |
| --- | --- |
| • HR owned and operated | • Line + HR owned and operated |
| • "Cover the waterfront" with education options | • Line leaders "interpret business strategy" into key development requirements |
| • Interview executives | • Target and focus/prioritize options to meet business goals |
| • Slow and deliberate | • Web-based diagnostics to engage large numbers of key stakeholders |
| • Long time to market–no urgency | • Cut time to market in half |
| • Hire a consultant to prescribe the solution | • Design process flexibility allows higher frequency updating to match changing business cycles |

Rapid-Cycle Design® is a method of engaging line leaders in needs assessment and design of executive and leadership development strategies and programs that not only increases senior line leaders' understanding, acceptance, and support of the solution by actively involving them in the process. It also enhances the business value of the designs and reduces the time to market in half.

The companies we work with have more and more frequently expressed a concern that their line executives don't have ownership in their executive/leadership development strategy or programs. Dependence on human resources (HR) for design, development, and delivery of executive and leadership development programs has come into question, as line executives seek to ensure that their development investment is clearly linked to and in support of company strategy and line management priorities. Too often, HR has been solely responsible for developing executive/leadership development programs that are then presented to line executives for review and approval. Since the line typically has little or no input to the solution, HR is put in a position of having to sell their solution to a skeptical audience, resulting in low sponsorship and support from the line organization.

In addition, over the past few years, many of our clients have experienced an increasing need to shorten the time to market of new executive and leadership development projects. This need for speed is in direct response to rapidly changing dynamics within organizations, industries and the economy. Traditional approaches to assessment and design involve conducting large numbers of lengthy executive interviews, and highly iterative design and development processes, and often require 6 months or more to complete. Emphasis is often placed on designing the *perfect* solution, giving too much attention to design elements that often change upon review, adding to the time investment with little return on that investment.

The concepts of the Rapid-Cycle Design® process enable us to address both of these critical concerns. Through RCD-based processes, we can quickly, and with a high degree of confidence, validate/identify specific executive/leadership capabilities needed to address marketplace challenges and achieve business objectives, generate creative strategy and program design options, and build early understanding and acceptance by key stakeholders by involving them in the process. RCD reflects the new realities of today's rapid pace of change in the business world, higher expectations of leaders, and the ever-growing demand that executive/leadership development be tightly connected to company strategy (see Table 1).

RCD provides a way to achieve greater results through the optimum combination of speed and engagement. This idea is best conveyed through the following formula: $Q \times A = E$, or Quality of the Idea times Acceptance of the Idea = Effectiveness of the Idea. The following graphic depicts this concept.

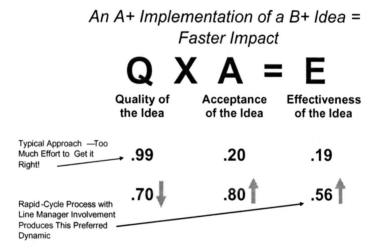

### An A+ Implementation of a B+ Idea = Faster Impact

$$Q \times A = E$$

Quality of the Idea     Acceptance of the Idea     Effectiveness of the Idea

Typical Approach —Too Much Effort to Get it Right! →   .99     .20     .19

.70↓     .80↑     .56↑

Rapid-Cycle Process with Line Manager Involvement Produces This Preferred Dynamic

In the typical approach, too much effort is expended to develop the perfect strategy or program design (to "get it right"). And typically, key stakeholders do not invest enough effort in generating acceptance of their concepts. Focusing too much effort on getting it perfect (a lengthy and ultimately impossible task), and not enough on generating acceptance, often minimizes the potential impact of a great idea: Quality (.99) × Acceptance (.20) = Effectiveness (.19). However, by generating ideas early in the process that are *directionally correct*, and then engaging line leaders in reacting to and validating them, we are able to increase buy-in (Acceptance) and generate a much higher impact solution for the organization: Quality (.70) × Acceptance (.80) = Effectiveness (.56).

The RCD process quickly produces a number of critically important outcomes, many of which would not be generated through traditional means:

- Enhanced understanding of the marketplace challenges, and the business' vision/strategy.
- Identification of the organizational and leadership capabilities required to achieve the business objectives.
- Prioritized areas of development and learning for executives/leaders based on the marketplace challenges and business objectives.
- An executive/leadership development strategy and/or program design(s).
- Design concepts and specifications for how and when the development/learning should occur (programs, processes, etc.).
- Identification of implementation challenges and ways to ensure organizational support for the development strategy, programs, and processes.
- Line leaders dedicated to the fulfillment of the leadership development plans—eager and willing to serve as on-going "advisors" to HR and the executive/leadership development team

Figure 1 illustrates the Rapid-Cycle Design® process, and each component of the process is subsequently discussed.

Rapid-Cycle Design® includes two complementary components: Rapid-Cycle Diagnostics and the Rapid-Cycle Design® Workshop.

## Rapid-Cycle Diagnostics

The Rapid-Cycle Diagnostics process allows us to identify and/or validate the capabilities that are needed to address the company's marketplace challenges and to achieve its strategy. In addition to traditional needs assessment methods, such as face-to-face interviews, Rapid-Cycle Diagnostics utilizes Web-based diagnostic surveys. This enables a broad reach into the organization to quickly obtain input from a large number of stakeholders regarding strategic business issues, marketplace challenges, competitive strengths and weaknesses, and required and current leadership capabilities. The process generates significantly increased engagement and ownership, and is completed in about 10 days versus the months a traditional process requires.

Rapid-Cycle Diagnostics is comprised of four critical components:

1. **Strategic Review:** Understanding the background of the business and its challenges so that the RCD methods can be tailored and focused. This involves reviewing reports, speeches and other relevant data to develop a solid understanding of the company's vision, strategy, and values. Some examples of the types of documents reviewed include:
   - Statements of company strategy / mission / goals / values.
   - Key speeches made during past few years.

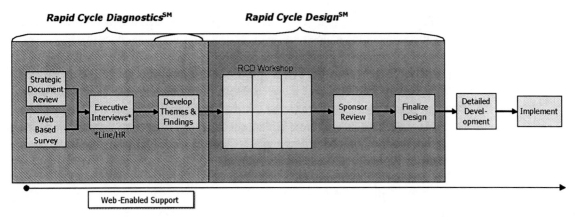

**Figure 1.  Rapid-Cycle Design™ process**

- Anything that describes key markets and competition.
- Company history.
- Relevant organization charts.
- Annual reports (stockholders and employee).
- Analyst reports (reports by company officers to security analysts and outside analyst reports of the company).
- Key human resource management documents, *e.g.,* appraisal forms, executive resource forms, incentive/bonus forms, etc.
- Descriptions of relevant existing or past management and executive training, education, or development programs and activities.
- Customer satisfaction survey/focus group reports/findings.
- Climate/attitude survey results.
- Bios on executives to be interviewed.

2. **Web-based Survey:** A brief survey that takes senior leaders less than 30 minutes to complete online, asking key stakeholders questions to:
   - Assess their understanding of and alignment around vision and strategy.
   - Identify their organization's critical marketplace/business challenges.
   - Identify required organizational capabilities.
   - Identify the leadership capabilities (mindsets, knowledge and skills) needed to successfully and effectively address the marketplace challenges, fulfill the vision, execute the strategy, and live the values.
   - Identify critical leadership capability gaps that could prevent/inhibit the organization from achieving its goals if they are not addressed.

The survey is customized to match the organization's needs, and is easily completed from any common, current Internet browser. The following "screen-shot"

(Figure 2) shows the beginning of our Web-based survey, which uses a variety of question types, including rating scales, rank order, prioritizing, and open-ended text responses.

3. **Executive Interviews:** Interview questions are designed to follow up on and clarify survey findings, and these in-depth interviews enable us to obtain top leaders' input and reactions to the survey findings. When an RCD workshop involves line leaders and there is enough time, the interview step can be eliminated in favor of an interactive review of survey findings during the workshop. Questions typically address topics such as:
   - Business Environment
   - Marketplace/Business Challenges
   - Vision/Strategy/Values

# Leadership Development Needs Analysis[51]

**Introduction**
This survey explores the business and leadership challenges of your organization and the leadership development capabilities needed to successfully address those challenges. Your responses are anonymous and will be combined with the responses of other executives. You will need about 30 minutes to complete this form.

**Context**
Begin by answering a few questions about your organization in general, its challenges, strengths and vulnerabilities. For the purpose of these questions, define the organization as the total enterprise overall (not just your area).

1. **Please provide your name and email address**
   Name: [                                    ]
   Email: [                                    ]

2. **In your opinion, which of the following marketplace challenges and changes will have an impact on the organization in the next few years? For each item, indicate whether you believe it will have no impact, a small impact, a substantial impact or a huge impact on the organization.**

|  | No Impact | Small Impact | Substantial Impact | Huge Impact |
|---|---|---|---|---|
| More competitors | O | O | O | O |
| Improved quality of competition | O | O | O | O |
| More globalization | O | O | O | O |
| More demanding customers | O | O | O | O |
| More sophisticated customers | O | O | O | O |
| Mergers and acquisitions | O | O | O | O |
| Strategic alliances and partnerships | O | O | O | O |
| Shorter product life cycles | O | O | O | O |
| Drastic reduction in prices | O | O | O | O |
| More strict legal and regulatory constraints | O | O | O | O |
| Increased competition for the best talent | O | O | O | O |
| More companies doing business through the internet | O | O | O | O |
| Rapid technological change | O | O | O | O |
| Increased pressure from shareholders | O | O | O | O |
| Meeting environmental requirements/goals | O | O | O | O |
| Changing employee lifestyles, values, etc. | O | O | O | O |

**Figure 2**

- Organizational Capabilities Needed to Fulfill the Vision, Execute the Strategy, and Live the Values
- Leadership Capabilities Needed to Fulfill the Vision, Execute the Strategy, and Live the Values
- Leadership Capability Gaps
- Desired/Needed Learning and Topics to Address in a Leadership Development Program

4. **Findings:** With a solid foundation of first-hand data, we are able to identify key themes, trends, and management issues, as well as executive/leadership development needs and priorities which will be used to "inform" the work of line leaders as they participate in a Rapid-Cycle Design® Workshop, the core element of the Rapid-Cycle Design® phase of activity.

# Rapid-Cycle Design® Workshop

*Rapid-Cycle Design® Workshop* processes utilize a blend of virtual activities and physical design workshops. The RCD Workshop engages HR and line leaders in defining the specific priorities and processes to be included in the ED/LD strategic solution. As a result, the ultimate solution is line leader owned and HR implemented. The Rapid-Cycle Design® Workshop is built on the belief that "If *they* build it, they will come."

The Rapid-Cycle Design® Workshop is comprised of four key components:

1. **Preparation/Pre-Work:** Workshop participants are invited to use a custom-designed Web site to prepare them for workshop participation to ensure that everyone starts at the same level of understanding. They can use the site to:
   - Develop an understanding of the project context, purpose, and objectives through review of documents describing the initiative.
   - Review findings from Rapid-Cycle Diagnostics. Summarized results of the Web-based survey and interviews (if available) are posted to the Web site for advance review to ensure participants understand the perspectives of their colleagues before the workshop begins.
   - Provide input to RCD Workshop agenda and focus. Participants review the workshop agenda and can provide input and suggestions to make the experience more valuable, and to start the engagement process prior to the workshop itself.

2. **Rapid-Cycle Design® Workshop:** This is a workshop that engages line and human resource/executive development/leadership development leaders in the work of converting business themes and capability gaps into the executive

development/leadership development (ED/LD) strategy and/or program design. Key features of the RCD Workshop include:

- Engage leaders from the target audience and other key stakeholders around themes and findings from Diagnostics. Line leaders participate for only the first 2 days of the typical 3-day workshop.
- Experts in executive/leadership development, from Executive Development Associates (EDA) and other sources, brief participants on trends and best/innovative practices in executive/leadership development. This serves to broaden and deepen participants' knowledge base around beneficial and impactful methods and approaches, and typically enables participants to think beyond their own personal experiences and to be more creative by seeing what other leading companies do.
- Other external speakers may be brought in as guest faculty if needed. For example, industry experts can provide up-to-date information and insights regarding trends and projected changes in the industry, enabling participants to compare their company to emerging industry issues and challenges, and helping them identify their own company's needs and priorities.
- Identify and prioritize executive/leadership development needs. Using the results of the Web-based survey and interviews with high-level executives (if they are conducted), as well as the new perspective they gain from presentations and discussion regarding ED/LD and industry trends, participants identify a list of development needs that are critical to their effectiveness in fulfilling the company's vision, executing the strategy, and living the values.
- Create high-level design options and guidelines for the "what" and "how" of ED/LD strategy and program development. In creating the what, workshop participants define the key topics to be addressed and the capabilities to be developed. In defining the how, participants recommend preferred learning methods, with an eye towards what will work in the company's culture and environment. They also provide input into who should receive/participate in what developmental activities and resources when using an integrated, systemic approach to the solution.
- After the workshop, the core team of ED/LD leaders and EDA consultants synthesize and fine-tune the large team's input, and create a recommended approach (e.g., strategy, architecture, program/s) to meet the identified and prioritized needs.

## Typical Rapid-Cycle Design® Workshop

The RCD Workshop is typically 2 to 4 days long, but varies with client need and circumstance. Workshops have ranged from 1 day to 4 days in length.

As mentioned, participants may be asked to prepare for the workshop by reviewing preliminary themes and findings online, at a custom-designed workshop Web site. Some clients have had line managers preview and comment on draft program design options online. Their comments are synthesized and presented to the entire group during the workshop for discussion.

A seasoned executive/leadership development consultant who is knowledgeable about the business and its challenges, best practices in design/development of ED/LD strategy, curriculum, programs and processes, and is a strong facilitator able to actively lead participants to achieve the workshop objectives facilitates the workshop.

Collaborative technologies, such as Web-based input and decision-making tools, are sometimes used in the RCD Workshop to engage the entire group of participants in virtual discussions, and obtain input on issues and questions from all members without undue influence from more vocal participants. It is particularly valuable to help manage large numbers of inputs in limited time.

A windowpane agenda for a Rapid-Cycle Design® Workshop focusing on design of an executive/leadership development program is shown in Figure 3.

# Rapid-Cycle Design Workshop
# Program Design Option

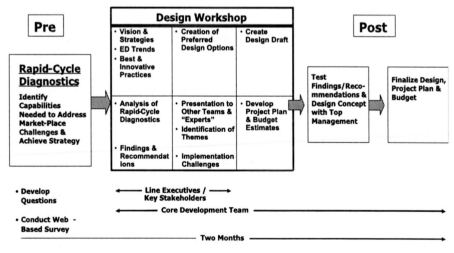

**Figure 3**   "Typical" Rapid-Cycle Design™ Windowpane Agenda

3. **Sponsor Review and Input:** Following the RCD Workshop, we encourage clients to review the recommended strategy and/or program design(s) with the sponsor(s) of the initiative and solicit their input. Developing support for the recommendations, and commitment of resources to implement the recommendations, is an essential step in the entire process. Review of the recommendations by sponsors ensures the proposed direction is in alignment with the company's strategic objectives and the sponsor's expectations of leaders, and creates another opportunity to obtain input from key stakeholders.

   At this stage of the design process, it is critical to ensure sponsor/stakeholder understanding of and commitment to implement the recommendations in order to build the momentum needed to execute.

4. **Final Strategy and Program Design–**After the sponsor's input to the recommended strategy and/or program design(s) has been obtained, the final version, integrating sponsor input and direction, is developed in detail. If the focus has been on ED/LD strategy, the team develops a detailed description of:

   - The ED/LD *Architecture*, in alignment with the company's vision, strategy and challenges, providing focus, structure, and priorities for development of targeted groups of leaders
   - A *Program Curriculum* that delineates proposed developmental resources (programs, processes, tools) based on top priority development needs, and linked to the company's vision, strategy, challenges and leadership capabilities needed to be effective and successful in today's and tomorrow's business environment
   - A *Plan to Implement* the strategy and make developmental resources available (build, buy) according to a schedule that is aligned with the company's strategy and operating plan, including a budget that specifies the investment needed to implement the strategy.

   - If the focus of the RCD Workshop has been on design of an ED/LD program, the team develops a detailed description of:
     - The Program Purpose, Objectives, Expected Outcomes, Business Need, and Target Audience(s).
     - A *Windowpane Agenda*, depicting the sequence, flow and timing of topics/modules in the program.
     - *Module Description* with objectives, topics/content overview, and potential faculty and other developmental resources for each module in the program.
     - A draft *Implementation Plan* describing the critical tasks needed to complete full development and implementation of the program.

# RCD IN ACTION

Based on our experience, Rapid-Cycle Design® is creating real value for organizations. For example, here is how it worked in one company.

- *Situation:* A major home improvement retailer made a commitment to develop regional and store leadership that would recognize and accept a new level of leadership expectations directly tied to the strategic and operational goals.
- *Solution:* With a "bias for action" already in the organization, a group of twenty from across the national retailer convened for a 3-day workshop. The mix of the group ranged from veteran district managers and store managers to corporate resources involved in the major strategic endeavors being driven by the new CEO. In the workshop, a vision for the outcomes of the strategic learning intervention was established, and over the next two days, through rigorous dialogue, presentation, critique, and facilitation, a "core design" was produced. This design was then provided to the executive/management/development staff who built the specific content and learning methodologies.
- *Outcome:* The ultimate program that was rolled out in the organization was at least 80 percent of the original core design as created by the line leader-based design team. With this there was strong ownership and excitement in the field to attend the session, and the pride of those involved was exceptional. For one RCD workshop participant, it was the first time he had experienced the power of a group process devoted to producing something so important in so little time. His comment was, "Not only have I helped with what we came together for, but I've experienced a process I can use in my own leadership role back in the store."

# CRITICAL SUCCESS FACTORS

Our experience using RCD has led us to uncover a number of Critical Success Factors such as:

1. Realize RCD is primarily a set of philosophies that when applied to real situations can produce major engagement and speed advantages. It must be tailored to the unique circumstances of the situation and company culture.
2. Be clear about the outcomes you are looking for. If it is for a program, focus all the diagnostics and pre-workshop processes around that. If it is for a more comprehensive leadership development strategy, the number of considerations increases dramatically, including RCD diagnostics and workshop design.
3. RCD may not be the appropriate approach in all situations. If a company has not had a culture of executive development, a more comprehensive, longer-range

investment in a change process is likely more important than the mere application of RCD to a specific problem. Issues of sponsorship, linkages across the HR systems, and other major challenges may be more foundational and need addressing.

4. If you have an existing executive/talent management steering committee or advisory board, try to use these stakeholders as much as possible, or have them sponsor individuals to be involved in RCD-related work.

5. Try to stimulate break-through thinking in the diagnostics and workshop, but respect the fact that with line leaders, you are also getting designs and concepts that are closer to what they will support, and will be pragmatic. Don't try to turn the line leaders into designers (this is a slippery slope), but stimulate them with perspectives about what they may not know about (*e.g.,* best practices, architectures from other companies, visits/talks by other executives, thought leaders, chief learning officers [CLOs] from other companies)

6. Always follow up and follow through. If the line leaders dedicate the time, they deserve to be informed and involved in the implementation. Because they helped you once, they will probably do so again.

## CONCLUSION

RCD is a powerful set of philosophies and tools that can significantly reduce the time required for needs analysis and design/development of executive/leadership development strategies and programs, while also significantly increasing senior line leaders' understanding, acceptance, and support by involving them in the process. Through Web-based diagnostics and a blend of virtual activities and an in-person design workshop, the time required for individual leader involvement is greatly reduced, although engagement in the process and acceptance of the outcomes actually increases.

# CHAPTER 6

# BUILD THE APPRECIATIVE CAPACITY OF ORGANIZATIONS

*David Cooperrider and David Bright*

## EXECUTIVE SUMMARY

This chapter presents a description of the Appreciative Inquiry Summit as a major organization development (OD) innovation. We describe how the Appreciative Inquiry Summit brings representatives from major organizational stakeholders into the same space and time for powerful, shared, positive, forward-looking inquiry that discovers and lifts up the best of what currently exists or could exist within an organization.

Appreciative Inquiry capitalizes on the power of words and images to shape creative conversations of the past, present and future. When an organization develops its appreciative capacity, it balances and transcends negative images through a focus on "what gives life to the system when it is most alive, effective, and synergistically connected in its ever expanding domain of relatedness." (Whitney and Cooperrider, 2000) Appreciative organizations value the fullness of organizing: the parts and the whole, the good and the challenging. They recognize the power of relationships to create opportunities for a better future. Because organizations evolve in the direction of the questions they consistently ask, every inquiry is an intervention. Organizations all over the world, like Roadway Express, have benefited from the practice of Appreciative Inquiry.

## OUR IMAGES AND THE ORGANIZATIONS WE LIVE IN

In the middle of a workshop not long ago, we conducted a simple exercise. We put one word on a flip chart: *wonder*. Without any other facilitation we asked people to simply turn to the person next to them, and share a personal story from any moment in their lives where they felt a real sense of wonder. Some recalled a profound sense of wonder they experienced when their child was born; others described a time they experienced the awesome splendor of nature. We asked them to listen deeply for insights. We planned for about 10 minutes.

The room was in a buzz. We tried to switch gears back to the scheduled agenda after the 10 minutes, and it was impossible. People were deeply into the stories. When they finally did come back, we asked people, in relation to the stories, to share adjectives and words related to wonder. These are a sampling:

**List 1.**

awe; surprise; full engagement; inspiration; sudden insight; emotional; hope-filled; terrifying; amazing awareness; humbling; meaning-filled; sense of discovery; sacred; uplifting; new understanding; demanding; feelings of new life; joy; deep relationship; satisfaction; change and wholeness.

We were surprised by the list. We found ourselves challenged by their work and we were moved to self-reflection. How often do we, in fact, feel these qualities when starting a new organizational development inquiry? What is the role of wonder in OD? Why is uninhibited wonder something we generally restrict to children? If doing good inquiry is at the heart of OD, why then so little talk of things like awe, curiosity, surprise, delight, amazement, and wonder when we are looking at organizations? What we did felt risky in this highly pragmatic business situation. Clearly it would be at odds with the accepted perceptual logic of the culture. Organizations are not generally magical, stirring, awesome, inspiring places where we talk about the experience of wonder. Or are they?

Intrigued with the list of descriptive words we asked the executives to prepare another inventory. We invited them to think back to the last time they had participated, with or without the assistance of consultants, in some kind of comprehensive organizational analysis. We asked them to recall their experiences (with the data collection, analysis, feedback) and how they felt about what they did and found. Consider these words and adjectives:

**List 2.**

disappointed; found big gaps; sense of threat; painful; overwhelmed; conflicted; sense of resistance; honest and disciplined; self-critical; differences of opinion, it provided wake-up call and marching orders; fragmented; sense of deja vu (we have heard all this before); valid identification of problems; challenged our complacency; eye opening; a bugle call; experienced doubt about our capacity for change; exhausting; what happened to follow through?; petered out; too slow; contentious; defensive relationships (it's that group's problem).

The contrast between the two lists was striking (we invite you to read the first list and second again) and gives insight into the power of questions to frame our description of the worlds we live in. Given a world characterized by the descriptors in each list, which version of reality would one wish to be a part of? How might the experiences in these two lists differ in their capacity to ignite long term, sustainable organizational change? What explains the difference in the two lists?

# Organizational Worlds

Understanding how organizational worlds are created is at the heart of Appreciative Inquiry. Its basis rests on several assumptions regarding the nature of human organizing. Organizational systems often appear to have their own minds, controlling the actions of individual actors who operate within them. It can be like watching traffic at 10,000 feet. When we look down and see thousands of cars moving around in coordinated action, it is as if there is a central intelligence directing the whole scene. "You sir! Stop at that light." "Now go." "Brake," etc. But of course, there isn't any such intelligence. The system functions because all the drivers have a reasonably similar scriptbook that tells them how to function when making individual decisions. So long as that script accounts for most contingencies, each person contributes their piece of the system, and it is created anew every instant of everyday.

Thus, the organization is generated when it is both represented as images or patterns in the minds of individual actors and when multiple players enact those patterns or images into existence. Indeed the patterns are reproduced not only in the minds but also in our language. For example, we talk about organizations as machines—"in need of fixing," "broken down," etc. Enacted and represented over a lifetime, these patterns of organizing become so automatic that they simply "are the way things should be done."

All organizing systems—whether traffic flows, governments, corporations, small groups or families—function on similar principles. Individual actors hold images of the system that they collectively enact. Enactment of such systems reinforces the images. With amazing swiftness, organizations emerge as the evidence of this process. Simply stated, organizations are centers of human relatedness with infinite creative potential. Organizations exist because they are held within the minds of interconnected and interdependent people. They are an elaborate demonstration of the potential for human imagination.

The way we think about the social world directly relates to the kind of world we "discover" and help to create. Managers and employees alike tend to approach their work from a framework of assumptions and vocabularies that are taken for granted. The new member of any organization quickly learns "the way things are done around here" through countless encounters with others at the water cooler and through real-time experience dealing with others. We quickly learn our tasks, the signals to watch for in our environment, and the implicit, unspoken, assumptions about why "things" exist as they do. We learn the organizational way of talking, the specialized vocabulary for survival. In time the conventional view can become so solidly embedded in us that it assumes the status of being real. As Weick (1995: p. 35, 37) puts it: "Over time, routines develop and the meaning of objects becomes fixed . . . people seem to need the idea that there is a world with pre-given features or ready-made information."

## ORGANIZATIONAL CHANGE

Seeing organizations from this perspective has intriguing implications for organizational change, especially if we want our change interventions to have a positive, long-term effect. Consider what it would take to change the traffic system described earlier. It seems obvious that we have to generate change in both the patterns of thinking and the patterns of action that generate the system. Focusing on one without the other is not sustainable. We might tell everyone that at midnight all traffic will flow in the opposite direction, but unless a substantial number of drivers actually followed the new paradigm, the fundamental change is merely an idea. On the other hand, if only a few drivers started functioning in their own new paradigm, they would be quickly brought into line by the majority of drivers who refuse to "think outside the box." The new reality can never emerge unless the images and are planted, allowed to germinate, and then cultivated and shared across a broad majority of the organization, and finally acted upon. Images matter, not just because they are ideas, but because the images we hold of ourselves and our organizations become reality. Appreciative Inquiry creates a forum where both patterns and images of organizing shift in dramatic ways.

## BUILDING BLOCKS OF APPRECIATIVE INQUIRY

### *The Power of Appreciation*

By now, it should be obvious that the words and stories we choose when talking about organizations have enormous consequences. Look again at the lists created in the workshop at the front of this chapter. Imagine now that these lists describe the word "organization." What would it be like if the adjectives of the first list were applied to your organization? Wouldn't you feel inspired to be part of a process that engendered wonder, even around seemingly simple tasks? Unfortunately, few organizations are self-described in these terms. Conversely, the second list seems familiar to many people. Far too frequently, vocabularies of deficiency are the norm, and often leave little room for the germination and cultivation of images of the positive. Without that space, images of the positive can never be transformed into the reality of shared awareness within an organizational system.

This does not mean that we ignore existing negativity, rather we look for ideal images that shape negativity. Organizational positives and negatives are two sides of the same coin. People don't react negatively to organizations unless they harbor some ideal of the way things *should* be. Energy is created by the perceived gap between the real and ideal, and the sense that the organization is designed to curtail one's ability to live in and create the ideal. True appreciation respects the wholeness of organizing, the good and the not-so-good. However, our experience suggests that organizations over-appreciate negative forces while severely depreciating those that are positive. When this tide of negativity is tipped in favor of the positive, our newfound language evokes images of potential, courage, excitement and innovation. Reframing problems as opportunities releases energy where people feel passion. When people have an avenue for expressing this passion, their creative potential can be limitless.

## The Power of Inquiry

Time and again, our experience suggests that every inquiry is an intervention, especially if it is widespread throughout organizations. Questions can literally change organizational systems and perceptions. We recently had a colleague who learned this lesson the hard way. A very good researcher, she had developed a questionnaire that had all the trimmings of an objective, non-intrusive survey. However, the organization where she administered the survey has a history of employee-bureaucratic tension. The questionnaire was simultaneously administered to over 2,000 employees. Several respondents quickly zeroed-in on questions they saw as intrusive. The survey quickly became the brunt of many insider jokes and threatened the success of an upcoming change initiative. Management quickly wrote a letter of apology and recanted on its sponsorship of the questionnaire.

Why are questions, even seemingly objective ones, potentially so potent? The answer is simple: Questions evoke images, sometimes never before imagined or considered. Indeed, the nature of our questions guides the answers we will discover. Consider the questions we posed to generate the lists at the beginning of this chapter. In the first inquiry, the simple word *wonder* evoked images of creativity, innovation, awe and humility. What might happen when the same question is repeated 2,000 times in an organizational system? Think about the effect of *ten* similar questions repeated throughout an organization. Now, what happens if those images, as suggested earlier, are allowed to germinate and grow? Quite frankly, the results can be astonishing. We have seen a Brazilian-based company achieve a 200 percent increase in profit in a single year. We have seen deep-seated animosity in union-management relationships turn into greater mutual respect. We have seen world religious leaders enter into meaningful dialogue and create new inter-denominational initiatives.

Inquiry can be a powerful tool for invigorating change, especially when coupled with appreciation. To appreciate means to value and to inquire means to search, to ask questions, and to discover. And this is what appreciative inquiry is about. It is based on the assumption that organizations, as centers of human relatedness, are alive with infinite capacity, infinite imagination, and possibility. Like the miracle of life on this planet—inexplicable, relentless, emergent, resilient, powerful—organizations are resourceful, living systems. What happens to our inquiry when we approach organizations, not as lifeless machines or problems to be solved, but as living systems—alive with capacity known and unknown? The core question for change leadership is not, "What is broken down here, where are the major barriers or problems?" The root question instead should be, "What is it that gives life to human systems when they are most alive and when they are symbiotically related in the most healthy ways to their worlds?" (Cooperrider and Whitney, 1999).

## IMPACT OF APPRECIATIVE INQUIRY INTERVENTIONS

When Roadway Express began using Appreciative Inquiry, there were many skeptics from all parts of the organization. Initially, 88 people convened in a 3-day summit in Akron, Ohio, the international company's home base. Representatives from the Teamsters' Union—dockworkers, truck drivers, and union stewards—met in mixed groups with supervisors, staff, and corporate managers. As the meetings concluded, a dockworker rose to make a remarkable statement. "For years here, I have come to work feeling that I could not say what I thought. In the past 3 days, I feel like everyone here has given me the opportunity to speak. I don't have to hold this in any more. I have actually looked forward to coming to work these past few days. It has been a long time since I remember feeling that way."

This was the first of many such meetings, and initial successes have led to the spreading use of Appreciative Inquiry throughout the dispersed organization of over 30,000 employees. Roadway is one of only a few remaining unionized trucking companies, but it is one where the managers and union employees alike are beginning to work together in remarkable ways. At a recent summit in Harrisburg, Pennsylvania, CEO Jim Staley talked about the *value* that the Teamsters' Union brings to Roadway—things like stability in the labor force, training of workers, and dedicated employees. These statements are indicative of fundamental shifts in the way managers and employees relate to each other.

Roadway uses Appreciative Inquiry as an umbrella that integrates several change initiatives. For example, they have instituted an employee education initiative to train all workers in basic finance and accounting. By coupling this with power of focusing on the positive core of what already exists in the organization, they hope to help employees realize how the small things they do at the local level can make a big difference company-wide.

Small-win stories are already having a big impact. For example, after the first summit at the Akron, Ohio facility, two union employees, a mechanic and a yard worker, worked together on a post-summit pilot initiative. Together, they noticed that a certain model of trucks were not capable of pulling as much weight as other models. With their newly gained tools they solved the mystery, created a solution, and implemented a change that has already resulted in a significant cost reduction to the company.

Other dramatic results are also starting to emerge, particularly in the way employees and managers feel about the company. At sites where appreciative interventions are underway, turnover and grievances have dipped, sometimes quite dramatically. In a recent follow-up study, we found that people feel more empowered, not just in word, but in action. They report "knowing what's going on" and that the internal dialogue of the organization is gradually shifting from negative to positive. Workers feel greater awareness about the impact of daily work, realizing that change can come from unexpected sources.

Even long-time employees are feeling energy for embracing change, particularly when they realize that Appreciative Inquiry isn't about trying to undermine the union, but rather to embrace the best of what the union has to offer. In a later interview, a Teamster recalled sitting in conversation with a supervisor. "You know, I always thought he was a hard-assed labor manager that I was going to have to go head to head with for the rest of my life. And here, I sat down next to him and talked to him for an hour back and forth, and realized that he was just another good guy trying to do his job, trying to work within the system, within the contract, which is the same thing I'm trying to do" (Powley, Cooperrider, and Fry, 2002). Obviously many employees also came to realize that managers also had a lot to offer the organization.

## PLAN AN APPRECIATIVE INQUIRY

Several critical features make for a successful Appreciative Inquiry. Perhaps one of the most important factors is awareness that long-term change will require more than an opportunity for high-level engagement. It also takes long-term efforts. As an OD intervention, Appreciative Inquiry Summit, a 3- to 5-day event, is the major forum for instigating change. The flow of the summit itself has four elements known as the

4-D cycle: (1) Discovery, describing the best of the organization's past and present; (2) Dream, a focus on the best of the organization's potential future; (3) Design, a movement toward framing bold initiatives for change; and (4) Destiny, the forming of action groups for post-summit work. Combined with pre-summit and post-summit efforts, the Appreciative Inquiry summit builds momentum for long-term change.

## AFFIRMATIVE TOPIC CHOICE

Having a clear topic and task for a summit is critical. One central premise of Appreciative Inquiry is that organizations evolve in the direction of the questions they consistently ask. Thus, the formation of a title and purpose for holding a summit make a huge difference to ultimate success. The summit topic should be a bold, well-articulated statement that embodies innovative, forward-looking thinking. In addition, three to five goals for inquiry give it substance.

The creation of an Executive Steering Committee (ESC) is a powerful way for establishing a theme and goals for inquiry. The ESC is a relatively small group and

**Figure 1.   THE 4-D CYCLE**

includes at least one or two representatives from all the major stakeholders who will be affected by the change effort, including customers, external stakeholders, etc. At Roadway, for example, the first ESC included union bosses, local supervisors, dockworkers, truck drivers, yard workers, external customers and senior managers. Often, this group comes together for two days of discussions, where they learn and discussion the philosophy and building blocks of Appreciative Inquiry. Their central task, however, is to create the central topic for inquiry.

The ESC also addresses the question of whom to invite to the larger summit. If possible, many smaller organizations shut down their operations for a few days and invite every member. Larger organizations typically invite a smaller, representative group of several hundred people. Whatever the case, it is crucial to have the *whole system* in the room, that is, to include the perspective of every major stakeholder group in the organization. The summit topic usually clarifies which organizational constituencies need representation.

During the pre-summit phase, it is also often helpful to conduct appreciative interviews with as many members of the organization as possible. Carefully crafted questions guide the interview process to focus on the discovery of positive stories in the organization. The results usually generate an abundance of positive stories that not only initiate positive reverberations throughout the organization, but also add to the creative potential of the summit. Simply doing the interviews is as important as understanding the information derived from them (Mohr, 2001).

Successful summit plans include arrangements that can enhance the ability for people to come together. The meeting area is ideally situated away from the normal work location in a very large room, where all the participants can be together, forming small groups around round tables. A comfortable, natural setting can also enhance the capacity for reflective, innovative, conversations.

## Day 1: Discover

Discovery injects the summit group with energy, focus, and anticipation for future work. Collectively, summit participants engage in activities that help them discover who they are as a group, including the resources each individual brings to the table. Questions focus on discovery of the best of what currently exists in the organization. Who are we? What does each person bring into this room? What is valuable and meaningful about what we do here? Participants express their hopes and dreams for the future, and look at external trends or forces that shape the organization's environment. By day's end, summit participants begin the process of imagining what opportunities are possible as they move forward together. They also map the organization's *positive core* by articulating existing competencies.

When conducted in a large-group setting, participants arrive to sit in pre-assigned seats around small, round tables loosely arranged in a large conference hall. Facilitators ensure that each table has a representative from each major stakeholder group. The small group encounter creates time and space for members of the organization to form relationships with people of vastly different perspectives. Often, people meet others whom they have never before encountered.

Summits seem to function better when we present a *holographic image* (Whitney and Cooperrider, 2000) of the summit that foreshadows the agenda, invites discussion, and equal voice, where every person has a perspective that is valued and shared. Another of the first activities is usually an appreciative interview, where each participant pairs up with someone they do not know. They ask carefully crafted, positively oriented questions of each other, usually probing for stories of peak experiences. In every case, this activity produces a sense of excitement as the room literally comes alive with a hundred or more interviews. Next, the groups reconvene and each individual introduces his or her interviewee, recounting something about the person's story. During this report, the group generates a summary of common factors in the stories, which builds a sense of interconnectedness.

Throughout the day, summit participants discover and more clearly define the life-giving forces in the organization. For example, they perform an analysis of *the root causes of success* (as opposed to root causes of failure), or identify the best practices of the organization when they are at peak performance. The day usually culminates in an activity where members have the opportunity to "map the positive core." This series of guided interactions leaves participants with an enhanced awareness of past successes that build a sense of potential for the future. It is easier to dream about the best of what might be when participants are well grounded in existing images organizational strengths.

## Day 2: Dream

The Dream phase draws on the best of the past and present to create powerful images of the potential future. A key question centers on building a sense of continuity (Whitney and Cooperrider, 2000). What is best about ourselves that we wish to preserve as we move to the future? This focus on the positive potential is a dramatic difference with other change initiatives that use analyses of deficiencies to inspire change through a fear of the future. Rather than focusing on what will happen "if we don't confront these issues in our organization," appreciative inquiry fosters change by evoking images of exciting possibilities. *Realistic* images of deficiency remain in the consciousness of the organization, but by focusing on images of abundance, the summit tips the balance in favor of ideas that often transcend deficiencies.

Looking toward the future, facilitators guide activities that excite the imagination and encourage innovative creativity. Participants consider in detail how the best of what presently exists might be leveraged and enhanced in the future.

A frequent exercise has summit participants imagine that they have fallen into a deep sleep. Ten years later, they awake to find that their organization has transformed into its perfect form. What does that organization look like? How do people get along in the new workplace? What does the organization produce and how well does it perform its work? What is it like to be part of something so great? Questions such as this excite the mind to think beyond the present horizon of possibilities.

Working in their groups, participants generate summaries of common themes that run throughout individual images. They have opportunities to share these themes with the larger group in several ways. For example, a spokesperson from each group gives a two-minute synopsis of a pictorial representation of common themes. Later, they might produce a skit, a poem, or a mini-drama that portrays the ideal world. The activities focus on sharing, enlivening, and enacting organizational dreams as if they were a current reality.

## Day 3: Design

The major tasks for Design are to identify concrete, actionable ideas that will move the organization closer to its potential and to form action groups around similar action themes. Questions now focus not just on images, but on possible steps. What inspires us to move toward the future? What provocative propositions might excite change? What bold initiatives might keep us on track?

Typically, organizational participants generate lists, goals, or actionable ideas. In summits at Roadway participants use these lists to create an opportunity map, an exercise in organizational mind-mapping. On a giant, wall-mounted poster, a facilitator writes up ideas as participants suggest them, clustering them into themes. The exercise concludes when summit members vote on hot topics by placing stickers on the poster next to ideas that hold particular interest for them. When completed, the map illustrates not only areas of conceptual convergence, but ideas where people feel common energy.

Next, summit participants reorganize themselves by "voting with their feet" to form action groups. Facilitators designate areas of the room as rallying spots for specific themes that are represented in the opportunity map. At this moment in the summit, the organization of the meeting literally reforms as participants gravitate to others who have similar interests. Because the images that guide this process are collectively generated, nearly every person finds a place where they feel interest or that have something of value to contribute. The new groups' centers of action form the basis for post-summit efforts to create change.

The phase concludes as action groups begin drafting a plan for their future work. They craft bold aspiration statements that challenge the organization to think more concretely about what it would take to bring about the ideal state. Statements are made in the present tense and usually include provocative propositions that describe details of what the organization would be like if the action group were successful. These activities create the foundation for the development of concrete goals, plans and action steps that will lead to the enactment of a new organizational reality.

## Day 4: Destiny

In the Destiny phase, action groups solidify their plans and begin thinking forward to post-summit work. Each group is invited to choose a name for itself and to propose a few bold initiatives centered on its theme of interest. Questions for this phase focus on building impact, commitment and momentum. What will a proposed initiative do for the organization? Who will be affected and how can they be included after the summit? What resources are needed for successfully fulfilling our goals?

Of all the phases, this is the most work-focused. The individual groups generate a list of possible actions and present those to the larger group for feedback. They then select actions that they feel are particularly inspired, and create an initial plan for carrying them out. Proposed initiatives usually include long-term, mid-term and short-range goals. Groups are encouraged to focus on at least one or two action items that can be completed immediately as well as those requiring more sustained effort. Ultimately, the intervention's success depends upon these groups' capacity to function long after the summit to bring about the future images invoked by the summit.

The summit usually ends on a high note where people have the opportunity to voice their overall thoughts and feelings about the whole summit. This continues a pattern, practiced throughout the summit, where open space is frequently provided for people to address statements to the entire group regarding their thoughts, stories, perceptions, and ideas. The real power of a summit is in its creation of time and space where people have equal voice to express themselves and their creative potential. The summit can be a particularly powerful moment in an organization's transformation experience.

## Post-Summit Work

The summit itself is merely a beginning (or an accelerator) to the unfolding processes of organizational change. Obviously, after having been removed from the normal flow of activities, participants have to return and reengage in their normal work. As summit participants continue working in their groups, they slowly create small, even tiny, wins that generate change in the organization. Successful teams meet regularly and work on or toward well-defined task lists. Action teams, because they usually draw members from various stakeholder groups, continue to foster new relationship configurations across the organization.

The chance for prolonged success is enhanced when teams achieve real gains, when they feel continued support from management, and when their accomplishments are acknowledged and celebrated throughout the organization as stories of success. When the organization's leadership frequently expresses belief that organization has the capacity to change toward the images of the positive, they facilitate the process of change.

## THE BENEFITS OF APPRECIATIVE INQUIRY

At Roadway, an organization with a long history, the change is coming about slowly, but is gaining more momentum as more and more sites hear about the successes in other parts of the organization and request their own opportunity to hold summits. If nothing else, the process creates awareness of the power of increased "positivity" within the organization's system. In daily interactions with each other, employees often report that small changes occur even in the way people relate to each other. This is more than positive thinking, it is a fundamental change in the way people conduct their work and how they get along.

All sustainable change efforts require courage, stability, energy, faith, and belief of organizational members. Remember again the lists at the beginning of this chapter. Which list evokes these attributes? It should be obvious. People create answers to the words posed in our questions. When the very nature of our intervention causes the reactions described in the second list, it shouldn't be any wonder that implementation is a painful, resistance-laden process. Deficit-based change depends on a model of motivation through fear. Abundance-based change depends on motivation through inspiration. When the whole system is brought into the endeavor in the same time and space, the positive, motivational effect on an entire organization can be far-reaching.

Our experience is that the benefits of an Appreciative Inquiry summit can be quite dramatic. Participants often come filled with apprehension, suspicion, or apathy. Usually they leave with sense of excitement, greater trust, and engagement. For this reason, Appreciative Inquiry is gaining momentum as an important OD innovation.

## WHERE TO FIND MORE INFORMATION

The study and practice of positive change is increasing exponentially. Additional information and resources is hosted can be found at the Appreciative Inquiry Commons at http://ai.cwru.edu, a site hosted by the Weatherhead School of Management at Case Western Reserve University.

## REFERENCES

Cooperrider, D.L, and D. Whitney. *Appreciative Inquiry: Collaborating for Change*. San Francisco: Barrett- Koehler Communications, 1999.

Mohr, B. J. 2001. "Appreciative Inquiry: Igniting Transformative Action," *The Systems Thinker,* 12, no. 5.

Powley, E.H., D.L. Coooperrider, and R. Fry (2001). "Appreciative Inquiry: A Revolutionary Model for Strategic Action." In *2002 Handbook of Business Strategy*. P. Goett (Ed.). New York: EC Media Group (pp.165–172).

Weick, K.E. 1995. *Sensemaking in Organizations*. Thousand Oaks, CA: Sage Publications.

Whitney, D. and D.L. Cooperrider (2000). "The Appreciative Inquiry Summit: An Emerging Methodology for Whole System Change." *Journal of Organizational Development Practitioner*, 32, no. 1 (pp. 13–27).

# PART II

---

# FUNDAMENTALS OF LEADING CHANGE

# CHAPTER 7

# HOW NATURE INNOVATES: THE COMPETITIVE EDGE FOR ORGANIZATIONS

*George Land and Greg Zlevor*

## INTRODUCTION

There is a natural process to growth and innovation. It is displayed in the physical and evolutionary record, demonstrated by atomic and molecular structures, seen in the growth of the simplest creatures, detected in cultural advances, and found in business. The first phase of this natural process is invention, which is a period of experimentation. At the end of Phase 1 a pattern emerges. In Phase 2 this pattern is maximized. The organism or organization utilizes this pattern to grow as much as possible. Eventually growth reaches natural and emerging barriers. As returns diminish, it is important to enter a process of innovation and invention. Phase 3, the next phase, is the time to innovate. It is also the time to begin a new process of invention or bifurcation. There are three phases, each with its own rules and processes. In business it is essential to wisely negotiate these three phases of change with their major shifts in processes, especially Phase 3 and the parallel process of bifurcation.

## HOW NATURE INNOVATES: THE COMPETITIVE EDGE FOR ORGANIZATIONS

The world is changing and it isn't. Before technology was nature. Surrounding technology is nature. Supporting technology is nature. Ahead of technology is nature.

Nature, growth, and change follow universal patterns. These patterns are observable and learnable. Once learned, these natural patterns can be followed to create sustainable and lasting change, as a process, within our organizations.

The world is changing but the process of change is not. The advent of technology and technology itself submit to the universal patterns demonstrated in Figure 7-1.

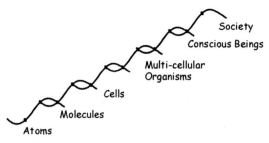

**Figure 1**

## Natural Wisdom

Nature goes through continuous cycles of creation and destruction, cycles of order and disorder, a process of flow occurring all the time. This is nature: the flow of energy and material through order and reorder into higher and higher levels of complexity. This cycle follows three phases, each with its own unique rules or characteristics.

This is also culture, societies, organizations, and business. History displays the inevitable shuffle and reshuffle of borders, beliefs, boundaries, and buildings into more and more complex webs. Connections and communication, by virtue of technology, have speeded up the shuffle but the rules remain.

The pre-Socratic Greek philosophers of Ionia were convinced the universe was the expression of a single force or pattern. Edward O. Wilson calls this belief the "Ionian Enchantment." George Land, co-author, developed the Transformation Theory to explain this pattern of cycles and its abrupt shifts. Stephen Gould then reinforced this discovery when he studied the fossil record. He discovered long stretches of stability punctuated by exciting bursts of growth and activity. Order and reorder. Stephen Gould called this "punctuated equilibrium." There is indeed a powerful pattern to growth and change.

Behold the noble flatworm, sacrificed by the billions in scientific labs around the world. Drop a flatworm in a nutrient solution and it darts about sampling nutrients throughout the solution. Suddenly, if the solution is rich with nutrients, we observe a change. The flatworm cells begin to enlarge and rapidly divide. It gets larger with each passing hour. This rapid development, depending on the amount of food, continues for some time.

Now if you were an investor and the flatworm was a business, you would buy stock. The growth looks unstoppable. It could become "The Flatworm That Ate Iowa!" But, the flatworm reaches a barrier to growth.

As we watch the worm, suddenly it changes again. Cells on the outside of the growing cells start to toughen and thicken. Cells on the inside form new structures and connections. A new flatworm is taking shape.

You invested in quantitative growth. It looked promising. Unfortunately, the environment limited the flatworm. There is a limit to how much of the environment the flatworm can turn into flatworm. When the flatworm could no longer grow quantitatively it evolved to qualitative growth. It created new cells and structures needed in maturity. The flatworm changed the way it changed. Now it can interact more creatively with the environment as well as make more flatworms.

What was the pattern of change going on during the development of the flatworm? There were three distinct phases of change, each with its own rules for development.

## Change Changes

*Phase 1.* The first phase is characterized by high levels of creativity, discovering the environment, and determining the appropriate pattern of growth. It involves testing and observing. What is this place like? What is available? What will work? What will not? What form will make the most sense? In the midst of this first phase even the embryonic cells do not know how they will be organized. The organism is experimenting. The flatworm will not make a decision until the first phase is fulfilled. It will eventually choose a form based on investigation, experimentation, and observation. These are the rules of Phase 1 (see Figure 7-2).

*Phase 2.* The second phase follows the Darwinian adage "maximize what works." In this phase the flatworm knows what is available and what is appropriate for the environment. Unlike the first phase of testing and experimenting (in order to pick the right form) the flatworm knows what to do and picks the optimal form. Once the optimal form is chosen it now maximizes and repeats it. This is the rule

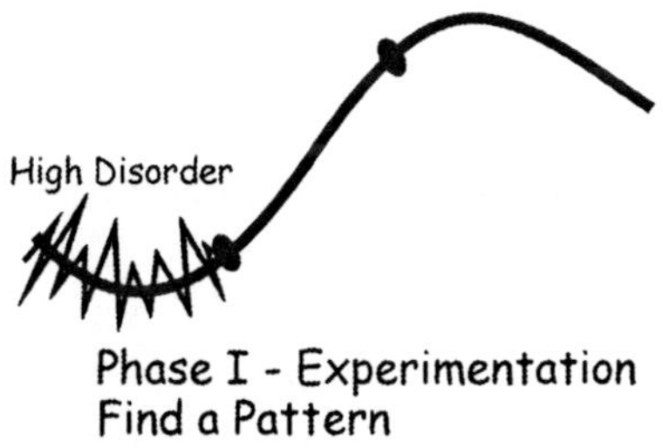

High Disorder

Phase I - Experimentation
Find a Pattern

**Figure 2**

for Phase 2: Pick what works and make the most of it. The flatworm improves its efficiencies of growth and extends itself further and further into the environment. The behavior becomes predictable and routine. The form and rate of growth can be calculated. The growth continues until the environment is significantly changed by the growing organism. Successful growth automatically begets barriers. As the environment exerts new pressure and stress the flatworm experiences diminishing returns. It goes through one last growth spurt to test the ultimate limits of the environment then shifts to another and very different phase. (See Figure 7-3.)

*Phase 3.* This is the integrative phase. In Phase 3 the rules change again. The flatworm, rather than continuing to grow larger and multiply, transforms internally and externally. Structures that competed in the nutrient rich environment now "mutualize," that is they shift to a cooperative relationship. Internally and externally new lines of communication develop and resources are shared. Cell growth becomes qualitative rather than quantitative. Differentiation is critical. The new cells are more dynamic and innovative. Instead of following the competitive and predictable behavior of Phase 2 they differentiate and creatively respond to a new environment. At this juncture, the system reaches a breakpoint. (See Figure 7-4.)

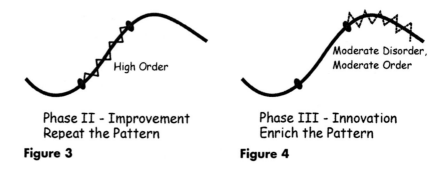

Phase II - Improvement
Repeat the Pattern

**Figure 3**

Phase III - Innovation
Enrich the Pattern

**Figure 4**

Parallel with the third phase a bifurcation occurs. It is ideal to initiate the bifurcation as diminishing returns appear at the end of Phase 2. A new form needs to emerge. At the bifurcation the system does two things:

• It enriches itself qualitatively.
• It transforms itself to a higher level of complexity.

For the flatworm, it may establish a cooperative colony or create a specialized adaptation. Whatever the outcome the process is known. In order to survive a higher and more complex form and relationship will emerge through bifurcation (see Figure 7-5).

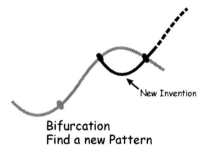

Bifurcation
Find a new Pattern

**Figure 5**

## Rules for Success

Three phases, three sets of rules for success. Try, fail, learn, and try again are the rules or mantras of Phase 1. At the end of phase one an optimal form or pattern emerges. With this emergence Phase 2, improvement, commences. Now the rules of growth are different. The mantras in Phase 2 are improve, extend, and maximize. Make the most of the new form or pattern. Repeat, improve, repeat. But nothing stays the same. The environment changes and the form so optimal in Phase 2 eventually loses its prominence and steam. This diminishing state leads directly to Phase 3—innovation and also preferably a bifurcation/invention. At the end of Phase 2 margins disappear, products are commodified, death or meager existence is impending. Phase 3 is coming. The only way out is to continually innovate in the core business and in parallel begin to create something that is new and more complex. Bifurcation, creating a new growth curve, is nature's way of creating the next level of complexity. The mantra or cry of Phase 3 is "The end is near begin again anew!" Integrate with the old AND create an entirely new pattern—a new Phase 1.

Invention requires the development of something completely new. It is a groundbreaking event, one whose true value may not be immediately recognized. Once that invention is successful (finds a connection in the marketplace), second phase improvement is necessary to funnel the system's energy into the most productive path. At this point, experimenting would drain the focus of improvement and maximization.

Improvement works as long as the environment supports it. Maximization requires such activities as increasing value, decreasing cost, eliminating waste, and process improvement. Study what is working and make it better. Maximization projects yield better, faster, cheaper, yet functionally similar solutions. Obviously, improvement only goes so far.

During the second phase, an "immune system" grows up around the system. Whether you are a flatworm or a dot-com start-up, this is part of the baggage you get with the second phase. And it makes sense. The immune system separates self from enemy or non-self and effectively eliminates it. This is useful for a growing system. However, it creates uncomfortable blind spots. These blind spots become obstacles in Phase 3.

Once a system enters the third phase it requires a very new and different form of creativity, one that allows for foreign elements to be incorporated in the system. The immune system does not go away, but is must become more porous. At the same time, sufficient resources and environment must be set aside to make room for innovation as well as invention.

In our consulting practice, we find this model critical to understanding what sorts of activities will be effective and what lies ahead for the client. It is useless to try and create process improvements or a quality program for a system still being invented. Tightening managerial controls can be deadly for an organization trying to transform itself.

It is easy to see why a person perfectly suited for Phase 1 can become bored in Phase 2. Invention is exciting, stimulating, chaotic, and unpredictable. Every moment is different. Phase 2 is quite contrary. Phase 2 is predictable and repeatable. In Phase 2 invention is distracting and problematic. Phase 2 is about continuous measurable improvement: "Time to shoot the entrepreneur." By the same token it is easy to see why the bureaucrats, so well suited for Phase 2, resist the onslaught of Phase 3. They despise disorder, loss of control, and chaos: "I don't care what is happening, make the numbers!" But the numbers can't be made the old way. The world is different and to be successful again will require a period of unpredictability. Phase 3 is about innovation and bifurcation in order to avoid decline. It is the time to begin inventing all over again: "Bring back the entrepreneurs!" The cycle repeats.

A challenge we frequently face is to help individuals in organizations achieve their creative potential. There are several components to this: environmental, cultural, and educational. We will deal with the educational approach first. To give every individual the chance to be creative, it helps to start with a common approach, language, and/or process.

## The Process

The transformation curve is the outcome of a creative system. Now it's time to look into the machinery. Let's return to the world of nature, and see if a single cell can teach us something about the most efficient way to be creative.

A cell can be said to have a goal, and that is to stay alive. The cell ingests nutrients from its surroundings. It then breaks these nutrients down into components through digestion. Some components go to storage, some go to waste, and some go to immediate use. By combining the products of digestion with the stuff in storage, internal proteins are synthesized. These are tested against molecular templates. If they pass inspection they are used to maintain or extend the system. The cell then optimizes its machinery to take advantage of the current environment.

In a perfect world, people create in the same way. People use information (knowledge, emotions, etc.) and nutrition. They are motivated by a Goal and use *Perception* to gather information about a problem or opportunity. They then *Analyze* the situation and break it down into manageable chunks. Possible solutions and plans are *Synthesized* from current information and past learning. These solutions are *Evaluated* against the criteria for success. Once a solution is accepted, *Action* is taken. Then the person *Responds* to what has been learned, and adjusts their strategy accordingly.

Alas, people aren't perfect. Most people try to bypass the creative process. They get caught up in a perpetual Perceive-Act loop, reacting to outside stimuli instead of innovating solutions. People often skip the information-gathering step, the careful analysis, the consideration of multiple solutions, the development of meaningful criteria, and the Response step where we incorporate what we have learned. (line about the importance of steps)

The educational prerequisite to organizational innovation, then, is to create a common process and language for solving problems, and to encourage the practice of those steps we often omit. Avoid omission and gain innovation.

As we described it above, the creative process is abbreviated PASEAR, which is Spanish for journey (see Figure 7-6). Thus we can wax metaphorical about the journey of creativity, life's journey, or whatever suits the mood.

PASEAR emphasizes certain steps in the process, depending on the phase of the system. A Phase 1 system (heavily involved in experimentation) is in the short cycle of Perceive-Act-Respond until it finds a way to connect to the environment (see Figure 7-7).

Once a pattern is found, it is necessary to be able to break down information to extract useful material, and to be able to evaluate product to make sure it fits the pattern illustrated in Figure 7-8.

Once a pattern is exhausted, a new means of growth must be found. The key feature of innovation is synthesis, combining the new and different with a successful core pattern illustrated in Figure 7-9.

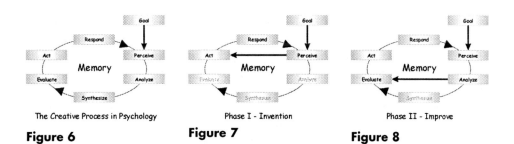

The Creative Process in Psychology        Phase I - Invention        Phase II - Improve

**Figure 6**        **Figure 7**        **Figure 8**

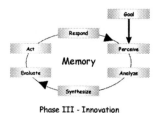

Phase III - Innovation

**Figure 9**

Our society, and many of our more mature organizations are in Phase 3, and desperately need help with innovation. Let's take a moment to discuss this particular skill.

We face an era in which we will continuously destructure and restructure the norms and rules of the past. Instead of looking the other way, or setting aside those things that are different, we will need to adopt a viewpoint that allows us to not only become aware of the things outside of our blinders, but also invite them in to cooperate with us in a creative and innovative way. Therefore, we need to shift from a repetitive pattern of predictable and measurable growth to an interactive mode of continual innovation.

In a mature and innovating Phase 3, the organization and the individuals operate by taking the old, opening it up for examination, redefining it, and combining it with the new. The result yields something that is beyond either. A + B does not equal AB, as it would in the second phase. The result is something both different from and better than either of its predecessors. Phase 3 produces not just win-win, but both/and. Based on the past, the "and" part of the transaction is unpredictable: It is a real innovation.

Thus, when individuals, departments, or organizations enter into empowering and creative partnerships, the results strikingly differ from anything we have seen before. In the world of biology, this is referred to as "hybrid vigor." Plant and animal breeders have long known that this process of combining "differentness" is a very practical way of "improving the species." That empirical wisdom of "outbreeding" now makes sense in the light of the new science of managing change.

This is half of the cultural solution to organizational innovation. The second half is managing renewal, which is the process of bifurcation.

An organization entering its third phase has yet another task to consider. Essentially, it is not only "maturing" in a third phase, but it is also beginning to re-create itself through a self-generated first phase. The main organization, department, etc., provides shelter for an internal "intrapreneurship" function. Under this protection, people and resources have an opportunity to completely rethink the business—to figure out a way to put us out of business (see Figure 7-10).

Every system contains the seeds of it own renewal. A successful mature business today needs to spawn its own second generation. This begins and is parallel

Transformation —A New Cycle

**Figure 10**

with the core business innovation during the third phase, not after it. It starts when the organization is healthy, growing, and creative. To a great extent, this is a direct replica of how biological organisms create offspring and shelter them with their accumulated resources, so that they have a better chance of getting off to a good start.

In American industry, companies (even whole industries) are replaced not by themselves but by outside forces—railroads did not create airlines, newspapers did not create television, telephones did not create e-mail. Today's businesses are learning from the science of change that they must re-create themselves even when they would like to believe that the old business will go on forever. As Peter Drucker put it, "The best way to predict the future is to create it." By not understanding and acknowledging this process of change and growth, we have permitted businesses and industries to be put out of existence by outside forces.

All of us must accept the simple fact that an individual or organization that has entered the third phase is unmanageable and unpredictable like weather. If we examine the central ideas behind second-phase management, we find that planning, organizing, directing, and measuring have to do with limiting an organization or an individual's performance while maintaining the boundaries of the normative system. That works very well in a second-phase, predictable, stable situation. In a third phase, management must shift to what we now see as "leadership."

Leadership-management empowers individuals and groups. It evokes the power latent and constrained by normal limits. A company growing in a third phase certainly needs some form of guidance, but that process must be one that allows the people and organizations within the system to respond to the dynamics of continuing innovation and change. Traditional, second-phase limits circumscribe people by a past that will never return. These limits disallow for the creation and re-creation of the future. In third-phase organizations the mechanism must shift from limits to purpose and mission.

Within this mission-directed framework, individuals and managers in organizations can make the day-to-day decisions in dynamic partnerships with customers, vendors, and other organizational functions to create the continuing innovations that will provide perpetual success—success beyond the normative boundaries. This is very different from that of "directing the attainment of objectives," or simply "increasing stockholder value."

The organization changes from "input" planned and managed direction to "outcome" directed. In other words, it "self organizes" in order to reach a destination. The organization is internally navigated.

This is the greatest challenge and biggest trap for organizations and business. It is difficult to relinquish the rules and order of Phase 2 in order to let the creativity and innovation flourish for a successful Phase 3. In Phase 3 it is necessary to add new and unthought-of value to the core business. True innovation produces high value and high margins. The core business or " knitting" needs to be reviewed and invigorated. This requires courage. It is not easy. It is uncomfortable and even frightening to challenge the core business but it must be done. Without adding something new and different, without providing additional value, without making the core business "new and better" the margins will continue to erode and disappear. In Phase 3 it is necessary to innovate the core business.

In addition, the organization needs to re-invent the core business altogether. This is a second and entirely different process of creativity. As a matter of fact, in order to do it successfully, it is necessary to develop a separate and independent group to discover how they can put the core business out of business. As a consequence, there is one group trying to innovate the core business (successful Phase 3 activity) while another group tries to find a way to put the core business, innovation and all, out of business. Hence, the business maximizes profits and opportunities on two tracks. On the Phase 3 track the business minimizes diminishing returns by innovating the core business. On a parallel but different track, bifurcation, an independent and autonomous group is finding a way to go beyond even the "new and better" core business.

Creating and maintaining two independent groups, to maximize the opportunity available in Phase 3 and bifurcation, is difficult to accomplish. This already difficult task is complicated Phase 2 baggage and rules. An organization needs to transform from a culture of order and repeatability to an organization of innovation (Phase 3) and invention (bifurcation) on two different yet parallel tracks. This is why most organizations either stumble or fail during the end of the growth process.

## CONCLUSION

As you can see there are three kinds of change, three kinds of creativity. It is essential to recognize and create the conditions for each phase to flourish and be successful. The most difficult transition is from Phase 2 to Phase 3 and bifurcation. Most organizations fail at negotiating this transition. The key to successful transition into Phase 3 is to adopt a creative culture focused on innovating the core business while setting up an independent group to re-invent the business entirely. It is all about having your cake and eating it too. It is nature's recipe for success.

## CHAPTER 8

# WHAT DO WE KNOW ABOUT TRAINING WORLD CLASS NEGOTIATORS?

*Lawrence Susskind*

## ABSTRACT

*Negotiation training is very much in vogue. Public, private, and not-for-profit organizations are investing heavily in both in-house and externally delivered negotiation training. Even a modest improvement in the negotiating capabilities of senior managers can translate into dramatic increases in profitability or organizational effectiveness. Much of what passes for negotiation training, however, is not based on the substantial body of theoretical knowledge compiled over the past few decades. In particular, too much attention is being paid to building individual skills and not enough to the organizational demands that tend to thwart even the most experienced negotiators.*

## INTRODUCTION

There is growing interest in adding to the negotiation skills of middle and senior level managers in every sector of society. To the extent that getting things done requires convincing others to do what we want, when we want, the way we want, negotiations appear to be central to the work of both public and private sector managers, in both large and small organizations. Since 1987, I have been involved in delivering negotiation training to senior executives through the Program on Negotiation at Harvard Law School. More than 30,000 senior managers have gone through various versions of our 2-day instructional session. In addition, through the not-for-profit Consensus Building Institute, I have been involved in providing training to more than 7,500 participants in tailored on-site programs sponsored by individual companies or agencies. Dozens of groups like ours have been operating in much the same manner throughout this period, and they probably reach an even larger number of middle-level managers every year than we do.

Much of what is being taught builds on a revolution in negotiation theory marked by the publication of Roger Fisher and Bill Ury's book entitled *Getting to Yes* (Penguin, 1991). The emergence of what they called "principled negotiation" or what we have now dubbed "a mutual gains approach" to negotiation turned the prevailing theory on its head. Prior to their book, most negotiation specialists presumed that any gain to one side in a negotiation required losses to others. The allocation of specific gains and losses was accomplished, so the conventional wisdom assumed, through an adversarial process known as "hard bargaining"—a kind of tug-of-war ending with a winner and a loser. Fisher and Ury suggest that by focusing on *underlying interests* rather than *demands* (or stated positions), and by proceeding in a problem-solving fashion, the parties to almost any negotiation can usually find mutually advantageous (*i.e.,* "all gain") outcomes—results that exceed what each side can realistically expect to achieve for itself if no agreement is reached. Their work, and parallel efforts by Walton and McKersie in labor relations; Schelling, Sebenius, and others in international relations; Raiffa, Axelrod, Rubin, and others in game theory and psychology; and still others in related fields, have demonstrated how hard-bargaining often undermines long-term relationships, wastes time, and produces inefficient (or at least, less than truly beneficial) results.

Over the last decade, negotiation (and, more generally, conflict management) has emerged as a field of study at a great many top-notch universities. Scholarly research is underway at numerous interdisciplinary centers, while books and journals summarizing the results of detailed studies of "what works and what doesn't" are published regularly. As our intellectual understanding of what takes place during negotiations deepens, negotiation training has become richer. What was once nothing more than a few "tips" on how to out-maneuver one's opponent, now offers systematic insight into frameworks and strategies likely to increase the odds of achieving better results under different sets of circumstances.

One of the key unresolved questions in the design of negotiation training is what importance to attach to culture. Multinational corporations want their senior personnel to be able to negotiate with potential partners around the world. Negotiation theory suggests that cross-cultural negotiation needs to take account of "special" communication problems in different locales or in different dyads. After all, no one is likely to be effective if they don't understand what is said by those who live by different standards and hold different beliefs. Moreover, there is very little chance of being convincing if others don't understand what is being offered or don't fully comprehend the meaning of various symbolic moves. The implications of all this for training are unclear. The general view is that negotiators "ought to be sensitive to cultural differences," but just how this should be accomplished in a training program, is not obvious.

Similar concerns are often expressed about the role of gender in negotiation. Should female negotiators be taught specific techniques or strategies for negotiating with male counterparts? Do women tend to negotiate differently from men (because of their upbringing or socialization)? Deborah Kolb and others have identified a variety of ways in which gender does, indeed, need to be taken into account in negotiation training. On the other hand, it may be that levels of professional education, social class, international experience or other factors have more to do with how someone negotiates than does their culture or gender.

Theory building proceeds in the negotiation field. Training programs abound, presumably, building on the growing stock of intellectual capital that has accumulated over the past two decades. Tailored negotiation training sponsored by individual companies or agencies seeks to take account of sect oral, cultural, and gender-specific insights. In the face of all these developments, one would expect the overall quality of negotiation to improve. It is not clear, however, that it has.

## THE MUTUAL GAINS APPROACH TO NEGOTIATION

The mutual gains approach to negotiation is easy to describe. It requires all negotiators to (1) prepare appropriately, (2) invest time and effort at the outset of any negotiation in trying to "expand the pie" (*i.e.* create value) through a series of cooperative moves, (3) ensure that the "division of the pie" is handled in a way that respects the needs and interests of the other side(s), and (4) anticipates problems of follow-through by crafting "nearly self-enforcing agreements." Of course, learning how to do each of these things requires some effort. The diagram below (Figure 1) spells out the tasks that need to be completed at each stage.

The Program on Negotiation at Harvard Law School has spent many years observing what happens when negotiators employ this four-step strategy, including situations in which one side uses this approach while the other continues to rely on hard bargaining. After studying many hundreds of negotiations, we have learned that a series of obstacles to the use of the mutual gains approach typically arises. Thus, negotiation training needs to focus not just on the four steps, but also on how to overcome the barriers or obstacles that arise along the way.

During preparation, mutual gains negotiators are supposed to put themselves in the other side's shoes and work hard to estimate each party's Best Alternative to a Negotiated Agreement (BATNA). They are supposed to clarify their own interests (*i.e.*, the kinds of thing important to them in rank order) as well as the interests of the other stakeholders. And, they are supposed to formulate possible proposals

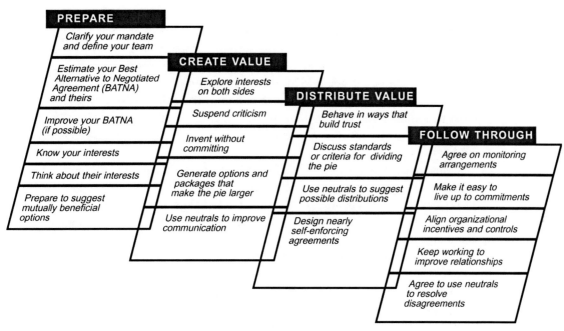

**PREPARE**
- Clarify your mandate and define your team
- Estimate your Best Alternative to Negotiated Agreement (BATNA) and theirs
- Improve your BATNA (if possible)
- Know your interests
- Think about their interests
- Prepare to suggest mutually beneficial options

**CREATE VALUE**
- Explore interests on both sides
- Suspend criticism
- Invent without committing
- Generate options and packages that make the pie larger
- Use neutrals to improve communication

**DISTRIBUTE VALUE**
- Behave in ways that build trust
- Discuss standards or criteria for dividing the pie
- Use neutrals to suggest possible distributions
- Design nearly self-enforcing agreements

**FOLLOW THROUGH**
- Agree on monitoring arrangements
- Make it easy to live up to commitments
- Align organizational incentives and controls
- Keep working to improve relationships
- Agree to use neutrals to resolve disagreements

**Figure 1    Mutual Gains Approach to Negotiation**

that would exceed each stakeholder's BATNA (*i.e.*, realistic walk-away option), while meeting other interests tolerably and their own interests exceedingly well.

In practice, most people under-invest in preparation (regardless of the stakes)! They spend far too much time fantasizing about what they want, and not nearly enough time thinking clearly about their realistic options if no agreement is reached at the negotiating table. They spend most of their time thinking about how things look from their own standpoint and not nearly enough time imagining how things look from the other side of the table. Finally, they come ready with proposals and arguments that meet their own interests, but they rarely develop proposals likely to be attractive to the other stakeholders as well.

As part of value creation, mutual gains negotiators are supposed to play the game of *What If?* by brainstorming options that might meet interests on all sides. This means probing interests through active listening and sharing one's own interests clearly. In practice, most negotiators are afraid to reveal their true interests and find it worrisome to look too cooperative (*i.e.*, appearing to want to help the other side meet its interests). They are afraid they will look weak, and that the others at the table will exploit this..

Value distribution is difficult for mutual gains negotiators for some of the same reasons it is problematic for hard bargainers. No one wants to see the other side get more than they get. Competitive instincts take over. Mutual gains negotiators are supposed to avoid a test of will and focus, instead, on the reasons that the distribution of value they are proposing is fair or appropriate. When stated convincingly, this allows all parties to feel good about the outcome of a negotiation, because they can explain, with their heads held high, why they got what they did. In practice, it is hard for inexperienced negotiators to pull this off. And, as a deal comes into view, most negotiators are very uneasy about flagging possible difficulties that might arise later on, even if this is the key to anticipating and solving the problems that are likely to occur.

Most negotiators only think as far ahead as a signed agreement. They don't realize that negotiations actually extend through implementation—when all kinds of surprises can and do occur (*e.g.,* personnel can change, market conditions can fluctuate, new laws can alter the rules of the game, new technologies may emerge, etc.). Handling these unexpected changes, as well as the other side's response to them (including failure to follow through on promises that were made), requires that dispute resolution mechanisms already be in place.

What this means in practice is that most negotiators fail to prepare adequately. They invest insufficient time and effort in value creation (because they are afraid they will look weak). They mishandle value distribution and, in the process, ruin the very relationships that will help them when problems that arise during implementation. And they don't do enough to anticipate the problems of follow through. If training only highlights what needs to be done at each step, and does not help build each negotiator's repertoire of responses to the obstacles that usually emerge, the impact of the training will be minimal.

## NEGOTIATION CAPABILITY IS A SKILL, NOT A GIFT

There are still many people who believe that skilled negotiators are born and not made. However, we have documented too much improvement on the part of people who have, through negotiation training, enhanced their ability to meet their interests by convincing others to act in certain ways, to share this view. Some negotiators may be more gifted than others, but in the absence of knowledge, skill, and strategy, even gifted intuitive negotiators are likely to fall far short of their potential.

Of course, there may be something to the notion that we are talking about a gift and not a skill if we focus solely on hard bargaining. After all, it takes enormous self-confidence (arrogance?) to act as if you are entitled to everything, when your negotiating partner gets nothing. And, bluffing with a straight face—which is essential to hard bargaining but anathema to those who practice the mutual gains approach—may well be akin to acting skills (with which some are blessed and others are not). Maybe being able to act in a self-serving fashion is a basic attribute that some people have and others do not. However, when it comes to employing the mutual gains approach, we know for sure that managers can learn to improve their negotiation skills.

Negotiators need practice. They need a chance to watch people more skilled than they are. They need feedback from colleagues who know what they are talking about. In short, negotiation training (like most other adult learning) needs to start with confronting the ways of doing things that people already have in mind. Then, they need to be given a road map or a model that offers a new (and hopefully better!) way of handling a certain task or assignment. Next, they need several chances to try the new approach in a protected learning setting, where the stakes are low. Finally, they need a period during which they are given the support and encouragement required to incorporate the new ways of doing things into their normal repertoire.

## "NOTHING IS SO PRACTICAL AS A GOOD THEORY"

The classic adult learning model described above (paraphrased from Kurt Lewin's "unfreeze-reframe-refreeze" formulation) hinges on the availability of a better way of doing things. Ideally, this new approach should be derived from actual practice. This means there ought to be many practical examples of what happens when a task is handled well or poorly. Adult learners are reassured if they can hear stories of what worked and what didn't.

Many of us who teach the mutual gains approach to negotiation rely heavily on simulations. Each trainee is given a detailed description of a negotiating situation (often based on an actual negotiation or a hybrid of several real situations). In addition, each person at a table of six, is assigned a specific role and given confidential instructions. These instructions are designed to accomplish three things. First, they guarantee that certain problems or difficulties will arise during the mock negotiation. Unlike role plays—that ask each person to imagine being in a specific situation and encourages choosing a way of acting that feels consistent with the circumstances—simulations guarantee that each player will act in a specific way. Second, they specify the interests and aspirations of each player. This means that individual negotiators can't be manipulated by the negotiating partner to whom they happen to be assigned. Third, they make it easy to compare results (and, more importantly, to analyze the relative effectiveness of different strategies) given exactly the same constraints and circumstances facing each pair. When a table of three or four pairs of negotiators, having completed exactly the same assignment, compare results, the ensuing dialogue is wonderfully instructive.

My colleague, Roger Fisher, argues that negotiation training all comes down to the fact that "there is nothing so practical as a good theory!" A set of techniques or moves, absent a theory that explains why certain actions produce particular effects, is too brittle. If things don't go according to plan, the negotiator is lost. Armed with nothing more than a script or a list of assigned moves, the novice negotiator who encounters unexpected behavior on the other side, is stuck. A negotiator working with a good theory, however, has the tools needed to respond regardless of what the others do or don't do. He or she knows *why* they are supposed to act in a certain way.

The following three checklists take the essence of the mutual gains theory and reformulate the key elements as questions negotiators must ask themselves. There is a checklist to use before contacting negotiating partners. There is another to use at the outset of face-to-face interaction, and, finally, there is a third checklist to use right before negotiators think they have concluded their dialogue.

## Negotiation Preparation Worksheet

(We suggest that you distribute this worksheet to everyone in your organization and encourage anyone involved in any important negotiation to put in the preparation time necessary to answer these questions.)

1. What authority do I/we have to make firm commitments in this upcoming negotiation? Who else do I/we need to have approve the analysis (below)?
2. What are my/our interests in the upcoming negotiation?
3. What are their interests?
4. What is my/our BATNA? How might I/we improve it?
5. What is their BATNA? If they have a strong BATNA how might I/we raise doubts about how realistic they are being about their BATNA?
6. What options (*e.g.*, packages) might I/we suggest for mutual gain (that meet their interests well and my/our interests very well)?
7. What arguments/criteria/reasons can I/we give for preferring the option (package) that is best for me/us? How can I/we help them "sell" this option to their second table?
8. What implementation problems are likely to arise if they accept my/our proposal and how might these be overcome?

## Creating Value: A Checklist

1. Have I/we listened carefully to and probed the interests of the other side? What did I/we learn that was surprising?
2. Have I/we prepared a series of "What If" proposals to present to the other side?

3. Have I/we identified issues I/we should emphasize that are likely to create value for the other side? What are they?
4. Have I/we identified issues that are likely to create value for us? What are they?
5. Have I/we clarified with the other side our intention to devote time early in the negotiations to "inventing without committing?" Do we have a clear understanding with the other side of how this will work?
6. Do I/we have the internal sign-off(s) I/we need to engage in a period of inventing without committing?
7. Have I/we considered various contingent options that could create value? What are they?
8. Have I/we sought outside assistance or a fresh perspective on possible ways of increasing value in this case?
9. Should I/we consider possible linkages between this negotiation and future negotiations with the other side?
10. Would the involvement of a neutral party facilitate further value creation?

### Anticipating the Problems of Follow-Through: A Checklist

1. Will it be necessary to monitor performance during implementation of the proposed agreement? If so, who will have this responsibility? How will disputes over interpretation of monitoring data be resolved? Who will cover the cost of monitoring and the cost of resolving disputes?
2. What relationship-building commitments might help to build trust and make it easier to deal with surprises in this case? What deadlines or milestones for reconsidering or reconfirming our commitments in this case will we build into the agreement?
3. What dispute resolution mechanisms will we rely on if problems emerge during implementation? Who will activate and/or pay for these?
4. What might be done to enhance the nearly self-enforcing quality of each element of this agreement?
5. What organizational incentives and controls are we promising to adjust in order to help ensure effective implementation of this agreement?

## CAN ONE-TIME TRAINING HELP? YES, BUT IT IS NOT ENOUGH

The goals of a short term (*i.e.*, one to three day) training programs in negotiation are: to present the mutual gains theory of negotiation; give attendees a chance to try their hand at mock negotiations (using simulations); to provide a setting in which questions can be asked and answered; and to offer an opportunity to see how others grapple with new methods and ideas.

Training can be highly tailored or it can be generic. That is, the simulations used in any training situation can be off-the-shelf and refer to generic negotiating situations, or they can be written for the occasion, presenting well-known negotiation problem in terms that the participants recognize immediately from their everyday experience. There are arguments for both options; however, the choice ought to reflect, above all, the learning style of the individuals involved. Some participants prefer to start with generic games and, before the training is completed, move to tailored games that reflect on-going negotiations in their industry or agency context. I have been in some training situations in which the participants were quite comfortable with the idea of cross-contextual learning. All the simulations were off-the-shelf. I've also been in situations in which the participants were skeptical about general lessons and needed to see the relevance of the mutual gains approach to their exact circumstances.

Training should provide convincing evidence that the theory of mutual gains negotiation is robust. That is, the mix of lectures, simulations, and stories about actual applications (*i.e.*, case studies) should give the participants a sense that what they are learning will be useful across a range of situations they are likely to encounter. This means that the instructor needs to have relevant "sect oral" experience. Senior trainees especially will rebuff anyone who tries to teach in too mechanistic or formulaic fashion. Questions (and skepticism) need to be addressed with specific stories or illustrations that seem realistic to the participants.

One of the more interesting versions of mutual gains negotiation training is what we call joint training. In the labor relations arena, this refers to negotiation training in which *both* the union and the management negotiating teams attend together. Exactly the same material is taught to both "sides" at the same time. In certain joint training situations, mock contract negotiations are used that involve a fact pattern far different from what the industry is facing, so that no one worries about giving away an upcoming negotiation strategy. Sometimes the union participants in such trainings are asked to play the management roles in the games and vice versa. This ensures that each comes away with a clearer sense of how the problem looks from the other side. In a work situation where the parties want to move away from a purely adversarial form of contract bargaining, joint training is an effective means of initiating a new approach.

In research studies prepared for the United States Department of Labor, we have been able to demonstrate the effectiveness of joint training. In addition, we have been able to use the joint training approach to bring regulators and those they regulate in the environmental, health and energy sectors together to learn a more collaborative approach to joint problem solving. The joint approach of the training adds an extra dimension and often some tension. The fact that each side sees the other learning what they are learning, however, justifies the tension because it enables both sides to shift to a new way of doing business.

# NEGOTIATION IS AN ORGANIZATIONAL, NOT AN INDIVIDUAL TASK

Even a terrific negotiator needs organizational support. Once negotiators are clear about the requirements of the mutual gains approach, they soon realize that at each of the four steps in the process, they need to interact with others in their company, agency, or organization. Indeed, they may be completely dependent on others, higher up in their organization, for certain information or approval. This can generate a new set of obstacles if the concept of mutual gains is not widely understood across the organization.

During preparation a negotiator needs to make a preliminary assessment of what he or she ought to set as a bottom line. That is, prior to arriving at a negotiation table, each negotiator ought to have a pretty good sense of what no agreement means to them. Put another way, each negotiator needs to formulate a clear sense of his or her BATNA (Best Alternative to a Negotiated Agreement). Even though they now this in theory, I have seen many senior managers direct their staff to "get the most that they can" in an upcoming negotiation, but "not to lose the sale under any circumstance." This, of course, badly muddies the calculation of the negotiator's BATNA. Being clear about when to walk away from a negotiation is a crucial part of preparation. When others, higher up in the organization, will not invest the time and effort up front to help set an organizational BATNA, it undermines even the most skilled negotiator's effectiveness. Deciding when to walk away is an organizational task. Too many senior managers are too busy to work with their negotiators before they meet with the other side. This, more often than not, dooms the negotiation to a less than ideal outcome.

During value creation the key is to play the game of *What If?* Often, however, organizations want their negotiators to veto all offers before they are made. They frown on improvisation for fear that their negotiator may inadvertently expose the organization to unforeseen legal or financial liabilities. This inhibits value creation in insurmountable ways. If organizations do not give their negotiators sufficient autonomy and a broad enough mandate, value creation will be undermined.

During the value distribution phase, getting the larger piece of the pie in a negotiation usually requires providing others at the table with reasons why the proposed distribution of value is appropriate or fair. An organization that pushes its negotiators to win at all costs, actually unempowers them in the value distribution battle. Instead, organizations should equip their negotiators with the evidence and arguments they need to justify a favorable distribution of value. In addition, organizations that second guess the results produced by their negotiators, no matter what the outcome or the context, teach them that they ought to inflate their demands in the future (to protect themselves from internal criticism). This, in turn, can lead to such unreasonable position taking down the line, that pretty-good results are lost when others leave the table in disgust.

During the follow through, it is important to think about the kinds of surprises that may occur during the implementation of any agreement. One way of heading off potential problems is to formulate contingent agreements. By spelling out ahead of time what each signatory will be expected to do under various sets of circumstances (including highly unlikely but extremely unpleasant events), little is left to chance and potential disagreements can be avoided. Some organizations, however, object to contingent agreements. They don't know how to "book" the value of contingent deals, and they don't like the potential exposure to uncertain liabilities, so a skilled negotiator may often be precluded by his or her organization from formulating appropriately complex (and self-enforcing) agreements.

Organizations need to make sure that they measure the right things in evaluating the success of their negotiators. Ideally, individual negotiator performance should be calculated against the BATNA agreed upon ahead of time by the organization. An outcome substantially above the value of the organization's BATNA should be rewarded internally. All too often, though, senior managers engage in "Monday morning quarterbacking," complaining that any and every result isn't what it should have been or could have been. Some organizations are also terribly shortsighted, measuring only the short-term monetary value of a successfully negotiated deal rather than the longer-term impact on market share, customer relations, or reputation. Whatever the measures are that an organization uses to gauge the success of negotiations, these ought to be made explicit before the fact and applied consistently.

## Coaching Advice to Senior Managers And Executives

Top management ought to do everything it can to improve the negotiating skills of its employees. This certainly includes providing training for those who are not clear about the theory that presumably informs their negotiation efforts. This is necessary, but not sufficient. Senior management also needs to do three other things. First, leaders ought to practice what their organization preaches. That is, senior managers ought to model the approach to negotiation that they want their staff to emulate–particularly in dealings with those same staff members! A senior manager who talks about mutual gains, but engages in nothing but positional bargaining in discussing possible pay raises with employees, sends contradictory, and ultimately self-defeating, messages.

Second, organizational leaders ought to give positive reinforcement and rewards to those who negotiate well while penalizing those who do not. I am constantly startled by organizations that reward negotiators who look and sound tough, but do not produce much by way of gains above BATNA. Moreover, leaders ought to praise those who prepare well, even though the absolute value of what they produce might be small (albeit well above BATNA). Attention ought to be drawn, not to those who get lucky on occasion (and produce spectacular results), but to those who stay the course and produce consistently good results because they know what they are doing.

Third, negotiation has to be an on-going focus of attention. Some organizational leaders get "a bee in their bonnet" about negotiation, insist on training for everyone, and then drop the subject. Negotiation improvements, because they are organizational and not just individual, take time to infuse the machinery of group interaction. They also take constant reinforcement. World-class negotiating organizations are built slowly and self-consciously.

## CONCLUSION

Most professionals yearn to improve. They seek advice and advanced instruction. Yet, whatever new approach or technique they learn is almost always uncomfortable at first. Thus, when the stakes are high, they are uneasy about trying a new way of doing things that they have not quite mastered. They revert; instead, to the old ways they know best (even if they don't produce the desired results). Change is slow in coming.

I've urged many organizations to draw attention to good negotiating practices inside their company or agency by publicizing success stories on a regular basis. A short 500-word email, once a month, highlighting meritorious preparation, value creation, value distribution or follow-through efforts keeps everyone's attention focused. I've also suggested creating a hot line or a Negotiation Preparation Office where a single person who knows the organization well is always available on short notice to help negotiators review their preparatory notes or strategic options. A long-term commitment to this level of assistance is often necessary to convince the staff that an organization is serious about raising the skill level of its negotiators.

## SUGGESTED READING

Fisher, R., W. Ury, and B. Patton, 1991. *Getting To Yes* (2nd ed). Boston: Houghton-Mifflin.

Lax, D., and J.K. Sebenius, 1986. *The Manager as Negotiator: Bargaining for Cooperation and Competitive Gain.* New York: Free Press.

Mnookin, R.H., S.R. Peppet, and A.S. Tulumello, 2000. *Beyond Winning: Negotiating to Create Value in Deals and Disputes.* Cambridge, MA: Belknap.

Mnookin, R.H., and L. Susskind, *Negotiating on Behalf of Others.* Thousand Oaks, CA: Sage.

Susskind, L., S. McKearnan, and J.Thomas-Larmer, *The Consensus Building Handbook.* Thousand Oaks, CA: Sage.

# CHAPTER 9

# VALUE DIVERSITY AND INCLUSION: LEVERAGING DIFFERENCES FOR BOTTOM-LINE SUCCESS

*Judith H. Katz*

## ABSTRACT

*An organization that not only recognizes, but also leverages the diversity of its work-force and creates an inclusive culture that supports everyone in the organization to contribute, will see positive, substantive change resulting in higher performance.*

## INTRODUCTION

Despite the fact that *diversity* has been a common word in the business lexicon for over twenty years, many organizations still do not fully grasp how diversity can be a key business tool that supports organizational success.

Diversity refers to the range of human differences that include ethnicity, age, sexual orientation, job function, race, range of ability, job level, gender, religion, nationality, education, class, family status, individual differences in work and leadership style, personality, and problem-solving methods. This definition *includes* white men. Every human being brings a unique set of skills, experiences, perspectives, and talents to everything they do. Organizations that tap into these differences and leverage the diversity of their workforce are seeing measurable results such as improved innovation and market penetration, enhanced customer loyalty, reduced cost, more efficient use of resources, increased retention, lower turnover, an engaged workforce, and significant impact to the bottom line. Organizations that do not leverage their diversity or remain blind to differences will not be able to compete in an increasingly demanding marketplace. Due to the technological advances and innovations of the last thirty years, customers and clients are more informed than ever before and they are demanding continuous improvements in products and services. Not only are competitors setting the standards by which organizations must measure themselves and consistently surpass, but increasingly, customers are driving the need for constant innovation.

## DIVERSITY IN A BOX

One of the biggest traps organizations fall into when they begin a diversity initiative is to relegate it to a few new policies and half-day training sessions. This approach is "diversity in a box," a compartmentalized, narrow approach that does not acknowledge the ways in which leveraging diversity and creating a culture of inclusion needs to permeate every level of an organization—every interaction, every communication, every practice and policy—in order to achieve the company's goals. Organizations that end up with a diversity-in-a-box strategy see diversity as getting in the way of success by forcing the organization to do something it does not want to do. Or they see diversity as something to be managed, shaping it to fit in the existing structure of the organization. Some organizations see diversity as a value and end in itself, an isolated box on the organizational chart, disconnected from the mission, vision, and strategies of the organization, which often results in a singular focus on representation or awareness.

Regardless of the reasons why some organizations begin a diversity effort, they often think of it as an extra—a package of programs and policies run by Human Resources or the in-house training department—unconnected to the bottom line. Change efforts that are not tied to the core business and goals of an organization, even if they are taken on with good intentions, are easily sidetracked or minimized when other priorities call or business conditions become challenging.

## WHY FOCUS ON LEVERAGING DIVERSITY AND CREATING A CULTURE OF INCLUSION?

In order for organizations to compete for market share they need to recruit, retain, nurture, and grow talented people. Over the last year The Kaleel Jamison Consulting Group has been conducting an informal survey with people across industries and levels, posing the question, "What percentage of your talents is the organization utilizing?" The average response is sixty percent. This means that a full forty percent of the ideas, vision, perception, talents, innovation, and efficiency *that currently reside in the organization* is being wasted. Organizations that accept the challenge inherent in this data and begin the work of creating a sustainable strategy for leveraging their diversity and creating an inclusion breakthrough are bound to be the big winners in the competition for talented people *and* customers.

The question for organizations is "How can you achieve higher performance, improved productivity, and increased innovation?" By leveraging the talent that already exists in an organization's greatest resource—people—overall organizational performance will improve.

The goals behind leveraging diversity and inclusion are relatively simple: organizations can achieve their greatest potential and highest performance when they have access to a broad array of skills, talents, and perspectives. The best way to achieve that broad array of viewpoints and expertise is with a diverse group of people who each bring different talents to the table—talents that complement, rather than duplicate each other. However, having diversity is not the answer—it is assuring that each person is included and that there is a breakthrough in the organizational culture, structures, and ways of doing business. Achieving such results does not occur by bringing in more people, conducting training programs, or communicating platitudes about the organization's commitment to diversity, but rather by creating an environment that allows diversity to thrive. It requires an inclusion breakthrough.

## WHAT IS AN INCLUSION BREAKTHROUGH?

The essence of an inclusion breakthrough is the engagement of people—and their individual and social identity group differences—as resources for today and tomorrow's success. When an organization creates a culture of inclusion that leverages diversity, it sees opportunities and challenges that cannot be seen when working from the basis of sameness. The breakthrough in performance and productivity comes from the combination of bringing people together while respecting and including their experiences, perspectives, talents, and differences. It comes in the transformation of an organization with a monolithic culture that supports sameness in style and approach to a culture that leverages diversity in its many dimensions and values inclusive behaviors. (see Figure 1)[1]

Inclusive behaviors change virtually every aspect of an organization's operations. People learn to work differently. Every project team scans the organization to make sure it has the best and right people for the work team. Disagreements lead to better decisions based on a 360-degree vision (multiple perspectives from diverse backgrounds) of the problem, challenge, opportunity, and possible solutions;

---

[1]Miller, Frederick A. and Katz, Judith H. "Diversity Consultation Skills." In *Handbook of Diversity Management: Beyond Awareness to Competency Based Learning*, edited by D. Plummer, 439-459. Lanham, MD: University Press of America, Inc., 2003.

---

**Figure 1 Eleven Behaviors for Inclusion[1]**

1.  Greet others authentically.
2.  Create a sense of safety for you and your team members.
3.  Address misunderstandings and resolve disagreements.
4.  Listen carefully to the person speaking until that person feels understood.
5.  Communicate clearly, directly, and honestly.
6.  Solidify the team's vision of its tasks and its relationship to the organization's mission.
7.  Hear all voices. Allow for options.
8.  Ask others to share their thoughts and experiences and accept their frame of reference.
9.  Speak up when people are being excluded.
10. Make careful choices about group actions and schedules. Treat everyone's time as valuable and their presence as critical.
11. Be brave.

---

and work assignments are made with consideration for outside-of-work responsibilities, so people freely give their whole selves without their jobs consuming their lives. Members of the organization and customers feel loyalty to the organization because of the quality of its products and services and also because of its values and behaviors.

An inclusion breakthrough happens when a critical mass of individuals begins to leverage diversity and inclusion as a central focus of their everyday business activities: thinking about people as partners and assets; solving problems by including all members who can bring a different perspective to the issue; enabling people at all levels and in all identity groups to feel they belong and can add their value; and inviting newcomers with their fresh vision to identify what others of longer tenure might not be able to see. The *breakthrough* comes from the inclusion (and all that goes with it) of *all* people.

## A DEMANDING BUSINESS ENVIRONMENT

The internal workforce may be the biggest differentiator among competing organizations. Many companies say that "people are our greatest asset," but few truly treat people as an asset. Investors know the value of a diversified portfolio; business leaders are just learning to apply that same philosophy to intellectual capital. Assembling a broad array of talents and knowledge gives organizations new assets that raise the value of the organization as a whole.

Business conditions are changing at a faster rate than ever. Markets have gone global. Competition has intensified. Customers are demanding better goods and services. Even the highest performing organizations know that they can't afford to sit still. With their greater vision and broader problem-solving skills, diverse and inclusive organizations have greater ability to meet the challenges of an ever-changing, highly demanding marketplace.

Addressing this marketplace requires re-examination of fundamental questions of marketing. Take something as basic as packaging, for example. Do you write the name of the products in the language of the country of the products' origin or the country where the products will be sold? Do you try to get the world to accept your language? And if you change the language, can you use the same illustrations? How have you integrated a diverse marketplace into your business model and approach?

# A CHANGING WORKFORCE

Work/Life/Family integration is having, and will continue to have, a huge impact on the way organizations function. More and more people are beginning to rebel against the 60- to 80-hour workweek that has become standard practice for many organizations. It is unrealistic to think that the baby boomers and the younger generation will be able to or would want to keep up the pace of work currently asked of them. It simply cannot be a long-term proposition. Younger people of all backgrounds and identities have a different attitude toward employment than their parents and grandparents did. They are interested in balancing their work lives with their personal lives and want organizations that respect them and create an environment that meets their needs. Today's workforce should be thought of as consumers with choices even in challenging economic times.

Many people feel they are being asked to give their lives to companies that are clearly not worthy of their trust, much less worthy of a life-sacrificing commitment. Once business starts to upswing again, many people will be ready to leave if they do not feel valued in their current organization.

Organizations need to be worthy of the contributions of their people by instituting the kind of policies and practices that value and support them. This may include welcoming the same-sex partners of lesbian and gay employees to company functions. It may involve paid paternity leave, on-site childcare, or adoption benefits to help support working parents. It might require new flextime policies or job-sharing options that give people the opportunities they need to contribute fully to the organization while still meeting their responsibilities in other areas of their lives.

A diverse population needs new organizational structures and approaches. Companies must be vigilant about hearing people's needs and bold in responding to them. Organizations are being faced more and more with complex situations that one perspective cannot sufficiently address—they need everyone's input. Part of creating an inclusive work environment involves changing the ways in which individuals and teams operate.

# NEW COMPETENCIES FOR A NEW CULTURE

In order to realize higher performance and bottom line benefits diversity and inclusion must touch every part of the business. Being comprehensive means being strategic. Organizations need to carefully plan their culture change efforts, enacting new policies, measuring results along the way, and holding people accountable for success.

The culture change process begins by identifying the new competencies and behaviors that are required to support a more inclusive environment. In the absence of effective skills for communicating and partnering across differences, organizations tend to marginalize the people who are most different from the dominant group. These people often feel unheard, devalued, and ignored.

Without effective conflict management skills, even organizations that are visibly diverse are unable to capitalize on the wealth of perspectives offered by their members. Such capitalization means basing decisions on careful analysis and synthesis of differing viewpoints, or on an informed debate on the relative merits of various peoples' proposals. Instead, many groups base decisions on who has the most seniority, grade or band level, or who is politically connected, thereby excluding potentially significant voices and insights. Without these skills, organizations may not be able to address the needs of an increasingly diverse marketplace and workforce.[2]

Senior executives, managers, and associates must learn and practice specific skill sets that foster a culture of inclusion. Organizations must identify the specific behaviors (see Table 1) that they expect of individuals at each level of the organization and then hold them accountable for demonstrating those behaviors. The competencies should be designated as components of a mission-critical imperative to leverage diversity and create a culture of inclusion.

Many businesses are looking more closely at how their organizations are operating, opportunities to cut back on spending, many are downsizing, and most are trying to develop strategies that will improve their long-term bottom line. Creating an inclusion breakthrough is a business strategy that will result in an organizational culture that yields higher performance and innovation, increased retention and development of an organization's people, and greater return on investment. All of these results from the change effort, however, must be measured in order to sustain support across the organization for the continued investment in culture change. Many organizations are be-

---

[2] Miller, Frederick A. and Katz, Judith H. *The Inclusion Breakthrough: Unleashing the Real Power of Diversity*. San Francisco, CA: Berrett-Koehler Publishers, 2002, 67.

**Table 1  Individual Competencies**

| ALL ASSOCIATES | MANAGERS | SENIOR EXECUTIVES |
|---|---|---|
| • Teamwork: Partnering with others | **Associate competencies and** | **Manager competencies and** |
| • Respect: Listening and responding to others | • Leading inclusive teams | • Connecting with all people |
| • Addressing conflict: Leaning into discomfort | • Developing and retaining people | • Integrating leveraging diversity and a culture of inclusion into business plans, strategies, and daily actions |
| • Straight Talk: Clear and direct communication | • Coaching and mentoring others | |
| • Belonging: Greeting and including people | • Modeling and creating a culture of inclusion | • Providing direction, focus, connections, and meaning to the inclusion breakthrough |
| • Being brave: Encouraging change | • Leveraging the diversity of all people | |

ginning to see the direct correlation of the investment in culture change to their bottom line and a breakthrough in the organization's productivity, processes, and approach.

# STRATEGY IS KEY

Many organizations still want to relegate diversity and inclusion to training programs, cultural celebrations, supplier diversity, hiring and recruiting efforts, or development and mentoring programs. All of these actions are needed; however, what is missing is a strategic initiative that addresses the very core of how business is conducted and the relationship of leveraging diversity and creating a culture of inclusion to organizational strategy, vision, and direction. Being strategic means moving from having a culture change effort that touches only one or two areas of the business to developing an organization-wide strategy that demands incorporating diversity and inclusion into every piece of the business.

## Kodak: Inclusive manufacturing

Kodak has invested a number of years in developing a "Winning and Inclusive Culture," a change effort focused on improving the ways people in the organization interact, creating more inclusive work teams, and strengthening their commitment to respecting and valuing the differences brought by each person in the organization. Kodak strategically expanded their change effort from first focusing only on how people in the organization work together to looking at how issues of inclusion and diversity can be integrated into other areas of business, such as operating systems. Kodak is taking the knowledge about the value of diversity and being inclusive that they gained through their pre-existing change effort and applying that knowledge to a process of improving their operating systems, a process of inclusive lean manufacturing.

The desire to examine operating systems and develop ways to make operations more productive, less wasteful of resources, and more inclusive came from people on the shop floor who were combining their knowledge of lean manufacturing with inclusive behaviors and practices. Getting management support for the change effort extended in this direction was critical. With this support the focus on changing operating systems to be more inclusive and more productive was viewed both as critical to improving business performance and integral to the company's overall change strategy.

Kodak began the inclusive, lean manufacturing process with the goals of eliminating wasted resources, improving workforce morale, and positively impacting the bottom line. With a focus on inclusion, Kodak brought together teams of people who are diverse across functions, experiences, and perspectives. These people all have some firsthand knowledge of how things happen on the shop floor, and Kodak gave them an opportunity to make positive changes in the operating systems. Each team underwent training on working inclusively and was then given a real business problem to address. Their task was to identify potential lean manufacturing improvements to operating practices. Through this process, Kodak solved problems and identified solutions inclusively using 360-degree vision.

Among the positive results Kodak has attributed to the process of lean manufacturing are: the reduction of all inventories totaling hundreds of millions of dollars; a cost savings in the tens of millions of dollars; greatly improved responsiveness to customers; and a substantially improved work environment with greatly-strengthened workplace safety. Reinforcement for the process has resulted in even more team activities at Kodak, and feedback indicates that the work in lean manufacturing is making the Winning and Inclusive Culture a reality.

Kodak took the step of widening the lens to see diversity and inclusion as an added value to the operating system. The indication is that Kodak is linking and aligning the Winning and Inclusive Culture initiative into the strategic work of the organization.

## MAKING DIVERSITY AND INCLUSION A WAY OF LIFE

For diversity and inclusion efforts to be meaningful and truly effective, they need to be woven into the very fabric of the organization itself. The behaviors and poli-

**Figure 2. The Way of Life Model**

cies associated with the effort need to become a way of life within the organization (see Figure 2).[3]

Several steps must be taken to achieve such a thorough integration in the organization's culture:

## Step 1: Develop a long-term strategic plan.

A comprehensive, multi-phase plan must be in place, one that reaches into every area of the organization. It is crucial that the initiative be linked to all of the organization's operations, process-improvement efforts, and bottom-line strategies.

---

[3]Miller, Frederick A. and Katz, Judith H. "Building Inclusion and Leveraging Diversity as a Way of Doing Business." In *Handbook of Diversity Management: Beyond Awareness to Competency Based Learning*, edited by D. Plummer, 461–485. Lanham, MD: University Press of America, Inc., 2003.

This includes customer service, product design, and market-development planning. Support for the initiative must begin at the top of the organization and extend to every person in the company. Achieving such widespread support necessitates that organizational imperative be clear and tied to the organization's vision, mission, and strategy. The imperative must speak directly to why it is critical for the organization to invest its time, resources, and accountabilities in such a change effort.

### Step 2: Create new competencies and formalize accountability for living the new competencies that create the new culture.

The need to establish new competencies at every level of the organization was discussed earlier in this chapter. Competencies without accountability, however, do not change a culture. Formalizing accountability might begin with the development of scorecards and other metrics that quantify results of the initiative and allow them to be tracked over time. In one organization an assessment was conducted of all managers to identify their skills and competencies given the organization's current and future objectives.

Using data from direct reports, performance reviews, and peers, each manager was assessed with a red light, yellow light, or green light as to their current ability and future potential to successfully manage and lead an inclusive work group. Managers who were assessed and given a red light were reassigned or terminated in some cases; managers with a yellow light were placed on a development path; and green light managers were seen as mentors and models for others. By identifying a new set of competencies for managers and then creating accountability for practicing those competencies, this organization is better positioned to achieve its current and future goals through the development, coaching, and retention of the organization's resources.

One recent client used a Diversity and Inclusion Index (an annual employee survey) to monitor performance along key dimensions related to their culture change goals. The results of the index not only allowed the company to gauge its progress, but also to tie incentives and rewards to improvements in the metrics, creating accountability among managers and all employees for achieving certain milestones outlined in the long-term strategic plan.

### Step 3: Work leveraging diversity and creating a culture of inclusion into all education/training programs, including those focused on business-critical initiatives.

People are being expected to exhibit new behaviors and function differently in a new culture. Education, therefore, is critical so that they can know what these behaviors are, why changes are being made, and how all will benefit from the new culture. Goals and expectations must be explicit. Since the issues and potential conflicts that diversity and inclusion initiatives encounter change over time, this education needs to be ongoing.

It is also important that diversity and inclusion not be seen as "add-ons" to the culture—another program akin to so many others. They should be regarded as part of the air that everyone breathes, or as a foundational element that supports all the other work in the organization. Accordingly, they should be a factor for continual education and professional development. When new policies or work procedures are enacted, the discussion around them should include an examination of how a change will affect people across the workforce.

### Step 4: Implement incentives and rewards.

One of the most effective means for illustrating that the organization is serious about culture change is clearly and publicly rewarding the behaviors the company wants to endorse. This sends a powerful message to everyone in the organization that the emphasis on change and new competencies isn't just lip service. The same kind of reward systems that work to promote all other desired professional behaviors (bonuses, promotions, gifts, public recognition, etc.) should be used to encourage good diversity and inclusion practices.

### Step 5: Enhance performance feedback systems.

One of the most important systems to be addressed is performance management. Few people in organizations are getting honest, candid, helpful feedback about their contribution and their potential growth and development. In many organizations systems are not in place to gather relevant data on managers' and others' performance regarding diversity and inclusion. Managers should be evaluated by their bosses, as well as by those they actually manage, to get feedback on how well they support an inclusive culture within their workgroups. This is tied to the notion of accountability. Performance feedback needs to incorporate how well managers are leveraging the diversity of their staffs, hiring, developing, and promoting a diverse cadre of individuals, and modeling inclusive behaviors.

### Step 6: Involve stakeholders.

Communicating business gains to the organization's stakeholders is a key to enlisting their support for institutionalizing change. Suppliers, vendors, board members, people from the community, and others who work closely with the organization all offer opportunities for the kind of partnerships that put inclusive behaviors into practice. For example, strategic philanthropy within the community builds on an organization's reputation and pull for a wider range of candidates who want to join the organization. Also, the use of diverse suppliers is crucial for assuring the organization is acting consistent with its goals. Diversity and inclusion are not confined to internal operations; they are methods for interacting with all stakeholder communities to improve working relationships and increase visibility.

## Conclusion

Diversity and inclusion are more than trendy programs or socially responsible frills. When viewed and implemented as strategic business strategies, they provide a competitive edge and a route to higher performance. To realize these benefits, however, organizations need to take a serious, strategic, long-term approach to diversity and inclusion, creating an environment in which individuals are respected and supported in bringing all aspects of their identities to their jobs. People must be educated about and held accountable for practicing the new behaviors and competencies that support a diverse and inclusive workplace, and the organization must undergo a process of change to make diversity and inclusion a way of life. Only then can the organization achieve an inclusion breakthrough that yields greater productivity, efficiency, and competitive edge.

## Summary

To keep up with the pace of change and the pace of their competition, organizations must innovate continuously. Creativity and innovation require a workforce that leverages diversity. As organizations position themselves for future success and viability, building a diverse workforce where people can bring their unique talents and perspectives to work with them everyday is critical to achieving higher performance. A diverse workforce functioning in an inclusive environment aims for a much higher utilization of skills. Organizations need to establish new policies and new competencies that support variation in approach and perspective, and foster teamwork and synergy among all members. The goal is an inclusion breakthrough: finding ways to tap into a much higher percentage of every person's capabilities and use their intelligence, vision, talent, and innovation to create both higher performance and greater employee satisfaction.

# CHAPTER 10

# UNDERSTAND AND APPLY SOCIOLOGY AND ANTHROPOLOGY: BUILD BRAND AND LEADERSHIP THROUGH BUSINESS ANTHROPOLOGY, MARKET RESEARCH, AND SCENARIO PLANNING

*Steve Barnett*

## ABSTRACT

*Market research is a field about to be fundamentally changed by consumer companies needing to develop deeper insights about their customers and by emerging technologies that will make real-time behavior and attitudes available for customer-driven management. Current problems in market research are discussed and solutions offered as future best practices. These solutions include ethnographic methods, outsourcing emerging digital and information technologies, providing real-time insightful data, the ability to use that data to hyper-differentiate brands and to develop/retain customer loyalty. Four futures for marketing research are discussed, with implications for best practices across all four, and within each.*

## INTRODUCTION

Market research is stuck in a time warp; new methods and technologies are available but researchers who haven't learned to deploy them effectively limit their use. To that extent, describing best practices cannot simply select from what is current, but should assess what will be effective in a transformed future. There are three fundamental ways that this time warp will vanish as market research changes in the near future:

- Increased use of anthropological methods and futures analysis tools (scenario planning) to deepen consumer insights.
- Digital technologies that allow data from any source to be integrated in a single database.
- Real-time information availability, including custom panels, so that clients and researchers can see (and act on) the same data,

This chapter will explore these opportunities in terms of real-time customer management that moves consumer research information into daily business operations. If the goal of brand differentiation is customer delight, then consumer research needs to provide ways to understand and act on profound customer desires rather than just identify traditional "need states" and product benefits. At the end of the chapter, I will use scenario planning to look at the futures of consumer research as a way to evaluate best practices in market research in an uncertain environment.

Our ability to understand consumer desires has dramatically improved in the past decade. We can obtain real-time information about behavior and attitudes. We can observe how consumers actually buy and use products without creating an artificial setting. We can integrate consumer data from any source into a single database. We can provide companies with real-time data and the ability to view, filter, and cross-tab that data. We can use pocket PCs to record consumer views and responses to open-ended questions. We can take consumer research and use it as a basis for developing future marketing and product development strategies without having to predict a single future—and emerging technologies promise to make all of the above much easier.

These possibilities are compelling and yet consumer research has not fundamentally changed during the last decade. The hard truth is that companies with successful marketing strategies and those with losing strategies basically rely on the same consumer data, typically gathered using methods available since the 1960s.

The tools of the trade remain the same—focus groups, mall intercepts, surveys by mail or phone, one-on-one interviews—with tiny modifications, like barebones online surveying or baby steps in observing how consumers buy and use products in their daily lives. Matters might even be worse; it is plausible to suggest that consumer research has devolved over the years as samples become less reliable with more consumers rejecting phone interviews and as the "closed feedback loop" syndrome expands. In this latter case, the interviewee feeds back to the interviewer information found in ads and other public sources. Consequently, nothing new is learned.

This stagnation has caused consumer research to commodify, with price-based competition increasingly the rule, since methods and results are similar across companies. In part, this is also due to a lack of analysis of consumer data. Unlike physics, everyone is an amateur social scientist. So, company marketers behind the one-way mirror of focus groups understandably seize on those phrases and views that support prior convictions. And questionnaire responses are mostly evaluated question by question rather than using clustering and factor analysis. Newer segmentation methods, like fuzzy sets, are almost never exploited.

There are, of course, companies that claim unique insights based on special approaches, including trending, mostly hidden from the client who must take the results on faith. Tracking trends is not the hard part; what is challenging is anticipating the inflection point (when the trend shifts decisively) and getting the timing of the inflection point right. At the same time, the need for at least some consumer research is being obviated by real-time consumer evaluations like collaborative filtering and CRM (Customer Relationship Management). But at least for now, collaborative filtering algorithms are too crude (like "nearest neighbor matching") to really provide individual consumer insight leading to cross and up-selling. And although CRM proponents claim almost magical results, CRM is very difficult to apply successfully. Most consumers resent being bombarded with many offerings they have not asked for, that are not really on target, and that seem blatantly calculated to entice them to spend more.

Something is wrong here. Not only are consumer research methods and results standardized, but there is little impetus for change even though the raw materials for major innovations are available right now. Future best practices in consumer research will not be limited to selecting the "best" from existing standards and methods, but rather will start by reframing the practice of consumer understanding. Here are my candidates for what will determine future best practices in consumer and marketing research:

- Anthropological research strategies
- Scenario planning
- Customized consumer panels
- Emerging technologies

# ANTHROPOLOGICAL RESEARCH STRATEGIES

All consumer research is to some extent intrusive, but some methods are more intrusive than others. Traditional qualitative research—focus groups—is significantly intrusive.

Gathering approximately ten people in a special room with microphones, videotaping, and a one-way mirror concealing an observers' room, hardly reproduces everyday life. Add to that a moderator asking probing, sometimes very odd questions ("If this car were a Hollywood star, who would it be?"), and any similarity to ordinary conversation vanishes.

Anthropology has refined fieldwork for the past 100 years and while academic fieldwork requiring a year or more is not realistic in a business context, adapted versions of fieldwork can provide profound consumer insights with limited encroachment on the consumer's everyday life.

There are two ways, based on anthropological methods, to reduce the extent of intrusion and increase the level of insight.

***Ethnographic observation.*** Anthropologists observe consumers using products at home, selecting products at POP (point of purchase), and evaluating products with family and friends. I recently directed a study of self-checkout at supermarkets and mass retailers where anthropologists observed customers scanning, then bagging their own items. The learning was significant and surprising. Younger people began to use supermarkets like convenience stores, just buying and self-checking out a few snacks. Moms with children avoided the whining for candy at traditional checkouts by having the kids help with checkout. The switch to self-checkout was not just a cost saving for the store, but transformed how customers perceived the store's value and resulted in organizing displays to reflect these new store opportunities. Observation is somewhat misleading, implying that anyone can just casually watch an activity. Skilled observers recognize patterns in behavior and attitudes; they don't just innocently view what is in front of them.

***Intensive Cultural Interviews (ICIs).*** Unlike focus groups, these group interviews do not use a moderator to *probe*, but instead create tasks for the group to complete on their own. A recent ICI was tasked with redesigning a clothing store to make it more customer friendly. Unexpectedly, they concentrated on the dressing rooms, typically a store afterthought—cramped, unflattering lighting, often without a mirror. The group created an exciting space with music, day and evening lighting options, the ability to see oneself in different environments using interactive videos, etc. This is important for stores where the conversion ratio of trying on to purchasing is often low. An improved dressing room could quickly pay for itself by improving the ratio.

## SCENARIO PLANNING

Predicting the future is business astrology; we have no way to make predictions and no methods that make predicting more "scientific." This of course doesn't stop consumer gurus from extrapolating and predicting all over the place. And just as astrologers make many predictions, hoping that a few will hit the mark and be remembered, some consumer predictions are on target. But as the old advertising saw goes, "I know 50 percent of my advertising works, I just don't know which 50 percent," so also for consumer predictions.

Consumer research is sometimes invoked as the basis for forecasting, using longitudinal surveys tracking the same questions and issues for months or years. While this does offer hints about the future, it begs two critical questions:

- What radically new products and/or services can fundamentally change the competitive landscape?
- When will a trend lose momentum; when will the inflection point on a trend curve occur?

Over time, these surveys lose value as they become locked into questions that have lost relevance but are basic to the questionnaire design.

Scenario planning is a more reasoned alternative, substituting "plausible" futures for the hubris of "probable" futures. Scenario planning was developed by the Hudson Institute, first applied to business strategy by Royal Dutch/Shell, and is now used by many *Fortune* 500 companies. Scenario planning workshops start with fundamental uncertainties and develop those uncertainties into coherent and very different futures.

A scenario workshop I directed 4 years ago focused on the futures of an innovative digital broadband application, enabling streaming video on cell phones. This was during the heyday of dotcoms, when almost any digital Web-based application was generously funded. As the scenario workshop starting point, we gathered consumer data on cell phone needs and desires. Surprisingly, even in that period of irrational exuberance, the workshop could only find one future out of five where this application was compelling enough to justify a large R&D outlay. We then developed early warning signs for each future scenario and tied R&D spending to the unfolding of those indicators. The indicators for the one positive future happened slowly, allowing R&D to begin with limited resources, expanding as more early warning signs unfolded, ultimately saving the company at least 15 million dollars in wasted expense.

I also participated in a small group of experts helping Steven Spielberg create the background environment for *Minority Report,* using scenario methods to anticipate what consumerism might look like 30 years from now. In that film, Tom Cruise is assailed by "personal" advertising messages (based on ubiquitous digital cameras scanning his retina) as he moves through public spaces. That future scenario is already emerging in real life as tiny, cheap digital cameras become available and as hologram technology is adapted to advertising.

Another example of scenario planning will be seen later when the futures of consumer research are explored from a scenario perspective.

## Customized Consumer Panels

Every company that makes a product or provides a service should have three on-going proprietary panels:

- Strong Loyalists–customers who will only buy the brand.
- Weak Loyalists–customers who will consider the brand as part of a set of other brands.
- Competitor Loyalists–consumers who will only buy another brand.

As far as I know, no company has them today.

These panels, typically online, can provide real-time information about product changes, promotions and sales, competitor strategies, and effective responses. They can be invoked as a competitor changes an offer (mark down, cross-sell, etc.), markets a new product or line extension (new model automobile, adding footwear to a clothing brand, etc.), or changes communications (new advertising campaign, direct mail, altering target segment parameters, etc.). Using panels this way allows more decisions to be fact-based as well as opinion and judgment-based. These panels bring customer data into real-time business activities.

A company that created these three panels used them effectively to assess a competitor strategy of becoming an "official sponsor" for a major sports league. As the sponsorship was rolled out in commercials, print, and at-game signage, the company queried its panels about awareness and impact. Surprisingly, impact was very limited for all panels. The conclusion was that since this competitor was not one of the leading sponsors (in visibility), they were lost in the overall "noise" of multiple sponsors, other advertising, and the general excitement surrounding games. This allowed the company to save money by not trying to develop its own sponsorship program or overreacting in other ways.

## Emerging Technologies And Outsourcing

We are at the bottom of S-curves of adoption for a number of technology applications that will directly affect the conduct of consumer research.

- Pocket PCs: Portable PCs can be used to administer sophisticated surveys and record open-end responses, with data that may be uploaded to an integrated online, real-time accessible database.
- Interactive TV: While interactive TV has had a spotty history (early experiments with poor samples and clumsy technology), technological improve-

ments promise to make the remote an attractive device for consumer surveying as well as sales.

- **Touch Screen Signage.** Mass retail aisles already have devices that provide on-the-spot coupons. The future will see touch screens in those aisles that allow customers to evaluate product concepts, join panels, answer questions, get information, etc. Touch screens will become a core tool for consumer analysis.
- **Voice Recognition.** Voice recognition technology reduces costs for sample acquisition and development. Instead of a call center with declining rates of consumer acceptance resulting in ever higher costs for sample preparation, voice recognition uses a recorded voice with verbal prompts, decoupling the number of calls needed to develop a sample from costs associated with having live operators making those calls.
- **Integrated Databases**. New software allows data from any source to be combined in a single database that can be accessed online and analyzed as a single consumer information source.
- **Real-Time Data Analysis**. Software now allows companies to view, filter, and cross-tab data as it is gathered in real-time, without waiting for it to be collated or cleaned (a process that can take weeks).

These technologies strongly imply outsourcing rather than trying to develop one or all of them in-house. Marketing research companies that tried to invent their own technologies have spent a huge amount for disappointing results. Either the bugs remain, making the technologies barely usable or the technologies rapidly become outdated and the in-house tech staff can't keep up. There is no reason for a marketing research company to go down this potholed road. Outsourcing to a company that specializes in developing and supporting emerging technologies is much cheaper, results are formatted and standardized, data are obtained faster, a wider range of information can be accessed, samples are more readily obtained, and next generation technologies quickly made operational.

Outsourcing these research and support technologies will create a sea-change in the marketing research sector. Like ADP for payroll, market research companies will no longer feel they have to do everything by themselves. Prior to ADP, companies did their own payroll, struggling through complex tax and benefit regulations, needing a significant staff to support the payroll process. After ADP, companies could prepare payroll with much fewer resources and with the knowledge that employee checks were accurate. Companies that offer back-office support to market research firms will have a similar effect and allow those firms to concentrate on their core competencies of client needs and analytical skills.

## SCENARIO-BASED FUTURES OF CONSUMER RESEARCH

Having invoked scenario planning as a powerful tool for exploring future options, let's use it to look at plausible futures for market and consumer research itself. The following four-cell matrix indicates four plausible futures for the evolution of consumer research, using scenario planning methods.

The matrix is the endpoint of a workshop exercise (with ten market research professionals) that starts with understanding critical uncertainties in the near future, converting those uncertainties into two axes and then describing the four cells that result when the axes are orthogonally related. Each cell presents a different future with its own demands for consumer insight and its own requirements for research skills.

While there are many uncertainties about the future of consumer research, the cost and efficiency-related concern about outsourcing is central. Digital and information technologies advance quickly and even large research companies cannot afford the internal staff to keep pace. On the other hand, these companies have invested in their own software and will find it wrenching to outsource.

The other critical uncertainty is the pace of adopting research innovations, in methods and technologies. In part, this is a generational issue—as older researchers and buyers of research retire, younger people will be more receptive and enthusiastic to change. But this shift will also be driven by the need for brands to find avenues of differentiation in a production world where commoditization becomes more common. The two orthogonal axes describe simultaneously critical and uncertain areas for the future of consumer research. They define the end points of whether market research firms will:

- Outsource research and reporting technology or continue to do it themselves.
- Develop innovative methods or continue marketing research as currently practiced.

The graph of these two uncertainities shown in Figure 1 illustrates the complex future paths for market research.

These axes generate the four plausible futures outlined in the diagram:

*New Life.* Sampling, surveying, and analytical software are outsourced as marketing research companies concentrate on their core skills of research design and consumer insight. Consumer panels for most products become routine practice as companies learn preferences, reactions to advertising, and promotions in real time. Some form of futures analysis provides a strategic way to assess current research findings for product positioning and new product development. As companies hyper-differentiate brands and products, insights from ethnographic

# CONSUMER RESEARCH COMPANY
# FUTURE OPTIONS

**Figure 1. The Complex Future Paths for Market Research**

observation assumes greater importance. Companies begin to use interactive TV to both sell and learn consumer desires. Collaborative filtering approaches continue, improve incrementally, but still fail to produce anticipated results. CRM also improves with best results for "loyalty cards" and creative partnerships across brands.

*Wild West.* While methods advance, market research companies still try to do everything in-house, resulting in confusion among manufacturers as findings are typically commoditized—any competent research firm will produce very similar findings. Companies are slow to outsource since their internal organization includes IT staff and they have become accustomed to doing things themselves. New research methods leads to greater specialization and clients choose research firms based on specific needs.

*Profit Taking.* Research methods do not progress, but market research companies increasingly outsource sampling, software, and analysis. Cost becomes critical since methods are standardized and clients evaluate proposals based on pricing. There are two possibilities here:

- Large research firms quickly outsource, small companies are slower and sector consolidation follows.
- Small research companies outsource first (since they can least afford internal support staff) while large companies struggle with sustaining their IT in-house, leading to a fragmentation of business as clients increasingly choose smaller companies that can under-price larger competitors.

***Business-As-Usual.*** This future is closest to what most market research companies do now. Companies increasingly select market research firms based on price, favoring large firms that can do quantitative research with relative efficiency. But over time, traditional market research companies lose to highly niched specialists who do only one thing, like observation or emotional and cognitive mapping. Much consumer research becomes obsolete as brands develop promotions, sales strategies, and product options in real time, testing and modifying on the fly.

Although each of these futures is plausible, there are patterns of evolution among them. Wild West can quickly move to New Life as research companies perceive the benefits of outsourcing. Profit Taking is viable for a time, but eventually research methods will change as clients increasingly demand deep consumer insights that will allow them to hyper-differentiate in crowded markets. Business-As-Usual is unstable; advanced research methods and new technologies are already here, rear-guard actions only make sense temporarily.

Since we cannot predict which of these futures (or what combination of them) will actually happen in the next 2 to 3 years, it is prudent to look at strategies that work (more or less) across all four scenarios. These strategies will become best practices for the next generation of consumer and market research.

- Consumer ethnography:
  - In New Life, this is a necessary marketing research skill as insight becomes the relevant currency.
  - In Wild West, it becomes a differentiator among companies seeking to uniquely position themselves to clients.
  - In Profit Taking, while quantitative methods are outsourced, qualitative research remains in-house and needs to develop new approaches.
  - In Business-As-Usual, niched specialists win and ethnography becomes a desired niche.
- Outsourcing:
  - In New life, outsourcing is the norm and research firms cannot submit a competitive bid without the cost savings of outsourcing.

- In Wild West, outsourcing is very much the exception, but those companies that see the savings and efficiency benefits do very well.
- In Profit Taking, outsourcing is expected as a cost reducer.
- In Business-As-Usual, outsourcing is only adopted by a few sector leaders; it is seen as risky by most who will likely change their minds over time.
- Sophisticated quantitative methods:
  - In New Life, quantitative analysis also evolves, enabled by outsourced technologies.
  - In Wild West, research companies need to be able to use advanced statistical methods, but they have difficulty to the extent that in-house technologies are flawed, slow, and costly.
  - In Profit Taking, quantitative methods advance very slowly, made easier by outsourcing cost reductions.
  - In Business-As-usual, some research companies will specialize in sophisticated quantitative analysis and clients will have to pay significant costs.
- Future strategic opportunities:
  - In New life, scenario planning is an expected part of a research presentation.
  - In Wild West, scenario planning is an unexpected delight as most research firms do not have the skills to conduct a scenario workshop.
  - In Profit Taking, scenario-based futures are typically outsourced to a specialized futures company.
  - In Business-As-Usual, generating plausible futures from consumer data is the exception, but clients more frequently use scenarios as a tool without consulting market research firms.
- Emerging technologies:

  - In New life, consumer research companies are constantly on the lookout for new methods that appeal to clients looking for deep consumer insights.
  - In Wild West, companies need to be aware of emerging technologies, but may be reluctant to adopt many of them due to cost implications.
  - In Profit Taking, these technologies can be more quickly utilized than in Wild West since outsourced costs can be controlled.
  - In Business-As-Usual, these technologies are very slowly adopted with little pressure from clients.

These opportunities and shifts define future best practices for market research. Research without intruding on consumers, making the most of information and digital technologies, going from research to consumer futures, and outsourcing everything but core competence, all will radically alter the consumer research business. As these best practices take hold in the next few years, we can expect more profound consumer insights, outsourcing as the norm, better use of panels and samples, real-time consumer data allowing real-time customer driven management, and the integration of research with futures strategies.

Consumer companies will be able to hyper-differentiate products, precisely target segments (including the segment-of-one), make more informed decisions about new product development and R&D allocation, and be in real-time contact with their customers (including advances in how to apply CRM). Finally, the CRM promise will begin to actually deliver. These developments in consumer research can be glimpsed and anticipated now, but making the actual changes will be challenging, as consumer research firms have to re-invent themselves in terms of skills, costs, client relations, and technology.

# CHAPTER 11

# RAISE THE BAR FROM CORPORATE COMPLIANCE TO TOTAL ORGANIZATIONAL INTEGRITY

*Scott W. Ventrella*

## ABSTRACT

*Total organization integrity is an organizational framework and mindset for creating corporate identities of the highest ethical standards. This chapter will identify the driving forces underscoring both the need and the urgency for establishing a fully integrated ethical framework. Further, using lessons learned from successful companies, it will provide a practical step-by-step approach for building a "culture of integrity" by building ethics into the organizational infrastructure, securing senior management commitment and aligning all employee's actions in congruence with ethical policy.*

*Traditional business ethics has focused primarily on legal and compliance issues. In short, the thrust was on "how to stay out of trouble," or if you somehow found your way into trouble, "how to get out of it." But legal and compliance codes represent nothing more than the minimum requirements. Companies desiring a more dynamic, holistic approach to ethics needs to go well beyond the basics and move toward total organizational integrity.*

## THE ETHICS LANDSCAPE

Historically, organizational focus on ethics has been on legal and compliance issues. Most corporations embraced ethics in response to periodic scandals and public distrust. The spotlight on corporate ethics practices and policies began to shine during the defense industry scandals of the early 1980s and intensified when the banking industry started making headlines.

This period, often referred to as the "decade of greed," triggered an onslaught of companies to adopt or revamp their codes of ethics. For the most part, their response was motivated out of fear, and served as both public relations tool, as well as an insulator from potential litigation. In 1991, under newly adopted guidelines, the Federal Sentencing Commission raised the stakes by introducing harsher punishments for corporate misdeeds; it significantly increased the maximum fines. The guidelines were again modified in 1995. At the time, the responsibility for creating, enforcing, and updating ethics code and policy rested primarily with the general counsel and senior human resource executives.

CEOs, of course, had input in code drafting as well as final approval, as in the case with Jim Burke during his tenure as CEO at Johnson and Johnson. In fact, by his own estimation, he spent close to 40 percent of his time related to J&J "Credo," a large part of which was devoted to communicating it throughout the company. J&J's "Credo Values" is a set of values and ethical standards to which the organization adheres. For more detailed information on J&J's Credo Values, see *Best Practices in Organization Development and Change Handbook* published by Linkage, Inc., and Jossey Bass in 2001, co-edited by Louis Carter and Marshall Goldsmith.

TGIF CEO, Wally Doolin, regularly reviews and updates the TGIF Credo with his management team to ensure that it reflects current (and evolving) business strategy, as well as changing social norms. The vast majority of CEOs rarely involved themselves beyond code drafting.

Focusing on legal and compliance code helps ensure that employees understand and stay on the right side of the law, and mitigates potential liability. But overall, the approach is limiting in several ways:

- Negative emphasis. Employees are basically given a list of "thou shall nots," and reminded that if for some reason they "do," that there will be a price to pay.
- Program mentality. Ethics becomes the job of a specific individual (or individuals) whose primary responsibility it is to oversee and enforce the program.
- Narrow focus. The emphasis is on the law and does not necessarily take an organization's policy, or vision/mission/values into consideration. It offers virtually no guidance on ethical decision-making for the gray areas and/or *right versus right* issues, the domain of most ethical dilemmas.
- Not progressive or proactive. The world is rapidly changing. Business ethics must keep up with issues associated with globalization, cyber-technology, social and environmental activism, investor scrutiny, and competition to name a few.

# MOVING BEYOND LEGAL AND COMPLIANCE

Many companies have already moved beyond the basics. Think of the ethical landscape as a continuum with legal and compliance issues on one end, and organizational integrity on the other. Most companies fall somewhere in between; however, in terms of a corporate mindset and culture, they find themselves in either one camp or the other.

In my experience, the companies that are the furthest up on the continuum are those which had a great foundation to begin with. It was the Total Quality Management (TQM) revolution of the 1980s and '90s that helped companies look beyond traditional ethics and broaden their purview. Texas Instruments (TI), which today has one of the most highly evolved ethics program I've seen, is a good example of this.

The company invested heavily in TQM during the early 1980s, and indoctrinated the entire company in its principles and practices.Leadership had a strong commitment and designated a vice president of quality to oversee the process. In 1987, the same discipline was used to create a formal approach to ethics. Although TI had been built on high ethical standards, they found that, due to growth and increasingly complex issues in the modern business world, it was time to introduce a more rigorous approach to their existing program. Interestingly enough, they appointed their VP of quality to establish a TI Ethics Office that had three primary functions:

- To ensure that business policies and practices continue to be aligned with ethical principles;
- To clearly communicate ethical expectations; and
- To provide multiple channels for feedback through which people can ask questions, voice concerns, and seek resolution to ethical issues.

These activities closely mirrored how they were already managing for quality. In fact, I would argue that TQM was a values-based approach to running an ethically sound, *and* profitable enterprise. In the early years of TQM, companies were interested in one thing: survival.

Foreign competition, mostly from Japan, was eating their lunch. In a desperate, reactionary mode, they adopted TQM to reduce waste, streamline processes, empower employees, and delight customers by offering goods and services that met or exceeded expectations. Unwittingly, this sowed the seeds for what I refer to as "total organizational integrity." Integrity is derived from the word *integer,* meaning *whole.*

TQM was a management paradigm that involved the *whole* organization, vertically and horizontally. Vertical in the sense that it was a top-down initiative, beginning with senior management and cascading down through the ranks, ultimately impacting all employees. Horizontal because it burst through corporate silos—it was cross disciplinary and not limited to any one function or department. It also considered and involved suppliers and customers.

The introduction of the Malcolm Baldrige National Quality Award in the mid-80s implicitly helped set the ethics bar higher, as well as broaden its scope. The criteria went well beyond product quality. It was also concerned with how organizations treated customers, employees, the environment, community, and so on. TQM helped pave the way to a more wholly integrated approach to business ethics. It also provided a useful framework for total organizational integrity.

## TOTAL ORGANIZATIONAL INTEGRITY

Total organizational integrity (TOI) is a comprehensive corporate value system that's embedded into organization infrastructure and driven by senior management. TOI is not a destination. Rather, it's an ongoing, continuous process that is distinguished by the following characteristics:

- Strategically-based
- Leadership Involvement
- Total Integration
- Tactical Deployment
- Review and Updating

Let's take a closer look at each.

***Strategically Based*** Legal and compliance code is generally drafted in response to external pressures and demands. TOI, on the other hand, is internally driven. It's part of the business strategy as well as the organization's identity. It's making a statement that's telling the world, "This is who we are, what we stand for, and how we will conduct ourselves."

A strategic view of TOI does not separate ethics from running the business. It sees them as inseparable parts. Nor does it give priority to one over the other. Raytheon Company's ethical policy makes this point very clear, where it states, in part, "At Raytheon, all our business relationships with customers, shareholders, employees, suppliers and host communities must rest on a foundation of integrity and trust. Our success is dependent on each individual's commitment to these enduring values and no success is worth the expense of compromising ethical behavior."

***Leadership Involvement.*** The U.S. Federal Sentencing Guidelines of 1991 specified that, "specific individuals within high level personnel of the organization" be assigned the responsibility for overseeing ethics. It was at about this time that we saw the emergence of a relatively new and unknown role in the organization; the ethics officer. I strongly endorse this function providing that the individual who fills it has a "seat at the table." In other words, the ethics officer needs to have sufficient respect and credibility in order to have the necessary impact.

If the ethics officer is too far removed from the senior management team, the culture will view the role as "window dressing." The ethics officer should be an active member of the management team with direct access to the CEO. At International Paper, Chairman & CEO John Dillon handpicked one of his most trusted managers, James Berg, to establish and run their ethics office. In his role as Director of Ethics and Business Practice, Berg has regular access to Dillon as well as to members of the board.

It is absolutely imperative that senior leadership be involved with, and committed to TOI. This includes the CEO and leadership team, as well as business unit presidents, general managers, plant managers, etc. It's also critical that the board of directors plays a role, especially in developing policy and programs.

One of the first "warning shots across the bow" was sent back in 1995. The Delaware Court of Chancery warned corporate directors that they could be held personally liable for subordinates' wrongdoing if they had failed to establish programs to enforce compliance with the law. Leadership sets the cultural tone for the organization. If leadership does not walk the talk, the rest of the organization will become cynical and distrustful. Leaders can ill afford to send mixed signals or behave in a hypocritical manner. Studies have shown that employees are more likely to behave unethically if they view their managers (leaders) as unethical. Concomitantly, they will behave more ethically if they view leadership as ethical.

The following is a short list of senior management's roles and responsibilities relative to TOI:

1. Determine Ethics Policy
   - Scope and range: This is what will be covered (legal, compliance, ethics, values, integrity, etc.)
   - Commitment: We're in it for the long haul
   - Rationale: This is our motivation for doing it (good business practice, changing business environment, competitive landscape, etc.)
   - Expectations: This is what we expect from the organization, and individual employees (accountability, responsibility, performance, etc.)

2. Authorize Infrastructure Requirements
   - Structure
   - Roles and responsibilities
   - Reporting relationships
   - Procedures
   - Processes

3. Provide Resources
   - Awareness
   - Education and training
   - Communications

4. Update Performance Management System
   - Performance planning and appraisal
   - Criteria
   - Measures

5. Develop Communications Process
   - Audience
   - Message content
   - Internal and external communication mechanisms

6. Monitor Performance
   - Audits
   - Assessments
   - Revisions
   - Updates

A closer examination of this list reveals that leadership is expected to manage for integrity exactly the same way it manages for other things of importance, such as finance, safety, quality, human resources, etc. If leadership is truly committed to organizational integrity, it will elevate it to a greater level of prominence.

***Total Integration.***  Once leadership has placed a stake in the ground, the organization must be in alignment. Organizational integrity is a *strategy*. Any change or update to the corporate strategy will have a domino effect in the organization. These changes must be reflected in corporate credos, vision/mission statements as well as the components that make up the organization (people, processes/procedures, and culture).

Each of these areas must be assessed to detect potential conflict and to ensure that they support strategic change.

- Recruitment. *Are we setting the right expectations at the outset?*
- New employee orientation. Are new hires indoctrinated?
- Training. *Are all our employees receiving the proper training, awareness, and education?*

- Performance. *Have we built this into the performance planning and appraisal process?*
- Support. *Do employees know who and where to go to if they have questions/problems/concerns?*
- Work Processes and Procedures. *Are there any functional areas (e.g. finance, sales, purchasing, etc.) particularly impacted, and if so, what process or procedural changes need to be made?*
- Culture. *What are the actual* habits, beliefs, attitudes, and practices that exist in the operating environment. Do they support the new strategy?

*Tactical Deployment.* Leadership, strategy, infrastructure, etc., are all necessary ingredients of organizational integrity, but ultimately you have to *make it happen.* The two most common methods for deploying ethics in an organization are communications and training both of which must be adjusted and adapted accordingly to meet cultural differences as a result of globalization.

Communication methods include:

- Posting code of ethics or business conduct information on walls, in annual reports, on the company Web-site
- Company newsletters, brochures, etc.
- Policy manuals
- Memos
- "Town Hall" meetings
- Employee handbooks

Many organizations have established hotlines, or help desks, to assist employees in real time.

Training methods include:

- In-house workshops
- Conferences
- Video-tapes
- Interactive software
- Web-inars

There's really no specific recipe or order. The best companies employ a "mix and match" method that best fits with their overall goals, objectives, and budgets. Surprisingly, few companies are using Web-based training, but I believe we'll begin to see an increase in the use of e-technology in the not too-distant future.

*Review and Updating.* Ethics policies, procedures, and practices should be reviewed periodically by senior management. It is the responsibility of the ethics officer to monitor ethics on a day-to-day basis and bring issues to the table for discussion, and resolution. If your organization does not have an ethics officer, I strongly suggest that you do have one. Lacking an ethics officer, the responsibility rests with your general counsel or HR executive. In a fast-changing world it is difficult to stay current on important issues that may affect your ethics policy and guidelines. This is especially important during times of change initiated by any number of factors.

For instance, due to the recent spate of scandals in corporate America (Enron, Arthur Anderson, Tyco, MCI, etc.) the NYSE's Corporate Accountability and Listing Standards Committee presented to the board of directors a report calling for significant changes in the way the NYSE-listed companies are governed.

According to the announcement, "The report centers on increasing the independence of corporate boards and giving shareholders more opportunity to monitor and participate in the governance of their companies. The report also includes recommendations to Congress and the Securities and Exchange Commission on policy and regulatory matters." One of the committee's recommendations requires companies to "adopt and disclose governance guidelines, codes of business conduct, and charters for their audit, compensation, and nominating committees." Senior management must also stay abreast of changes in international, federal, state, and local law. Changes in social norms and values need to be addressed, and decisions made relative to them (*i.e.,* marketing tobacco to kids). Any significant change warrants review and discussion at the highest levels. Decisions made to address these changes need to be communicated to the culture in a timely, clear manner. Subsequently, the existing organizational infrastructure must be assessed to see if they accommodate and support the changes.

## INDIVIDUAL INTEGRITY

When it's all said and done, ethics and integrity comes down to making a personal choice. It's about good decision-making and taking responsibility. Most unethical behavior is not based on a conscious decision to do "bad."

People are basically good and want to do good. Employees certainly need to be aware of the law and understand where the boundaries lie, but laws, standards, policies, and guidelines do not cover every possible ethical dilemma, nor do they provide employees with the guidance to make an ethical decision.

Most ethical dilemmas are not black and white; and ultimately, every individual has the responsibility for making in-the-moment decisions based on gray areas, or right versus right situations. It becomes incumbent upon the organization to remove ambiguity from the decision-making process by initiating *dialogue* around ethical topics and issues using some of the following methods:

- Case studies
- Experiential exercises
- Role-playing
- Scenarios

No matter which method is used, it's important that it be very carefully planned and facilitated. Through dialogue, employees can:

- challenge their individual and collective beliefs, values and attitudes on ethical issues in a respectful, non-judgmental manner.
- understand the impact and consequences of certain decisions.
- provide feedback to management on the "fuzzy" areas.
- determine the best course of action in a given situation.

On the other hand it enables management to:

- communicate and reinforce organizational core values and standards.
- visually demonstrate leadership commitment.
- remove some of the guesswork for their employees.
- assign the responsibility of ethical decision-making to *all* employees.

## THE THREE-POINT ETHICS CHECKLIST

Finally, management must equip every employee with a framework for making decisions on the firing line. An effective tool is the "three-point checklist" of which there are many variations. Here's mine:

When faced with an ethical dilemma, employees must ask themselves the following three questions in order:

1. Am I breaking any law?
2. Am I in alignment with company code (policy, credo, values, etc.)?
3. Am I in alignment with my own "platinum standard"?

The first two questions are objective. If the issue is clearly illegal or against company code the message should be, "Don't do it!" If employees don't know the answer, they should still be instructed not to *do* it until confirmed. Sometimes employees want to do the right thing but may fear retribution. In these cases, employees should have someone in a position of authority with whom they can confide. Finally, a negative answer to the first two questions means that an employee must refer to a subjective measure, a personal platinum standard, before taking any action. Sometimes the answer, "don't do it," comes, not because an action violates the law or company code, but because it just doesn't feel right. At one time slavery in the US was legal, but that didn't make it right.

Doing business in China, or putting soft drink machines in elementary schools may be legal *and* in-line with company policy, yet may still prick the conscious of some individuals. The decision for the employee then becomes, "Do I challenge the law and/or policy, or go against my conscience?"

A platinum standard is a personal ethical framework that serves as an anchor and guide, giving us a sense of right and wrong. It's based on an interwoven set of morals, principles, values, and standards that evolve throughout one's life. I use the word platinum because platinum is the most precious of metals. It does not corrode, rust, expand, contract, or break down in any way. I always remind people that, "Whenever in doubt about an ethical decision, default to your platinum standard and compare. Then make your decision."

Ethics is not compliance; it is executing a highly integrity-based belief system. The strategy for achieving total organizational integrity transcends the traditional obedience to corporate standards of action, where companies are constantly walking the fine line between getting in trouble and staying "safe." Ethics challenges organizations to reach for moral excellence. This is no longer what sets the best apart from the rest; rather, it is the key ingredient for survival, success, and longevity. One Texas Instruments executive puts it this way, "A reputation and track record for ethics and integrity is vital for establishing the trust that is the basis for all successful business relationships . . . ." Adopting total organizational integrity as a corporate way of life will help ensure that you and your company leave no margin for error in living consistently with what you stand for.

## CONCLUSION

Simply "staying out of trouble" is no longer good enough for companies—the stakes are too high. Shifting the corporate focus away from legal and compliance issues towards total organizational integrity makes good business sense. It will help companies attract and retain top talent, enhance corporate reputation and image, and better prepare them to address issues associated with globalization, technology, and changing social norms and values.

# CHAPTER 12

# VALUE SKILLED MANAGEMENT: BE A SKILLED MANAGER, NOT A MANAGER OF CORPORATE TENURE

*Bill Hawkins and Lori Riordan*

Technological advantage is fleeting. Rapid advancement in communications and technology in the last decade has virtually assured organizations that any technological advantage enjoyed today will be quickly copied (and most likely improved upon) by the competition within the year. Intellectual assets provide the greatest long-term strategic advantage. Skilled people—especially at senior management levels—provide a competitive edge that is hard to duplicate. Recognizing this, you would expect companies to focus a lot of attention on selection, development, and retention of this key asset, particularly those in management positions.

In our experience, companies don't give the focus or attention to this asset they do other assets deemed important to the daily management of the business. It is not unusual to see a company take months to do extensive analysis researching a new inventory system, then promote someone to run this system simply because he or she has been with the company longer than any other employee and has demonstrated technical competency. Little attention is paid to what skills are actually needed in this new role. Managers promoted because of "tenure" are frequently unskilled in their new role.

Although promotion of unskilled managers can occur in any organization regardless of size, age, or stage in the life cycle, it most frequently occurs in start-up and high-growth companies. In these organizations the pace of change is fastest and the pool of available talent just isn't as large. There is a particular appreciation for technical competence and an allegiance to people who were there through the difficult and turbulent times. This tenure is translated into knowledge of "how things are done here." Technical proficiency translates into the ability to address the current crisis quickly—often without regard for anything other than achieving results. Of course, this skill was highly valued in the start-up mode, but may not be optimally effective, in a midsize company, and might actually be counterproductive in specific situations (during a merger, for instance).

## WHAT IS HAPPENING IN COMPANIES

Failure to recognize a combination of unique skill sets (by position and by level) can derail a carefully planned reorganization or promising career. Obviously, technical skills are critically important for first level management, but not so important at the top. People and conceptual skills dominant the needs list at the executive level. Placing unskilled people into new positions might be all right if the critical competencies and skills were identified and the newly promoted people developed to improve them. Research shows that this is not what is happening.

Michael Lombardo and Bob Eichinger surveyed 3,000 people in over 130 companies, comparing multi-rater feedback on 67 competences of individual contributors, managers, and executives. What they found was troubling. The transition required in moving from individual contributor to manager is considerable. Results, however, showed that little change occurs in the actual skills demonstrated on the job. With a few small differences, the multi-rater results of managers looked like the individual contributors (differing on only 8 of the 67 competencies). It appears that those with awful people skills or a serious lack of technical skills do get weeded out at the individual contributor level (or at least not promoted), but no new skills are developed. The people who are promoted arrive in the management role prepared to do what they have always done. Although success in the new role always requires new skills (build effective teams, develop direct reports, deal with conflict), as a group they are no more skilled at doing this than individual contributors.

It looks only slightly better at the change from manager to executive. Skills that are absolutely essential at the executive level, such as dealing with ambiguity and paradox, motivating others, or managing vision and purpose are in the bottom half of all competencies for managers. They are also in the bottom half of skills ranked for executives.

Even though the skill and competency requirements change rather dramatically with level, in most organizations few people are expected to develop other than technical job skills. Managers and executives, who were originally hired to be software engineers, sales people, or financial analysts, get promoted. In this new role they find themselves in situations where they must lead unenthusiastic people through complicated change processes that impact nearly every area of the organization. Many fail because they simply don't have the skill set to achieve success in the new role. It is little wonder that studies estimate executive failure rates at between one-third to one-half.

# How Do You Know if This Is Happening in Your Company?

Waiting for failure on the job is waiting too long. There are early warning signs. Turnover is one of the most visible signs that a company has established a management team based on tenure/technical proficiency. Formal exit interviews of every departure, both voluntary and involuntary, provide valuable information. While most departing employees will try to be positive—"I have a better opportunity that pays more"—analysis of exit interviews conducted with specific targeted questions and categorized answers will provide a useful tool to uncover specific issues. The relationship with the boss usually has a lot to do with turnover. Most people want to work for someone who is fair and well-respected, creates a productive and team-oriented environment, provides a vision and map for the future and allows them to do their jobs. Poor management plays out in many ways that have a ripple effect in the company.

An effective turnover analysis will cut data in two ways, horizontally and vertically. A horizontal cut of data shows tenure of departures and the reasons for it. A typical analysis divides the data into four categories of employees leaving within: 0-3 months, 3 months to a year, 1 year to 3 years, and 3 years and above. Although poor management skills of the boss provide an umbrella for many of the turnover issues—ineffective communications, poor hiring practices, unprofessional behavior—this analysis by tenure frequently provides insight into specific skills needed in specific managerial positions.

The vertical cut will show the ratio of promotions to departures for the overall company by management level and by department. The aim of this analysis is to determine whether there are more departures than desired and if the right promotions occurring. It is typical for high growth companies to have 20:60:20 ratios. Twenty percent of the employees are promoted; 20 percent leave and 60 percent remain in their current position. In more established companies this ratio can fall to 10:80:10. An analysis comparing these ratios provides insight into where problems might exist.

Each level in the organization has certain unique demands, from performing specific technical tasks to managing people and processes to forming and motivating others toward a vision and direction. While everyone may do all of these on occasion, the amount of time spent, the emphasis on the skill and the nature of the responsibility change dramatically across levels. The point is that people do not join organizations with all these skills no matter how talented they may appear. They need development.

# WHAT CAN YOU DO ABOUT IT?

The first step is to search out the core competencies and skills that drive business success for key positions at each level in the organization. This really isn't as hard as it may seem. Do some reading. There is a lot of literature on the subject. Get a panel of "experts." This can include senior leadership in the organization, outside consultants, and people currently in the role or a similar role who are successful. Have them come to some agreement on the importance of various skills needed. What does competence look like? Identify those behaviors that separate the people who are simply competent from those who excel and agree on measures.

Once you have identified the requisite skills needed for success, focus development around them. Most research indicates that at least 75 percent of learning takes place on the job. So the question becomes, "In what type of job experiences are the people in your organization involved?" Tenured, but unskilled, managers draw on the same skills, tackling roughly the same challenges over time. They hone current skills, but little real development takes place.

# DEVELOPING SKILLS

Development involves four types of skill building experiences:

*Jobs that take the person out of the comfort level.* Jobs that are the least likely to teach and develop are straight upward promotions doing the same type of work at a higher level. Development takes place when people are challenged. To prepare for executive management, for instance, high-potential candidates need jobs that require learning totally different skills than used for previous success. Look inside the organization for opportunities to move people into "turnaround" situations. Employee conflict and morale issues are a good starting point for a "turnaround". Move a person in this situation, to a staff position where he or she must learn to influence without authority.

*Mentors.* We all learn from bosses, both good and bad. Mentors add another dimension to learning from others. They are men and women who take younger people and personally help guide their career. Mentors need to check for how the learner learns. Some people learn best by having this type of one-on-one coaching from an experienced role model. Others prefer to learn by doing and making mistakes.

Same-sex and ethnic background mentors can be especially effective for women and minorities who may have few role models in their immediate workplace.

*New challenges in the current job.* If there is no developmental job available, create a new context in the current one. Increase the visibility or the complexity of the current job. Add new products, change the reporting structure, add to the number of people managed, put the job holder on a project or task force. Again, the key is to select the challenge that will broaden the experience and develop new skills, not necessarily use current skills, for successful task completion.

*Outside resources.* Although most development takes place on the job, don't overlook other resources available. Two weeks at Harvard or a well-run leadership development course can provide the tools needed for development back on the job. The key is timing. People learn best when they see how the new tool, information, or learning can be used immediately to perform more effectively back at work.

## CONCLUSION—BEST PRACTICE TOOLS AND STRATEGIES

This book provides best practice strategies and tools for changing your organization. As you read the chapters that follow, you will see practices that apply to many areas of your organization. They confront a variety of issues with diverse solutions—and you will notice a common theme: You will see organizations that fully understand the importance of a skilled management and executive team. Look closely at the processes and you will see leaders and developers creating skilled managers through leadership development and change.

# CHAPTER 13

---

# LEADING DIALOGUE PROCESSES TO BUILD COMMITMENT AND REACH SHARED UNDERSTANDING

*Jodi Knox*

> *"We should not attempt to change people's behavior. Rather, we should reach an understanding over how the relations that determine our behavior can be changed."*
>
> —Wolfgang Schnelle

## INTRODUCTION

*Action dialogue is the accumulation of parts—insights, ideas, observation, awareness, and so on—leading to shared understanding and committed action.*

In the relentless effort to accomplish objectives and achieve results, the most common complaint you hear from leaders is that "nothing's happening" or "things aren't moving fast enough." Creating and maintaining action is central to success. There is the kind of action where people go through the motions and get things done yet there isn't much energy behind it. This yields a going-along type action where you may get what you ask for but seldom more and often less. To get whole-hearted action for an initiative where people are energized and behind a plan involves a process that builds commitment and generates action. Moderating dialogue processes builds understanding and support across critical stakeholders and creates committed agreement for action. In effectively moderating actionable dialogue everyone gets involved quickly and you achieve appreciative understanding and results far beyond business as usual. Learning to conduct and moderate dialogues is a critical leadership tool. The process is simple, but putting it into practice is not.

## BACKGROUND

Rhythms and patterns of daily life in organizations today have changed. The tempo of business innovation has increased toward discovering new rules and rapidly applying vast resources to play the new or better game. Executives and leaders today must dare to break up engrained ways of thinking and attitudes to find these new pathways. With today's business environment made of increasing partnerships, alliances, technological advances and, innovation, leaders are challenged to manage increasingly complex relations and a rapid pace of problem solving and execution. This can leave even the best of today's executives disoriented very often with a splintered community of followers.

As innovation becomes a rising force in accelerating the need to understand and meet business challenges, it requires changes in the opinions, values, thinking and working patterns of individuals and companies. The prized ability to sense, respond and rapidly create meaningful new forms and strike alliances to drive business growth is now a coveted source of competitive edge. Deal making of various forms—mergers, acquisitions, all types of strategic alliance activity—continues at a fevered pitch. Now, it has become even more important to lead tasks across departments, across businesses and alliance networks, and to achieve cooperation and committed action.

This requires business leaders to collaborate on complex problems in a structured way to tackle business issues, generate new insight, and create new possibilities for action. For this reason it becomes even more important to be able to reach a shared understanding with other people. A vital attribute of any business leader today is the ability to *build understanding and support* across critical stakeholders and create committed agreement for action. This process and skill set is critical for successful implementation of projects and initiatives relying on interdependency between players without hierarchical subordination.

This requirement drives one of today's greatest challenges faced by every leader—building commitment to initiatives and generating action. In companies today, it is critical to build the quality of decisions made and rapidly develop a critical mass of supporters who understand and appreciate what is necessary to be done in order to succeed.

## THE COST OF LOOSE COUPLING
## BETWEEN TALK, DECISION, AND ACTION

The typical requirement for laterally leading a project or initiative in today's organizations is marked by cross-departmental cooperation, networks, flat hierarchies, teamwork, and group work. Much costly time can be spent making sure that people in a targeted community are aware of the challenge and decided action steps. This typical condition is made even more difficult where bringing about a shared understanding and commitment for action is with other people we do not command, where there is no direct authority to influence. For many practitioners or meeting leaders in today's organizations, the traditional approach to laterally leading cross-business teaming is establishing common ground and building consensus. The thinking is admirable and simple: If we build support for our initiative, and communicate what needs to be done, contributors will "get it" and execute according to plan. Yet often this doesn't occur; "face agreement" is reached in meetings, that is, heads are nodding yet no real action results.

A second pitfall that some practitioners or meeting leaders develop is a zealous attention to establishing "appreciation", or building consensus, without any theoretical rhyme or reason to their approach. Promoting appreciation or support for an initiative where there has been little can, itself, generate a wave of energy and enthusiasm that will go away just as quickly as the next challenge or trauma to the system rears its head. The issue is raised to caution against the indiscriminant application of a facilitated discussion process which lacks a theoretical basis and structured method to its practice. Leading dialogue processes to build commitment and reach shared understanding calls for a disciplined and reasoned approach to its use.

A moderated dialogue process for complex problem solving is a form of active consulting that creates new practices/ideas/images that aid in the developmental change of a system. If you want to go down new paths with people, you need visions that can be changed as new developments arise. Leading dialogue processes structures your debates, within your company or with your business partners, to develop a shared understanding and appreciation for action-oriented solutions and improve creative problem solving skills. A structured dialogue process promotes the infrastructure that enables people to work together effectively and accomplish the expected results.

Dialogue techniques for leading and moderating discussions bring structure to the complexity of unpacking a wide variety of challenges for a central business issue. The process enables all players to constructively interact and evaluate the problem or issue at hand. The dialogue leader, or moderator, provides each party the ability to maintain their power and contribute actively to the development of ideas and solutions. The complex business challenge and issues are collectively discussed in order to create new, generative ideas or images that aid in developmental change of the collective group discussing them. The result is appreciative and shared understanding rather than a circular dispute, or worse yet, nodding heads signaling consensus and no action to follow.

This chapter is meant to encourage critical reflection about the role of discursive dialogue for helping leaders advance complex problem solving and committed action. It is not that difficult to defend an opinion; it is much more difficult to really understand one. An approach has to be identified to enable the stakeholders themselves to understand and sustainably solve the problems and bring commitment to action. An approach where to be successful there is occasion to lead laterally across cooperation partners to be brought to take steps together in a desired direction.

The chapter is organized by three main parts. The first part, the background, describes the challenge and explains why leading dialogue processes to build shared understanding continues to draw attention. The second part defines how dialogue differs from discussion and outlines the main characteristics of the unique methodology and technique to carry out an actionable dialogue session. The third part challenges you to think beyond the moderated dialogue process, to understand the latent issues impeding progress in the organization. The fourth part summarizes the value and outcomes you can expect from a practice of dialoging on differences offering key insights and lessons learned.

# It Is Not That Difficult to Defend an Opinion; It Is Much More Difficult to Really Understand It

## *Moderating Actionable Dialogue*

Derivations of words often help to understand a deeper meaning. Participation means both "to partake of" and "to take part in." If we could be taking part in communicating and creating a common meaning that would be participation. In this type of participation a common mind arises. Dialogue comes from the Greek word *dialogos*. Logos means "the word," or in our case the "meaning of the word." Dia means "through," it does not mean two. A dialogue can be among any number of people, not just two. The image this suggests is of a stream of meaning flowing among and through a group of people and between them. (David Bohm) This makes possible a flow of meaning in a whole group out of which emerges some new understanding. It is something new that may not have been conceived of at the starting point. It may be a new idea, strategy, understanding of business threats and opportunities, or a set of actions necessary to achieve market dominance. In any case, it is something new and creative. This new shared meaning, shared understanding is the cement that holds people and groups together and committed to a cause.

In a dialogue session, individuals might hold a separate opinion but that opinion is expressed and then absorbed into the group and one final group meaning would be seen. Insofar as people having opinions or assumptions they defend, there is something that interferes with innovation. If you are defending an assumption, you are pushing out whatever is new. Differences in opinions and assumptions must be shared and understood so that something can move between them and the collective group can move beyond them in another direction toward coherence—into something new and creative. The product is something created, agreed to, and owned by the collective party.

Dialogue is often used interchangeably with discussion, as in "Let's have a dialogue." Yet in group meetings where there is only discussion, issues are typically broken up for analysis and batted back and forth until somebody wins enough points to get their way. Very frequently in the case of a discussion a few ideas are emphasized where one person picks up someone else's idea to back up their own and the end result is not very much further beyond the various points of view. Problem-solving sessions or meetings of this sort conclude with perhaps, at best, trade-offs or a negotiated solution lacking the cement of new appreciation for what needs to be done and serious commitment. Those who take part are not really open to questioning their fundamental assumptions and rather end up trading off minor points.

Problem-solving discussions and decision making often leave out active reflection. Leading a structured dialogue process which visually captures an argumentation flow, forces reflection points, uses inquiry to challenge the participants on assumptive thinking styles and propels the group beyond limited thought styles (i.e. why they actually do something) to arrive at an appreciative understanding for what needs to be done, and finally stretches decisions and agreement on action steps. It is making individual and group thinking visible. Within the disciplined process, one intellectualizes the idea, clarifies their thinking, reflects on what has been revealed, and then is challenged to inquire more deeply and break closed thinking before moving to action. This brings the increased structure needed for addressing a wide-variety of challenges around a complex, central business issue and builds a convergence of interests.

Companies do not only pursue economic aims. There is a mixture of varied, often diverging, aims, values, and interests which are either created by the organizations themselves or already in existence, but which are in a constant state of flux. Leaders at companies try to represent this mixture of aims and interests in strategy documents, with full knowledge that varying objectives, values, and interests cannot be reduced to a common denominator, and that this is not in fact necessary for performance. This creates tension and conflicting interests between departments, functions, and individual players.

Leaders aware of natural and healthy tensions in organizations take this as a driving force rather than an impediment for progress. They set themselves the task of engaging a communication process for bringing these incompatible viewpoints to light to enable power and action. Structuring a targeted communications process to involve all viewpoints and diverging interests lifts these factors from a latent state and triggers a productive problem-solving process. The achievement is shared understanding and sincere agreement. It makes the invisible thinking, of individuals and functional areas, visible. This results in appreciative decision making and action.

To make the needed changes, the company's leadership would be required to focus beyond the boundaries of their more traditional silos and business units and work together with internal and external partners to create environments where higher levels of performance are more easily achieved and sustained. They would now have to focus well beyond the one-on-one encounters and management of their own groups and develop broader and deeper skills in strategy and scenario development, building engagement with stakeholders who may have competing interests and agendas, as well as deal with complexities that could not be addressed by traditional problem-solving approaches.

# WHAT MAKES THIS APPROACH DIFFERENT, INTERESTING, AND INNOVATIVE?

The consulting procedure is a process of group dialogue. In discussions with groups of people from affected areas, the problems are brought to light, which become the focus of the dialogue process. The suggestions for solving these problems are also elaborated in group discussions and workshops with those involved. The group moderator is able to make people feel safe so that participants allow their viewpoint and thought structures to be challenged. This builds a common foundation for leaders to focus on issues and challenges and creates a climate for team learning and action. The necessary communication for building shared understanding and commitment is accelerated.

A structured dialogue process creates opportunities for leaders to think together to resolve complex organizational issues in order to do more intelligently what is necessary. Naturally in discussions, each participant focuses on their own objective, interests and agenda. The moderator organizes communication between players and intellectually influences the patterns of thinking of the group. A moderator is not neutral. She will give structure to collective thought, will generate new insights and create new possibilities for action. By skillfully searching for differences of opinion or assumptions, the moderator is able to turn hidden or unchallenged issues into manageable problems to be prioritized and solved.

During a workshop, the dialogue moderator intervenes in the group discussions either indirectly or directly. "Indirectly" means that she formulates the questions and propositions of which the discussions are about and architect the blended flow of inquiry, dialogue and challenge throughout the session. The moderator intervenes directly by taking part in the discussion with her own opinions and recommendations in a provocative manner. She always does this if the indirect method is not successful in breaking closed thinking. These indirect and direct interventions are the points where consulting takes place: She is simultaneously both a moderator and a consultant. Skillfully using questions to trigger doubt and contradictions opens critical dialogues to analyze and bring to light what is really is behind the problem.

In leading dialogue processes one of the end goals is supposed to be "reaching an appreciative understanding." This means the challengers and the challenged arrive at an agreement that favors new ways of acting. Reaching an understanding can certainly be a complete agreement, a consensus, but in most cases this is unlikely. For this reason effective moderators take a whole systems approach and do not direct their interventions towards creating a consensus as a specific objective of the moderation. During the process of reaching a shared understanding, it is perfectly possible and legitimate for participants to accept disadvantages and losses if this opens up ways of acting that help to avoid even greater disadvantages and losses. This is why it is termed *appreciative understanding*.

In order to reach this appreciative understanding, it is necessary to remove mental blocks and guide participants towards new insights and openness of mind. To achieve this, one must lead the discussions to participants' differences and "blind spots." Even if the consulting procedure focuses on the communication between those present, it still needs both prior and accompanying diagnoses to select the dialogue topics and tailor them. These are topics that the practitioner or meeting leader brings in to the discussion or, even better, the participants bring up themselves. For this to happen the organizational patterns and structures have to be investigated.

Generally it does not take long to identify the obvious patterns or structures. The organization charts, plans, and available statistics/data are used in the assessment. Yet, the hidden organizational structures are mainly identified in exploratory discussions with groups from the various areas and levels of the organization. The insights gained are complemented by active observation and studying texts (self-descriptions, minutes of meetings, specialist articles, etc).

To find the hidden structures, the practitioner pursues certain question sets that are suitably formulated and put to the relevant parties in the exploratory meetings. Mostly these are questions on *differences,* unearthing discrepancies between talk, decision, and action. Examples of such are as follows:

- Why is action not taken, although a decision has been made? Or why are decisions made even though people know that no action will be taken? Or even, why are decisions made so that no action will be taken (e.g., by setting up a working group, or task force, which nobody then consults)?
- What three key influencers may have a different opinion then you on the issue(s)? Talk with them.

- What key influencers may share your opinion on the issue(s)? Talk with them.
- Which views (people's own rationale) do certain people put forward to the others?
- Why is there so little cooperation even though there is so much coordination?

It is important to encourage interests that are not easily convergent with that of another in order to create distinctions. Distinctions create a deep, ingrained awareness that automatically changes the way you think and act. Distinguishing the various perspectives and interests enables you to create possibility, action, and relationship. With each new distinction comes new power for understanding and new effectiveness for building solutions to successfully transform thought patterns into actions. Through the dialogue process, and building on differences and distinctions, evolution of the solution is created and shared by all. In this way, the outcome has a much higher frequency of impact because there is an intense coherence of understanding and all are "in phase". This is the way to get whole-hearted action behind it.

# METALLIC BRIEFCASE OR A BROWN ROLL OF PAPER

## *Visualization*

When working in companies, we usually do not take space into account as a key factor for empowered thinking. A successful use of a moderated dialogue approach requires a different use of space. For example, each participant needs 60 square inches for a group size of 5 to 25 people. This means that if you work with 20 participants, they will actually occupy 200 out of 1,200 square inches (with the seats). What is the remaining surface used for?

The purpose is to have enough space to spread out on large boards, covered with brown butcher-block paper, the thinking process of that group. Information inputs and interaction contents (individual ideas) become visible on posters as we lead the dialogue process. After two hours, you may have 10 such boards/posters visually capturing the thinking of the group: Everything available in front of you is used to deepen reflection, allowing connecting ideas and encouraging participants to find their own solutions. This allows for areas and ideas to be clustered and more immediately identified and selected for next steps. Some ideas spring to light; some cook. Visual argumentation capture is one way to literally bring the relevant issues to light in order to find the explanations and ideas that move the group forward.

Visualization is a well-known creative tool used to draw maps of your thinking on a given topic to get the overview. Metaplan's contribution to leading active dialogue processes was to define practical solutions to use this powerful technique, with 20 people simultaneously, by connecting an interaction method and a visualization system. Coming back to our example of 20 participants, in a room of 1,200 square inches

with 10 boards/posters filled with ideas in front of them, it is interesting to note that these 10 boards account for a "thinking space" of almost 20 square inches each. Or, said differently, our group is using a vertical surface of 200 square inches to develop their thinking graphically over 2 or 3 hours! This process can go on for 2 days, which is what ultimately makes it a powerful instrument for working on highly complex issues that span multiple stakeholders. This demands that a structured flow be used so that the dialogue moderator and participants do not get lost in the meantime. In the Metaplan approach, such a flow is called a "dramaturgy."

The Metaplan group work method is a moderated dialogue program where all the participants are actively involved in the discussion. This affords each person an opportunity to develop his or her reasoning pattern in depth. Using data from the diagnostic phase, the practitioner or meeting leader identifies the things that may distort or limit participant views. What this means is that it is important to see the different opinions held that are a result of past thoughts, experiences, what others have said, and so on. In this way the practitioner uncovers the myths, dogmas and fictions participants believe in which support can limit their thought structures. The objective of a spirited dialogue process is not to definitely know or define something, but to see it in all its dimensions.

For example, organizational myth is the label given to legends which have been passed down and people take for granted. These myths can limit new thinking and consequently new actions that may result from innovative thinking. Similarly dogmas (rules which go unquestioned) and fictions (beliefs for actions which lack evidence) can be thought limiters when assumptions remain uncovered and thinking unchallenged. In this way the moderator acts as an *agent provocateur:* She is there to inject the group with a unique perspective to stimulate thought and drive active dialogue.

In this way the moderator serves in the following role:

- To facilitate the expression of divergent viewpoints, reserves, and clarify contradictions enabling a convergence to be built.
- As ideas are formulated in detail, the moderator team writes them down and places them in order. With this approach, we can follow the development of the reflection as a whole. Participant frameworks become vivid and clear.
- To focus discussion on the key points: The moderator leads it towards the aspects that must be debated to reach the stated goal.

A thorough and structured preparation of the workshop is crucial to achieve a result-oriented outcome and to prevent and overcome numerous obstacles that are difficult to tackle. The moderator must give very careful consideration to developing the meeting scheme, or dramaturgy, so that it will warrant active participation, open up perspectives, make the group discussions more effective, and lead to a shared understanding. Here, "effective" has a double meaning: On the one hand it implies saving time. In workshops moderated with dialogue techniques, results are achieved faster than by traditional methods. On the other hand, it also implies that the participants are more deeply involved in the group process, in considering all opinions, and in working towards jointly supported results.

Certain rules governing the dramatic process assist the moderator in thinking over the course of the discussion in advance, in order to lead the group down a continuous path to a conclusion. Workshop planning involves design in the following areas:

- How to reach a shared understanding by planning meeting dramatics
- How to trigger appropriate reactions from a group
- How to compose an argument
- How to formulate questions eliciting interactions

For a discussion using the Metaplan approach, visualization tools are needed to make the group members' thoughts and arguments visible to all. Visualization helps participants follow the oral discussion more easily. Propositions, comments, criticisms, doubts, objections, and difficulties are all rapidly captured visually and clustered by theme, issue, and real-time relevance. This works to focus the group, force reflection and advance the discussion toward weighted areas of dialogue. At the end of a workshop, the entire flow of the discussion is represented as a record in photominutes. This not only ensures accurate representation of the meeting discussion, making all frameworks and possibilities vivid and clear, but also captures the atmosphere of the discussion and demonstrates the methods used to achieve those results. Photominutes are produced to reduce the large posters to a standard, useable A4 format that is handier for follow up work.

# FLASHMARKS: HIGHLIGHTING THE HOT SPOTS

If you object: flash. There are various visualization techniques for creating a visual image of the discussion, interaction, and dramaturgical planning tools and techniques the moderator relies on for designing a results-oriented dialogue session. A critical interaction technique is termed a "flashmark."

Flashes are catalysts for reaching a shared understanding. Qualifying additions or objections to a statement are called out and marked with a lightning bolt on the respective poster. Flashmarks denote areas of controversy or distinction that warrant more discussion time. At these points, there is a need for debate or to understand each other better. The participant that flashed then adds his argument or clarification to the debate. In this way flashmarks open up the dialogue to other people's arguments and encourage participants to express deviating opinions.

Questions about a poster may also be posed with a flash. Flashing alone is not enough though; the moderator should be careful to precisely extract the arguments behind the flashes. Those arguments, as well as any ensuing sequence of replies and additional arguments need to be captured and clustered next to the original statements. This way various viewpoints are visibly juxtaposed where they are written down and made objective. The participants come to terms with the contribution of others and can integrate them better into their own way of thinking. Flashes help to precisely formulate the idea and express it exactly; they also reveal weaknesses in concepts.

Through chains of contradictions, the idea is developed further. Others' arguments are complemented and tested by contradiction and participants contribute something to the idea. An individual recognizes his contribution, and the flashmark brings a sense of relief where a participant can see that he has contributed to an idea and to some extent made it his own.

# Using Questions for Helping the Birth of Ideas

Effective dialogue schemes use questions to open a debate among participants. Each group member should be curious as to what the others in the group will say, and be stimulated to also take a stand and explain it. It is critically important to get the group to diverge on the topic or related issues before moving toward convergence of agreed-to solutions. Diverging allows all participants to share their expertise, convictions and interests so that they all contribute to the development of solutions.

To trigger interaction in the group a good question has to meet certain criteria:

- *It should ask for opinions or suggestions,* not for expert knowledge. Each participant should be able to provide answers. A question that only an expert can answer will not result in a group dialogue.
- *It should be open, allowing several answers* from each participant. It is always wrong to ask a question answerable with "yes" or "no," because the discussion would quickly be over. On the other hand, blatantly leading questions such as "Why is piecework the only way?" or any question that might insult the participants should be avoided. A question that "strikes home" will be accepted by the group and will result in a stimulating discussion.
- *It should challenge and concern.* The question should be relevant to the personal experience of the participants, it should not ask for information anyone can read about in the newspapers. If it concerns me directly I am much more interested in contributing answers. In a discussion with manufacturing managers a question such as "What difficulties are inherent in participative management?" should not be used, but rather "What difficulties could arise if we let our workers have more of a say in our decisions?"
- *It should guide in the intended direction.* When phrasing a question, possible answers should already be anticipated. The direction of the discussion triggered by the question should be in accordance with the goals for the meeting. The moderator decides whether to pinpoint problems in a work area, ask for ideas and solutions, or collect pros and cons to a known suggestion. These considerations help to decide whether the expected answers will lead towards the discussions intended results.

There are different types of questions. One must consider in advance with what question one will trigger the desired interaction. The following examples of types of assertions and/or questions formulated for different responses and interactions:

| | |
|---|---|
| Proposition | Best Brand Company is broadly recognized as an industry leader in sales and marketing! <br> (using dots, opinions are rated on a scale) |
| Call-Out Question | What are current shortcomings that impede our ability to grow talent? |
| Card Question | To be excellent in 2004, what are the topic areas in which we could impact performance further? <br> What characterizes excellent "customer insight"? |
| Weighting Question | If business unit effectiveness today = 100, where will it be in 2004? <br> (scale provided) |

To keep an active dialogue session going, a moderator must consider how to intervene, provoke and mediate the discourse at the right times. Once well-phrased questions are identified, there are various techniques for using questions effectively in the dramatics and architecture of a lively dialogue session.

There are traditional problems with leading dialogue processes as well. Limitations can emerge which stall an intended lively, healthy problem solving session. To a skilled moderator, these limitations typically point to latent issues in the organization that can be symptomatic of a greater problem. This provides the opportunity to address bigger challenges that are impacting high performance. For example, an active dialogue session will reveal the conditions that influence behavior. Identifying these latent issues in the organization affords leaders the opportunity to change conditions so others can behave differently. In the end, leaders gain deeper insight in to their own structures to change conditions for a better result.

## An Open Process

The type of changes that result from leading dialogue processes have a character of social transformations that take place within the organization or across professional communities. This process of change is often described by professionals as being an open, contingent, and political process. It is *open* because the target, or goal, may evolve during the project and room is left for all interdependent players involved to contribute and influence the project. This is a priority for leading the dialogue session.

Leading a dialogue process is also *contingent,* in the sense that there is not one perfect way to organize a given change. For effective sessions, it must be understood and expected that large parts of the solution, or what will be achieved, are left open to being defined. Generating new insights and breakthrough thinking can produce original explanations, paths, and ideas.

Often a desired outcome for leading a dialogue process is to construct some temporary arrangements between players who may have diverging interests and ideologies. The process has a political dimension to stress the public debate of those involved representing views and interests of their group. There must be enough room for the far superior form of spontaneous order to arise than decided order. Decision makers may get easily tempted to define plans well in advance in a small committee. Leaders of dialogue processes grow in confidence that there are alternatives which will emerge that follow a certain rationality and special form of intelligence involving all without, however, running the risk of losing control. This is the path to achieving a common understanding.

# CONCLUSION

Mastering the skill of moderating dialogue not only enables you to lead more effectively, it gives you access to areas in organizations that many struggle to influence and change. Creating and attending to things that exist in language is the work of a leader because it is words, conversations and actions that motivate people and drive most behavior. For example, you can gain access to things such as culture through organizational language.

Moderating toward shared understanding removes conflicts, develops room to act and encourages venturing into new territory. Managers and leaders in companies tend to underestimate the ability of other's to find solutions, to place trust in others. Yet people need to feel confident with what they are doing. Engaging actionable dialogue, working together, building buy-in and appreciated understanding produces enthusiastic and energized people. When you need good answers, you must ask the right questions through a constructive dialogue process. Fostering buy-in and committed action through dialogue will help build a new future for yourself and your business.

# CHAPTER 14

## BE A TRENDSETTER: THE FUTURE OF BRANDING, MARKETING, AND ORGANIZATIONAL COMPLEXITY

*Ryan Mathews*

## INTRODUCTION

Branding—at least branding as we've become used to it—is obsolete. Like a square dance caller at a hip-hop club, branding is out of sync with the rhythms of commerce in the third millennium post-industrial world. The projection of often-superficial claims and vaguely defined efficacy statements onto a passive and unsuspecting public who mindlessly purchase with unquestioning belief is an artifact of historical commercial imagination. And, in the same way that branding has changed forever, so has the marketing that supports brands and the organizational structures that birth and nurture them. The assumptions that formed the bedrock of the classical industrial economics are all up for review. The combined force of discontinuities is rapidly overtaking the entrenched bastions of demographic determinism and the established wisdom of long-term longitudinal studies. And, in the midst of what can only be described as revolutionary change, the paradox of innovation—the dynamic tension between creatively deviant thinking and the impulse to ""get back to basics"—struggles to resolve itself.

The lines that have artificially separated work from the society at large have dissolved. The institutional prophylactics that business has used to keep itself safe from the infections of the culture that house it have failed. A generation from now, business scholars will look back and marvel that anyone ever thought of the institutional pursuit of wealth creation by individuals and corporations as different from other cultural expressions such as art, literature, media, or religion. No doubt they will be equally as surprised that a commercial system ostensibly engaged in the endless pursuit of innovation should so strenuously reject the most obvious sources of creativity and how organizations charged with the growth of branding managed to campaign so effectively against the very forces that could have advanced their stated goals. The collapse of the so-called New Economy has brought temporary solace to the forces of retrenchment and tradition, but the future of branding belongs to the deviant. Before we consider the future of branding, marketing, and organizational complexity, we need to establish some clear models of both innovation and the dynamic social and commercial market, or the context in which innovation manifests itself.

# POSITIVE DEVIANCE: THOUGHTS ON THE ROOTS OF INNOVATION

Innovation is by definition something new, a departure from established practice or perception. Deviance is by definition also a measurable departure from the norm. For the sake of this chapter we will be concerning ourselves exclusively with deviations that are positive, that is, those measurable departures from social convention that result in social and/or commercial advances. As Watts Wacker and I suggest in *The Deviant's Advantage: How Fringe Ideas Create Mass Markets* (Crown Business, 2002), every product, idea, or person who comes to enjoy commercial success at the heart of what we call "Social Convention" advance down a measurable, predictable, and linear path from what we term the "Fringe"; to a place we describe as the "Edge"; to a state we call the "Realm of the Cool"; passing next to a stage we describe as the "Next Big Thing"; and finally arriving at Social Convention. Let's examine each of these stages of innovation and then tie them back to our analysis of the future of branding, marketing, and organizational complexity. We'll start our journey at the Fringe, a vast and hostile land populated by true, authentic deviants.

Fringe dwellers are individuals so certain of their own vision that sometimes they are disinclined to share it, fearful that it will be corrupted in the hands of less than true believers—which, by the way, is exactly what happens almost 100 percent of the time. The Fringe is a place of pure passion, more often than not fueled by creativity rather than commercial concern. The Fringe dweller may or may not choose to communicate his or her vision to others. Jesus lived on the Fringe but chose to share his vision. Henry Ford was also a product of the Fringe. So were Leonardo and Michelangelo and so are Bill Gates, Steve Jobs, Larry Ellison, and almost every entrepreneur past or present that you can name. Corporate America's cool hunters never quite reach the Fringe. It's too primal for their tastes, too unrefined, and not quite commercially viable enough. And the truth is that much of the innovation born on the Fringe dies there before it ever impacts the larger commercial world around it. But, almost miraculously, some innovation manages to sustain itself and find it's way to the Edge where it begins to build a small but fanatically dedicated audience.

The Edge is the first public showcase for the deviant idea, personality, or product. Sometimes audiences are built by accident, someone "discovering" a new artist happily working away in obscurity or a new musical sound taking shape on the proving ground of street culture. Occasionally the originating deviant may come seeking an audience for financial or emotional support. This helps explain the evolution of social movements and radical political parties, of new schools of art and music, and even the origin of products like the television that we now take for granted despite our inability to determine who it was that actually invented them. If there's media coverage at the Edge, it's almost always negative——a story of how some undesirables are attempting to threaten the safety of the status quo. Society's first impulse is to eradicate deviance by eliminating the deviant. But innovation cannot be denied forever and so some deviance (and sometimes even the originating deviant) move to the next phase, the Realm of the Cool.

The Realm of the Cool is where Corporate America (or Europe or Asia for that matter) looks for its next big commercial breakthrough. The audience for innovation at the Realm of the Cool is greater and less orthodox than the tightly knit true believers who inhabit the Edge. Edge dwellers often let go of innovation as it becomes popular. The Realm of the Cool is populated by the "beautiful people" whose opinions, while not directly embraced by anyone outside their circle, shape and determine what products will be coming down the commercial pike. Think of the difference between an haute couture fashion show and the designs that eventually find their way onto the racks at Macy's, Nordstrom's, and even Wal-Mart. The fashion show runways are populated by drastic and radical design innovations, lionized in the media but all but unsalable in Anytown, U.S.A., or Great Britain, Italy, or Spain. It is the essence of these chic designs, perhaps only their colors, that makes its way to market. The runway starts and stops in the Realm of the Cool but the lines are distributed everywhere. There is intense media and corporate interest in the Realm of the Cool, but the reporting back to Social Convention still reads more like "look what those wild people are doing" than "here's what you ought to be doing." The problem with looking for innovation in the Realm of the Cool of course is that everyone else is also looking for it there. It's convenient, far more accessible than either the Fringe or the Edge and decidedly safer in more ways than one. Imagine rushing into a senior marketing meeting of any well established organization accompanied by a person so obsessed with a new idea they could easily be cast as the local crackpot. Now, by contrast, imagine walking into that same meeting with a cassette of a new sound being featured at "all the right clubs"." Your odds of corporate survival just increased exponentially. Like all the other stages, innovation can stop at the Realm of the Cool. Some "cool" concepts never really catch on commercially. But, some do and those advance to a place we call the Next Big Thing.

A great deal of attention is paid to the Next Big Thing. It is the breeding ground where Seth Godin's "Idea Viruses" trigger an epidemic of acceptance and the catalyst for Malcolm Gladwell's "Tipping Point." But whatever it is called, it's the stage innovation occupies before it reaches Social Convention—the on-deck circle of creativity. The audience for innovation is much larger and less exclusive. The object of their attention is more marketable and therefore often less authentic. The stakes are higher and the competitive pressure to be "first to market" with a scalable offering is far more intense. Media coverage here switches from "look what the beautiful people are doing" to "look what you'll be doing . . . soon." Many products and ideas seem to emerge full-blown from the Next Big Thing because the vast majority of the market doesn't bother to track their progress from the Fringe. This tendency to only look at innovation after it has—for all intents and purposes arrived—can cause even the most tuned-in to miss major commercial opportunities.

This is how IBM managed to understand the market potential of the interface they leased (rather than bought) from Microsoft. This is how Microsoft in turn managed to miss the commercial potential of the Internet. This is exactly why Detroit's "Big Three" automakers—Ford, General Motors, and Chrysler—managed to let the Japanese and, to a lesser extent, the Germans steal the domestic American car market and why Xerox, which developed commercially scalable versions of the computer mouse, the software programs we've come to know as Windows, and the portable computer itself, managed to not only fail to monopolize the computer industry but lose a staggering portion of its share of the copying business. It also probably explains why England, Spain, Portugal, the Netherlands, and France managed to lose their colonies. Nothing is apparently as easy to overlook as an idea whose time has really come.

It's only a branding hop, marketing skip, and commercial jump from the Next Big Thing to Social Convention, the place where "look what you'll be doing . . . soon" becomes translated into "this is what everybody's doing." We don't need to spend a great deal of time describing Social Convention. It is, after all, the stage of commerce most of us are most familiar with, the brass ring so many of us spend our entire careers praying to capture, at least just once. It is capitalism's nirvana, the promised land of plenty where economies of scale and a commercially acceptable version of creativity give rise to the maximum number of units sold and gross dollars collected. Oh, sure the innovation is still there underneath all those line extensions, but it's sometimes so well disguised that it's all but unrecognizable.

# THE ABOLITION OF CONTEXT AND NOTES ON A NEW THEORY OF BRANDING

So, what does all of this have to do with branding? Be patient just a little while longer. The "Sturm und Drang" of innovation has increased in intensity. Not only as Alvin Toffler suggested over 30 years ago in *Future Shock* has there been an increase in the rate of change, there's also been a parallel increase in both the depth and breadth of change. Things are just moving much faster from the Fringe to Social Convention and having a much shorter run on commercial center stage. Changes are literally coming so fast to many markets from high technology to biotechnology that it's all but impossible to sustain market interest before a new contender to the throne emerges. The result has been what we call the "Abolition of Context"—the elimination of the cultural footholds and connecting points that commerce has historically utilized to build new markets.

For example, let's suppose you're a beauty care company attempting to brand a new cosmetic product. Historically you would have taken a breakthrough in some form of research and then analyzed trial and use data, demographic trends, past sales histories, and other conventional tools to see what, if any, commercial applications might be marketable. You would then scour libraries of past beauty references or troll the waters of popular culture looking for the right brand identity, often a word such as Obsession or Passion. The brand identity would then be applied to the commercialized R&D and the result would be a product virtually guaranteed at least measured success.

Now let's use this new model on our same example: Cosmic Cosmetics discovers a new technology, say a translucent foundation that provides an excellent base for other makeup. They go to market their new brand, which they call Atlantis, conjuring up visions of the mysteries of lost classical civilizations. They find a classical Mediterranean beauty to be the model spokesperson for the brand and launch their new campaign. The problem is beauty is at best an arbitrary concept. With so many innovations competing with each other it's increasingly difficult to understand which approach to branding will be the most successful. Does Atlantis speak (as a brand concept) to women of color? Do aging baby boomer women want to put something on their late 40-, 50-, or 60-year-old skin that reminds them of sunken ruins? Will young professional women even bother with a product they may determine to be a reminder of the artificial standards of conventional beauty imposed on them by a male-dominated society? Will groups of consumers boycott the brand because one of Cosmic Cosmetics down stream supply chain partners does substantial business with another company that exploits child labor in the developing world? What is the right brand position in a post-September 11, 2001, America where our most fundamental assumptions about ourselves, our way of life, and the world have been so substantially shaken? How, indeed, can you ground a branding concept in a world that yo-yos hourly between war and peace?

We think it was exactly these kinds of pressures that were at least partially responsible for the collapse of the New Economy. Innovation, in this case high-technology innovation simply hit Social Convention far too rapidly for the existing commercial social context to evaluate it. Suddenly, before we knew it, the rulebook was thrown out and we found ourselves in a blind, mad race to throw dollars at ideas simply because we had never heard of them before. We were intoxicated with innovation and eager to fill our glasses, no matter what the cost. We had no real, proven way to evaluate business plans, and the context of traditional investing and financing simply collapsed. The result of this Abolition of Context was that the New Economy skyrocketed and then crashed. We had never known what we were doing and the truth of that came home with sobering certitude. And the sobering certitude pattern we witnessed in the high-technology world will repeat itself with alarming frequency until we develop a bolder vision of what we need to develop to cope with our future. Now, let's turn our attention back to what this all means for brands.

## DEVIANT BRANDS AND THE FUTURE

In America brands used to belong to the manufacturer. In Europe brands were often the province of the retailer, but in the future brands will be increasingly defined by the consumer. Brands used to the carefully nurtured fruit of corporate cultures. Today they are bartered like commodities; co-mingled with sometimes antithetical products; and diluted beyond recognition for a few points of market share. Licensing agreements have moved from logical co-offering to relationships so fanciful and tenuous it's almost impossible to imagine how they ever came into being in the first place. You can buy Harley-Davidson condoms and Eddie Bauer wallpaper and diaper bags. Brands like Bailey's Irish Cream are born in a laboratory and supplied with artificial and elaborate "histories" before being unleashed on a less than critical public. And brands like Hello Kitty have become products licensed to facilitate the marketing of other products. There never was a Kitty—the image is the whole product.

Want to become a deviant brander? Study brands that either reinvent themselves like Spam or Arm & Hammer or brands, like Snapple, that manage to maintain their authenticity and market appeal regardless of ownership. Deviant brands, and deviant branders, just seem to make their own opportunities rather than wait for mass-market acceptance. Deviant branders also know the value of the authentically iconic, which explains why every generation seems to reinvent Betty Boop and Betty Page to serve their own needs. The power of the authentically iconic becomes a critical element in ensuring brand success in the Abolition of Context. True, authentic deviant brands create their own context. They ride out market highs and lows because they know they'll always be back. This ability to self-define context is what makes deviant brands so successful over time. They survive the persistent waves of change precisely because they never identify with externals, standing always slightly off center even at the height of their popularity. The secret of their "return" is that they never leave.

Many branders argue that a brand is a promise. Well, deviant brands are more than that; they are the essence of authenticity. They don't promise anything beyond themselves because they aren't interested in anything beyond themselves. It takes a truly deviant brander to think in these terms, the lure of those inauthentic gross dollars is just too strong for most to resist, which is why deviant brands need the support of a truly deviant marketing system.

## THE DEVIANT MARKET

Deviant marketers flourish by eliminating the distinction between the message and the target. What they never lose sight of is the fact that what people believe to be true is always more forceful than what you tell them is true. Truly deviant marketers allow consumers to form demand on their own. The tricky part of this, of course, is that it forces a whole new discipline on marketing. To begin with, deviant marketers have to tap into media that consumers use rather than traditional media choices. This might mean a Web site, or it might mean distributing free tee shirts, but in all cases it involves intercepting the consumer where and how they live.

Want to be a trendsetter in marketing? How about starting by selling people what they want on their terms? Seem like a farfetched idea? Look at the growth of cause-related marketing from sales tie-ins with local schools (which work) to cause-related credit cards (which generally don't) and hundreds of marketing programs in between. Many of these efforts fail. Why? They fail because, in part or sum, the tie to the cause is artificially conceived and/or inauthentic. Consumers are smart enough to recognize when they're being patronized. Offer them a credit card that promises to save the whales and consumers expect to see a saved whale or two. This is especially true in the current market environment where consumers have come to distrust almost everything about large and prosperous businesses. Remember, there's no traditional context to latch onto here. Marketing campaigns stand or fall on their own, but the fastest way to kill one is to base it on a claim that consumers can easily see through. So, if everything is changing and the old tricks of the trade don't work, is there any hope? The answer is an aggressive, yet somewhat hesitant, yes. Aggressive because they way is clear and hesitant because it involves rewriting most of what they teach at your average business school.

## BUILDING THE BETTER CORPORATE MOUSETRAP

The problem with becoming a trendsetter is the frighteningly high mortality rate among corporate pioneers. The structure of most businesses prevents people from making the contributions they are capable of. In a word the enemy is culture. The sad truth is that most corporate cultures hate innovation despite all the mountains of annual reports and CEO speeches to the contrary. Corporate culture loves the idea of innovation but hates the reality of the innovative employee who refuses to be molded into the company image. Real diversity (educational, experiential, lifestyle or stage, economic) is avoided with the same passion as more traditional forms of diversity such as gender or ethnicity. So companies developed a series of obvious and hidden screens to weed out those who differ from the norm.

It begins with the human resources departments who only hire from certain schools and weed out those who don't seem to exhibit the proper team spirit (won't conform easily). Then there are the more subtle forms of stamping out the outré— not promoting them, assigning them to boring or thankless tasks, or, if all else fails, public ridicule or termination. We're reminded about the story of Lotus cofounder Mitch Kapor who one day became so concerned about the fact that his company was building sales but failing to innovate that he devised a little test. With the help of some fellow corporate co-conspirators, Kapor arranged to have the resumes of the original 40 employees of the company (including his own) suitably doctored and sent through the personnel department. The results were unilateral. Not one of the 40 people who had built the company was even called in for an interview! The revolution Lotus had launched had swallowed its children. So how do you avoid the trap Lotus built for itself?

The first step is to isolate all the impediments to innovation in your company and eliminate them. This may require you to survey employees that have left the company (whether it was their idea or yours) and those who you pursued but refused to accept your offer. The next step is to constantly contaminate your corporate culture with foreign spores in the form of people engaged in businesses mildly or radically different from yours. If you manufacture potato chips, odds are there's a lot to be learned about marketing from a guy who makes microchips. Why? Because you can listen to their voice without all the assumptions, baggage, and negative culture of your own industry. Several years ago DowBrands commissioned a body of environmentalists to help them with their consumer products. These weren't just any environmentalists. They were in fact people who believed most corporations were evil and most commercial products were ecological disasters waiting to happen. The great gift they brought DowBrands wasn't specific advice, it was proximity to another, often hostile, voice and view. By the same token, when Apple was in trouble it turned to Steve Jobs, the leader many blamed for the company's initial fall from grace. Why? The Apple management team was betting both Jobs and Apple had changed enough they could once again be good for each other.

Although it's almost too much of a cliché to use, it's also true that none of this is possible without the agreement of the corporate powers that be. Traditional leaders simply do not lead in nontraditional manners. If you want to find out where a company stands on innovation, study its senior management and the metrics they've put in place. Or, better yet, analyze how they got to the top and you'll understand exactly who and what they'll reward or punish. If, on the other hand, you want to really change a corporate culture you only have two choices: change management or change metrics.

## COMFORT BRANDS

In terms of branding, this means throwing out the volumes and volumes of branding lore and conventional wisdom and thinking of a brand as a dynamic, almost organic, entity that evolves and will one day die. There's little or no point in investing millions of dollars to prop up a heritage brand in a commercial world where the Abolition of Context has eliminated the power of tradition. There's even less of a point in treating consumers in the age of Ozzy Osbourne as if they were still living in the age of Ozzie and Harriet Nelson. A brand isn't so much a promise as it is a placeholder, a temporary reflection of a world of radically changing values.

Marketing then is less of an exercise in selling the market than an attempt to capture its soul, if only for a moment. Marketers have to quit acting like frustrated advertising executives and begin acting more like corporate cultural anthropologists whose job it is to describe a newly encountered tribe. The marketer's job is not to impose a false sense of meaning but to help consumers whose lives are increasingly difficult to achieve at least a temporary sense of satisfaction. For generations in business we have assumed that we were immune from changes in the social milieu. The truth is that we're all in this together.

The successful brander and marketer of the future, indeed the successful corporation of the future, will adopt an essentially biological approach to their business. They will see consumer markets not as fixed, static, and waiting to be exploited, but rather as complex adaptive systems constantly in motion. They will understand that evolution belongs to the deviant gene, that sometimes subtle changes can create rapid shifts in markets making this year's "hero brand" next year's "also ran." They will realize the perishability of brand claims in a society undergoing exponential change. But most concisely they will come to see the Abolition of Context as an ally, not an obstacle.

And, perhaps most importantly, in a world of rapid social and commercial change corporations, branders, and marketers will have to begin developing the ability to look beyond the Realm of the Cool, beyond even the Edge to face innovation at ground zero—the Fringe. Everyone in business will have to develop their skills as Fringe miners. This will demand the development of a whole new sensibility and a whole new set of personal and organizational talents. Perhaps the most critical of these new talents will be a tolerance for embracing risk and celebrating failure.

Earlier in this chapter we said that not all ideas make it from the Fringe to Social Convention. Playing on the Fringe will involve banking on ideas and individuals that won't pan out over time. This means we have to stop punishing people involved in projects that don't work out, brands that fail to gain traction, and campaigns that somehow miss the mark. If branding and marketing are indeed organic processes we must remember at all times that life is messy and evolution is full of dead ends.

If, on the other hand, all this seems a bit too New Age, a bit too soft and squishy, consider the alternative—business as usual. Now there's a scary thought. We've witnessed the collapse of the New Economy and now the Old Economy seems to be having a bit of difficulty of its own. Our modest prediction is that things are likely to continue to stay dicey until we learn to look at the market, and the opportunities it offers, in fresh new ways and with fresh eyes.

Brands can flourish in the future because they can serve as safe havens in otherwise chaotic lives. One day we may see the notion of comfort foods extended to comfort brands—goods people purchase simply because they remind them of a better, simpler time. But this will only happen when marketers learn to constantly, and effectively, monitor the public pulse.

## THE PERILS AND POTENTIALS OF TRENDSETTING

So what can we conclude about trendsetting in the future? First, it will be dangerous. Second, it will be the only way to gain significant market advantage. Success will involve staying ahead of the market and the market, as already mentioned, is a target in perpetual motion. Successful branding and marketing will be an exercise in creating and deconstructing meaning. If endurance over time was one of the keys to branding in the Industrial Age, flexibility will be key to future branding success. If deviants had to be eliminated to keep the wheels of commerce turning in the past, then they will have to be cultivated and lionized in the corporation of the future. If homogeneity was the key to past business success, then a more heterodox approach will be the key to future survival. Brands can no longer afford to be promises of meaning; they must offer meaning. Brands can't function in a fixed context; they must provide their own context. And trendsetting brands will construct promise and meaning in clear and deliberate ways. Fail to adopt this approach and brands will increasingly slouch en masse towards commodification identifying generic categories like "Kleenex" and "Xerox" rather than unique sources of value that have the right to command a premium from consumers.

We'll have to adopt new criteria for brand introduction and new metrics for brand success and failure beginning with our expectations of brand survival. Branding may be more of a serial activity—that is the introduction of successive products rather than the promotion of individual items. In such an environment corporate branding is likely to be far more critical than the branding of individual items, since individual items are likely to have severely truncated life cycles. We're already seeing signs that this is happening. The brand Microsoft is far more valuable than any individual iteration of Windows. By the same token, the Dell or Gateway brands are infinitely more important than any individual model of laptop or desktop computer. This is because to a large extent the world of high technology already operated under the rules of the Abolition of Context. "Best of class" high-technology products aren't those that have just arrived at market, they are those who have yet to arrive at market. In a world where we have moved from the planned obsolescence of the Industrial Age to the inherent obsolescence of the Information Age the brand promise of individual technology products is transitory at best and hollow at worst.

## CONCLUSION

In the future more and more products will fall into the branding model that's beginning to unfold in the high-technology arena. It will require deviant thinking to take advantage of these changing market conditions and a different approach to corporate organization to maximize future opportunities. Branding and marketing will have to be redefined and essentially reinvented. The skills of the past may actually represent impediments to future progress. As that great corporate theorist Bob Dylan once noted, "The first one now shall later be last, for the times they are a changing."

# CHAPTER 15

# WANT ADULT LEARNING?

## Practice in Simulated Realities

*Stu Noble*

## INTRODUCTION

Although there may be widespread acceptance that learning is, and will continue to be, a key differentiator between short and long term business success, there are few definitive answers as to how this learning can occur. The unique learning styles and preferences of the new generation of employees and management populating our organizations, as well as the growth of passive e-learning approaches, provides added complexity to the equation. This chapter will provide one answer to this multi-faceted question . . . the use of well-designed business simulations to accelerate high-impact learning and facilitate change.

## WRITING ABOUT SIMULATIONS: A PARADOX

Writing this began as an attempt to explore the value that experiential approaches, and specifically group simulations, have in the training and organizational development landscape. As I framed out how to approach this task, within the inherent boundaries of the next several pages, I came face-to-face with a fundamental paradox: "How do you describe in words the power of learning through the experience of a well designed simulation?"

Ironically, this is also a core aspect of why experiential-oriented learning is talked about more than designed and implemented. While few would dispute that experience-based learning is how adults learn best, it is still relatively rare (though growing) that these approaches find themselves integrated into training and development curriculums.

Dynamic, high-impact, and practical learning approaches, such as group simulations, are critically needed for building the performance, agility, and innovation necessary to allow organizations to thrive in the future, as well as to keep our in-house learners interested and challenged in a way that takes full advantage of classroom opportunities. This chapter will provide a window through which to explore the following aspects of this multi-dimensional paradox.

# THE CONTEXT OR "WHAT'S GOING ON?"

The world of learning cannot be differentiated from the context within which it resides. This is a world that can be characterized by speed, information overload, technology, and knowledge acceleration at warp speed, globalization, and an enmeshed world economy that demands performance under rapidly changing conditions. No doubt, we could add others to fill this page.

The implications of this for the field of organizational training and development are both profound and simple. Learning, at the individual, group, and organizational levels, is widely regarded as a key performance factor, as well as a differentiator in achieving (and/or maintaining) competitive advantage. The profound aspect must address the question "*What* do today's learners need and *how* can this be best achieved?" And the simple approach just focuses on applying what we already know about how adults learn best and responds, "Just do it".

Learning needs can be segmented into several categories, each of which having implications for both the profound and simple responses to this critical challenge. These include:

- Technical skill building (how to)
- Conceptual, information-based knowledge (why)
- Process and procedural know-how (what systems)
- Personal development (soft skills)
- Group and organizational development (soft and hard skills)

There is one more component of this abbreviated environmental scan worth noting. This has to do with the changes that have occurred in the learning styles and needs of those entering the workforce over the past 10-plus years. This new generation of employees, many of whom are already in leadership positions, have grown up in a world of high stimulation, readily accessed information, and, for many, a computer game orientation. While the baby boomers have experienced a shift of pace and complexity in the work world, this new generation only has speed and rapid change as their context.

The implications of this from a learning standpoint are manifold. Most relevant to this discussion is the fact that traditional-style learning techniques will not be sufficient for these and the learners of the future. Meeting their learning needs must go well beyond information delivery. And the performance pressures and pace of work require any learning "interlude" to be simultaneously compelling, relevant, and practical.

There is no silver bullet to best address the learning needs in the world described above.

For some of these however, the use of well-designed, properly positioned, and effectively facilitated experience-based approaches, especially group simulations, can have a uniquely powerful learning impact.

## WHAT ARE GROUP SIMULATIONS ANYWAY?

A group or organizational simulation, by definition, is a working model of some actual or theoretical organizational dynamics. Sometimes a simulation is closely related (in look and feel) to the system being simulated; at other times, it is analogous only in its replication of a particular dynamic, process, or feeling.

From a learning standpoint, what matters most about a simulation is that the participants who are using it are able to meaningfully connect their group experience to the aspects of the world they care about. To create this effect, organizational simulations typically must reduce or eliminate some aspects of a situation in order to enable participants to focus on a manageable number of variables. This approach allows us to go through a few simulated years in a few days, a product development cycle in eight hours, or the redesign of an organization in a half-day. If this reductive process is done well, the core elements of complex organizational processes are highlighted and consequently more understandable.

Historically, the traditional approaches we've used to diagnose organizations have provided us with a sequential (or linear) understanding. But, as we've come to realize, these approaches usually are inadequate for creating an overall patterned comprehension. Swedish simulation designer Klas Mellander in *The Power of Learning* likens this approach to "trying to solve a jigsaw puzzle by starting in the upper left hand corner and then putting all the pieces in place in the right order, from left to right and from top to bottom."[1] Simulations, on the other hand, start by creating a frame of reference (e.g., the edges in Mellander's puzzle within which we can locate our fragmented bits of knowledge [the specific puzzle pieces]). With regards to organizations, simulations help us make sense of key details within the

---

[1] Mellander, Klas. *The Power of Learning*. Homewood, IL: Business One, Irwin, 1993, p. 111.

larger frame and set an appreciation of the gestalt, rather than focusing on the various pieces. By doing this, simulations provide us a means to expand the limited perspectives of our daily life orientation.

Well-designed simulations can provide people, who must act sensibly within the increasingly complex and confused landscape of modern organizations, a means to overcome provincial understandings. They offer what one could call a "bird's-eye view." This view is one that can be studied and restudied from different perspectives and in different degrees of detail. This broader view that simulations offer also enables exploration of the interrelationships between various elements within the whole—a greater systems understanding—which enables choices and actions with a better understanding of their implications.

Finally, to truly understand what a simulation is (and what it isn't), it's important to distinguish between simulation and games. There has been some debate over the years about what to call experiences that somehow involve interaction with, or within, an operating model, that is whether to call them simulations or games. We prefer to make this distinction based on the primary intent of their use. If it is a contest with winning or losing as its primary goal, or an experience where the primary goal is to have fun, then we would call it a game. An experience that models an aspect of real life, with its purpose being to learn about a system, about the consequence of various actions/decisions, or about one's self, we would call it a simulation. So here's your pop quiz. Are you familiar with Monopoly? Based upon the above, is it a game or a simulation? (*You can find the answer at the conclusion of the chapter.*)

Of course, there is an overlap between these two distinctions. Many excellent simulations have built-in elements of competition and gaming. And many great games give rise to meaningful learning. We tend to draw our definitions from the depth and breadth of the learning experience itself and the nature of the primary learning objectives.

## How Simulations Help

Simulations can provide powerful and positive contexts for applying both individual and collective learning principles. For instance, simulations can take advantage of the opportunity to maximize active and enjoyable involvement in the learning process. They can generate creative, emotional tension and they can encourage us to explore, conceptualize, inquire, experiment, and critically analyze while using multiple senses. They can make us the agents of our own learning, shifting a classroom into a learning laboratory. With a focus on learning rather than teaching, they can build upon and integrate the participants' knowledge and life experiences. They can also provide an opportunity to explore from various new perspectives and behaviors.

Simulations also can create opportunities for open exploration of tough issues and differences without the repercussions that might be resulted from confronting certain issues directly. Simulations create safe conditions and can thereby reduce fear of the unknown. They can promote the discovery of new possibilities for action and facilitate finding common ground. They can allow for and engage different learning styles, giving us a kind of "practice field for collective experimentation and decision testing."[2]

Good simulations are very engaging. Simulations are unique in that the activity of participating in a simulation contains its own goals and motivation, and the learning involved is not just a means to some external end (e.g., passing a test, performing a task at a later date). They provide the learner the opportunity to operate from various rules and perspectives. (That is, the learner is not just a recipient of information, but is also an agent and referee.) Simulations enable the learner to be free from dependence on the authority of a teacher. Learners reason for themselves, test that reasoning in various ways, and get prompt and often quite tangible feedback on the quality of their reasoning.

Thus, interactive simulations focus less on the teacher and more on the learning that occurs among participants. As Mellander puts it, "they create conditions where learners can learn more than they are taught—where the learning content is greater than the teaching content."

Good simulations also allow for different learning styles, usually involve both the intellect and the "gut," and generally take advantage of the previous knowledge/life experience of the participants. They create learning situations that are responsive to the participant's actions . . . giving them feedback and encouraging them to be reflective about their own learning and/or progress.

## SIMULATION-BASED LEARNING: FROM THE INSIDE OUT

A great deal has been already written offering the core reasons why well-designed and competently facilitated experiential-based group simulations are effective learning vehicles. In this section, I add a new dimension—why simulations make sense for the inner world of the individual learner. Here we can draw heavily upon the wonderful research that has been done about the nature of intelligence.

---

[2]McAteer, P. F., *Simulations: Learning Tools for the 1990's*, Training and Development, 45(10) 1991, pp. 19–20.

## Intelligence and Experiential Learning

Thiagi, leader and most widely recognized in the world of simulations and games, provides the following research findings from cognitive sciences when asked to explain why simulations are effective.

## Of Two Minds

Seymour Epstein of the University of Massachusetts, with his groundbreaking theory of intelligence called Cognitive Experiential Self Theory (CES), suggests that we have an experiential mind and rational mind. Our experiential mind learns directly, thinks quickly, pays attention to outcomes, and forgets slowly. Our rational mind learns indirectly, thinks deliberately, pays attention to the process, and forgets rapidly. Epstein's contention is that you need both minds. Interactive learning strategies appeal directly to the experiential mind. When combined with debriefing discussions and relevant, practical concepts and application, they provide a balanced approach to whole-brain learning.

## Three Intelligences?

Robert Sternberg, IBM Professor of Psychology and Education at Yale has determined that practical and creative intelligence can be added to analytic intelligence as measured by IQ tests. Sternberg's research has shown that practical and creative intelligence are a better predictor of job performance than analytical intelligence. Interactive, experiential techniques such as simulations develop these practical and creative intelligences. An experience of a simulation design and implementation context.

## Would You Believe Seven?

Professor Howard Gardner at Harvard has developed the revolutionary concept of multiple intelligences (not to be confused with multiple personalities). A total of seven, they are

- Linguistic (thinking in words and using language)
- Logical-mathematical (quantifying and working with hypotheses)
- Kinesthetic (acquiring physical skills)
- Spatial (three-dimensional thinking)
- Musical (working with pitch, rhythm, timbre and tone)
- Interpersonal (interacting with others)

- Intrapersonal (understanding one's self)

Traditional training caters mostly to the first two intelligences. However, most work requires at least some of all seven. Simulations and other interactive activities involve all of one's intelligences and, thus, help prepare for the total world of work.

## And What About Emotional Intelligence?

Daniel Goleman has identified that being "smart" goes beyond IQ and involves emotional intelligence. Elements of which include self-awareness, impulse control, persistence, motivation, and empathy. Traditional training does little to address these elements. However experiential and interactive approaches do.

## THIAGI'S SEVEN LAWS OF LEARNING

In trying to understand what differentiates an effective group simulation or learning game, I turn once again to Thiagi who has articulated his own perspective within a framework of seven laws that has guided his prolific simulation and game development work for over 30 years. It is easy to see how the following of these laws would lead to experiential designs that address all of the various intelligences referred to in the above models. You will also note a direct correlation with the widely accepted (though rarely followed) principles of adult learning.

Law of Reinforcement: Participants learn to repeat behaviors that are rewarded.
Law of Emotional Learning: Events that are accompanied by intense emotions result in long-lasting learning.
Law of Active Learning: Active responding produces more effective learning than passive listening or reading.
Law of Practice and Feedback: Learners cannot master skills without repeated practice and relevant feedback.
Law of Previous Experience: New learning should be linked to, and built upon, the experiences of the learner.
Law of Individual Differences: Different people learn in different ways.
Law of Relevance: Effective learning is relevant to the learner's life and work.[3]

---

[3]Thiagarajan, Sivasailam. *Thiagi's Thinking on Experiential Learning (and Its Benefits)*. Accessed in 2002 from www.thiagi.com.

Next I will add my own to the case for revealing the power of group simulations made by the above wisdom, experience, and research focused on the individual. This places the individual in the context of their relationship with others.

## Learning as a Social Act

People have a need to learn, as well as to belong. For most, the act of learning is a social activity that addresses these fundamental human needs. Most classroom learning forums offer this potential, but the closer they are to the mental models of learner passivity imprinted from an early age, the more this potential is left unmet. Ask most employees attending company-sponsored training and they will tell you that what they often found most helpful are the discussions over breaks, lunch, or at the bar late at night.

The explosion of e-learning resources (whether they are effective or not is a topic for others to debate) provides another opportunity to consider the impact of this social aspect. If learning is both a social and community-building process, then how will this need be met through computer or Web-based approaches?

## Design Challenge Part One: Interrelated Dynamics

Understanding the deeper structure of what is being simulated (i.e., a specific or broad array of organizational dynamics, such as the process of aging, a court room trial, a manufacturing process, etc.) takes a great deal of work. The ability to translate an often complex or confused bunch of parts into an intelligible working model that gives it a clear sense of the essential cause and effect relationships at work is a design challenge unlike any other form of training or instruction.

In my case, along with Brent Snow and Ken Victor, I have spent the past six years creating a simulation that reflects an experience of a self organizing system, while offering very practical and focused tools for leadership effectiveness, organizational agility, and team performance (see insert). Talk about a complex set of organizational dynamics!

Did we, as designers, need to fully comprehend the complexities of an organic system? Of course not; yet, as designers, we must understand enough of the core essence to build a credible model. But how much knowledge of reality is enough? If the answers to three questions—(1) Can we represent the most important in a way that makes sense to others? (2) Can we account for how the dynamics could change under different conditions? (3) Do others understand these dynamics better as a result of his simulation?—are yes, then perhaps we know enough.

Organizational simulations, as we have previously stated, become operating models that define a significant aspect of a complex organization, or a condition within an organization. That is, they emulate three things: (1) the state of a particular organizational system; (2) the way that system changes; and (3) the way different elements within this system interact with each other.

Another challenging aspect of designing a robust simulation is creating relatively consistent conditions and results, while at the same time building in the ability to flex with the uniqueness of a group and the dynamics they create. In other words, providing a structure that yields predictably consistent learning, although that learning is uniquely different for each group. This is especially true for open-ended simulations in which a wide range of possible outcomes is built into the design. (As opposed to closed-ended simulations in which a single outcome or limited set of possibilities predictably occur.) The best simulations, as well as the facilitators who use them, seem to be able to balance the design of the simulation while supporting the participant-centered, discovery-based learning that emerges.

# DESIGN CHALLENGE PART TWO: WALKING A FINE LINE WITH REALITY

If simulations come too close to reality itself, their learning potential dramatically diminishes. Discovery of new possibilities within the safety of a laboratory-like environment is soon replaced by the complexity of organizational patterns, personal experiences, and historical baggage. On the other hand, if the variables in a simulation are made so simple as to seem simplistic, or reduced to the level of being pointless, then the experience will feel trite, too elementary, and/or unrelated to the real world. In either case, we will have trouble traveling across conceptual bridges that provide insight and learning.

Consequently, the art of designing a simulation lies in finding the balance, the emotional and/or metaphorical connections, between the simulated experience and reality. Generally, the further the simulation experience is from actual reality, the more the facilitator needs to build the metaphorical bridge through questioning and other approaches. The closer the simulation is to reality, the more the facilitator needs to help participants gain their own "reflective distance." Barry Oshry, in his organizational workshop simulation that explores the world of tops, middles, and bottoms in organizational systems, has coined the term "TOOT," or "Time Out of Time'" for the structure that artfully enables this balance.

# THE SIMULATION FACILITATOR: STILL ANOTHER PARADOX

The effective simulation facilitator wears many seemingly contradictory hats. He is a teacher, as well as a fellow learner; a stage manager, as well as a "real-time" designer; a guide, as well as an explorer. As such, many feel that the leading group simulations, particularly open-ended ones, require a higher order of skill than most other types of facilitation. In part, this is because so much must be understood: the simulation model with its various nuances, the dynamics of the referent situation, and the simulation's larger context as well as the connection between it and these dynamics. In addition, there are the required stand-up skills, the ability to listen, ask good questions, and so on, along with the ability to treat each experience with the self-confident creativity of an artist working with a new piece of canvas.

Thiagi explains the deeper levels of facilitation skills with a musical analogy:

> A beginning musician plays the instrument, a master musician plays the music, whereas a wonderful musician, a world class musician, plays the audience. Similarly, in the facilitation of simulations, the beginning facilitator manages the simulation the way it is designed to be run, whereas an expert facilitator facilitates to get the kinds of outcomes or the goals that are desirable for the group. However, the best facilitators I have seen are those artists who can truly play the participants and accomplish all of these things![4]

This suggests to us that the art of simulation facilitation is virtually invisible to the participant/learner. Here lies the core of the paradox. As we have often realized after an exhausting day of this invisible work, there is no harder task than managing the creative tensions of learning, the unpredictable and always unique group dynamics, and the logistical detail—often all at once!

Despite what we have said thus far, simulation-based learning is not a free-form process. It requires deliberately conceived elements and a framework that, when integrated, produces a predictably impactful learning experience. To achieve this effect, the simulation facilitator needs to have a clear understanding of the learning outcomes expected, as well as the boundaries that, if crossed, could be counter-productive. The potential for powerful learning that sometimes emerge may not be aligned with the facilitators stated objectives. Yet, the facilitator must always work to the overall intent and desired result for the organization. The balancing between these potentialities, and the intended learning results, is at the heart of the dynamic tensions we have explored above. Indeed, another paradox.

For even the most skilled facilitator, managing these tensions often involves an emotional roller-coaster that challenges one's ability, instinct, and integrity, and requires a great deal of trust in discovery-based learning processes. There simply is no way to disengage and stay outside the laboratory; being in the room, one is part of the process. It is impossible to be either the guide or the learner in this scenario. Paradoxically, one must be both.

---

[4]Thiagarajan, Sivasailam. *Thiagi's Thinking on Experiential Learning (and Its Benefits)*. Retrieved in 2002 from Workshops by Thiagi, Inc., Web site: http://www.thiagi.com.

# THE VALUE OF GROUP SIMULATIONS

The information provided in this section makes a strong case for the inclusion of group simulations as a key aspect of developing an effective learning approach. However, one doesn't have to go far to access their own personal evidence.

Here is an exercise that, if you are willing, you can do to explore this question in yourself.

### Reflection Exercise
1. Think of a time that you had a powerful learning experience.
2. Close your eyes and imagine yourself back in that experience.

   i. Imagine what were you doing? If there is a teacher, what were they doing/ co-learners?
   ii. What did it feel like? Any smells or sounds associated?
   iii. We you stationary or moving? Any interactions with others?

3. Review the Seven Laws just discussed. How many of these laws applied to your experience?
4. Overall, what made this learning experience memorable?

I often introduce people to the world of simulations through using a performance frame of reference. Most people have some experience in their lives of performing or playing a sport. It doesn't matter whether its ping-pong or baseball, golf or tennis, swimming competitively or drama, a piano recital or basketball, etc.

Here's the point: Performing in all of these venues requires a certain amount of practice and, in some cases, simulation of the ultimate "game." A Broadway show doesn't open without months of countless rehearsals and dress rehearsals. Tiger Woods didn't become the greatest golfer of all-time without a commitment to relentless practice and repetition. American football players rehearse under simulated game conditions all week for their 60-minute weekly performance. I think you get the idea.

However in the game of business, the expectations are for individuals and teams to practice and play at the same time, on the same field. Unreasonable? Perhaps. However, the reality is that there are neither the appropriate forums nor time to do otherwise. This becomes another case for the use of relevant, practical, and well-designed group simulations to be incorporated within the work landscape. Exceptional performance requires practice. And the closest this practice comes to simulating the conditions and expectations of real life challenges, the better prepared the players are for whatever happens in their unfolding game.

# THE NEXT FRONTIER: EXPERIENTIAL LEARNING AT A DISTANCE

OK. It's finally time to address the "other e-learning" and how it fits in this discussion. The same environmental conditions and learning context stated at the beginning of this chapter are equally relevant when assessing the value proposition of technology-enabled distance learning. As communications technology has become more sophisticated and bandwidth limitations stretched, translating traditional instructional designs into cyberspace will continue to evolve. For economic reasons alone, the value of people accessing information and enhancing their know-how without the cost of travel and resources associated with classroom settings becomes evident. As the need for staying up to date with an explosion of information and knowledge becomes more and more difficult, the importance of effective e-learning forums becomes, perhaps, even more important. As more and more computer-based literate new employees enter the workforce, the overall comfort with these e-learning approaches may also increase.

I was struck by comments I recently read in an excerpt from a report published by Branon-Hall, experts in the field of e-learning simulations. The purpose of this report was to inform learning specialists about the simulation-based tools and resources that exist in the market. The underlying message, however, is a clear message that off-the-shelf, page-turning courseware often fails to produce their intended learning results, especially when high-level skills are involved. The addition of simulation-based e-learning courseware not only would greatly enhance effectiveness but also represents an enormous growth segment of the e-learning market in the coming years. This is illustrated by the following taken directly from the report commentary:

The demand for simulation-based e-learning is poised to become a distinct and powerful revenue generation engine in the e-learning industry. As a stand-alone product category it will generate about 8 percent of revenues in the 2006 market, estimated to be worth more than $83 billion ($6.6 billion). By 2011, it will represent 17 to 18 percent of the overall market.[5]

The message is loud and clear. Interactive, engaging learning approaches, whether they be designed within face-to-face classroom environments or integrated within e-learning coursework, greatly enhance the potential for impactful learning. The growth of this aspect of the e-learning market just cited reinforces its perceived value.

In moving into a more focused view, the Brandon-Hall report goes on to identify six main categories for potential e-learning simulation use, including

- *Software simulations* for IT/application training
- *Technical simulations* for learning about physical systems, equipment, and/or processes

---

[5]Brandon Hall staff, *E-Learning Simulations: Tools and Services for Creating Software, Business, and Technical Skills Simulations*, www.Brandon-hall.com.

- *Procedural simulations* which teach step by step methodology
- *Business simulations* for teaching management skills, running mock companies, accounting practices, etc.
- *Situational simulations* for building interpersonal, communication, leadership, and other soft skills
- *Virtual worlds* for teaching by recreating environments, workplaces, etc.[6]

I found the definitions of these six categories helpful in relating what are described as e-learning simulations and the other type of group simulation experiences being discussed in this chapter.

There is no question in my mind that the social learning dimension is best addressed in live, face-to-face design approaches. In looking at the six distinctions, social learning would probably fall into business, situational and virtual categories. I am also aware that my own perspective about the limits of electronic interaction are, perhaps, much more conservative than reality suggests. To illustrate, I must admit that over the past several years I have been very surprised at the level of intimacy found in many of my email-enabled relationships. And, as I watch my teenage daughter in her very social world of instant messaging, I know that we are rapidly moving toward a time when electronic interaction has greater potential to meet both learning and connection/belonging needs.

In the meantime, the paradox of e(xperiential)-learning amidst all of this becomes even more pronounced. Rather than address this as an on-or-the-other matter, the conversation is best approached as "one and the other." (Which is labeled "the other" depends upon the side from which you look.)

Just as there has been, in response to the variable success of the investment in e-learning methodologies, a greater emphasis upon blended learning strategies, so too do I look toward a blended solution as the next frontier of experiential learning. However, by "blended" I am not merely referring to adding face-to-face active learning designs to compliment electronic approaches. I also believe that even well-designed simulations can compensate for poorly constructed or highly traditional learning designs. This is especially true when addressing the soft skill learning needs mentioned above.

While well-designed, face-to-face, engaging, challenging, and relevant experiential-based designs would no doubt greatly contribute to the transition to maximizing the potential of blended learning, the next frontier is perhaps found in a new simulation-based design format. I believe that, due to a variety of environmental, organizational, and cultural factors, the ability (and/or willingness) of learners to meet in face-to-face venues will continue to diminish. The question then becomes

---

[6]Brandon Hall staff, *E-Learning Simulations: Tools and Services for Creating Software, Business, and Technical Skills Simulations*, www.Brandon-hall.com.

how we apply our knowledge, experience, and creativity associated with adult learning into the world of distance learning.

My own answer is simple and quite exciting. As educators, organizational consultants, learning designers, and facilitators, we have no choice but to create dynamic, highly socially interactive, relevant, and easily accessible group simulation-based designs that are technology enabled. Stepping forward into a new paradigm or frontier is never a comfortable act. Our personal assumptions, beliefs, and capabilities must be challenged during the process. For me, this has been both an exhilarating and frustrating process. Perhaps this paradox becomes the most relevant one of all!

## CONCLUSION

Increasing an organization's collective intelligence and capacity for positive action is the task of much organizational development focus today. In this regard, the power of simulations to create the baseline conditions for group dialogue and inquiry is particularly important. Well-designed simulations can surface symbolic maps of some multi-dimensional organizational phenomena. This map can serve as a basic reference system. It can become the foundation for understanding the whole. Only then can the bits and pieces of detail, which are uncovered or transmitted later, can be appropriately placed.

This power to create a framework is important for both dialogue and inquiry, which are key elements of learning. A simulation map can assist in the formulation of meaningful inquiry from a variety of different angles or perspectives.[7] This better enables people to both think about and discuss with others about complex and difficult issues; it enables a kind of practice field for collective experimentation and decision testing[8] and it provides a metaphoric structure for analyzing future circumstances.

The challenge of navigating ourselves and organizations within these turbulent times calls for learning opportunities that stretch our ability to understand both the elements and dynamic interrelationships in our environment. This equates to a generalized systems awareness. Improving organizations requires more that one person moving in the same direction. We all must be able to authentically share our different perspectives and really listen to each other in order to develop the shared and genuine understanding necessary for collective movement in a coherent forward direction.

---

[7]Greenblat, C. S., and R. D. Duke. *Practices and Principles of Gaming-Simulation.* Beverly Hills: Sage Publications, 1981, p. 13.

[8]McAteer. 1991, p. 22.

The collapsing of time and space found in a well-designed and artfully facilitated simulation makes it possible to recognize what is often clouded or seemingly invisible. Whether used as a tool for work redesign, leadership development, team building, or countless other organizational development (OD)interventions, this mode of action learning is consistent with the core values of self-determination, teamwork, collaboration, and inherent in our profession and belief in the human spirit that is deeply ingrained in our humanity.

We also know that there is no panacea or silver bullet that, alone, can possibly address the complexity and expected chaos of interrelationships in a complex work system. Yet we have found that experientially based, well-designed simulations that incorporate the concepts and principles outlined in this paper have the potential to significantly accelerate the transformational learning of individuals, groups, and organizations.

### Answer to "What is Monopoly?"

Based upon my definitions, Monopoly can be either a game OR a simulation. An example of the latter would be if a group of learners were in a situation where they were trying to understand the challenges and dynamics involved in the world of real estate. A time component might be added, requiring rapid decision making, as well as periodic focused discussions about real estate principles, strategies, approaches, etc.

There could be a strategy component that would also provide an opportunity for learners to test their assumptions in a safe world of Monopoly money.

## SIMULATION EXAMPLE: THE VORTEX SIMULATION™

## *Introduction*

The Vortex Simulation, from *3D Learning,* is a fast-paced, uniquely engaging action-learning approach for leadership development and skill building. Participants actively explore and discover what it takes to build effective, agile, and innovative organizations amidst today's rapidly changing marketplace.

| | |
|---|---|
| Purpose/Intent | The Vortex Simulation workshop is designed for managers at all levels. It provides an excellent learning platform for those within a single department or unit, individuals from throughout an organization, and cross-functional and/or interdepartmental project teams or work groups. It can be run with groups of 18 or more, with design variations that can accommodate well over 100. An ideal group size for the basic workshop is 25 to 35 participants. |

The basic workshop design is facilitated in one day, with other versions ranging from ½ day to 2 days. It can be readily customized to address a client's business issues, concerns, and learning objectives.

**Learning Objectives**

After experiencing Vortex, participants are able to:

- Apply an understanding of organizations as dynamic, living systems (a systems perspective), and how to maximize flexibility, innovation, *and* performance. (Incorporates the 3DL Performance Model[sm])

- Reexamine their own leadership role and learn ways to enable leadership to emerge throughout a work group and/or an organization.

- Understand the significance of personal accountability in organizations and how to build an environment of collaborative individualism.

- Improve the ability to effectively work across individual, group, and/or organizational boundaries.

**Design / Process**

*During Vortex, subgroups ranging from three to eight participants assume one of seven different organizational roles in a startup division (called The Vortex Division) launched by a company (Star Enterprises) that is in a rapid decline.*

After an engaging and high-spirited "New Employee Orientation," participants run their division for several months of their startup journey. The work of this high-paced, dynamic organization—being bombarded by information from the global business environment—requires individual contribution and accountability, maximized collaboration, and leadership at all levels to achieve their mission.

During this engaging workshop, participants have several opportunities to exchange ideas and plans, give and received feedback, and provide coaching to each other in maximizing how to practically apply new strategies and approaches in their work.

Between each quarter, participants engage in facilitated discussions, performance analysis (The Vortex Scoreboard), as well as other activities that anchor learning. Real life application work is integrated throughout the simulation-based learning experience, guided by brief facilitator presentations, self-directed learning maps (incorporating the 3DL 9 Performance Model[sm]), and the helpful Participants' Workbook.

Specific desired outcomes are easily accommodated through customized use of the real life, application-focused group-learning activities built into the workshop. A structure is put in place that readily supports on-going learning groups to work together after the simulation experience through the availability of a follow up dialogue and information-sharing forum

| Focus | Analysis: How does this apply to Vortex? |
|---|---|
| Thiagi's Seven Laws | |
| *Reinforcement:* | Several opportunities exist throughout the design. These range from the focus of facilitated debriefs, small group discussion, and planning, Reflection-in-Action journaling, use of a Performance Scoreboard, and application-planning activities. |
| *Emotional Learning:* | The scenario, level of individual and group challenge, and highly interactive and intensity of design, Reflection-in-Action, and assessments are all intended to stimulate feelings, as well as thinking. Participants care about the outcome of their individual and performance. |
| *Active Learning:* | Design approach is primarily discovery-based and learner-centered. The overall design requires participants to take responsibility for their own learning and involvement. This tone is set right from the beginning. |
| *Practice and Feedback:* | Overall design addresses this need. The exercise is set up as a learning laboratory to practice new thinking and behaviors. Feedback comes from other participants, as well as the facilitator. |
| *Previous Experience:* | Participants draw heavily upon their own experience. Their approach, planning, and decisions require them to bring their knowledge and experiences into the process. These either help or hinder them as they are challenged during the exercise. |
| *Individual Differences:* | The design and facilitation is focused upon the importance of recognizing, enabling, and supporting thinking, behavior, learning, and cultural differences. This is made explicit during the Orientation segment of the simulation. |
| *Relevance:* | The scenario provides a universally accessible and relevant challenge. Participants are given frequent opportunity to discuss and write how their experience relates to their real lives. Learning Application Activities, interspersed throughout the design, provide a focus upon immediate real life relevance. |

| Intelligences | |
|---|---|
| Epstein (Two Minds) | The simulation design integrates a focus on the experiential and rational minds through its discovery orientation, multi-faceted group activities, and application discussion and exercises along with financial analysis, organized planning, and concept presentations. |
| Sternberg (Three Minds) | *Practical:* The task is tangible. The learning and discussion throughout the process is readily applied to real life situations. Several application and planning exercises are interspersed throughout the design. (Participants move in and out of simulation to focus and anchor learning) A Participant Workbook provides a resource for both in-simulation and post simulation. |

*Analytical:* The group's performance is measured at the end of each 30-minute quarter along several quantified scoreboard criteria, including Profitability, Capability and Agility. The use of an optional pre-workshop survey, along with measurement using an in-process assessment instrument, provides an analytical component to the process.

*Creative:* The open-ended design, along with the emergent quality of the participants' group experience, stimulates and reinforces risk-taking and innovation. The work itself of the organization promotes creative expression.

When incorporated, the participants create images of their imagined future in building visual Strategic Scenarios.

Gardner (Seven)

*Linguistic:* Extensive verbal and written, as well as reflection opportunities

*Logical-Mathematical:* The Vortex Scoreboard, along with quantitative analysis

*Kinesthetic:* The hands-on, highly interactive style of the design is supplemented by real work that involves physical manipulation of paper and other materials. The design also includes a great deal of movement around the room.

*Spatial:* A strength of the simulation is its emphasis, through participant experience, upon shifting perspective. This creates opportunities to begin exercising the minds ability to perceive and think in multiple dimensions. We use the metaphors sea level, above the trees, and bird's-eye view for easy reference and as a common language around strategic/systems thinking.

*Musical:* The pacing and rhythm of the simulation forms a repetitive pattern. In addition, a variety of music is incorporated throughout the workshop.

*Interpersonal:* The design involves extensive group, small group, and individual interaction, both formal (seven pre-determined functional groups, mixed group application exercises, small group discussion, and report outs, etc.) and informal manner (self-organizing groupings and participant-directed interactions).

*Intrapersonal:* Several opportunities for individual reflection, journal writing, and dialogue.

Goleman (Emotional)

See previous descriptions for examples of how emotional intelligence is incorporated within the simulation design.

A Social Act

The learning that occurs within Vortex is highly dependent upon the complex interpersonal interactions that take place. This provides the platform for the conceptual and practical exploration.

Blended Options

As a simulation engine, Vortex has been designed into a Virtual Team Effectiveness workshop in both a face-to-face and distance format. Each design incorporates several technologies, including phone and an Internet enabled communications and decision-making platform.

## Suggested Readings

Handy, C. *The Age of Unreason.* Cambridge, MA: Harvard Business School Press, 1990.

Noble, Stu and Brent Snow. *Using Simulations to Accelerate Organizational Learning and Change.* OD Practitioner, 1997.

Vaill, P. B. *Managing as a Performing Art: New Ideas for a World of Chaotic Change.* Jossey-Bass: San Francisco, 1989.

# CHAPTER 16

---

# MANAGE YOUR WORK AND VALUES

## Go Beyond Replacing Executives and Manage Your Work and Values

*William Rothwell*

## INTRODUCTION

I have spent growing amounts of time fielding client requests to launch programs that allow for qualified replacements of executives. And the replacement issue has emerged as a burn issue at exactly the same time that many corporations have been downsizing due to a business slowdown. There is reason for that concern. Corporate leaders are testing their bench strength because of the risks posed by threatened terrorist actions, inevitable demographic change, increasing cynicism about organizations, and restricted immigration levels. And, of course, that bench strength has often been found wanting.

This chapter is meant to encourage you to reflect critically about the role of executive replacement. The chapter explains why succession management has garnered increased global attention and is likely to continue to do so for some time. Secondly, it defines succession management and summarizes how it is usually carried out. Thirdly, the chapter is meant to challenge you to think beyond succession management to how work can be accomplished. Lastly, I suggest that values modeling is likely to become a driver, along with competency modeling, for future succession and work management efforts.

## THE CALL TO ACTION

Four major reasons seem to account for the recent, and growing, interest in succession management. Reviewing those reasons is worthwhile.

## Reason 1: Terrorism and the Aftereffects

The fallout of September 11, 2001, has been widely felt in government and business. When the World Trade Center collapsed, 172 corporate vice presidents lost their lives. Decision makers became more keenly aware, perhaps more so than at any time since the 1996 airplane crash of U.S. Secretary of Commerce Ron Brown and the executives of 32 large companies, that key people can be lost without warning. Heightened concern about the possible loss of executive lives has prompted renewed interest in succession management as part of an organization's total risk-management strategy.

## Reason 2: Demographic Changes

Almost everyone is aware that the U.S. population is aging. This demographic change is a major reason for growing interest in succession management. Organizational leaders in business, government, and nonprofit organizations are scrambling to find qualified replacements. That is made more difficult because years of corporate downsizing have depleted the ranks of experienced managers.[1]

The National Council on Aging summarizes what is happening to the U.S. workforce as follows:

> The population aged 65 and older is projected to double over the next three decades from 35.3 million to nearly 70million. In 2030, people 65-plus are expected to make up 20 percent of the population. The Census Bureau projects the 65-plus population to be 39.7 million in 2010, 53.7 million in 2020, and 70.3 million in 2030.
>
> The population aged 85 and older is the fastest growing segment of the older population. In 2000, it was estimated that persons 85-plus made up 2 percent of the population, and by 2050, the percentage of this age group is projected to grow to be 5 percent of the population. The 4 million 85-plus population in 2000 will grow to 19 million in 2050.[2]

As the U.S. population ages, there will be an increasing need to replace existing workers. By one estimate, about one-fifth of the largest U.S. companies are already beginning to lose up to 40 percent of their senior executives.[3]

Perhaps not so well known is that the aging crisis is actually a global issue. The G7 nations—the leading industrial nations that include Canada, France, Germany, Italy, Japan, the United Kingdom, and the United States—are simultaneously facing this crisis. These nations emerged from World War II at about the same time,

---

[1]Geber, B. "Who Will Replace Those Vanishing Execs?" *Training* 37, no. 7 (2000): 48–β53.

[2]"Facts About Older Americans," http://206.112.84.147/content.cfm?sectionID=106. Accessed April 7, 2003.

[3]Caudron, S. "The Looming Leadership Crisis," *Workforce* 78, no. 10 (1999): 72–79.

and they all experienced a post-World War II baby boom. The implications are profound. For instance, consider the following statement released by the Center for Strategic and International Studies:

> As a result of aging and depopulation in the world's most productive regions, economies that today account for two-thirds of global output face decades of slowing growth amid rising old-age dependency.
>
> With the retirement of the post-World War II baby boom generation later this decade, many developed nations will see an unprecedented decline in their working age populations. Between 2000 and 2050 the working age populations aged 25 to 64 of Europe and Japan will decline by 28 and 34 percent, respectively. If compensating gains in productivity fail to materialize, these countries will spend much of the time after 2010 in recession.[4]

Nor are the G-7 nations alone. After year 2020, an aging crisis will also affect nations of the Far East, Southeast Asia, and Latin America:

> East Asia and Latin America also will see significant increases in their over-65 populations after 2020. By 2030, China and Korea will have older population age structures than the United States.[5]

According to a 1997 survey of 773 CEOs in 23 countries conducted by Watson Wyatt Worldwide, more than 40 percent of responding CEOs around the world reported that their companies are now accounting for the aging workforce in their long-term business plans.[6]

## Reason 3: The Crisis in Confidence About Business Leadership

Scandals are taking their toll on public confidence. Political scandals have long been the norm since Watergate and later politically motivated efforts to impugn the integrity of leaders.

But the most recent scandals that have rocked business, government, the church, and the media have eroded public confidence in all institutions and, more importantly, in leaders generally. A 2002 survey conducted by the Conference

---

[4]The Center for Strategic and International Studies, "A Global Aging Initiative." Retrieved from the CSIS Web site: http://www.csis.org/gai/index.htm. Accessed April 7, 2003.

[5]The Center for Strategic and International Studies, "A Global Aging Initiative." Retrieved from the CSIS Web site: http://www.csis.org/gai/index.htm. Accessed April 7, 2003.

[6]"Aging Workforce Emerges as Concern for Employers Worldwide," *Relocation Journal & Real Estate News* 12, no. 4 (April 1998). Retrieved from the *Relocation Journal & Real Estate News* Web site: http://www.relojournal.com/apr98/aging.htm. Accessed April 7, 2003.

Board predicted between 12 and 20 more scandals following the announcement of the Enron debacle.[7] Of particular interest in the same survey was this: "When asked what happens to great performers who don't live up to their organization's ethics values, 23 percent [of the surveyed corporate ethics officers] said 'we tolerate them.' Nearly 30 percent responded: 'we coach them.' Eighteen percent said: 'we fire them.' And 8 percent said: 'we promote them.'"[8] In short, unethical behavior is not consistently managed.

Phil Clements, a managing director of Towry Law Invest, was quoted as saying that the WorldCom affair "has damaged investor psychology. Normally at this point in the cycle you would expect investors to buy in expectation of an earnings recovery." Clements added, "This time no one believes earnings. Corporate America has been lying for years."[9] A June 2002 survey, conducted by NBC News and the *Wall Street Journal* reported that 6 in 10 Americans no longer trust corporations.[10]

## Reason 4: Tightened Immigration

Relying on immigrant talent has been the traditional response by U.S.-based corporations when faced with labor shortages. But this time that strategy may not be as workable as it has been in the past. As a direct consequence of September 11, 2001, and its after effects, immigration in the U.S. has been tightening up. "Heightened feelings of uncertainty and threat as a result of the September 11th terrorist attacks might cause North Americans to develop unfavorable attitudes towards immigration, according to an expert at The University of Western Ontario."[11] Drawing on experienced executive talent from abroad is not likely to be the effective strategy that it could have been just a few years ago. That is especially true because the most likely source of such talent—other industrialized nations—will be experiencing the same problems at about the same time.

---

[7]The Conference Board. "Corporate Ethics Officers Predict More Scandals," Retrieved on June 17, 2000, from The Conference Board Web site: http://www.conference-board.org/search/dpress.cfm?pressid=4713.

[8]The Conference Board. "Corporate Ethics Officers Predict More Scandals," Retrieved on June 17, 2000, from The Conference Board Web site: http://www.conference-board.org/search/dpress.cfm?pressid=4713.

[9]Scott, Maria, and Jill Insley, "Corporate America Has Been Lying for Years," *The Observer,* June 30, 2002. Retrieved in 2002 on *The Guardian Unlimited* Web site: http://www.guardian.co.uk/worldcom/story/0,12167,746392,00.html.

[10]Steven Thomma, "Polls Show Americans Losing Trust in Nation's Institutions," (June 2002). Retrieved in 2002 from SmartPros Web site: http://finance.pro2net.com/x34490.xml.

[11]"Terrorism May Have a Negative Impact on Immigration Attitudes," *Media Newsroom,* (November 26, 2001). Retrieved from the *Media Newsroom* of the University of Western Ontario Web site: http://comms.uwo.ca/media/archives/releases/2001/sept_dec/nov26.htm. Accessed April 7, 2003.

## Defining Succession Management

Succession management is a means by which to build internal bench strength systematically. But why is it requested? What is it? How is it carried out? What are some traditional and emerging problems with it? Why is succession management not sufficient to meet organizational talent needs?

### Why Succession Management Is Requested

When confronted with pending vacancies—such as a wave of expected retirements—many managers think of only two possible ways to solve the problem. One way is to step up external recruitment, including executive searches. The second is to build internal bench strength through a succession management effort.

### Succession Management Defined

*Succession management* "assures that key people are not just identified but also developed to move into future leadership roles."[12] Succession management is now the preferred term for such efforts in the private sector,[13] just as *workforce planning* is the preferred term for such programs in the public sector. Terms such as *replacement planning* and *succession planning* have fallen into disfavor. One reason is that they are associated with other, sometimes ineffective, planning efforts. Another reason is that developing people for the future should be a continuing effort that is built into daily decision making, since people develop through on-the-job experience. Succession management thus recognizes that talent is cultivated through ongoing efforts and should not be regarded as a separate, isolated activity.

### How Succession Management Is Carried Out

Most authorities would agree that succession management includes at least four key activities: "(1) building a competency model; (2) evaluating the team; (3) discovering hidden potential; and (4) fast-tracking candidates."[14]

The *STAR model* that I first presented has been widely accepted as a way to conceptualize the succession management process.[15] That model requires decision makers to: (1) commit to making the effort to plan for succession; (2) identify how work is presently performed; (3) examine current performance levels using an effective performance management system; (4) plan for how future work will be car-

---

[12]Byham, W., "Grooming Next-Millennium Leaders," *HRMagazine* 44 no. 2 (1999): 46–50.

[13]Leibman, M., R. Bruer, and B. Maki, "Succession Management: The Next Generation of Succession Planning," *Human Resource Planning* 19, no. 3 (1996): 16–29.

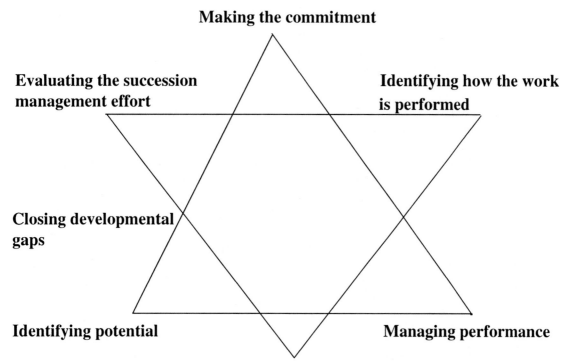

**The Star Model**

*Source: Adapted from William J. Rothwell, Effective Succession Planning: Ensuring Leadership Continuity and Building Talent from Within. 2nd ed. (New York: Amacom, 2000).*

ried out; (5) identify potential; (6) close developmental gaps; and (7) evaluate the succession management effort continuously.

Each step is logically related to the others. *Making the commitment* means that senior executives are personally committed, willing to devote time to the effort, make the business case, and clearly establish the goals for the succession management effort. *Identifying how the work is performed* means identifying the competencies of exemplary (best-in-class) performers.[16] *Managing performance* means measuring individual achievement. *Planning for how future work will be performed* means identifying the competencies essential to achieving the organization's strategic objectives.

---

[14]Byham, W., "Grooming Next-Millennium Leaders," *HRMagazine* 44 no. 2 (1999): 46–50.
[15]Rothwell, W. *Effective Succession Planning: Ensuring Leadership Continuity and Building Talent from Within.* 2nd ed. New York: Amacom, 2000

*Identifying potential* means assessing individuals against future work requirements. *Closing developmental gaps* means developing individuals to bring their abilities in line with the present and future competency models. *Evaluating the succession management effort* means determining how well the effort is working.

## Traditional Problems with Succession Management

There are many problems with traditional succession management efforts. Implementing each step of the STAR model, I have found, is prone to common problems.

Perhaps the most common problem is a failure of leadership at the top. That affects the first step of the STAR model. I have learned that, until the CEO (in the private sector) or the senior career officials of an agency (in the public sector) are willing to own the effort, it is most likely doomed to failure. A typical misstep is to define succession as an "HR effort." Thoughtlessly, handing it over to the HR Department is a big mistake. While HR does have an important role to play, HR professionals cannot "run the show" by themselves alone.

Another problem is a total lack of understanding about what competency models are and why they are used. That affects the second step of the STAR model. Identifying competencies is hard work and takes time. Too many senior executives, however, would like to rush the effort. Their sense of urgency is misplaced. One consequence is that it leads to many bad competency modeling efforts. A second consequence is that too few organizations derive the full benefits of discovering what distinguishes exemplary (best-in-class) performers from fully successful ("average") performers. Looking for the "quick and dirty" solution is all too common.

It is also common for organizations to experience difficulty with measuring current performance. (In the memorable words of a client who shall remain nameless, "our performance management system here is broken—and will never be fixed.") That affects the third step of the STAR model. My experience in private and public sector organizations has been that many decision makers really have no idea who their exemplary performers are for the simple reason that their performance management systems do not reveal, in objective ways based on measures of output or results, who is performing the best. Instead, the performance management system is sometimes force-fit for compensation reasons. (At one company, which shall remain nameless, the leaders admitted that they force-fit performance appraisal ratings to hold down compensation costs.)

---

[16]Rothwell, W., and J. Lindholm, "Competency Identification, Modeling, and Assessment in the USA," *International Journal of Training and Development* 3, no. 2 (1999): 90–105; Dubois, D., and W. Rothwell, *The Competency Toolkit*, Amherst, MA: HRD Press, 2000.

Senior leaders may have some sense of who are the best performers near the top of the organizational hierarchy. But the deeper down they go, the less aware they are of the exemplary performers. Too often, I have found, performers are left guessing about what goals they are expected to achieve or how their results will be measured. It is a truism that people should not be named as successors if they are failing in their current jobs. But, if there is no way to tell how well anyone is performing, then the question is moot.

Discovering the competencies needed for the future and identifying future potential are also prone to problems. (These are, of course, the fourth and fifth steps of the STAR model.) Few organizations have built a future competency model for each department or job category that aligns strategic objectives with necessary performance requirements. And identifying future potential, which often uses 360-degree assessment as a method, is not coupled with intensive coaching, mentoring, or counseling. The result is that these efforts are not nearly as effective as they could be in cultivating talent.

But by far the most common problem that afflicts succession efforts is a failure in closing developmental gaps. That is the Achilles heel of even the finest succession management programs. When the year is up, many people have not fully achieved their developmental objectives. The question is: *What are the consequences of that failed achievement for them and their managers?* If there are no consequences—such as reduced pay raises or bonuses—then the individuals targeted for development, and their managers, conclude that pursuing developmental objectives is a waste. Ensuring follow-up—and consequences for success or failure—are keys to overcoming the most common problem to afflict even the best-practice succession efforts.

Finally, few organizations have established effective, comprehensive evaluation systems for their succession efforts. While almost everyone talks about the need to demonstrate return-on-investment or other metrics for training,[17] few organizations have done much to evaluate succession management efforts. Too often the goals of the program in step one of the STAR model were left vague. One result is that nobody knows how to measure results if the goals guiding the program were never made timely, specific, and measurable.

Of course, other complaints have been raised about succession management efforts.[18] Some observers claim that they take too long, cost too much, and require too much time. Various ideas have been offered to overcome these objections and deal with these challenges.

---

[17]Phillips, Jack. *Return on Investment in Training and Performance Improvement Programs.* Burlington, MA: Butterworth-Heinemann, 1997.

[18]Byham, 2002; Sorcher, M., and J. Brant, "Are You Picking the Right Leaders?" *Harvard Business Review* 80, no. 2 (2002): 78–85.

## Why Succession Management Is Not Enough

Give a little boy a hammer, and he will find all manner of things that need hammering. This so-called *law of the hammer* is just as relevant to succession management as it has been shown to be relevant to training.[19] In training, much has been written about the need to distinguish between problems that lend themselves to training solutions and problems that require management action.[20]

My experience has been that HR practitioners often face a similar dilemma with succession management requests. The fact is that there are far more approaches to meeting the organization's long-term and short-term work management needs than simply implementing a succession management effort. Indeed, succession management should be regarded as only part of a comprehensive solution and not as a panacea.

## MANAGING WORK

Good consultants will help their clients see that a plea for a succession management effort is usually just symptomatic of a greater problem. The consultant's challenge is to help clients discover a range of approaches to meeting their talent needs and managing the work. While succession management is important—and has too often been neglected in the slimmed-down staffing of many corporations—it is not sufficient by itself to achieve the real goal of getting the work done. Finding ways to get the work done is the real goal.

## Managing How to Get the Work Done

Recall that I mentioned earlier that managers who face the need to fill a pending or existing vacancy will often think of only two ways to meet the need. One way is to hire from outside. The second way is to promote from within.

But the reality is that there are many more ways to get work accomplished than that. In addition to those two choices, ask managers to consider a broader list of alternatives. Use the worksheet appearing in Figure 16-2 to help them accomplish that. Suggest that using this checklist, or one like it, should become routine when filling vacancies.

---

[19]Geis, G. "Human Performance Technology: An Overview." In *Introduction to Human Performance Technology*, 1–20. Washington: National Society for Performance and Instruction, 1986.

[20]Mager, R., and P. Pipe. *Analyzing Performance Problems: Or You Really Oughta Wanna*. 3rd ed. Atlanta, GA: The Center for Effective Performance, 1997.

**Figure 2. A Worksheet for Considering Alternative Approaches to Getting Work Accomplished**

*Directions:* Use this Worksheet whenever a vacancy occurs in your organization. Ask the manager who is experiencing a vacancy what strategy would be most effective to meeting the need to get the work done. For each alternative listed in the left column below, ask the manager to consider how well that alternative might be successful in achieving the desired results. Indicate "yes," "no," or "maybe" for each alternative by checking a box in the center column. Make remarks in the right column about whether two or more alternatives might be combined to get the work done.

| *Approach to Getting the Work Accomplished* | *Is This an Approach That May Get the Work Accomplished?* | | | *Remarks: Can Two or More Alternatives Be Combined to Get the Work Done?* |
|---|---|---|---|---|
| Could the work be accomplished by: | Yes ✔ | No ✔ | Maybe ✔ | |
| 1  Recruiting externally? | ❑ | ❑ | ❑ | |
| 2  Using internal promotion or internal recruitment through a method such as job posting? | ❑ | ❑ | ❑ | |
| 3  Outsourcing all or part of the work or work process? | ❑ | ❑ | ❑ | |
| 4  Insourcing all or part of the work by giving it to other workers as part of their jobs or to other departments? | ❑ | ❑ | ❑ | |
| 5  Using temps or contingent workers? | ❑ | ❑ | ❑ | |
| 6  Using contractors? | ❑ | ❑ | ❑ | |
| 7  Using part-time workers? | ❑ | ❑ | ❑ | |
| 8  Using retirees of the organization or other organizations? | ❑ | ❑ | ❑ | |
| 9  Using telecommuters? | ❑ | ❑ | ❑ | |
| 10 Dividing the work up for teams? | ❑ | ❑ | ❑ | |
| 11 Having it done by task forces committees? | ❑ | ❑ | ❑ | |
| 12 Eliminating the work so that it does not have to be performed any more? | ❑ | ❑ | ❑ | |
| 13 Simplifying the work so that a replacement worker is not necessary? | ❑ | ❑ | ❑ | |
| 14 Automating the work? | ❑ | ❑ | ❑ | |
| 15 Making the work self-service so that customers have to absorb all or part of the work? | | | | |
| 16 Using another approach? (*Specify*:) | ❑ | ❑ | ❑ | |

As the checklist shows, getting work done can be accomplished in many ways. Of course, one way to meet that need is to recruit talent from outside the organization. A second way is to source talent by promoting from inside the organization. But beyond those two obvious approaches of satisfying the need, there are alternatives. Among them: outsourcing the work; insourcing the work; and using temps, contingent workers, part-time staff, consultants, retirees, telecommuters, teams, taskforces, committees or others. The need for successors may also be influenced by simplifying the work processes, automating the work, eliminating the work completely, or shifting some work to consumers or customers. The point is this: There are many ways by which to achieve the goal of getting the work done.

## Predictions

My prediction is that, as employers begin to experience the staffing crunch they will inevitably face as a result of pending retirements, they will find many ways to get the work done. Succession management will be just one option. For one thing, I expect that employers will become much more effective in inventorying their pool of retirees and finding ways to tap them. I also predict the creative use of flexplace workers, some from international settings, some who are flextime workers, and some who work unusual hours. Employers will also become more effective at inventorying the competencies of their existing workers so that they can be tapped in real time to address immediate challenges while also being developed for the future.[21]

## What These Alternatives Will Do and Will Not Do

Succession management builds the intellectual capital of the organization. I believe it is worth the investment. Alternatives to it do not always do that. But, on occasion, alternative methods do get results faster. And that is precisely my point.

## MANAGING VALUES AND ETHICS

In the wake of corporate scandals, managing values and ethics is growing increasingly important. Traditional approaches of establishing corporate value statements or codes of conduct must give way to those that are more effectively integrated with competency identification, modeling, and assessment efforts. Values and ethics are

---

[21]Rothwell, W. *The Action Learning Guidebook: A Real-Time Strategy for Problem-Solving, Training Design, and Employee Development.* San Francisco: Jossey-Bass/Pfeiffer, 1999.

growing more important because scandals like those associated with Enron and Arthur Andersen have eroded public confidence in business and could create a tougher regulatory climate in which it is more difficult to do business.

## How Organizations Establish Corporate Value Statements and Code of Conduct Statements

Many organizations establish corporate value or code of conduct statements in executive or board of director meetings. Hicks indicated that a corporate code usually addresses: "an overall statement of the company's objectives, a mission statement or a summary of the company's basic philosophy; responsibilities to shareholders and the financial community generally; relations with customers and consumers; relations with suppliers; employment practices; personal conduct, which may include references to bribery, inducements, commissions, gifts, and handling conflicts of interest; responsibilities to the community; and monitoring of compliance with the code and the means to be used in ensuring compliance."[22] To develop a code, Hicks suggested that the board of directors should take the lead and should authorize an ethics audit, draft a code, communicate the code, and administer, enforce, and review the code.

Unfortunately, such codes that are developed from the top-down often do not address the daily challenges encountered by the people who do the work. More than one observer has complained that what exists today in many organizations are not statements of corporate values but of executive values[23]—and that they are notoriously shallow and useless.

## How to Improve, and Integrate, Values and Ethics Modeling with Succession Management

In the future, more attention should be paid to developing value and code of conduct statements based on actual research about the ethical dilemmas faced by those who perform the work. That can be done, for instance, by using critical incident surveys or reengineering competency modeling approaches that use interviews to isolate exemplary ways of handling ethical challenges. Prospective leaders can then be assessed, and developed, in line with the actual ethical challenges as well as the performance challenges they face in their corporate cultures.

---

[22]Hicks, B. "Developing a Code for Corporate Ethics," *Australian CPA* 69, no. 9 (1999): 22–23.
[23]French, S. "CEO Values Replace Corporate Values," *Canadian HR Reporter* 15, no. 7 (2002): 5; Urquhart, J. "Creating Meaningful Corporate Philosophy," *Journal of Property Management* 67, no. 3 (2002): 68.

## *Predictions*

I predict that value modeling will become more rigorous. Drawing on methodologies similar to those already used in competency modeling, such value-modeling efforts will be necessitated by the increasing pressure that leaders are likely to feel in the future to serve as role models who adhere to high moral and ethical standards. Individuals will be rated on their adherence to such standards. When found wanting, they may be given developmental assignments to help them build their ethical awareness in the same way they are now given developmental assignments to build their capacity to perform.

## CONCLUSION

As a consultant, I have found growing interest in succession management. Interest goes beyond simple executive replacement to include concerns about developing people at all levels over the long term. However, organizations are not deriving maximum benefit from competency models because their leaders have a misplaced sense of urgency. They prefer quick-and-dirty card sorts or short-term focus group experiences for competency identification to the hard work involved in discovering the differences between exemplary and fully successful performers. And yet that is precisely where the real benefits can be derived, since having a blueprint is essential to building leaders of the future.

In the future, too, I believe that leaders will be forced to go beyond results-oriented competency modeling to include a more rigorous approach to modeling values and ethical issues. That is driven not so much by a back-to-basics mentality as it a more holistic view of what is involved to achieve good performance. Results cannot be achieved at a sacrifice of values, principles, morals, rules, laws, regulations, or company policies. In short, the order of the day is to get outstanding results while still playing by the rules.

What does all this mean to me? It means, I think, that consultants must do a better job of mounting convincing arguments to show the benefits to be derived from doing more rigorous research around competencies as blueprints for performance. It also means taking a broader perspective of what clients need, since pleas for succession programs are sometimes merely disguised pleas for help in figuring out how to get the work done.

# PART III

## SUSTAINING CULTURAL CHANGE AND LONG-TERM RESULTS

# CHAPTER 17

# DEVELOP LEADERS WHO BUILD MARKET VALUE—THE RIGHT RESULTS THE RIGHT WAY

*David Ulrich and Norm Smallwood*

## INTRODUCTION

The purpose of leadership development is to build leaders who know how to increase organization capability that delivers current and future earnings consistent with firm values. In this chapter we argue that it is the job of leaders at all levels to create sustainable shareholder value and to be able to communicate this value to all interested parties, namely, the shareholders, the investment community, the regulators, the customers, and the employees of the organization. Accomplishing this purpose requires an integration of ideas from a number of different disciplines. It involves an understanding of the new role that intangibles play in company valuations and new shifts in thinking in organizational theory. It invites line leaders as well as those in Human Resources, Accounting, Finance, and IT to consider new dimensions to their roles. Ultimately it challenges the reader to become a new breed of leader who can become an architect to build intangible value for his company. After reading this chapter, the reader will have a practical approach for designing a high-impact leadership development process that builds leaders who increase organization capability to deliver results.

## HOW LEADERS LOST MARKET CREDIBILITY

It's easy to think that we used to have better, trustworthier leaders. Since the early 1990s till late in 2001, a bull market raged throughout the global economy. Large and small investors were making good money on their equity investments in publicly traded companies and many senior business leaders were making a lot of money. We admired our business leaders because they were responsible for our swelling retirement accounts. We believed there was a link between executive pay and performance. Many executives attained celebrity status. These executives were seen as business geniuses that deserved their high pay and perks due to their performance. Ten years ago, in one of the first big windfalls, Roberto C. Goizueta, the chief executive of Coca-Cola received $80 million in pay and prepared to explain it at the annual meeting. Shareholders did not need convincing. During his speech, he was applauded four times, and no one criticized his pay since it was tied to their personal stock value as well.

By late 2001 a series of bad things began to happen that has ultimately reserved at minimum and reversed in many cases faith in business leaders. The technology dot-com bubble burst and a mild recession followed. Terrorists attacked the World Trade Center and the Pentagon. The situation worsened in the Middle East. The mild recession turned worse and so did other business news. We found out that Enron and Arthur Andersen had colluded to "cook the books," and falsifying earnings, revenues, and expenses. The reason for the cheating? We would assume cheating was for immediate personal gain, but in fact some of the cheating was to increase the perception of business performance. Over time, increased business performance would lead to higher individual executive pay and stock options. Enron turned out to be the tip of the iceberg. WorldCom, Tyco International, Rite Aid, ImClone Systems, and others turned out to be led by greedy executives who also cheated and cooked their books.

Clearly, leaders in these companies have destroyed billions of dollars of market value for their own companies and have eroded the public's perception of the entire market. The public mood is currently one of confusion and distrust about the stock market because of the dishonest actions of a few. In a short period of time, we have witnessed the double-edged sword of how business leaders impact market value. Leaders can infuse the markets with optimism, most of them honestly, and increase the market value of their businesses. Leaders can also destroy market value through deceit and mistrust.

We believe that there has been a change in the components of market valuation that have become magnified by these recent events. The traditional viewpoint is that when a firm earns more money its value goes up. The more it earns, the more investors value it. In recent years, however, the logic has begun to twist. Firms in the same industry and with similar earnings may have vastly different market values. Increasingly, the intangible value of a company reflects its inflated or deflated stock price.

## THE ARCHITECT OF INTANGIBLES—WHERE LEADERS SHOULD START

One might conclude from recent events that intangible value is a function of the economic cycle. We disagree. When the dot-com bubble burst, the recession occurred and stories of dishonesty grew, some firm's market value fell more than others. We believe that firms that survived the market credibility crisis did so because their leaders made the intangibles tangible. These leaders met financial goals, had a strategy for growth, created core competencies aligned with strategy, and ensured organization capabilities. Intangibles often exist within an industry, not across industries, so the patterns of P/E (price to earnings) ratios of firms within an industry offer evidence of leadership intangibles in both up and down markets.

The concept of intangibles has a history outside business. Successful sports teams are often characterized by intangibles: the drive among teammates, the quality of coaching, the ability to win, and the like. Leaders of sports franchises build intangible value by promising and then delivering on successful seasons. They invest in PR and often make key players larger-than-life modern day heroes and heroines. Then they sell memorabilia that further solidifies their fans' identification with their team. They work hard at selecting the best coaching and player talent possible and then invest even more in building a team culture for winning. Players and coaches are held accountable for performance. High performance results in bigger salaries and longer tenure. Poor performance leads to trades with other teams or getting cut.

In business settings, understanding and being able to leverage intangibles is of enormous interest to leaders. When intangibles are defined, leaders may make choices that affect not only what happens inside their firm, but also how investors value those decisions. Other work offers more precise financial definitions of intangibles. We define intangibles as either the positive or negative value of a company not accounted for by current earnings. Companies with high intangible value have higher price/earnings multiples than their competitors. They have earned the perception that they can be trusted to deliver on their promises about the future. Companies can also have negative intangibles when their market values decline with negative reputations.

The vast majority of the research about intangibles has been aimed at trying to measure them. Baruch Lev, a professor at New York University, is the foremost authority in this area. We highly recommend his books and articles. Our interest is elsewhere. We want to understand how leaders build intangible value for their firms. As a starting point, we propose Figure 17-1, The Architect for Intangibles.

This figure suggests four layers of intangibles in which leaders make choices that have impact. In our consulting work, we have witnessed leaders use the ideas with great impact. The CEO of a large insurance company explained his e-business growth strategy to investors using the framework. The next day analysts wrote up the presentation in the trade journals using phrases such as, "At last, XYZ Company is putting its money where its mouth is" and "XYZ has a significant insight into how to build these new distribution channels." The financial impact—$1.7 billion dollar increase in market value! Unfortunately, XYZ did not invest in building real capability and within a few months had lost the entire gain. Others have

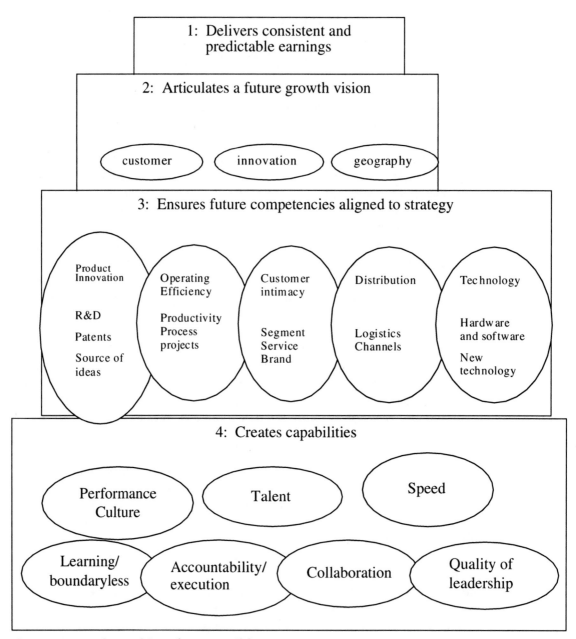

**Figure 17-1    The Architect for Intangibles**

told us that this framework helps them understand Jack Welch's behavior at General Electric. He became a master of building intangible value. His secret? The market trusted him to keep his promises. He told customers, investors, and employees exactly what he planned to do and then he worked very hard to ensure that real capability was put in place to deliver it. Earnings were delivered as promised. No excuses. GE leaders at every level have spent the last twenty years building strong capabilities for speed and accountability that outpaces competitors. Over time, GE leaders have earned a brand identity for developing leaders who deliver on promises. When Jeffrey Immeldt succeeded Welch and two senior GE leaders left for Home Depot and 3M last year, the stock of Home Depot and 3M increased at a much faster rate than the rest of the market due to raised expectations about future success.

Bob Hargadon lives in Paris and is a senior human resources executive with Boston Scientific. Bob is using the Architect for Intangibles to redefine the role of HR at his company. He has partnered with line executives to understand the firm's strategy. Based on this understanding, he has crowned HR responsible to deliver on the two organization capabilities most critical to implementation of the strategy. This includes coordinating with Finance, Accounting, and IT in a much closer way and deploying global "centers of excellence" led by HR. Within these centers of excellence HR professionals will provide education, coaching, tools, and consulting aimed at increasing impact and value.

With the Architecture for Intangibles, leaders can hype their company and get a temporary blip in value or they can use the Architect for Intangibles to get leaders at every level clear about how they must contribute to build a stronger organization that is differentiated from others in their industry. The hype will be short term and gains will be lost; the sustained intangibles come from leaders actively engaging in and changing the items in the Architecture for Intangibles.

The implications of the Architect for Intangibles are enormous for leadership development. An overall implication of increasing intangible value is that market value is measured at the corporate level where the company stock is traded while intangibles are developed and built by every team and individual throughout the company. This means that senior leaders must clearly articulate where the company is going and what it stands for and that other leaders at every level must do their part to fulfill that promise to employees, customers, and shareholders. Earnings must be delivered as promised. Financial and intellectual capital must be invested where it builds business competencies consistent with strategic direction. Organization capabilities of speed, talent, collaboration, shared mind-set, and accountability must be delivered not discussed. To do this requires building better individual leaders and also building a leadership system that ensures that all leaders understand their part in what value should be built, their role in delivering it, and a process for developing their capability to succeed. Building value is a job for everyone and success in that job benefits everyone.

## BUILDING A LEADERSHIP SYSTEM

In the two other books we have written together, *Results-Based Leadership* and *Why the Bottom Line ISN'T: How to Build Value Through People and Organization*[1] we describe the content for how leaders can deliver balanced, strategic results and increase market value. Rather than repeat this, we will describe how to set up a leadership development process that supports this content and impacts positive market value—a process that delivers the right results the right way.

Our approach to develop leaders has six components that are depicted in Figure 17-2. Each of these components is interdependent with the other components. We have numbered each of the components because there is a sequence to the data collection required for each component in order to optimize individual development and business impact.

## STEP 1. BUILD A CASE FOR CHANGE

Money to invest in leadership development too often comes from the "it's the right thing to do" fund. Building a case for leadership change is usually skimmed or even skipped altogether. When it is clear that leadership matters to the company's success, investment in leadership is sustained. A case for leadership creates a baseline for measurement and shows how better leaders relate to the company's future success. Stakeholders of the leadership development process must understand the value of their investment in order to continue investing when money gets tight. When the case for leadership is made, leaders willingly allocate time and resources to, improving the quality of leadership. Building a case for the importance of leadership comes by identifying the current state, desired state, and the value of bridging the gap between the current and desired states.

Ideas for conducting a case for change:

### Current State
1. What is our current market value?
2. What are our top five change initiatives?

---

[1]*Results-Based Leadership*, authored by the contributors to this chapter—David Ulrich and Norm Smallwood, published by Harvard Business School Press of Cambridge, MA, copyright 1999; *Why the Bottom Line ISN'T: How to Build Value Through People and Organization*, authored by the contributors to this chapter—David Ulrich and Norm Smallwood, is published by John Wiley & Sons of Hoboken, NJ, copyright 2003.

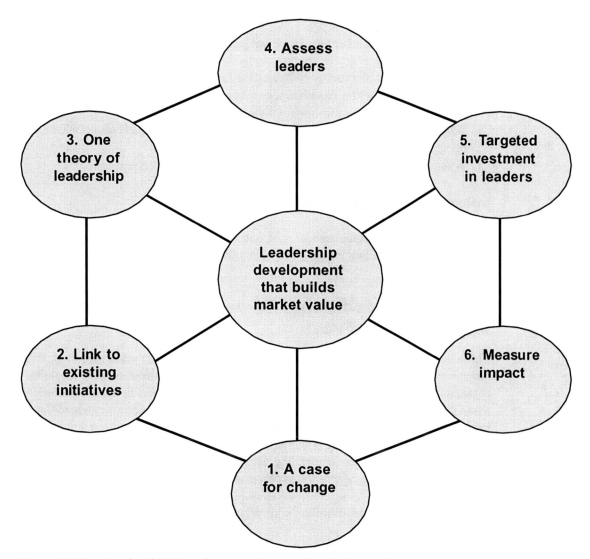

**Figure 17-2   Leadership Development Process for Business Impact**

3. Describe cases where we have not kept our promises to employees, customers, and investors and the impact.
4. Describe the current level of alignment at each leadership level: from the boardroom to the front line.
5. What are our most significant business challenges?

### Desired State

1. What would our market value be if we increased our price to earnings multiple by 10 percent?
2. What is the impact of successfully implementing our top five change initiatives?
3. What is the impact on customers, employees, and investors if we had a track record of keeping our promises with them?
4. What is the value of getting alignment at all leadership levels about what performance really matters?
5. What is the value of resolving each significant business challenge?

### Value of Bridging the Gap

For each delta between the current state and the desired state, take a shot at describing both the tangible and the intangible value of closing the gap.

## Step 2. Tie Leadership Development to Existing Business Initiatives

There is nothing wrong with leadership education for its own sake. However, this type of education does not have as much impact on the business as education that is tied to business needs. A first step towards greater impact is to have knowledge about the current, important initiatives that are critical to your company. Once these initiatives are identified, leadership development can be tied to these initiatives. For even greater impact, key initiatives should be tied to action learning projects formulated as part of the leadership development process. Skills, tools, and a shared language can be taught to leaders at every level for implementation of key initiatives.

For example, we are familiar with a large manufacturing company that has three major initiatives:

1. Grow revenue by $10B
2. Cut expenses by 10 percent
3. Achieve Six-Sigma quality standards

These initiatives should drive the selection of action learning projects in leadership development. They also suggest key business and organization capabilities that leaders must build in order to deliver on these expectations. Finally, these initiatives demand alignment around priorities and resource allocation for growth, cost reduction, and defect elimination.

# Step 3. Articulate One Theory of Leadership for Leaders at Every Level

A theory of leadership is simply a way to talk about leadership in general, and specific leadership outcomes and attributes. There are many theories of leadership to choose from: situational leadership, competency- and principle-based leadership, Great Man theory of leadership, Theory X and Theory Y, and so on. We advocate a theory we call "leadership brand." Leadership brand occurs when a sufficiently large number of leaders exhibit distinct leadership practices over time. As a result, the organization creates leaders who are branded—that is, distinct from leaders in other firms.

Leadership brand lies at the heart of a firm's identity. Imagine observing two leaders at any level doing much the same job at competing firms. How long before an investor, customer, or employee could distinguish one firm from another because of the leader being observed? Branded leadership communicates to all stakeholders both the means (how work is done) and ends (what the goals are) for any firm.

Conceptualizing a firm's brand to include the image of branded leadership helps us to extend the current thinking about what makes an effective leader. When we run leadership workshops, we often start by asking participants to fill in the open-ended statement: "In the future to be successful at this firm, a leader must . . . " The responses are consistent with current thinking about how to be better leaders: set a vision, have energy, energize others, mobilize commitment, manage teams, coach, have integrity, think globally, and so on. After we generate this list of what we call attributes of leadership, we ask, "Who is surprised by this list?" No one is. The list makes sense and can be turned into behaviors, which can then be assessed through 360-degree feedback and woven into development experiences. But then we ask, "What if we did this exercise in twenty companies?" or "Compare your list of attributes with the competency models of other companies? Would they differ?" And the answer we inevitably get is, "No, they are much the same."

Many of the current efforts to be or build better leaders have fallen prey to the trap of generic models of leadership. Even the rigorous competency models based on key informant methodologies with high reliability and validity tend to generate similar lists of behavior-based competencies that might be expected of leaders in any number of firms. These competency models fall short because they are not linked to customers, shareholders, and business results. They are often tied to past behaviors and not to future performance. They focus on what leaders are like rather than on what they accomplish.

For leadership to be a brand, leaders must exhibit more than generic competencies. Generic brands do not receive a premium price; they do not attract customers; they do not commit employees. Likewise, generic leaders who demonstrate universal competence cannot deliver the unique results they are expected to deliver. Turning generic into branded leadership is both simple and complex.

At a simple level, branded leadership requires a new definition of leadership: *attributes X (Multiplied by) results.*[2] Our redefinition of leadership as the outcome of both attributes and results explains some of the causes of ineffective leadership and the challenges faced by effective leaders. Leaders who either embody attributes or achieve results will not have sustained success.

Leaders who score high on the attribute (or character) side of this equation but low on results do not truly lead. These leaders do good works, relate well to others, and act with honor and integrity. However, even when people exhibit the behaviors most expected from leaders, if they fail to deliver desired results, they will not be seen as effective leaders. They are generic and not branded leaders, having mastered the language of leadership but not the essence.

Other leaders who score high on results but low on attributes also face enormous risks. They often take or receive credit for results they did not produce, so they have difficulty replicating or extending those results. They lack the leadership goodwill required to get results in the face of obstacles. They find the going tough when they try to focus attention on new initiatives or strategies. These leaders do not create long-term legacy because their results cannot be sustained by their behaviors.

Effective leaders need to have both attributes and results. All the integrity, character, and goodwill in the world will not cover a lack of results. But in delivering results, leaders must also do it in the right way. As evidenced with the lack of confidence in many business leaders, building character sustains results, particularly when the getting of results is difficult. So to leaders who get high scores on employee surveys or 360-degree feedback, we say, be wary. Leadership is more than a popularity contest. Without clear and visible results, leadership cannot endure.

Leaders who demonstrate attributes and deliver results become branded leaders. Branded leaders possess appropriate attributes. They have a point of view about the future of their business, build teams, manage change, and have personal integrity. But they are also able to turn attributes into specific results required for their business to succeed by providing a "so that . . . " explanation for each attribute they demonstrate. Focusing on results requires understanding the unique competitive requirements of a firm. Firms win with strategies that differentiate themselves to customers and the financial markets; results should reflect these differences. For example, leaders at Qantas have a vision *so that* traveler satisfaction will stay high enough to gain a sizable share of frequent travelers' dollars spent. Leaders at the

---

[2]Ibid, 1999. Results Based Leadership

Olympics have a vision *so that* they attract committed employees and volunteers who will manage the large masses of event attendees. Leaders at Disney have a vision *so that* guests will return home from the Disney theme park experience with positive memories and stories for their friends. Each "vision" becomes branded when it is coupled with a "so that" statement that makes it specific to the unique requirements of the business.

## Step 4. Assess Your Leaders Using Your Leadership Brand as the Goal

The use of 360-degree feedback instruments to assess leaders is a trend that we believe will, and should, continue. However, traditional 360-tools measure behaviors linked to a company-specific competency framework. As we have already pointed out, these are usually generic not unique leadership competencies. 360-degree feedback should be tied to a statement of the company's desired leadership brand.

Building a statement of desired leadership brand involves the articulation of five business issues. First, you need to be clear about your strategy. Strategic clarity exists when leaders, employees, and customers have a clear and shared sense of the how the firm allocates resources to win in the future.

Second, the strategy should lead to a shared mind-set. A shared mind-set represents the firm brand, or identity, to the best customers in the future. Crafting a shared mind-set comes when leaders think about what they want their organization to be known for in the future by their best customers. Building unity of mind-set helps shape a unique culture inside the organization and a firm brand outside the organization.

Third, articulate desired leadership attributes. Others have studied the attributes and behaviors of leaders extensively. For example, in recent work, James Kouzes and Barry Posner have synthesized over twenty years of research around the world with thousands of leaders. They find that over time, admired leaders seem to have four enduring characteristics: honest, forward-looking, competent, and inspiring. Other characteristics are important, but they are not as consistent over time: intelligent, fair-minded, broad minded, supportive, straightforward, dependable, cooperative, determined, imaginative, ambitious, courageous, caring, mature, loyal, self-controlled, and independent.[3] Similar lists have shown up in other studies. One of the more interesting approaches to attributes comes from research by Jack Zenger and Joe Folkman.

---

[3]Kouzes, James, and Barry Posner. *The Leadership Challenge*. 3rd ed. San Francisco: Jossey-Bass, 2002.

They find that leaders judged as more successful in 360-degree instruments focus on their strengths to pull them to success more than on their weaknesses. In focusing on strengths, Zenger and Folkman describe "competency companions," areas where strength in any single competence may not ensure high performance, but the combination of competencies yields multiplicative effects.[4] These competency companions are not intuitive. For example, if a leader scores low in technical skills, one of the ways to improve this perception is to increase the perception of interpersonal skills.

Attribute models should be tied to the future, not the past; linked to strategic goals, not be generic; and focused on behaviors, not ideals. In addition, attribute models should be integrating mechanisms for HR practices. With a clear leadership model, leaders can be hired, promoted, trained, developed, appraised, and compensated against the criteria implied in the model. Attribute models are more likely to be used by leaders who participate in creating them than by those who have the attribute model created for them by a human resource team or outside consulting firm.

Most firms we know have explicit or implicit leadership competency models. In speeches, 360-degree feedback instruments, and performance appraisals, the attributes become a part of a firm's theory of leadership. But, as we noted earlier, attributes are only half of a leadership brand statement. Too often, they are generic, not tied to the business strategy or results. One test of a leadership brand is the extent to which the statement that completes the phrase "What makes an effective leader here is . . . " is not a generic list of ideal behaviors but a clear statement of how leaders can and will help accomplish the strategy. By reading the statements about expected leadership, employees, customers, and investors should be able to know the firm's strategy. Too often leadership statements are too generic and fail to distinguish one firm's strategy from another. By reading the leadership brand, anyone should be able to discern the strategy of the organization in which the leader works.

Fourth, define desired results. Branded leaders possess attributes and produce results. While most efforts to be better leaders focus on the attributes of leadership, leaders also need to turn their attributes into sustainable results. But because results themselves can be difficult to see on a day-to-day basis, it helps to look for their vital signs, much as a doctor uses selected tests to assess human health. Clinical experience has shown the medical profession that among the hundreds of available tests, some work best as leading indicators of overall health—pulse rate, blood pressure, blood composition, EKG results, and so on. Likewise, vital signs of leadership results can be specified. Based on recent theory and research on balanced scorecards and our own hands-on experience, we suggest four domains for leadership vital signs that should be defined, assessed, and manifested for every results-

---

[4]Zenger, Jack, and Joe Folkman. *The Extraordinary Leader*. New York: McGraw-Hill, 2002.

based leader: employee, organization, customer, and investor. Leaders generate employee results when they identify specific ways to increase both employee competence and commitment. They achieve organizational results by assessing the capabilities needed to win and then creating those capabilities, thereby ensuring that the organization has a unique identity. Leaders generate customer results when they identify target customers, customize their services for these customers, and integrate customers into HR practices such as staffing and training. Finally, they produce investor results by managing their balance sheet through profitable growth, reduced cost, and increasing shareholder value through management equity. Branded leaders master and can be measured by the vital signs in each result area.

Fifth, link results and attributes into a leadership brand statement. Any leader trying to be more effective must have both the right attributes and the ability to get results. Sometimes leaders start with attributes that then must be turned into results; at other times, leaders start with results that must be accomplished through attributes. By linking attributes and results, leaders create a brand that distinguishes them from leaders in other firms. Part of the brand comes because leaders can choose from the potential result vital signs in each of the four areas and pick those that are most aligned with the goals of their business. With results clearly defined, leaders can then ensure a virtuous cycle that connects attributes and results by starting either with attributes or results but then ensuring the connection of the two.

When individual leaders are assessed against their company's leadership brand, they get specific development feedback that points them to where they should build on their strengths in areas that have been pre-defined as having the most value. Further, it is straightforward to aggregate this feedback data to find out areas of strengths as well as areas needing improvement for all leaders.

A complementary leadership assessment approach is what Dave Hatch, former vice president of executive development at Pepsi and at IBM calls "experience-based assessment." Experience-based assessment methodology identifies existing skills and experiences that a leader has developed and matches these experiences against the experiences, skills, and capabilities required for future leadership roles. These experiences can be overlaid against critical leadership transitions to identify potential gaps and missing experiences. These transitions include individual contributor to new supervisor, supervisor to functional manager, functional manager to general manager, and general manager to officer/multiple businesses.

## Step 5. Targeted Investment in Leaders

Step five is where most leadership development efforts start. With the information and buy-in from the previous four steps, this step is much more likely to have a significant impact on business results. There are at least four areas to target for investment:

1. Leadership development
2. Leadership selection
3. Performance management
4. Retention of highest performers

Leadership development efforts build a shared language and common tools accessible to leaders at every level. A common mistake is to provide different language and tools to different leadership audiences. If leadership actions are to be coordinated and have impact on key initiatives, then it is critical that leaders can talk to each other and apply a common set of tools.

Job assignments can be a critical source of leadership development. Leaders can be systematically rotated through jobs that might give them experience in different business settings. Jobs can be classified along a series of dimensions. in which emerging leaders can be given job assignments that familiarize them with diverse work settings.Such job assignments include: growth versus turnaround, line versus staff, small versus large, capital intensive versus service oriented, consumer focus versus business-to-business focus, start-up versus mature business, and so on.

Effective leadership selection efforts include the integration of desired attributes and firm values into the selection process. It is much easier to select leaders with the predisposition to certain attributes than it is to develop them. Nordstrom selects leaders and staff based on their predisposition towards a service orientation. Southwest Airlines selects leaders who have a "fun DNA" and who find ways to celebrate employee success.

Performance Management practices must appraise and reward leaders for acting consistently with leadership brand intentions and for implementing the right results in the right way. Finally, it's critical to retain leaders who embody the leadership brand. This means there must be assessment tools that allow leaders to identify and keep the right talent.

## Step 6. Measure Impact of Investment in Leadership Development

There has been much progress in measuring the impact of investments in training and development over the last few years. Some researchers describe five levels of measurement to assess the impact of education:

1. Reaction and planned action—Measure the extent to which participants enjoyed the experience.
2. Learning—Measure the extent to which a skill or competency was improved.

3. Application—Measure the extent to which learning was applied to the participant's actual job.
4. Business impact—Measure impact of learning through impact on the business with tools like the Balance Scorecard or certain performance measures or quality improvements.
5. Return on Investment (ROI)—Measure a return on the investment of leadership development dollars spent such as cost reductions or revenue improvements.

There is also a sixth level that can be measured:

6. Impact on Market Value—Measure the extent to which leadership development activities can be tied to building the capabilities that will deliver future results and increase investor confidence.
   In summary, the six components ensure that the leadership development process is systemic, sequenced, and integrated. Components are integrated vertically to the strategy and business needs of the firm as well as horizontally to one another. The nature of a creative development process is that there will be iterations across the components and within specific components. The framework of these six components reduces complexity and allows for clearer communication about what is going on and why with key stakeholders.

# CONCLUSION

Leadership is one of the most visible intangibles. Investors, customers, and employees can identify and observe leaders and ascertain if they add value or not. Leaders wanting to create leadership depth must start with themselves. They must be the kind of leader that they want others to become. Then they must give emerging leaders the opportunity to produce leadership intangibles. When leadership intangibles exist, a leadership brand pervades all levels of the organization. To create a leadership brand, leaders need to clearly articulate strategy, translate the strategy into a shared mind-set, articulate desired leadership attributes, define desired leadership results, and link the results and attributes in a leadership brand statement. With a brand statement, leaders can assess and invest in future leaders.
   Leaders who generate intangible value:

- Take personal responsibility for being effective leaders. They are willing to model the leadership that they expect others to follow.
- Craft a leadership brand that defines the attributes and results expected of a successful leader.

- Create formal and informal mechanisms to assess leaders against the brand.
- Find ways to invest in emerging leaders through training, development, and support systems.
- Ensure that the leadership brand permeates all levels of the organization.
- Encourage leaders who model the brand to be public and visible to investors, customers, and employees.

When leaders build leadership brand the right way, they increase trust in the business. Investors, employees, and customers believe that the company can and will deliver what it promises, when it promises to do it. When this happens over time, market value is positively impacted. When market value is positively impacted, investors are wealthier, employees are more committed with secure retirements, and customers prefer to do business with companies that have greater capabilities to give them what they want.

Ultimately this is the test of whether we have developed better, trustworthier leaders.

# CHAPTER 18

# PUT ACTIONABLE RESULTS INTO LEADERSHIP DEVELOPMENT

*Richard Lynch and Jim Dowling*

## INTRODUCTION

In this chapter, we suggest blending three essential organizational capabilities to maximize the impact of leaders: individual learning, organization learning, and delivering desired results. To do so, Action Learning is taken to the organization level and enabled through information technology. We provide an operational model and an array of technology tools that encourage and leverage learning at every level. This chapter will provide leaders with a better understanding of the direct connection between leadership development and the actions that result in desirable business outcomes.

## ACTION LEARNING DEFINED

Learning through action predates medieval times. Maturing through the novice, apprentice, journeyman, and master, arises a model of learning. Scientist turned educator Reg Revans introduced the term Action Leaning to business in England about 50 years ago. However his success in the UK failed to catch on quickly, and when his book, *Action Learning*, was published he ended up buying most of the copies.[1]

Revans observed educated bright people at work and saw that they learned by working in a very collaborative manner. He saw how those people applied and discussed the knowledge that they had acquired through formal education and individual leaning while they worked. The way that they worked, solving problems,

---

[1] Crainer, Stuart. "Interview with Reg Revans." *Financial Times,* April 12, 1996.

sharing ideas, and in effect connecting the "learning dots" catalyzed the learning reaction. He created a simple equation to capture this observation:

$$L = P + Q.$$

Learning (L) occurs through a combination of programmed knowledge (P) and the ability to discuss insightful questions (Q). It is scary to some that learning revolves around questioning. By definition, there can be no assumption that leaders know best.[2]

More recently students of Revans have defined Action Learning as a "continuous process of learning and reflection, supported by colleagues, with the intention of getting things done"[3] and a "process which brings people together to find solutions to problems and, in doing so, develops both the individuals and the organization."[4] Others began applying Action Learning for executive development and business strategy.[5]

Why is Action Learning an idea whose time has come? The underlying radical learning philosophy is well suited to foster the kinds of collaboration and speed of change required to compete in a global environment. Furthermore, technology has advanced to enable inquiry, advocacy, coaching, community, and sharing of ideas connected to desired results.

## APPLICATION TO LEADERSHIP DEVOLVEMENT

Action Learning is an essential component of leadership development. It transforms generic leadership education into an integrated change agenda targeted on the right business results. When transformed from a learning philosophy to a knowledge management system, Action Learning accelerates a company's rate of organization learning. It helps institutionalize learning by promoting interaction among participants and through assessment and reinforcement of leadership development objectives.

## *Report From the Field*

Although in various disguises,[6] Action Learning has taken hold in many organizations:

---

[2]Ibid.

[3]McGill, I., and L. Beaty. *Action Learning*. 2nd ed. London: Kogan Page, 1995.

[4]Inglis, S. *Making the Most of Action Learning*. Aldershot, England: Gower, 1994.

[5]Dotlich, David, and James Noel. *Action Learning: How the World's Top Companies Are Recreating Their Leaders and Themselves.* San Francisco: Jossey-Bass, 1998.

[6]The way some proponents describe *Action Learning* sounds a lot like Six Sigma, Work-Out, or other improvement programs. We take the more broader definition that includes inquiry, advocacy, coaching, communities, etc.

## Analog Devices

Chairman Ray Stata and Art Schneiderman, former vice president of quality and productivity at Analog Devices, developed and implemented components of an Action Learning system that included a balanced scorecard with enterprise goals, problem-solving methods, tools, and measures of organization learning. Through this program, their active role in developing improvement targets and guiding process improvement teams increased the ability of Analog's leadership and organization to sustain improvement efforts and business results.

Stated in terms of defect reduction, goals were set by establishing half-lives (the time in months it should take to cut a defect count in half) for achieving business goals.[7] To Schneiderman, the half-life is the speedometer for the rate of improvement and Stata labeled it the organization's learning rate.

Analog institutionalized an interactive questioning and learning process in its top-down and side-to-side goal deployment system (called Hoshin Kanri). During the business planning cycle, current trends were used to establish the baseline performance level for a few key performance measures (e.g., on-time delivery, parts per million defective). Next the half-life was chosen based on inquiry as to technical and organization complexity. The discussions around the theoretical capacity and the half-life typically involved several rounds of discussion between senior management and the individuals responsible for the end result—another organization learning method.

Once the goal was accepted, specific budgets and plans for problem solving were drafted To ensure congruency, a senior manager was assigned to a steering committee comprised of leaders from several problem-solving teams—each focused on contributing to a piece of the larger goal (e.g., cut late deliveries in half in 12 months). In this way the day-to-day problem-solving activities were coordinated and focused on the highest leverage points and individual and organization learning resulted.

## GE Capital

In 1996 GE Capital launched its Six Sigma program, outwardly a process improvement initiative, but truly an organization development initiative involving leaders and teams working directly to improve business performance and indirectly to build leadership bench strength and organization capabilities.

In addition, GE Capital created a knowledge management system that was instrumental to the program's high payback. By 1998, Eric Mattenson and Mike

---

[7]For additional information on half-lives and goal setting see Arthur M. Schneiderman, "Setting Quality Goals," *Quality Progress* (April 1988) or visit Arthur M. Schneiderman's Web site: http://www.schneiderman.com.

Markovits had designed and implemented an online intranet site that included dashboards of key metrics, problem-solving tools, education support, and an inventory of projects generated from its training programs and forums to showcase team results and how they got them.

## StorageTek

Action Learning (learning by doing in a controlled environment) is at the foundation StorageTek's leadership development program. Developed by Roger Gaston and Susan Curtis of the human resources department and their team, their program was based in part on a highly interactive senior leader workshop, where key assumptions about its business and initiatives were questioned openly. The team's Action Learning was to define key anchor points such as its primary business focus and primary customer value proposition that all leaders would share and respond to.

These key guidelines were used to tailor StorageTek's "Leading for Results" workshop and direct the alignment of the next 400 leaders through their 7 days-7–week-7 month action plans. Questions raised during the workshop are captured by instructors, answered by the executive team, and posted for all participants. An online leadership toolkit is also made available to sustain learning.

In addition, StrorageTek provides a variety of activities and learning opportunities such as succession management interviews that center on experiences. After action review, advocacy, and inquiry are all part of StorageTek's Action Learning practices. In a nutshell, action creates learning and learning creates action.

## Brady Corporation

Laura Aubiodun, director of Individual & Organization Effectiveness at Brady Corporation recognizes that most companies don't flounder because of poor strategy. The culprit is poor execution of the game plan. The problem is that strategy, developed and written in the language of a few visionaries, gets lost when the rank and file tries to interpret it in operational ways.

Her solution: develop shared mind-set around the strategy and get leaders at all levels aligned to it. Brady workshops introduce key strategic concepts in a down to earth manner and take strategic thinking to strategic action. These workshops are structured to challenge the status quo as well as underlying assumptions so that leaders who participate can learn from and about each other. Action plans developed through these workshops will be used to launch improvement projects that will be tracked in the company's knowledge management system and linked to both desired results and development interventions.

The common threads in these initiatives: Individual and organization learning are coupled; business results and learning are coupled; and Action Learning is used by leaders to execute strategy.

## DESIGN GOALS FOR AN ACTION LEARNING CENTER

The lessons from these examples suggest the following key elements of an Action Learning Center (ALC):

# ALC Serves as the Glue for an Integrated Change Agenda

State strategy in terms people understanding and rapidly communicate these key anchor points to leaders at all levels. Anchor points should include:

- Company purpose and mission that are in line with future goals
- Company value propositions for employees, customers, investors, and the organization
- A clear description of how the business units of the company should interoperate
- Statement of the business focus and customer value propositions
- Statement of firm brand—how the company wants to be known by its best customers.

Engage leaders at every level. Action Plans demonstrate desired capabilities and these capabilities are woven into the companies enabling systems:

- Recruiting and talent identification programs that consider future organization and business capability requirements
- Succession planning is experience based
- The ALC provides a platform for integrating leadership, business capability, and organization capability development into all major change initiatives.

# ALC Promotes Organization Learning

By providing up to date information, common language, and tools, learning is accelerated. The ALC becomes the source for:

- An inventory of essential business capabilities at the enterprise level
- Tracking a balanced set of measures at the business unit and function level
- An inventory of essential leadership attributes and organization capabilities
- Leadership effectiveness assessment and development instruments
- Employee performance assessment tools linked to desired business and organization capabilities

- Skill and attribute development programs tailored to organizational and individual needs and delivered to obtain business results

By providing tools and forums for discussion, collaboration, and learning among:

- Senior executives
- Emerging leaders at all levels (e.g., high potentials and high professionals)
- Front-line leaders

## *ALC Enables an Organization Learning Model*

3M Company is well known as a learning organization. Part of its success comes from experimenting and sharing knowledge through its innovation center. We have mapped observations of 3M's operating model to one put forth by Ulrich and Smallwood[8] in which the combination of generating ideas with impact and generalizing solutions forming those ideas is the basis for individual, team, and organization learning.

## Extending the Beneficiaries of Action Learning

Organization results impact stakeholders and should drive individual results. In training parlance this matches organization learning to the Level 4 evaluation hierarchy (business impact); while the individual learning and development addresses Level 1 (reaction), Level 2 (learning), and Level 3 (application).

Action Learning drives evaluation Levels 1 to 4 and when integrated into leadership development extends the list of beneficiaries to include the organization and investors (Levels 5 and 6).

Sustained return on investment comes with sustained learning. Leaders who are continually engaged in the education and development of others are the backbone of vital organizations. So, Action Learning is not a series of events used to develop competencies through experience. Rather, it is a work-style that can be embedded in the business culture and a competence that leaders strive to perfect.

As described above Action Learning processes carry some administrative overhead. It takes time to document goals, approaches, successes, failures, and results for each learning experience. Evolutionary developments in information technol-

---

[8] Ulrich D., and N. Smallwood. *The Bottom Line ISN'T!: How to Build Lasting Value in Your Company.* Hoboken, NJ: John Wiley & Sons April, 2003.

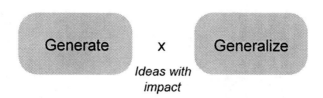

| Generate | x | Generalize |
|---|---|---|
| | *Ideas with impact* | |

| | |
|---|---|
| Process of discovery | Trial-and-error is part of the challenge |
| Creative | |
| | So-called mistakes can offer vital clues that lead to success |
| Risk takers | |
| New ideas | |
| | "See" patterns and fit through Innovation Center |

*"Management that is destructively critical when mistakes are made kills initiative. It's essential that we have many people with initiative if we are to continue to grow."*
*- Former President and Chairman of the Board, William L. McKnight.*

**Figure 18-1**

| Generate | x | Generalize |
|---|---|---|
| | *Ideas with impact* | |

| | |
|---|---|
| Diverse membership | After Action Review: |
| Brainstorm | Trained many people who sustain the technology and keep reinventing it |
| Stretch goals | |
| Utilize new members | |

**Figure 18-2**

| Learning Organization = Leaders Ability To ... | |
| --- | --- |
| GENERATE x GENERALIZE<br>ideas with impact | |
| **Defininition** the ability to create new practices, insights, and applications within the organization | the ability to share the ideas across boundaries within the organization, e.gg., time, geography, function, etc. |
| **Key Finding** A belief in encouraging experiments and discovery ... 3M has many programs that encourage employees, including the 15 percent rule, which allows employees to spend part of their work time exploring experiments.<br><br>In addition, technical employees can apply for 3M Genesis Grants, which provide corporate monies for innovative projects that are not funded through standard channels. | 3M technology platforms are core elements of 3M innovation and springboards to meeting customer needs. In countless combinations, 3M technologies come together as core elements of innovative new products. |

**Figure 18-3**

ogy have cut into administrative and creative overhead and, at the same time, have enabled Action Learning at the organization level.

## VISIBILITY TO THE RESULTS AND THE ACTIONS THAT DRIVE THEM

A search of the World Wide Web for "Action Learning Center" will take you to a number of retreats with rope challenges, bridge building, and meditation aimed at building stronger teams. What organizations need is a virtual Action Learning Center, a place where everyone in the organization can learn together as they take action and drive their business strategy to achieve desired results.

We surveyed the field of information technology products that companies have used to construct elements of a virtual Action Learning Center. We also examined

## Learning Evaluation levels

Level 1: Planned Action
    Smile Sheets and After Class
    Action Plans

Level 2: Learning
    Skill competency assessment

Level 3: Application
    After action reviews, OTJ
    performance, 360 improvements

Level 4: Business Impact
    Balanced Scorecard or
    Performance Measures &
    Quality Improvements

**Action Learning**

Level 5: Measuring Return on
Investment
    Cost reductions, Revenue
    improvements

Level 6: Impact on Market Value
    Investor confidence in future
    earnings (Results-Based
    Leadership)

**Leadership Development
Action Learning**

**Figure 18-4**

several products during their development phase, products that will in the future add vital components. The current state is immature, but prospects for enabling organization level Action Learning are very good.

We envision a workspace that is oriented not to managers, supervisors, and workers but to leaders and leadership, whatever their position on organization charts. This workspace is designed to enable the principle work that leaders do: develop a strategic perspective, build relationships, make connections within and outside the organization, champion change, and so on. At the same time, the workspace exemplifies how leaders work: They aim for results and they model and encourage desired behaviors. Our Action Learning Center has six major components as shown in Figure 18-5:[9]

Education, Work-Out, Feedback, Anchors, Lessons, and Measures act as sources and repositories of information used throughout the organization in their improvement work. The documents in the center represent actions being taken.

Early platform efforts employed Lotus Notes and hand-cobbled Web pages. These solutions either failed to support new features or fell out of favor as the platform du jour among technologists. Knowledge management systems have been employed and found to fall short in their ability to interconnect with other desired components such as scorecards and learning management systems. The current platform of choice is the Inter/intranet portal. Portal servers as they are called readily accept plug-in modules and readily interconnect with existing internal and external systems.

Another type of platform is the learning management system. Such systems manage data about development goals, course offerings, participant progress, and assessment of learning and utilization of education resources. As such, these systems provide an integrating platform for education components and provide data to support Level 1 and 2 evaluations as previously described.

*Education*—A programmed knowledge component that represents a collection of more or less static information about why the center exists; who is participating; and what is going on. It also acts as a gateway to online learning and tools that participants are encouraged to use. Almost all e-learning systems provide this component, as do some knowledge management systems. Although education in the form of online tutorials, examples, and simulations is plentiful, access to enabling tools is rare.

*Work-Out*—A programmed knowledge component that provides participants with methods to share. Whatever business improvement discipline(s) a company chooses to become really good at (Six Sigma, Lean Manufacturing, Work-Out, total quality management) will introduce administrative overhead. At the same time, they may introduce dozens to hundreds of improvement actions throughout an organization. This component represents the gathering point where actions are structured, oriented, documented, and made visible. Common tools encourage uniform action structure and minimize overhead.

*Feedback*—An observation, reflection, and insight component that provides leaders with a window through which they can observe actions and provide

---

[9]"Action Learning Center." Retrieved from the Results-Based Leadership Web site: http://www.rbl.net/alc.html.

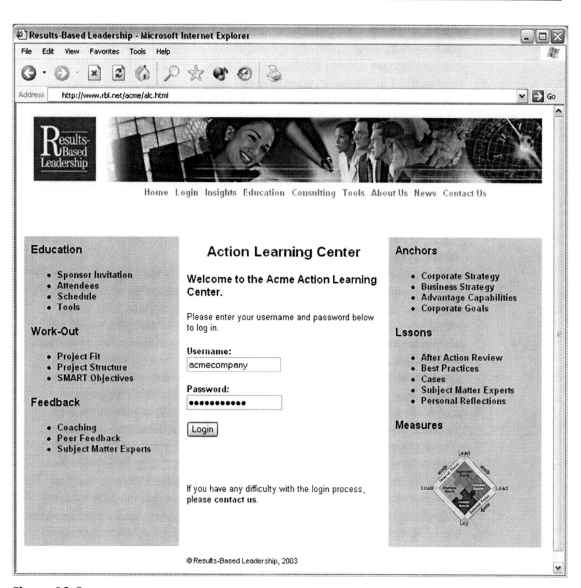

**Figure 18-5**

coaching. The feedback component allows leaders to communicate tips, guidance and, other notes of encouragement to action teams and individuals. Leaders who are several levels away from the teams organizationally and thousands of miles away geographically can use a combination of private and public message boards to reinforce commitment and recognize desired behaviors. Note that this mechanism seems to work best when people close to the action tip off the top executives that a complement or two would be appropriate.

*Anchors*—A programmed knowledge component that provides direction by setting boundaries and focusing action. It communicates in simple terms what the company is trying to do, how, for whom, and to what extent. The goal here is brevity and clarity. Anchors combined with Feedback create an empowering environment for Action Learning without the pitfalls of over-innovation and excess improvement.

*Lessons*—Another insight and questioning component is the main repository for knowledge and new questions. Knowledge management systems of various types have filled this role quite well. The more simple ones with strong search capabilities seem to be more valuable than the complex neural networks that can't explain how they arrive at their conclusions. Value is maximized when it is simple to populate and simple to locate information. In some environments, corporate library or technical library functions have found a new and even more productive life managing this component.

*Measures*—Scorecards and scorecard systems provide the organization with feedback that keeps Action Learning on track. Most scorecard or measures systems snap in readily and serve well. Currently there are three ways that companies acquire scorecard technology: embedded in an Enterprise Resource Planning (ERP) system—least desirable because all data must be moved to the technology and access is generally through the ERP system; Executive Dashboard Systems—okay but often they are architected to allow line of sight down but not up or across; and true balanced scorecard systems—provide line of sight in all directions and snap into both portals and ERP systems alike.

*Actions*—The work that catalyzes learning and business results is represented in Figure 18-5 as a stack of forms representing Action Plans and project descriptions. Here is where the power and value of the virtual Action Learning Center reveals itself. Background information is collected from the Education, Lessons, and Anchors sections and Actions result. In the process of creating an Action Plan, the models and methods of process improvement are applied to provide structure; experts and interested parties are engaged through Feedback; actions are tied to the Anchors and Measures; and when the Action is completed, Lessons are recorded and shared. Along the way, Feedback/coaching is connected to Actions and changes to Anchors and Measures are communicated immediately to allow course correction.

## ACTION LEARNING CENTERS IN THE FUTURE

The future of Action Learning Centers is promising. It can be built from technologies that exist today. However, there will be new and evolved technologies in the future. Intranet/Internet portals will hold the platform seat. Learning management systems will extend and then likely collapse under their own weight in all but the largest implementations just as ERP has experienced. Smaller learning management system components will find their way into Action Learning Centers.

The major advance to current technologies will be the development of tools that sustain online education through application to daily work. Most e-learning suppliers are building static simulations (generic data) and are working towards live simulations (real company data).

There are three companies offering a glimpse of the more distant future. EngageThoughtware (UT), PerformaWorks (MA), and mGen (MA) are pushing the envelope. mGen is taking education to the community level by emphasizing the value of broad involvement and communication of learning. This represents a strong model for organization learning. EngageThoughtware is leveraging the value of community even more strongly through a technology that enables collaboration across an extended enterprise around actions. PerformaWorks's goal deployment and alignment system addresses three issues of business performance: goal clarity, action alignment, and talent. The reader is encouraged to explore these cutting edge business solutions each based on proven and adaptable technologies.

## CONCLUSION

Action Learning is the way that leaders convert life and work experiences into leadership competencies that build strong organizations. It can and should be integral to every organization's leadership and operational systems: It is the way to "operationalize" this essential organization capability.

1. Adults learn quickly when lessons are relevant to immediate work and when they work in a collaborative environment.
2. Customer, investor, and employee results are the responsibility of leaders, and the pursuit of those results provides excellent context for leadership development.

3. Results-oriented leaders can be empowered with clear goals and tools that eliminate administrative overhead.

4. Information technology tools can be used to create an action learning culture that is results focused.

5. The tools are positioned and capable of supporting early adopters.

6. Technology-enabled Action Learning in this context is a necessity for competitive companies and an advantage capability for the winners.

Judy G. Zettergren, Ph.D., with S.C. Johnson brought this quote by Donald H. McGannon to our attention: *"Leadership is action, not position."* The quote defines the future of both the way that leaders will develop and what leaders will do. Action Learning will not only be the way that people progress through the leadership pipeline, it will be their core value to the organizations and the constituents that they serve: employees, customers, investors, and the organization itself.

## CHAPTER 19

# KEEP GOOD COMPANY: NEW WAYS TO A SUSTAINABLE, BLUE-CHIP CREATIVE CULTURE

*Ivy Ross and David Kuehler*

## INTRODUCTION

Martha Graham, the mother of the modern dance movement, expressed that "No artist is ahead of his time. He is his time. It is just that the others are behind the time." The same underlying philosophy can be applied to successful organizations. It is often said that an artist's work mirrors society. It has to reflect both the reality of social life and the needs of the individual to find resonance with a large audience. Like the inspired artist, a good company must also hold up the looking glass and align it's ecology to reflect the current realities of culture as well as the needs of the individual—it's consumer—if it hopes to remain vital and avoid the costly misstep of becoming, as Graham puts it, "behind the time."

What follows is a first hand account of how the girls division at Mattel successfully reinvented how the world's number-one toy company innovates by creating a groundbreaking product development process called Project Platypus. Platypus is a dynamic process for bringing out human potential in an organization through the synthesis of collaborative experiences resulting in new business opportunities. The lessons learned from this process are valuable for any company or community seeking new ways to insure a healthy, sustainable, and innovative future.

Ivy Ross, senior vice president of design and development for the girls division, had been at the company for about three and a half years. She had witnessed and participated in many re-engineering processes. Mattel already dominated most of the traditional toy categories. It was clear that in order to keep growing, they needed to start looking for new opportunities. This meant exploring emerging patterns in the marketplace or creating new ones.

Based on known realities of Mattel's processes, Ross's instinct told her that a new path to innovation had to be created, not re-engineered. She believed it was important that the new process leveraged all the human assets that Mattel had. As Margaret Wheatley describes, "If we want to succeed with knowledge management, we must attend to human needs and dynamics. . . . Knowledge [is not] the asset or capital. People are."

Ross believed, that innovation lay in creating a community where everyone feels valued; with passion and trust at its core. The end result must be something greater than any one person could have created alone. The process must be as innovative as the brands it would produce. It must mirror society from both a cultural and humanistic point of view.

She hired David Kuehler to lead the project. Together, they assembled a pilot program to apply these overarching theories. "We just did what we thought was right. We followed our hearts and designed a program that was reflective of society. It was the way, we believed, people really wanted to work and create," says Ross and Kuehler.

Project Platypus is a distinctive way of creating new opportunities for Mattel. The deliverables include a new brand that can deliver at least 100 million dollars in revenue by the third year in the market place. The final presentation includes tested products, packaging, merchandising ideas, and a full financial analysis.

This is accomplished by choosing 12 Mattel employees from different areas of the business unit. They leave their existing jobs for 12 weeks and shed their titles and their hierarchical way of working. They work in the Project Platypus space as a living system in a postmodern way. Alumni are released back into the system where they utilize their newly acquired skills to share the process with their managers and colleagues. Each session is unique. The participants and the business opportunity will change with each initiative.

## THIRTEEN WAYS TO A SUSTAINABLE CREATIVE CULTURE

### 1. The Right Mix

They say, "It's all in the casting." It's true. Like great stories, successful groups require the right mix of people with the right chemistry. Spend the time building a team of individuals who are representative of your company's evolving culture. Choose individuals who are passionate, collaborative, excited about creating the next thing, and willing to go outside their core skill set to try some thing new.

Project Platypus was composed of individuals from all areas of the company: design, model shop, marketing, engineering, online, hair, packaging, and copywriting. They were encouraged to use the opportunity to take on cross-functional roles and view the process from a different point of view. As a result, individuals found renewed passion in their work, which brought new perspective to the initiative. In addition, we were building a community of hybrid talent that was able to react quickly and effortlessly to change.

We are swiftly moving into a postmodern society, where hybridity and ethnic ambiguity are becoming part of the cultural landscape. "America is becoming truly 'post-racial.' Where ethnic difference does not divide but actually brings diverse constituencies together," states Leon E Wynter, a journalist and former *Wall Street Journal* columnist. "Marketers have to think about biracial or trans-racial groups, a fast growing category," says Marilyn Halter, a Boston University professor of American studies and author. The 2000 Census found that 6.8 million Americans claimed they belonged to at least two racial groups. In entertainment, characters and celebrities are purposely trying to remain ethnically ambiguous. Even family structures have adapted to the new social patterns of the 21st century. According to the "We Are Family" article in *Viewpoint* magazine, "New types of family trees are emerging. In a process that the Future Foundation has dubbed the 'flexibilization' of family roles and ties, new family networks are becoming the social paradigm."[1] This trend tells us that, like society, we can no longer divide our employees into pure silos of marketing, design, manufacturing, etc. There is no "typical" family anymore nor should there be a typical organizational structure. Companies need to learn to tap into the richness that diversity brings.

## 2. Environment

*A new process requires a new environment, a place that will inspire collaboration, play, and creative thinking. To shift your mind you must shift your space.*

A unique space was created for Project Platypus. Grass green flooring was installed, and skylights were punched into the roof providing bright sunlight. "It feels like a meadow," said one of the construction crew. The furniture consisted of bean-bag chairs, ergonomically designed office seating, and large rubber balls to sit and bounce on. All of the desks were on wheels so they could be moved around to create a variety of group configurations. An adjacent room contained a sound chair, developed by Dr. Jeff Thompson, that would encourage maximum creativity by aligning the right and left halves of the brain using music embedded with binary beats. Finally, a 12-by-40-foot pushpin wall was installed, to act as a living journal of the process.

---

[1]Raymond, Martin. "We Are Family," *Viewpoint*, vol. 12 (2002) p. 46.

The best kind of creative community is "emergent." It's organic and unplanned. The design evolution of a space is reactionary. It should align itself to emergent ideas at a moments notice. There is a trend towards creating both public and private spaces with this in mind. New office furniture lines are designed knowing that many activities will co-exist within the same locale. The same is true of our private environments. In the last 10 years, domestic furniture lines have been introduced that are designed for multitasking. Beds convert to become part of an office, chairs flip over to become tables, and couches transform into an entire living center. Nothing is stagnant. Clearly, consumers today don't want things that are boring and predictable. New designs are providing us with flexibility, customization, and a place to dream. Our workspaces must mirror this trend.

## 3. Create Big Challenges

There are challenges, and there a big challenges. Create meaningful initiatives that people will feel passionate about. Raise the bar so that a group realizes they will have to learn to rely on each other for success. The end results are innovative products that are far greater than what any one person could have created alone.

The mission for each session of Platypus is to create a completely new brand in three months that includes strategy, product design, financial analysis, and marketing recommendations—a daunting task for an individual, but an achievable one for a committed and talented group of people. For some, this concept was threatening. They were used to working in an environment where they would have a meeting, disappear into their cubes, and emerge when they had the solution. "My idea is ready now!" Their process was isolated and invisible. In Platypus, each individual knew they were working as an organic whole, a living system where each member had a say and a stake in the process. Most importantly, they had the support and trust of each member of the group, which allowed them to rise to the occasion and relish the challenge before them. Jean-Paul Sartre, the French Philosopher put it best: "Immerse people in universal and extreme situations which leave them only a couple of ways out, arrange things so that in choosing the way out they choose themselves, and you've won—the play is good."

People today are looking to do big things. They want to have an impact on the world in order to bring meaning to their lives. And they are finding ways to connect to the people that hold similar values. In today's society people are attaching themselves to personal causes at a very young age. Joseph Campbell says, "The heroic life is living the individual adventure." We need to allow people to move beyond their self-imposed limitations and to do great things. Corporations must create an environment where one's true identity and gifts are celebrated. People will rally around what they feel passionate about and what holds meaning for them. Creativity exists in everyone; when it is not surfacing, it is usually being suppressed by judgment. Failure to innovate is often a result of an organization that is paralyzed by fear. It is afraid to let passion out of the bottle.

## 4. Time to Graze

The group was given time to graze, to learn, and to develop meaningful relationships. Many organizations don't allow employees the time they need to prepare for an initiative. The process is often mechanized and impersonal. "Here's the objective and the deadline. You, you, and you work together in this way." Imagine the innovative ideas that are lost because people become slaves to a process.

> If we drew a line to represent a creative occurrence the only portion that would reflect measurable productivity would be a short segment at the end of the line: This line segment is the equivalent of the cow's time in the barn, hooked up to the milking machine. But the earlier, larger part of the event, when the milk was actually being created, remains invisible. The invisible portion is equivalent to the time the cow spends out in the pasture, seemingly idle, but, in fact, performing the alchemy of transforming grass into milk.[2]

The first two weeks of the project (immersion) allowed the group time to prepare for the initiative. The leaders shared the project vision with the group. Then the seedlings of knowledge and culture were planted by bringing in outside speakers and experts that personified the core values of the process. There were no schedules or deliverables. The group's job was to simply graze and to allow a unique creative culture to unfold.

We are shifting from a service-orientated culture to a knowledge- and creative-based one. Consumers are demanding more than just a purchasing exchange. They want information, experience, and value. In order to deliver this to the consumer, we must model our companies in the same way. We need to let employees venture out and learn about the world they serve, rather then sitting in a cubicle and making educated guesses. As leaders, one of our primary roles must be to inspire them and feed them with information and experiences that will inform their task. We should create a relaxed but stimulating environment for true creativity to emerge. We must pay attention to the quality of our conversations with our customers. Multidiscipline and multi-viewpoint dialogues are equally important because we are,

---

[2]MacKenzie, Gordon. *Orbiting the Giant Hairball: A Corporate Fool's Guide to Surviving with Grace.* New York: Viking Press, 1996, p. 64.

in a sense, co-creating custom experiences with them. We also must do the same for our employees. They are being asked to serve the customers in this same way.

## 5. Shared Experience

This is where cultural DNA is born. It guides a group's behavior, thinking, and decision making. Many companies implement quick-fix initiatives referred to as team bonding or team building hoping to achieve similar results. Unfortunately, they often fall short. Creating a healthy, productive, and creative community requires time, commitment, and care.

Immersion sets the field for a unique culture to organically unfold. Speakers, participants, and experiences were programmed with great detail. First, the leaders shared the project vision with the group to give them a sense of mission. Second, they provided the group with a collection of shared experiences: shared experience, shared knowledge, and self discovery.

*Knowledge Speakers* provided the group with a 360-degree view of the vision. If you're trying to design a car, you don't just look at other cars. You look for knowledge and inspiration in out of the way places. We consulted with Dr. Michael Conforti, a Jungian analyst a doctorate in child development, to hone the team's observational skills, a Japanese tea master. The collection of speakers provided the group with the information and context they needed to approach the project with fresh eyes.

*Self-Discovery Speakers* helped each "Platypi" re-discover their dreams and individuality. A participant said, " This process helped me find a way back to myself." Some of the speakers included a practitioner in collaborative living systems and a researcher in music and brainwave activity. Members were encouraged to spend time in a sound chair to stimulate creativity. The objective was to help each participant discover a renewed sense of self and expressiveness.

*Creative Culture Speakers* set the groundwork for a productive living system. A cultural mythologist discussed the significance of archetypes in story and culture, and an improvisation artist led the group in a variety of theatrical games to teach them the fundamentals of group storytelling, brainstorming, and collaboration.

By the end of the immersion, the change in many of the individuals was noticeable. People began to dress differently; they laughed more. Relationships were forming and people were more comfortable expressing their feelings and ideas. This is often referred to as the "Inclusion Phase" of a living system. The culture was beginning to emerge.

In the book *The Evolving Self*, Mihaly Csikszentmihalyi uses the expression "memes" in contrast to "genes" to identify the origins of human behavior. "Memes are born," Csikszentimihalyi notes, "When the human nervous system reacts to an experience. They are the information units in our collective consciousness and transport their views across our minds. A meme contains behavioral instructions that are passed from one generation to the next, social artifacts and value—laden symbols that glue together social systems."[3] Memes are so vital they reach across whole groups of people and begin to structure mind-sets on their own. People are beginning to spend money on experiences as opposed to just "things." The things that we find the most memorable and valuable are the experiences we have had with others. The shared group experience has a life of its own and will contribute greatly to the success of the output of the "group mind."

## *6. It's About Trust*

The group connected on a daily basis, which held them in relationships of trust and respect. When people are vulnerable, they are the most open—free to create. Traditionally, employees have been told to "leave your feelings at home. This is business." When organizations strip humanness from the workplace they strip away human potential and creativity as well.

To maintain relationships of trust, a check-in called "Face-to-Face" was created. The group met each morning and simply connected with each other, as humans, before the work commenced. Face-to-Face served three purposes. First, it provided people with a forum to connect with each other and to be "in relationship." Second, it was to name and resolve conflict. Someone once said, "Spouses should never go to bed angry." Theirs was, "Never go through the day in conflict." It gave people the opportunity to name their differences and seek resolution within a healthy and respectful community. The third purpose was planning. It allowed the Platypi to evolve with the process as it evolved. When 12 people are connected, their combined intelligence and ability to solve complex problems is remarkable. Face-to-Face permitted them to realign their process and create customized solutions as required.

American political scientist Francis Fukayama suggests, "The ability of a nation, a community, or a company to compete economically is instrumentally influenced by the inherent level of trust among its members. Trust represents an intangible form of social capital." Trust is the binding force that connects every aspect of our lives. In our relationships we look for trust and unconditional love. In companies, we spend too much time worrying about "who we can trust." The time spent worrying is taking away from the time that should be devoted to creating.

---

[3]Csikszentmihalyi, Mihaly. *The Evolving Self.* New York: HarperCollins Publishers, 1994, p. 120.

Trust is becoming something we demand from our brands as well. Consumers rely on them to be trustworthy and have integrity. Companies that have earned the consumers trust are able to branch into areas outside of their core competency. One example is Amazon.com. Originally known as an online book retailer, it has now expanded into clothing. It worked hard to gain the consumers trust, and it understands the importance of maintaining it. Consistent with the movement to simplify one's life, consumers are looking to consolidate their resources in both goods and services. They are looking to do more business with fewer companies. You can bet that the companies they choose will be those with whom they build a relationship based on meaning, values, and trust.

## 7. Storytelling

How do you find a common language that connects groups of people from a variety of different backgrounds, disciplines, and skill sets? Story. A strong narrative can help build and guide a brand strategy. It provides meaning in a way that people can truly internalize, retain, and communicate to others. In some companies, the brand story is held by a chosen few. They consider it their property. If all employees had a stake in the story then they would be more willing to share ideas and promote the brand.

The group was comprised of people from multiple disciplines. Some expressed their ideas visually, others through words or technology. The fundamentals of storytelling (What does a person want or need? And what is keeping them from getting it?) were used as common language to begin developing a brand. The following storytelling techniques were applied.

### Subjective

Find your passion in the vision. Create a story about what this initiative means to you in a very personal way. Platypi were asked to participate in an exercise called "What if?" For example, "What if we could create a brand that helped children understand their emotions?"

### Objective

Tell a story based on something you have observed. Platypi went into the field to perform observational research. They created stories by watching children play. They identified the physical, mental, and emotional aspects of what was taking place and developed stories to fulfill the needs they observed.

Platypi shared their stories with the rest of the group then posted them on the wall. They analyzed them and looked for emergent patterns. The patterns provided the sparks for the emerging brand story.

"Stories, fairy-tales, and corporate narratives have become the latest way to encourage organizations to develop more human and emotional networks," as noted in the "Storyville" article from *Viewpoint* magazine.[4] Charts and spreadsheets are still very important. However, we need a more human approach. Linear and non-linear storytelling are being applied more and more in advertising to get and hold the consumers attention. As a research tool, it brings insight into a product or service. More relevant information is acquired when consumers are asked to tell a story about why a product is appealing and how it relates to their everyday lives.

## 8. Joy

A common mantra at Playtpus was "Work is personal and personal is work." Gone are the days when an employee arrived at nine, put in eight hours, and then left at five to begin their "other" life. People are looking for meaning, balance, and joy in their lives as well as their work. The company that helps employees find purpose and meaning in their jobs will find that it pays dividends in the long run.

At Platypus, people aligned themselves around ideas they felt passionate about, and they were challenged to pursue ideas that inspired them. In addition, they were encouraged to take time out and play each day and try to see life through the eyes of a child. Great ideas come from a relaxed place of fun and whimsy. Coming up with great ideas doesn't have to be painful.

In the past consumers demanded products that were dependable, predictable, and functional. That has changed. Consumers still desire functionality, but they want products that provide them with meaning and pleasure. The well-known industrial designer, Philippe Starck is acutely aware of this trend. His "Excalibur" toilet brush elevates an ordinary household object into a whimsical, "Sword in the Stone" toilet cleaner. He transforms the mundane into something meaningful by applying story, surprise, and humor. In addition, there is a new group of consumers called "balance seekers." These people want to lead a rich life versus wanting to get rich. The questions being asked are "What makes me feel good?" and "What is giving me joy?" Current figures show that balance seekers make up almost 50 percent of the adult population. Contrary to past beliefs, people are now looking for a joy that comes from within, not something external that puts joy into them. Joseph Campbell says, "Do what you love and love what you do. Work begins when you don't like what you're doing."

## 9. The Individual and the Group

As in society, there has to be a balance between the needs of the individual and the needs of the whole. Companies should take the time to learn who each of their employees really are and find a way to tap into their individual gifts. This boils down

---

[4]Raymond, Martin. "Storyville." *Viewpoint,* vol. 12 (2002) p. 60.

to truly honoring people for their uniqueness and recognizing it as a corporate asset that can by leveraged by the organization.

So much of the team's work was centered on group thinking and collaboration. The team leaders had to allow time for a people to take a step back and let all of the knowledge and experiences they had acquired sink in. They wanted to let their unique voice and point of view come forward so they could feel fulfilled and bring fresh insight to the whole. Some people chose to work individually and others in smaller groups. The alliances formed organically around the idea. The group's physiology was always expanding and contracting, with the emerging brand story at the center.

Once upon a time, people wanted brands like Gucci, Prada, and Calvin Klein. Wearing these logos signaled that you were part of a certain collective status. They were your identity. Sagra Maceria De Rosen, head of JPMorgan, says, "Even before September 11th, the logo as a status symbol was beginning to wane. What happened at the Twin Towers accelerated the process."[5] Currently, there's a strong desire for people to discover their own individuality. They are choosing things and fashions that reflect the uniqueness of who they are, rather than relying on a brand to create their identity for them. That is why there is a return to clothing that makes a more personal statement, such as vintage items and street clothes. Years ago, fashion magazines dictated what the "uniform" of the season was going to be. Now magazines are helping us curate our essence. They show us how to be more eclectic and unique through the expression of fashion. Tee shirts are becoming fashion billboards. Just by passing someone on the street, you can tell a little bit about who they are and what is important to them. All this points to a burning desire for people to express themselves.

## 10. Collaboration Not Competition

Organizations often rely on competition to act as a catalyst for innovation. Employees are left feeling unfulfilled, burnt out and isolated. Viola Spolin, the author of *Improvisational Theater* notes, "Imposed competition makes harmony impossible; for it destroys the basic nature of playing by occluding self and by separating player from player."[6]

A renowned product development firm and an improvisational artist were asked to share their perspectives on the creative process. The combination of improvisational theater exercises and product development brainstorming techniques

---

[5]J.P Morgan analysts report 2002.
[6]Spolin, Viola. *Improvisation for the Theater*. Evanston, IL: Northwestern University Press, 1963, pp. 10–11.

gave the group the tools they needed to define their own ideation process. Brainstorms were a daily activity at Platypus. People broke into small groups and aligned themselves around the stories they felt most passionate about. One person facilitated and acted as the scribe while the rest of the group added ideas and built on those of others. A playful atmosphere based on mutual respect, trust, and openness took center stage. Competitiveness and egos were set aside.

Participants began to give each other "gifts." If someone created an idea that seemed right for another person, or group, they would draw or write it and pin it next to their work on the wall. Since everyone felt a sense of ownership over the process gifts were given away freely. Sam Hamill, poet and editor of Copper Canyon Press notes, "I live in a gift-giving economy. Once you create a gift and give it away you are empty and free to create again."[7] The group experienced the power and fulfillment of creating something together through play. It strengthened the bonds between individuals and competitiveness slipped away.

There is a movement towards former competitors creating partnerships and relationships that serve the same consumer. Companies are realizing that another option to competition is collaboration. They create partnerships and offer the targeted consumer the convenience of a more "wholistic" or one-stop shopping experience. This is also practiced on the Internet; Web sites will direct you to other Web sites that contain like-minded information. In the past, this was a rarity. Today, it makes sense. Organizations are beginning to grasp a principle that scientists have been on to for years: Relationships are the organizing principle of the universe. The worldview of modern physics is now a systems view. David Bohm states, "Everything is connected to everything else. We are not sure how this connectedness works, but there is certainty that there is separation without separateness—this envelopes human beings and atoms alike."[8] Organizations can find great power in surrendering to the operating principles of the universe.

## 11. Chaos Is Good

Organizations often experience chaotic moments on the path to innovation. Rather then support the novel forms that arise from chaos, they become nervous. They switch to plan B, the tried-and-true process. Who knows what could have emerged if they had only remained supportive and committed to the process.

At one point in the process the Platypus group experienced frustration and disorder; they were trying to make sense of their efforts. They could see the light at

---

[7]Excerpt from interview with Sam Hamill, Editor, Copper Mountain Press. (NPR/KCRW, Los Angeles, CA).

[8]Bohm, David. *Wholeness and the Implicate Order*. London: T.J. International Ltd., 1995, p. 11.

the end of the tunnel, but they couldn't get there. The leaders remained supportive and trusted the people and the work. They, too, had to surrender to the chaos; it was a necessary and essential part of the process. According to John Van Eenwyk, author of *Archetypes and Strange Attractors*, "Chaos theory proposes that when repetitive dynamics begin to interact with themselves they become so complex that they defy definition. Yet, from these 'complex dynamics' there eventually emerge new patterns that are based loosely on the old. In other words, while chaotic systems break down order, they also reconstitute it in new forms."[9]

Like strange attractors, the research, brand, story, and product were orbiting on the wall. The Platypus group looked back upon their experiences and compared the patterns of knowledge they acquired earlier to the evolved work and macro-patterns on the wall. They were close, but they couldn't make sense of it. They just had to trust that a new order would emerge. Two days later, a Platypi gifted the group with the skeleton of a unique system. Then someone else added an idea, then another. Without warning, an order emerged.

All living systems go through periods of chaos in order to reach a higher level of connectedness. According to Mukara Meredith of MatrixWorks, an organization specializing in Group Dynamics, "A living system goes through three stages to interconnectedness: inclusion (forming), chaos (conflict) and mutual connection (Trust). Out of the chaotic state a new form of meaning emerges."[10]

## 12. Intuitive Leaders

A new kind of process requires a new kind of leader. They are servants to the idea, the process and the people. Old reporting structures and hierarchies must be set aside to make room for corporate Sherpa who guide the process of innovation.

The leader at Platypus took their cues from the role of a director in the theater. Like the director, the leader's job was to serve the people while also serving the project vision. They set the field and then worked to get out of the way. They were still "present;" however, they kept things on course by sending impulses rather than orders. They let the individuals discover their hidden talents and helped them grow. What's good for the individual is good for the group. There was a stage in the process, as in theater, when the group began to take on a life of it's own. They developed their own language, rules, and customs. They were "flowing." The leader recognized this and took a step back to allow a deeper spontaneity and creativity to emerge. To an outsider, the leader's role is often invisible. After one seminar a guest

---

[9]Van Eenwyk, John, R. *Archetypes and Strange Attractors*. Toronto, Canada: Inner City Books, 1997, p. 43.

[10]Interview with Mukara Meredith, MatrixWorks Inc., November 22, 2002.

speaker commented on the leader's role, " You have so many wonderful things to add. Why don't you take the lead more?" The leader responded, "I am."

In fast-paced competitive environments, the best decisions come from experience and intuition. This observation is backed by research from economics, cognitive psychology, and neurology. What we call "gut instinct" is learning without awareness, which is a real form of knowledge. Today's leaders must look for emerging patterns at every level, then trust their gut to act on what they feel, whether its a new business opportunity or responding to a personnel issue. Consumers are using their gut to decide what products feel right to them, and so should the companies that create the products. An quote from the "Think with Your Gut" article in *Business 2.0* hits the nail on the head, "To sharpen your intuitive thinking, you have to get out of your own way; to foster it among those around you, you have to get out of their way too."[11]

# 13. An Evolving Culture

True, sustainable cultural change is not achieved from a top-down corporate mandate. It spreads from within an organization—person-to-person, department-to-department, division-to-division. Pay attention to what your employees need and serve them. Start small and create and commit to a meaningful pilot program that likeminded people can rally around, and let it grow. Given time and nurturing, the network will spread the news.

The network society is one of the most important developments of our time. Networks are a series of linked points that work toward a collective end through informal communication. There is no hierarchy, no beginning, and no end. We are living in a multilayered and complex global society. The Internet has reshaped our lives. In Mark Buchanan's book, *Nexus*, he says, "Social networks turn out to be nearly identical in their architecture to the World Wide Web, the network of Web pages connected by hyperlink links. Each of these networks shares deep structural properties with the food webs of any ecosystem."[12] Marketers are using network thinking to discover new ways to reach audiences. The "right" consumer is no longer reached through TV or print advertising. Instead, companies are locating the 20 percent, or vital connectors, in a targeted network that can start a trend among the other 80 percent. The same can be true when one talks about cultural change in a corporation.

---

[11]Stewart, Thomas, A. "Think with Your Gut." *Business 2.0* November (2002): Accessed from the Web site: www.business2.com/.

[12]Buchanan, Mark. *Nexus*. New York: W.W. Norton & Company, 2002, p. 15.

## CONCLUSION

Project Platypus will influence the culture of Mattel more and more as each group of employees is released back into the system. They become creative catalysts, bringing new ways of being, doing, and creating back to their previous jobs. There have been sightings of walls being taken down, dialogues replacing meetings, stories being told, and gifts being given every day. The understanding of intuition and the ability to read patterns in the field suggests "future possibilities" and "imagination" as qualities of observation. Designers and marketers are collaborating and networking in a different way, and there is a level of intimacy and freedom of expression among those who have participated in the program. Most importantly, there are a growing number of people in the division who have experienced the magic that can transpire when they come to work as "who they really are," giving all they can give, having fun, and being inspired at the same time. As a Platypi once said, "All our truth is welcome here."

# CHAPTER 20

# DOES YOUR ORGANIZATION HAVE CRUCIAL CONVERSATIONS AND TRANSFORMATIONAL MOMENTS THAT RESULT IN ORGANIZATIONAL CHANGE?

*Larry Peters and Joseph Grenny*

## INTRODUCTION

We have been part of hundreds of conversations about what it takes to create an effective organization, an organization that not only survives in today's tough business climate, but one that builds a platform for future prosperity. We've both felt a nagging ambivalence from people in these conversations. When discussing what sets effective organizations apart the conversation reflects both the spectacular results these great companies consistently produce and the behavior and attitudes of the people who produce them. And yet, when we ask the question, "How do we get there from here?" our primary methods are limited to adopting the structures, systems, processes, and practices of some of these best-in-class organizations.

The assumption that seems to hold us hostage in these conversations is that while new behaviors and attitudes are the goal, the best—or only—method for getting there is through influencing *nonhuman factors* such as organizational structure, work processes, or performance management systems. The change literature is filled with cases of failed change (e.g., TQM, BPR) based on this assumption. After scores of experiences working with senior leaders to create significant, meaningful, and measurable change in their organizations, we've concluded that there is good reason for this history of failed change: It is because this assumption is deeply and dangerously flawed.

The flaw is deep in that it draws attention away from a far more powerful assumption—that the best way to influence behavior is for those with the vision to begin behaving differently; to live the vision. Organizational change begins with *personal* change.

The flaw is dangerous because it siphons off precious leadership attention and scarce organizational resources on change strategies that are doomed to fail. Changing structures and systems and policies and other "external" factors may help an ineffective organization become somewhat better, but changes such as these cannot make it a great organization—unless and until people change their behavior! And, because changing structures and systems do not automatically change behavior, prior change efforts based on this assumption are likely to have created a seedbed of doubt and cynicism. Employees make a decision to participate only when they start to see others do so. They wait for evidence that, this time, something really will change. In this way, prior failure breeds a cynicism in organizations that increases the chance of failure of the next attempt at change. And in this climate of mistrust and cynicism, even if later change efforts reflect a sound change methodology, these efforts will have a hard time taking root.

# THE CASE OF A NEW CEO

A few years ago, we worked with the senior leaders of an insurance company. A new CEO had been tapped to head up the organization that had been recently formed through combination with three others. Stacy, the new CEO, was itching to lead the organization in a bold new direction. She and her senior team were convinced that enormous growth was possible if the organization could gain a more profound understanding of client risks and offer customized insurance solutions to match them. The problem was that this organization was so beset with parochial attitudes that it was impossible to rapidly create customized insurance products. Individuals were so identified with their functions that no one felt enough ownership of a particular customer to gain the profound understanding required to drive this strategy. In short, the culture was perfectly misaligned with the new strategy—in fact, it was pointed 180 degrees in the wrong direction.

In order to foster a more client-focused business, Stacy did what many leaders do. She championed an effort to benchmark companies that were known for their ability to work cooperatively across functions and develop deep relationships with customers. Six months later, the company was reorganized into strategic business units, matching a "best practice" they uncovered in their study. They had broken down functions into multi-skilled teams that focused on specific market segments. They had overhauled the pay system to reward those who could perform multiple roles (e.g., risk assessment, underwriting, claims, service) in serving customers. And yet, in spite of all the shuffling and changing, behaviors and attitudes were mostly unchanged. While old conflicts continued within the new multi-skilled teams between various functional players, conflict also emerged elsewhere. New battles for resources, rewards, and respect emerged between the multi-skilled teams. Those vying for different customer segments competed for capital in the budgeting process and for investments in marketing. Teams that could have created cross-selling opportunities for other teams with existing customers rarely did so. In brief, while processes, work design, performance management, and structure had completely changed, behavior was stuck in the past.

Were the new structure and systems good ideas? Yes, the plan was clearly focused on the new business strategy. Did it work elsewhere? Yes, again. Stacy and her executive team found evidence that this approach to customizing their product offerings could work because they saw it work elsewhere, in best-practice organizations. Could it work at this company? Yes . . . but not by first changing what's "out there"—the nonhuman structures and systems of the organization. The path to organizational change is through personal change.[1]

## SO, WHAT'S A LEADER TO DO?

The benefit of installing new structures, systems, and processes is that there is a clear, concrete set of *deliverables*. Focusing on "things" lends an illusory feeling of substance to a change effort. But without the opportunity to flow-chart, design, and install something, leaders are left asking, "What should I *do* to influence change?"

We have already stated that we think the path here is for leaders to "live the change" they want to see in others. In practical terms that means, "walking their talk." This often-stated bromide means more, however, than personally behaving in a manner consistent with the change; it also means leading. Leaders care enough about the changes that need to occur that they say and do the many things that are needed to influence others and outcomes. They get the attention of others in ways that not only clarifies desired outcomes, but also clarifies everyone's responsibilities to be a part of producing those outcomes. It's acting toward others in ways that make a difference.

We suggest that the best place to exert this influence is in the conversations we hold. Not in any conversation, but, for example, in conversations aimed at surfacing assumptions, clarifying responsibilities, identifying and removing barriers, and providing meaningful and honest feedback to people on their actions to date. These types of conversations can create transformational moments, when people no longer can easily excuse themselves from being a part of the change effort. They surface the dilemma and clarify the need to make a choice between contributing to

---

[1]We are not arguing that changes in the organization will not be needed; we are arguing that we need to focus *first* on the people whose behavior needs to shift and only later on the context that will have to support those behavior changes.

creating a new future or co-conspiring with those who would desperately hold on to the status quo. *It is in these types of conversations that reality is confronted on a personal level, and personal change becomes possible.* The best way, and maybe the only way, for leaders to address these issues, then, is to examine whether they approach or avoid conversations that are crucial to the change process.

Our contention is that self-correction—growth, progress, and change—is the natural order of things in life; it is not some unnatural occurrence that requires brute force to bring about (as it often seems in many organizational change stories). People will naturally choose to act in response to changing realities if they see and understand those shifts and their implications, and if they see their roles in producing the conditions that make the status quo unacceptable. If this is true, then the question should not be "How do I drive positive change?" rather, it should be "What is restraining it?"

Our conclusion is that what keeps relationships, teams, and organizations stuck from the natural path of self-correction and growth is our inability to foster dialogue around a few crucial conversations. The corollary, then, is that the strongest lever for leading to breakthroughs is to first influence how leaders—and later, how everyone—approaches opportunities to create these transformational moments.[2]

## THE PIVOT POINT

For example, the problem in the financial services company was *not* that people were not cooperating. That happens everywhere from time to time. The problem was that people—beginning at the top of the organization—seemed incapable of discussing this lack of cooperation. People had so come to expect a lack of cooperation that no one discussed it anymore—beginning with the leaders. When a vice president felt stonewalled in a request for support from a corporate function, he would shrug his shoulders and work around the problem. By so doing, he was not only colluding in perpetuating the problem, he was providing the key resistance to self-correction and change. No change in the structure or work design or anything else out there could matter if he would not talk about the core issue that held him, and the company, back.

We watched, for example, a budget planning discussion between senior executives in this company. It was the first such exercise these executives had been through since the rollup of the three companies. In the months prior to the session

---

[2]Transformational moments can come about for many reasons (e.g., crisis, a stretch assignment, and benchmarking to find new possibilities). We are arguing that we, as leaders, can produce needed transformational moments by holding the kind of candid conversations that make ineffective mental models/behavior subject to scrutiny. Although not a new concept, it is a powerful one and one that is within our circle of influence.

each executive appeared to jockey for position with Stacy. Some were concerned that the two vice presidents who arrived with Stacy—Bruce and Frank—from her previous company were "untouchable." So with this mixture of politics, tentativeness, and self-interest, the discussion began. It started out as "business as usual." Each vice president prepared a budget that demonstrated clearly why his/her division was the only sensible place to invest precious capital dollars. They would grossly overstate what they expected, argue for it as though it were rational, and then return to their division with a compromise that hopefully resembled what they secretly expected.

They were stuck in a rut of their own making all because they avoided the conversation that could get them unstuck. We came to call these "crucial conversations," because they offered a transformational opportunity for change. If the CEO's vision of a truly cross-functional, client-focused organization were ever to come about, these vice presidents would have to address what kept them stuck. Only when individuals, beginning with leaders, actually talk candidly about behavior that is detracting from their goal—directly, specifically, and immediately—can real change occur.

We learned this by seeing, time and again, how real change began when leaders stopped averting their eyes or ducking their heads when potential transformational moments presented themselves. Here's how it played out at the insurance company.

Stacy began this meeting by reminding everyone that their success as a company depended on their success as an executive team. She urged them to examine each budget request carefully and ask themselves whether it made sense for the company as a whole. Everyone nodded in agreement.

The ritual began predictably. As Fred presented his budget, other executives asked fairly tentative questions and pushed only gently. No one wanted to throw the first punch, lest punching be declared fair game when they were in the ring. Bruce, a previous peer of Stacy, was to present his budget next. After he did so, and questions began, Stacy violated protocol by answering many of the questions asked of Bruce. To most in the room, the message was clear—Stacy was there to defend Bruce's budget. Her "boy" couldn't be touched.

Had the meeting ended this way, the top-drawer effort to change behaviors and attitudes in the company would have continued to flounder. This very conversation would have been one more example of how turf, politics and position were more important than the customer focus and teamwork propaganda that had accompanied the process, or the pay and structural changes of the previous months.

It was at this pivotal moment in the merged company's evolution—as we later saw—that the attitudes of company leaders hung in the balance. The question was, "Would anyone step up to the crucial conversation that was hanging there in midair?" Would anyone dare to question Stacy's actions, or would they instead act out, rather than talk out, their concerns. Would this event become one more justification for talking the "teamwork talk" while walking a "functional, self-interested" walk?

But that's not where it ended. While a few vice presidents began to fidget and others looked on with a ceramic game face, one spoke up. Kevin, in a respectful but direct way, pointed out what had just happened. He went on to describe the effect he thought it was having in the room. And he did so in a way that made it clear that his whole motive was to support Stacy and the team's vision and goals.

Kevin's intervention was followed by what seemed like a long and very uncomfortable silence, as everyone waited to see what Stacy would do. Then, finally comprehending what Kevin was saying, Stacy smiled broadly, then laughed, and then apologized. She went on to describe how Bruce had been out for minor surgery the previous week when budgets were prepared. Since she had previously led his division, she prepared his budget for him, and so was more prepared than he to answer questions. She apologized for not explaining this before, and asked the group to cycle back and hammer hard on Bruce's budget.

That moment was a turning point for the team, a transformational moment. Kevin took Stacy at her word and asked some very direct questions about the budget. Others followed suit. The participants later described that as their first true experience as an executive team looking at a budget from a company perspective. And, from that beginning, they started to have the kind of dialogues that turned conversations into levers for change.

## DIALOGUE DURING CRUCIAL CONVERSATIONS IS WHAT REMOVES BARRIERS TO CHANGE

Time and again we've watched as organizations that were stuck in their capacity to release the potential of their people make great progress by creating dialogue around the crucial conversations that are keeping them stuck. We helped executives understand that investment in other changes could, realistically, only have marginal and/or short-term returns. And we helped them learn how to create the mind-set, skill-set, and heart-set needed to help themselves and their people identify and to hold crucial conversations.

For example, we worked with an organization that had spent millions of dollars on Six Sigma efforts without realizing any appreciable gains in cycle time, quality, or productivity—the benefits you'd expect to achieve from such an effort. They had successfully implemented two small Six Sigma pilot projects by focusing enormous organizational attention on these areas. But aside from these "brute force" success cases, there was little evidence that Six Sigma concepts and tools were integrated as a new way of doing business.

At that point the company began to focus on some specific crucial conversations that released people's natural desire to improve quality and performance in their teams. It turned out that what was sapping people's desire to use Six Sigma processes was their belief that these tools would never deal with the *real* barriers to improvement. These barriers included:

- Peers who were wasteful or unproductive
- Supervisors who weren't walking the talk
- Senior managers who didn't give the time, resources, or support required to make real changes

Over a period of 18 months, we worked on enabling people to candidly discuss these and related tough issues to help them confront reality by creating transformational moments. The result was remarkable. Areas of the company that were previously rife with cynicism (i.e., a chorus chanting "This place will never change!") began to make rapid progress in implementing significant improvements. In short order, Six Sigma tools became useful vehicles for advancing ideas and desires people naturally wanted to promote. As we interviewed various teams in the organization, it was clear that the areas where these three crucial conversations were held most effectively were the areas where the most improvement was achieved.

In this case, we collected data to examine any impact on bottom line business results. Our results revealed more of a widespread recognition that tough subjects were now open to dialogue and hard performance indicators where the needle was moving in the right direction. More importantly, the data showed that performance rose more in those units that reported better dialogue, where people spoke about what mattered. We cannot pinpoint any one transformational moment that occurred, but suggest that in this company, any conversation that allowed people to address the real issues they faced would have been regarded as transformational. Anecdotal evidence from write-in responses to surveys suggested this was the case: "Who got inside my supervisor's body? He actually asked us to find a better solution since the one standard one was not (and never had been) working!"

## CRUCIAL CONVERSATIONS CREATE TRANSFORMATIONAL MOMENTS

Great companies produce great results, consistently, and over long time frames. Collins and Porras[3] recently called such companies "visionary companies" and said they were built to last . . . and built to win. These companies surely have many

---

[3]*See* James C. Collins and Jerry I. Porras, *Built to Last: Successful Habits of Visionary Companies* (New York: HarperCollins, 2002).

lessons to teach and best practices to offer. But, leaders who set out to emulate those that are built to last are living in hope, not reality, if they only focus on the contextual factors that are easy to see in those visionary companies. *It's not the structure, systems, processes, and practices . . . it's the people that matter.* It's the people who make those contextual factors work. And, as tempting as it might be to try to transform a company by adopting these best practices, it is a failure path for greatness. Imagine transplanting the people from an also-ran company into a visionary company. Would the structures, systems, processes, and practices win out or would those great companies slip to becoming good companies, to becoming also-rans? We think the latter.

We have come to believe that the first question leaders should ask when attempting to address significant business challenges that require new ways of behaving is not "What structures, systems, processes, or practices must we make to drive change?" Rather, we believe that a more fruitful approach to releasing people's natural desires for change and progress come from asking transformational questions:

- "What crucial conversations are we not holding or not holding well that are keeping us stuck?"
- How are we as leaders failing in these same conversations?
- How will we hold others to our new standards for making a difference?

Real change in our organizations requires personal change. This is not a new theme. Bob Quinn makes this point powerfully in his recent books on leadership.[4] Change leaders confront emerging reality; they understand, own, and act on their responsibility; and they help others do the same—they lead themselves and others. What may be new is the notion that we can create transformational moments by engaging our people in conversations that are, at the same time, at the limit of our collective dysfunction and to our power to create meaningful, sustaining change.

When we confront reality by holding a crucial conversation, we disturb habit and call attention to the gap between what we say and the results we actually produce. For many people this is a transformational moment. When we give honest feedback to teammates, we do the same. When we help our peers see the story that excuses them from acting with responsibility, we create the opportunity for change. To be sure, these crucial conversations only hold the promise for transformation; some people may not respond in an adaptive way. But, to also be sure, without holding these crucial conversations, nothing will change. We need to disturb the thinking of our people in ways that help them see the choices they've made and that give them the opportunity to choose again, to choose adaptive responses that produce

---

[4]*See* Robert E. Quinn, *Deep Change, Change the World* and *Letters from Garrett* (San Francisco: Jossey-Bass, 1996).

the results we want and need. This requires transformation and we believe that, in turn, requires holding crucial conversations.

## CHANGE ME—CHANGE US

So, how do we begin? We believe that personal change must begin at the top if our organizations are to fully realize the full potential of the people that constitute them. We become individually more powerful to confront emerging reality when we improve our ability to talk about the emotionally and politically risky issues that remove the barriers to change. And the first step toward influencing how everyone holds crucial conversations is for leaders to change how they hold theirs. In doing so, we become more collectively powerful.

The crucial conversation we described in the insurance company turned out to be a watershed event. The remaining budget discussions in that meeting rose to a higher standard of candor and engagement than previous ones had. Executives asked more penetrating questions, confronted fallacious assumptions, and challenged each other to embrace a higher standard of "enterprise-level focus"—beginning with the pivotal moment when Kevin chose to confront rather than avoid what he perceived as hypocritical behavior from the CEO.

As the meeting was about to wrap up, Fred, who had made the first budget presentation, took the group to a new level. He suggested that capital funds that he had been given earlier in the meeting were excessive given the growth potential of his division. "If this is really about building the company rather than just my division, then I suggest we take $5 million from my budget and move it to Bruce's where the real growth opportunities are." The meeting went another two hours and the entire budget was reallocated—this time with a *true* team view driving the discussion.

Transformational moments can occur suddenly and can be short in duration, but they, nonetheless, can cast a shadow far into the future. In the insurance company, for example, people did get around to making the new structure, work design, and processes work, not because of the new performance management system, but because out of transformation comes an understanding of the right things to do, and the will to do them.

And it all started with a crucial conversation.

## CONCLUSION

Organizational change isn't magic; it's just hard. And, it's hard because we make it hard by focusing our attention on externals—structure, systems, processes, and practices. These seductive change targets appear to be appropriate—they are seen in our books about best practices and are the take-aways from our benchmark visits. It is our contention, that, as targets for change, they are distractions, at best; they do not have the power to create change.

Organizations change only when people change—when hundreds, or even thousands, of people behave differently. We get the new outcomes we want and need, not because of the new structure, strong focus on teams, or strategic reward system. We get the new outcomes we want and need because people produce them!

We believe these new outcomes come about when, and only when, we hold the kind of conversation that speaks to our dysfunction as individuals or as teams. When we help people see their integrity gap (between what they espouse and actually do), we give them an opportunity to make new choices—to choose between continuing to be "stuck" or to move forward in a more effective way.

Remaining "stuck" demands collusion and codependency. Everyone has to turn their backs if people are to be allowed to continue their individual and collective dysfunction. In this way, people collude to not just allow mediocrity, but to create a self-sealing pattern that fights against improvement . . . fights against real change. To borrow from a well-known saying, "It takes a village to produce continued mediocrity!"

The only path that breaks old patterns is one that confronts them. And that takes courageous leaders, starting at the top, to step up to the challenge of holding crucial conversations, to help others see their roles in producing the results they get, and to help others understand that new results require new behavior on their parts.

So, how do you transform a large organization? We think that they can only change one crucial conversation at a time.

# Chapter 21

MANAGE ORGANIZATIONAL EMOTIONAL
AND BUSINESS CHAOS FOR EXCEPTIONAL
BUSINESS PERFORMANCE RESULTS

*Deborah Rozman and Doc Childre*

## Introduction

Best practices for business often refer to the importance of creating alignment between mission, vision, values, goals, strategy, and tactical plans. Alignment is viewed as critical for achieving bottom-line results and increasing shareholder value. In most organizations there are serious breaks in alignment, contributing to chaos, complexity, and unpredictability: mission statements that decorate company walls but don't impact day to day business; visionaries out of touch with marketplace realities; values paid lip service but not lived; long-range goal planning sacrificed to fighting fires and short term needs; staff meetings as pep rallies to boost enthusiasm but resulting in cynicism. The result is emotional and business chaos. The chaos becomes more exacerbated in times of economic uncertainty. Personal and organizational security both are threatened, causing increased emotional stress and lack of clarity. This scenario describes many organizations today.

Emotions are one of the last taboos in business to be addressed. Some leaders are realizing the need to deal with toxic emotions, but don't know how. Fortunately, there are best practices based on new research, tools and methodologies that allow people to develop emotional management skills quickly, with almost immediate stress relief and performance benefits. These tools enable people to shift perceptions and break through mindsets that confine them to tactical issues without the larger overview.

## Emotional Alignment

Creating, managing, and sustaining organizational alignment is a signature of leadership. The mental, emotional, and physical (action) alignment within an individual has to come first, before alignment with others can be sustained. We need only look to physics to understand how this works. Alignment is the proper adjustment of components for coordinated functioning, in a machine, an electronic circuit, a laser, etc., or a state of agreement or cooperation among persons. When alignment occurs there is *coherence* between parts, and intended results are likely to be achieved. Coherence is the orderly and harmonious relationship of parts that generates increased clarity and power. For example, when light photons are aligned, they emit highly amplified and coherent radiation—a laser—that has more power to shed light and cut through densities than the incoherent, non-aligned photons in an incandescent light bulb.

To shift a business from chaos to coherence requires the mental and emotional as well as physical (action) alignment between all stakeholders. Often the emotional component is ignored and the mental/action alignment breaks down. Some might question whether emotional alignment is possible if personal goals and objectives differ from boardroom to front line workers other than the common denominator of making money. But even making money will fall short if there's emotional bankruptcy. When a company is under siege from emotional chaos, mergers fail, commitment erodes, productivity wanes, and innovation languishes. Emotional mismanagement obstructs the coherent energetic momentum needed to achieve goals.

Many leaders today recognize the need to mine and develop the knowledge capital of employees, to increase and utilize the intangible assets of the company. The ability to develop or extract latent assets is impacted by the organizational emotional climate. Emotions are where passion, care, meaningfulness, and satisfaction are experienced. Emotion fuels creativity or innovation and provides the juice for going the extra mile. Without emotional alignment, the needed power, clarity and intuitive feeling that can laser through complexities or make the impossible possible is lost.

Emotions may be the most wasted and neglected resource in business. They are left to go whichever way the wind blows or stack in a toxic dump. In the best of times, people waste emotional energy in pursuit of emotional vanities such as one-upmanship, greed, self-centered ambition, and manipulation, which lead to backbiting, undermining, and organizational chaos. Negative emotional energy pumps out like an uncontrollable fire hose until it is spent. Or it quietly leaks away in resentment and blame, like a dripping faucet that no one sees until it has rotted the floorboards under the sink. In difficult times, when people need a full reserve of emotional energy to stay buoyant, what's left is disarray, anger, anxiety, depression and burnout. Internal emotional chaos costs businesses far more than they realize. It is only starting to be quantified, yet its effects can be seen in soaring health care costs, increased absenteeism, slowed productivity, missed goals, customer complaints, and poor product quality. When employees are just trying to survive emotionally, the company gas tank is running low or near empty. This eventually translates as losses to the bottom line. At this time in history when the speed of change is unprecedented, emotional chaos is having lightning-quick and devastating consequences.

The AOL/Time Warner merger is a seminal example of a merger gone awry due to lack of emotional alignment between stakeholders, with billions of dollars lost as a result. The scandals of Enron, Tyco, and WorldCom are graphic illustrations of the impact of emotional mismanagement and unbridled vanity on employees, shareholders, and society.

James K. Clifton, chairman and chief executive officer of the Gallup Organization, is speaking out on emotions as a critical factor for business success. In a *Gallup Management Journal* article, titled "Winning Business in the Emotional Economy," Clifton cites statistics on how successful organizations can build sustainable growth by harnessing the power of human emotions. From the statistics he concludes, "The success of your organization doesn't depend on your understanding of economics, or organizational development, or marketing. It depends, quite simply, on your understanding of psychology: How each individual employee connects with your customers; how each individual employee connects with your company."[1] He further explains that companies have learned how to be lean and mean to cut prices but know very little about how to grow margins. Now, faced with extreme competition and customer relationships based solely on price, they are headed down a path toward continuous margin erosion unless they discover a new way to manage human nature and unlock new potential. This requires understanding human emotion.

Peter J. Frost describes the emotional pain in today's workplaces and the strategic and financial imperatives for developing compassionate management in his thought provoking book, *Toxic Emotions at Work.* (Harvard Business School Press, p. 30). He reports that study after study has shown a distinct correlation between a harmonious workplace and company profits. David H. Maister, a former professor at the Harvard Business School, surveyed more than 5,500 people from 139 offices in 29 firms in 15 countries on quality of client service, quality of work, market reputation, long-term client relationships, profitability, and growth. Financial performance of each office was measured by an examination of margin, profit per-employee, revenue growth over two years, and profits over the same period. Results showed that *employee attitudes actually drove financial results*, not the other way around, and that 23 percent of all the variations in financial performance

---

[1]"Winning Business in the Emotional Economy," *Gallup Management Journal.*

could be explained by the degree to which employees agreed with the statement, "We have an uncompromising determination to achieve excellence in all that we do." More than 50 percent of all variations in profit performance were explained by nine key attitudes, none of which had to do with technical skills or financial acuity. Maister concludes that by raising employee satisfaction 20 percent, a company can boost its financial performance by more than 42 percent.[2]

So what actions can organizations take to turn around emotional chaos? First, they have to recognize, admit, and even measure its draining effects. Companies create balance sheets to account for financial assets and deficits, but it's time to also do cost accounting on mental and emotional gains and drains, since that's too often the source of financial drains. Money is energy. Mental, emotional, and physical energies move and flow within and between individuals and between organizations. A tirade of negative thoughts, judgments and blame, can keep emotional and physical energy draining all day. As the speed of change accelerates and disrupts work-flows, emotional reactivity accelerates and can spread like a virus in the workplace—an *emotional virus*. Emotional virus symptoms include ongoing negative attitudes, blame, griping, us-versus-them behavior, office politics, and widespread defeatism. When you hear people gossiping about they, them, she, or him with a negative slant, there's a virus spreading. An emotional virus is a contagion that erodes teamwork, blocks problem solving, and generates an atmosphere of incoherence and stress.

## THE STRESS EFFECT

Organizations of the future that seek to build and sustain high performance will diligently address its prime disabler: emotional stress. Stress, rather than being an external event which can cause us to feel stress, is actually an internal physiological and emotional response to our perception of threat, resulting in a series of adaptations by the mind and body. Simply put, the body creates a stress reaction in response to our perceptions and emotions. Too much stress becomes disabling.

Stress in organizations is just starting to "come out of the closet." In the post-September 11, 2001, world of gnawing economic, political, and social anxiety, people are needing to talk more openly about chronic feelings of anxiety, tension, being overwhelmed, and helplessness that have become commonplace. Some companies are providing employee assistance programs, counseling services, wellness programs, and flexible work schedules to reduce employee stress. While tremendously

---

[2]Maister, David H. *Practice What You Preach: What Managers Must Do to Create a High Achievement Culture*, New York: The Free Press, June 2001.

helpful, these accommodations don't in themselves address the source of emotional or business chaos in the work environment—let alone make it a place you want to be and feel productive. Job stress is highest when feeling overworked is combined with feeling you have little or no control, unfair supervision, feeling undervalued and unappreciated, and few opportunities for career advance.[3]

A 2002 Cigna Behavioral Health survey found 45 percent of all workers say their job is more stressful than ever and they either considered leaving their job, left their job, or plan to do so soon. Many do the minimum to get by. When asked to describe their workplace attitude, 47 percent say "choppy waters" while 11 percent describe themselves as "man overboard" They cite several reasons: uncertain economy, worries about job loss, heightened distrust in corporate America, and the reduced value of their retirement savings and investments. Only 5 percent say global terrorism is a contributor to their stress. Their decision not to leave their stressful job is based on a need for a steady paycheck or a fear of the unknown. "These figures should catch the attention of employers across the country," says Dr. Keith Dixon, president of CIGNA Behavioral Health. "It's hard to build productive and cohesive work teams when more than a third of your people would rather be doing something else."[4]

Another 2002 study by the National Institute for Occupational Safety and Health found that the number of people who called in sick due to stress has tripled from four years ago and 42 percent of employees—double the percentage in 2001—say their coworkers need help managing their stress. This is a cry for help. The American Institute of Stress estimates that stress and the ills it can cause—absenteeism, burnout, mental, and physical health problems—now cost American business more than $300 billion a year. Workers who report high levels of stress cost health care systems almost 50 percent more than their less-stressed colleagues.

## THE ROLE OF LEADERSHIP

It will take courageous leadership to buck the growing stress momentum and create coherence out of chaos. People are looking for leaders who care and have compassion. They are tired of answering to emotionally unmanaged, self-serving masters who lead themselves and those around them into chaos. In his book *Primal Leadership,* Daniel Goleman demonstrates through numerous research studies

---

[3]Reaney, Patricia. *The British Medical Journal* (2002).
[4]CIGNA Behavioral Health, "Worried At Work: Mood and Mindsets in the American Workplace," KRC Research, 2002.

how leaders' emotional states and actions profoundly affect how the people they lead will feel and therefore perform. He astutely states, "How well leaders manage their moods and affect everyone else's moods, then, becomes not just a private matter, but a factor in how well a business will do."[5]

Combining sophisticated health and performance testing with a psychometric tool called the Personal and Organizational Quality Assessments (POQA), the Institute of HeartMath, a non-profit research and education organization founded by stress and performance researcher, Doc Childre, has identified how critical emotional coherence is to personal effectiveness for individuals and organization. HeartMath's research with an organizational development model called Inner Quality Management (IQM) shows how leaders set the emotional climate of the organization, and it is their own personal coherence that is a critical precondition for organizational coherence. Measuring various stress symptoms, emotional attitudes, and feelings toward work and senior management, provides a clear window into the state of organizational performance.

Unfortunately, it's still taboo for most executives to admit a stress problem, although their physician, coach, corporate medical director, or spouse may know the problem only too well. After all, leaders are supposed to thrive under stress and employees are expected to perform better under the goad of stress. It's traditionally been seen as a sign of weakness to admit chronic anger, anxiety, depression, or panic attacks, or to acknowledge the effect of their lack of emotional management on others. The net effect is "People are absolutely nuts, stressed off the map . . . I've never seen it this bad." says Dr. Stephen Schoonover, author of *Your Soul at Work* and head of a firm that helps executives combat stress in their lives.

So what are workers doing to cope? When emotional chaos gets to a certain point and people have nowhere to turn, they either breakdown, blow up, or go to the heart to find some intuitive direction. As a result, many are saying no to ludicrous work schedules and taking more time for family or vacations or just having fun. Others are taking time for meaningful reflection, getting more involved with spirituality, and taking up exercise programs or hobbies. They are turning away from the workplace as a place to learn and unfold their potential. It's time for leaders to seize the day and transform chaos into coherence. This starts with emotional alignment to laser through the chaos. Rigid business structures will have to change and process improvements implemented that foster emotional alignment. This will free up a tremendous amount of energy for internal and external growth and mission alignment. Fortunately there are tools, instruments, models, and measurements for achieving emotional alignment and coherence, step by step.

---

[5]Goleman, Daniel. *Primal Leadership*. Cambridge: HBS Press, 2002, pp. 18, 26.

# THE ROLE OF THE HEART

Since 1991, Institute of HeartMath has researched and developed scientifically based business tools to improve the stress/performance ratio. This research includes the impact of emotions on physiology and decision making. It draws from a promising new field called neurocardiology and maps how the heart and brain communicate. What is significant is that this research has proven that the heart is an intelligent system with its own nervous system and processing capacity and that it is part of the emotional system. Feelings do affect the heart. Sayings like, "listen to your heart," "put your heart into it," and "follow your heart" are not mere metaphors; they are performance tools based on sound physiology. Neurocardiologists discovered in the early 1990s that the heart has an intrinsic nervous system—a complex an independent system referred to as "the brain in the heart." This heart-brain has neurons that sense, feel, and remember. It receives and relays information from the heart to the brain in the head. The heart has been found to be a convenient access point for creating positive emotional change, and ultimately, organizational change. Attitude and perception shifts happen quickly when heart and brain are brought into emotional alignment. Great leaders intuitively know this and use this knowledge to galvanize passion and action when a new mission or direction is needed. Heart-brain alignment results in higher mental and intuitive functioning for better performance—like running higher octane gas through your system. Because of the promise this performance research has for individuals and organizations, it's helpful to explain a little about its scientific underpinnings.

# GETTING ALIGNED—HARNESSING THE POWER OF FEELINGS

The experience of feelings transforms the world from a series of events and facts into a living, dynamic experience that gives meaning to life. When feelings are strong, they can be detected in the changing pattern of people's heart rhythms or heart rate variability (HRV). When frustrated, afraid, worried, angry, or upset, people's heart rhythms become uneven and irregular. Viewed on a computer screen, they look like ragged mountain peaks. This jerky pattern is called a chaotic or incoherent pattern and is typical of feelings of anger or frustration. When upset, it's hard to feel or think coherently and people are more likely to say or do things they later regret. When feeling confident, secure, cared for, or appreciative of someone or something, people's heart rhythms become smooth and even. HRV takes on a highly ordered or coherent pattern, which is an indicator of nervous system balance and good health. Scientists have found that a smooth, coherent heart rhythm pattern also makes it easier to self-manage emotions, think clearly, and make better intuitive decisions.

The autonomic nervous system connects the brain and heart. It controls many of the functions of the internal organs and glands that secrete hormones. The autonomic nervous system is also involved in the ability to feel and experience emotions. Negative emotions like anger, anxiety, or worry, cause the signals going down the two parts of the autonomic nervous system to the heart to become out-of-sync with each other and cause heart rate to speed up and slow down in a jerky manner. Being out-of-sync from negative emotions can be likened to driving a car with one foot on the gas pedal (the sympathetic nervous system) and the other on the brake (the parasympathetic nervous system) at the same time. Just as it causes extra wear and tear on a car and burns more gas, being out of sync causes extra stress in the body and drains energy. Everyone has negative emotions occasionally, but too many over too long a time keep heart rhythm patterns incoherent and keep people on mental and emotional stress overload. This affects attitude, health, and performance. Perception gets distorted (e.g., the boss looks at you funny, and you're sure that he's being critical or that you'll be fired). Without thinking you react—get upset, scared, angry, and are ready to quit. Long-term studies have revealed that chronic stress reactions and attitudes such as anxiety, hostility, and fear degrade physical health and dramatically increase the risk of cardiovascular disease, cancer, and other chronic conditions. The link in this chain to the underlying heart rhythm patterns represents a breakthrough for understanding and transforming chronic stress reactions.

It is now clear that positive emotions, such as appreciation, care, and compassion allow the two branches of the nervous system to get in sync and the heart's rhythm pattern to become more ordered and coherent. Heart rhythm coherence drives heart–brain synchronization or alignment. There is a direct correlation between one's degree of heart rhythm coherence and cognitive performance outcomes. Research shows that increased heart rhythm coherence increases flexibility in the way one thinks, improves decision making, increases creativity and intuitive problem solving, improves immunity and hormonal balance, and lowers blood pressure. Most leaders and anyone who has been successful has intuitively understood this and created personal strategies to do things they enjoy in order to bring more balance and coherence into their systems. Scientific research is now confirming the physiological value of positive feelings.

Getting in sync is smart business. Heart–brain synchronization (alignment) gives people the coherent power they need to control emotional habits and impulses. It increases awareness and focuses scattered emotional energies. People gain clearer intuition to see and make choices based on what's best for the whole situation. The concept of emotional intelligence, popularized by Daniel Goleman in a book of that title, promises these outcomes but its implementation into the workplace has been slow. His book spawned a movement that injected enthusiasm and hope into those responsible for transforming the emotional chaos of their organizations. His framework for developing emotional capacity and leadership excellence has been synthesized into four key constructs: self-awareness, self-management, social awareness, and relationship management.[6] However, the challenge for most organizations is to turn conceptual frameworks into practical tools people can apply in their work and day-to-day lives.

HeartMath's Inner Quality Management system (described in more depth below) blends a strong conceptual and physiological research framework with simple, field-tested tools that are easy to apply in developing emotional capacity and self-management. HeartMath's research has shown that emotional awareness involves integrity, courage, and commitment to acknowledge what you are feeling about yourself, others, and issues, and then to manage your emotions from the coherent heart rhythm state to bring them into alignment to find clarity. People are accountable for the effects of their emotions on their bodies, minds, work products, and careers.

Creating emotional alignment within oneself and the workplace does not have to be a squeamish or arduous task, but it does take practice. The fear of many leaders is that it will be like uncovering a nest of roaches that scurry every which way when exposed to the light of day. However, there are proven methodologies that can guide individuals and businesses through the paces of emotional alignment. Once emotional alignment is improved, even incrementally by an individual, a work team, or organization, it geometrically accelerates achievement in other areas. The ROI can be significant. One effective effort yields a 10-times or more return in results, intangible and tangible. As emotional ROI is increased, it improves the stress/performance ratio and lifts an individual, team, or organization out of emotional deficit spending. The reduction in backbiting, mistakes, time waste, and stress, and improved organizational climate can be felt by all.

There will always be unmanaged emotions in the workplace, always people who feel under-appreciated or feel company policies and actions are unfair. Effectiveness in building organizational coherence is not about having idealistic expectations, but about systematically increasing emotional alignment in steps and stages. This frees energy to stay focused on a mission, inspired by vision, living meaningful values, and achieving goals in an iterative process with other stakeholders. It increases job satisfaction and gratification, refueling passion and commitment that act as a buffer during challenging times. Increased coherence allows

---

[6]Goleman, Daniel. *Emotional Intelligence.* New York: BantumBooks, 1997.

organizations to surf the inevitable ups and downs with minimal energy loss—mental, emotional, and physical—and that means money to the stakeholders. Emotional alignment is the substrate of sustainable peak performance.

## TOOLS TO CREATE COHERENCE OUT OF CHAOS

HeartMath's Inner Quality Management (IQM) system is a blueprint for creating emotional alignment within the individual and the organization. It encompasses four dynamics: internal self-management, coherent communication, boosting organizational climate, and strategic processes and renewal. The tools of IQM enable individuals to quickly stop emotional stress in the moment, shift their heart rhythms into a more coherent pattern, and align heart and brain for clearer perception and intuition. The tools empower both leaders and workers to shift out of frustration, anger, worry, and anxiety into at least a neutral state, to depersonalize and assess a situation with more awareness and objectivity. They foster appreciative, compassionate, or caring modes that improve communication, satisfaction, and performance outcomes. Often one intuitive insight gained from using a HeartMath tool has solved a problem that has kept an individual or workplace embroiled in chaos. The results of practice are not only beneficial in the moment of crisis or challenge, but because they are based on fundamental physiological principles, they also create a re-patterning of old habits and behaviors which can be life-changing. From an organizational perspective, as individuals' coherence and resilience increases, workplace climate, creativity, morale, and productivity are all enhanced.

One of the core HeartMath tools is the Freeze-Frame® technique, which can be used any time you find yourself in a stressful or potentially stressful situation. Based on this simple emotional coherence technique, a computer software system, called the Freeze-Framer®, has also been developed which shows, in real time, changes in the user's heart rhythm coherence level (reflecting emotional alignment) as the individual uses the technique. The Freeze-Frame technique on its own develops increased heart rhythm coherence so you can quickly recoup from drained emotional energy. Use of the computer software system in combination with Freeze-Frame can train the individual to gain the high performance state at will and sustain it for longer and longer periods, much like an athlete or performer trains himself for high performance on demand.

For example, if you pause right now and focus on something in your life that you appreciate, perhaps your spouse, child, pet, garden, new car, or anything that evokes a genuine feeling of appreciation, you can smooth out and bring more coherence to your heart rhythm patterns. Just focus on the positive feeling of appreciation and let it expand through your body. If you do this for an entire minute it could change the rest of your day. What you perceive, how you feel, and what you decide to do next could be different than before you did this simple exercise in appreciation.

An executive in a *Fortune* 100 high-tech company describes Freeze-Frame as follows:

> "I think of Freeze-Frame as a business power-tool. After using it in my work for a couple of years, I find it indispensable for creative planning, problem solving, making clear decisions, and maintaining a high level of stamina during long days. I'm able to gain access to more clear, creative, and intelligent solutions. My work throws me into lots of situations that I have to plan for but can't control. Freeze-Frame has helped me to generate creative solutions in unexpected situations that required clear 'thinking on my feet.' A side effect of using Freeze-Frame at work is it's nice to have some energy and creativity to take home with me at the end of a long day!"[7]

Another core HeartMath tool is called the Cut-Thru® technique. It empowers individuals to literally cut through patterns of overcare, insecurity, anxiety, or depression to perceive new options. This tool aligns the heart, brain, and gut for more coherent power and brings in a higher organizing intelligence. A senior leader at Motorola attributes the creation of six new patents in a short time frame to his team's practice of the Cut-Thru technique. In the book, *Overcoming Emotional Chaos,* Doc Childre and I describe how the Cut-Thru technique can be used to unlock creativity, innovation, and satisfaction in the workplace.

The IQM system and other coherence-building tools and strategies for energizing teams, project planning, and leadership are described in *From Chaos to Coherence: The Power to Change Performance*, by Doc Childre and HeartMath CEO Bruce Cryer. HeartMath LLC, an innovative training and consulting company specializing in human and workplace performance since the early 1990s, also provides organizations with pre- and post-training Personal and Organizational Quality Assessments (POQAs) which are statistically analyzed to evaluate emotional assets and deficits and track the progress in achieving alignment and coherence. The POQA is an 80-item self-report inventory with 14 separate dimensions designed to reflect key elements that underpin performance and quality. Assessments are collected just prior to HeartMath training and again six to eight weeks after. It includes personal data (e.g., I feel angry, annoyed, tense, anxious, depressed, exhausted, etc). Each question includes a five-point response scale (e.g., often, most of the time, occasionally, almost never, never). It also includes business data (e.g., My supervisor and I communicate well with each other) with response options (e.g., agree, strongly agree, disagree, strongly disagree, etc.)

---

[7]HeartMath LLC, Hunter Kane, Ltd., United Kingdom, 2001.

## ASSESSMENT OUTCOMES

World-class companies, such as Sony, Shell, Cisco, Boeing, Unilever, BP, and Liz Claiborne, are providing HeartMath programs to executives and teams, training in-house trainers to deliver the programs, and providing Freeze-Framer heart rhythm software to employees. Stakeholders from main board members to executives to middle managers to front-line workers have significantly decreased their anxiety, anger, feelings of being overwhelmed, and intent to leave their job, as well as significantly reduced their stress symptoms, and have been able to sustain these improvements through practice of the HeartMath tools long after the training. For one *Fortune* 100 technology company, pre- and post-data showed that the percentage of employees who frequently experienced anger was reduced from 42 percent to 9 percent after 3months. Surveys of nearly 1,400 employees at five global companies showed the following pooled results after 6 months:

- 60 percent reduction in anxiety
- 45 percent reduction in exhaustion
- 41 percent reduction in intent to leave the job
- 24 percent improvement in the ability to focus
- 25 percent improvement in listening ability
- 17 percent improvement in home/work conflict[8]

Many individuals reported finding a new rhythm when under pressure and used the emotional alignment and coherence tools not only at work, but also in many aspects of their personal lives. All of this adds up to increased productivity, improved performance, health, and satisfaction, and cost savings to the organization.

Below is a published case study of outcomes from these five global companies.

## COMPOSITE CASE STUDY

### *Five Global Companies—Pooled Results*

#### Sample Size: 1376

The data presented here represents the impact of the HeartMath's Power to Change Performance, an Inner Quality Management program (IQM), on nearly 1,400 people at five global companies.

---

[8]HeartMath LLC, Hunter Kane, Ltd., United Kingdom.

Prior to attending the course, all participants completed an extensive psycho-metric questionnaire, the Personal and Organizational Quality Assessment (POQA). The POQA was administered again six weeks after the training and again at 6 months to determine the impact of the IQM program. The POQA is a self-re-port inventory designed to reflect the key psychological and workplace elements that contribute to the overall quality of an organization. The instrument provides a concentrated yet comprehensive assessment in the two main topic areas listed here.

# PERSONAL QUALITY

Personal Quality scales directly reflect employees' day-to-day moods, attitudes, and stress-related symptoms. The stress symptom items possess clinical relevance as valid measures of stress, which can exert a significant negative impact on em-ployee health and work performance. Scales include: positive outlook, depression, gratitude, anger management, motivation, resentfulness, calmness, stress symp-toms, fatigue, and anxiety.

# ORGANIZATIONAL QUALITY

Organizational Quality scales are comprised of questions concerning such areas as strategic understanding, goal clarity, and work attitude. Organizational Quality scales also examine key areas that influence employee job involvement, perfor-mance, and important factors related to employee behavior and ability to perform well. These include: freedom of expression, confidence in the organization, job challenge, value of contribution, communication effectiveness, manager support, morale, work intensity, productivity, time pressure, and intention to quit.

The main findings of the POQA are presented in Table 21-1. Some groups were also followed up at 12 months. The data gathered found that the improvements seen at 6 months were sustained at 12 months.

In addition to the subjective POQA assessment, some groups underwent ob-jective assessment of their blood pressure and heart rate variability before and af-ter the IQM program.

# BLOOD PRESSURE RESULTS

Attendees on the first pilot study had their blood pressure monitored over a three-week period prior to the program. The group average was 126/80mmHg. Six weeks after the program, with no other lifestyle changes, the average blood pressure had fallen to 118/78mmHg. That is an 8mmHg drop in systolic blood pressure and a 2 mmHg drop

**Table 21-1**

| 1. Personal Data | Pre-IQM Before | Post-IQM 6 weeks | 6 months | (Sample Size: 1376) |
|---|---|---|---|---|
| I feel tired | 49% | 31% | 32% | Often/Most of the Time |
| I feel exhausted | 38% | 20% | 21% | Often/Most of the Time |
| I feel anxious | 35% | 14% | 14% | Often/Most of the Time |
| I feel worried | 33% | 12% | 15% | Often/Most of the Time |
| I feel annoyed | 29% | 12% | 11% | Often/Most of the Time |
| I feel angry | 17% | 7% | 5% | Often/Most of the Time |
| I feel tense | 41% | 15% | 21% | Often/Most of the Time |
| I experience sleeplessness | 29% | 16% | 11% | Often/Most of the Time |
| I have aches and pains | 25% | 14% | 17% | Often/Most of the Time |

| 2. Business Data | Pre-IQM Before | Post-IQM 6 weeks | 6 months | (Sample Size: 1376) |
|---|---|---|---|---|
| Intent to leave job | 22% | 19% | 13% | Agree/Strongly Agree |
| I am focused | 63% | 68% | 82% | Often/Most of the Time |
| I am satisfied | 47% | 56% | 67% | Often/Most of the Time |
| I am an excellent listener | 66% | 71% | 88% | Agree/Strongly Agree |
| I am perceptive | 65% | 72% | 85% | Agree/Strongly Agree |
| Home/work conflict | 54% | 44% | 45% | Agree/Strongly Agree |

in diastolic blood pressure. One individual, whose blood pressure was very high prior to the program (160/100mmHg), had the first normal reading (130/80 mmHg) for the first time in 15 years according to the company's Chief Occupational Health Physician. This individual's blood pressure has remained normal for the 2 years since the IQM program.

This level of blood pressure reduction, if repeated in a large clinical trial, would reduce the incidence of stroke by approximately 60 percent. The reduction in blood pressure in this pilot study was in keeping with the reduction in blood pressure seen in other groups who have run the IQM program.

# HEART RATE VARIABILITY RESULTS

Heart rate variability (HRV), as measured by the beat-to-beat changes in heart rate derived from a 24-hour electrocardiogram (ECG), is a sophisticated measure of autonomic nervous system activity and balance. It has been repeatedly shown to be a powerful predictor of all-cause mortality. The scientific literature suggests that HRV should remain stable over time with a gradual deterioration with increasing

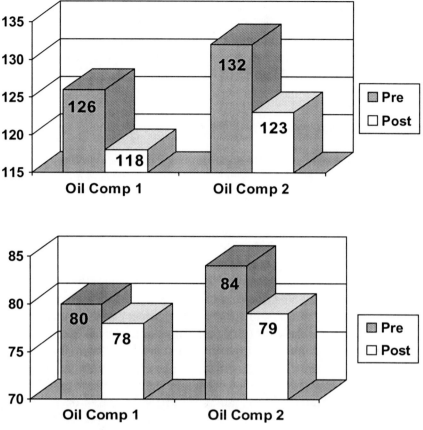

**Figure 21-1    Systolic Blood Pressure / Diastolic Blood Pressure**

with age. Significantly reduced HRV suggests an increased risk of disease and premature aging.

## CONTROLS

A number of individuals in the pilot studies had their HRV measured before and after the IQM program. In one pilot study the entire management team underwent an executive assessment with HRV analysis. All 10 subjects who started to apply the tools after the IQM program saw an objective improvement in their nervous system function and balance. These significant objective improvements as measured by a range of HRV indices, occurred despite the management team being in the middle of a major divisional re-organization (see Table 20-1). The improvements in HRV ranged from 10 to 195 percent and were achieved in just eight weeks. This represents a reversal of the normal age-related decline in HRV data and demonstrates that individuals can indeed improve their nervous system synchronization and balance through practicing emotional self-management.

Source: HeartMath LLC, Hunter Kane, Ltd., United Kingdom.

# RETURN ON INVESTMENT (ROI)

The financial ROI to organizations from HeartMath programs has been significant. The average cost to recruit and train one employee is estimated at 30 percent of an employee's salary. In many cases, if even one or a few employees decide not to leave the organization due to HeartMath training, the cost of the program has been covered. In addition, reduced stress symptoms save companies money in reduced absenteeism and health care expenditures. HeartMath helps organizations chart and track ROI and cost savings following HeartMath leadership and employee trainings.

Delnor Community Hospital near Chicago has worked with the HeartMath since 1999. The first year following HeartMath training, Delnor reduced employee turnover in a staff of 1,000 from 28 percent to 20.9 percent overall and down to 5.9 percent in the 400 HeartMath-trained staff. Delnor realized $800,000 in annualized savings from these turnover reductions. In addition, their customer satisfaction improved from 73 percent to the 93 percent and Medicare length of stay decreased by 9 percent, totaling $1.4 million in annualized savings to the hospital. Delnor was ranked number 1 in employee satisfaction based on Sperduto and Associates national database of more than 300 health care organizations.

In the second year of HeartMath implementation, Delnor's employee turnover rate went down to 14 percent overall and to only 1.3 percent among HeartMath-trained staff. In 2002, Delnor was awarded the prestigious Corporate Health and Productivity Management Award for demonstrating the relationship between health and productivity through intervention initiatives and measuring the resulting changes. Delnor is now incorporating HeartMath training in new employee orientation programs. Tom Wright, Chief Operating Officer at Delnor, says, "HeartMath has given us tools to make the difference between required courtesy and genuine care. We have achieved our benchmarks in excellence in patient satisfaction and employee satisfaction. I believe without HeartMath, we could have not reached our potential."[9] Business Heart

---

[9]Tom Wright, COO, Delnor Community Hospital, 2002.

A climate of increased organizational coherence is palpable and can be felt by all. A work environment where people move and flow with greater equilibrium and warmth, treat each other with compassion and care, and have more available intelligence to cut through challenges in a way that's best for all concerned is a satisfying place to spend eight or more hours a day. HeartMath's tools help organizations establish such an environment and achieve these results by providing leaders and managers with tools to develop what we call "business heart." This means aligning heart and brain for effective decision making.

In today's world, leaders need to be smarter and more intuitive than before. They need to enable people to maximize their potentials A leader with business heart is not soft, but knows that a strong heart and clear head are both essential. As Daniel Goleman so eloquently puts it, "No creature can fly with just one wing. Gifted leadership occurs where heart and head—feeling and thought—meet. These are the two wings that allow a leader to soar."[10]

It's time to for leaders and organizations to understand the role of the heart in human physiology and performance and to develop the heart, not as a soft skill but as a measurable hard skill, an inner technology needed for coherence. People are hard-wired for coherence, but it takes the heart to activate it.

## CONCLUSION: BUILDING COHERENT BUSINESS MODELS

Coherence is an alignment of energies that facilitates the higher organizational intelligence capacities of the human brain. Coherence in individuals and between teams can cut through decision-making and business processes that are complex and time consuming. As the physiological basis of coherence becomes more widely understood, companies will see coherence as a key performance indictor. New business models and systems will emerge. It will be just common sense to structure organization charts, write job descriptions, and conduct performance reviews with coherence as a benchmark The use of 360-degree feedback evaluations will become what they were intended to be—an iterative process to further growth rather than a release valve for incoherence, griping, and blaming. A leader is responsible for managing the equity—developing the assets and resources of the company—internal as well as external. It is the executive leadership who are mandated to develop an organization's knowledge capital, which must involve its emotional capital, or its knowledge will be non-optimized and wasted.

---

[10]Goleman, Daniel. *Primal Leadership*. Cambridge:HBS Press, 2002, p. 26.

A leader's job is to see the bigger picture, hold the vision, energize others, inspire commitment, manage and coach, satisfy customers, and improve shareholder value. There has to be emotional alignment and organizational alignment for leaders to achieve this. Coherence develops these attributes and skills quickly. In the new business models, leaders will structure organization charts and appoint positions and players who can build coherence and sustain alignment between the organization's mission, vision, values, strategies, goals, and tactical plans. It's organizational coherence that bridges values with measured outcomes, which is often the missing element to actualizing strategy and achieving results.

# CHAPTER 22

# YOU CAN'T BE A CHAMPION UNLESS YOU KEEP SCORE—MEASURING THE IMPACT OF GREAT PEOPLE PROGRAMS

*Dr. John Sullivan*

## INTRODUCTION

If this were the Olympics, it would be obvious to all that you couldn't become a champion without measuring results. In fact, the definition of a champion is "the one with the best results." In the general business world the use of numbers and metrics is part of life. CEOs, CFOs, and shareholders all measure results using numbers and dollars. Within all major firms all projects, products, and business units are evaluated on the basis of numerical results. However, in direct contrast, we within HR resist using metrics, almost like developing them was the equivalent of a root canal. After over three decades of studying the dramatic differences between the two approaches, I have concluded that there are three primary reasons why HR professionals resist the use of metrics:

1. They protect the "human resources" of their firm. The inherent "human" nature of HR people forces them to resist anything that might in anyway reduce an individual to "just a number."
2. Most enter the field of HR without a business degree and as a result they are uncomfortable with business ratios and measures. Their lack of understanding with regards to common business ratios and sometimes business in general leave them uncomfortable with metrics.
3. They are so unsure of the results of their HR programs that they are afraid they'll get an "F" on the scorecard if we begin to measure. ("A" students love being graded.)

*"Without data, it's just an opinion."*

### An "Unreal" Definition

*Metrics—A derivative of the Latin word metri, meaning a series of numbers designed primarily to strike fear in the hearts of HR people while simultaneously making CFOs happy.*

### Our Fear of Reducing Humans to Numbers

Most people enjoy working in HR because they enjoy working with people and helping others with people problems. This is especially true in the "softer side" of HR including such functions and activities as organizational development, coaching, mentoring, training, and leadership development. Our concerns for "dehumanizing" people started in the 1950s with the fear about the possible introduction of universal IDs and forcing everyone to have a social security number. Historically many argued that universal ID's and the application of numbers to individuals in general created a situation whereby the unique aspects of our individual characters would be minimized. In reality, in most cases, the opposite turned out to be true and those who continue to cling to this excuse are behind the times. The world has changed. Credit card companies, insurance companies, political parties, and even your local grocery store have realized that delivering "individualized" service requires that you have data to help you distinguish wants, needs, and behaviors unique to each person. In a global fast-changing world, numbers and data have become king, They have become the "key" measure of business success and the determinant of whether you will get future funding.

# YOU CAN'T TELL IF YOU'RE ACTUALLY HELPING PEOPLE AND IMPROVING THEIR LIVES WITHOUT METRICS

Although most utilize metrics primarily to build their business case, strong "people advocates" need them too. As a strong people advocate you care about people and improving the quality of their work/life balance. But how can you know what their actual needs are without the use of metrics that identify what is needed? Metrics derived from surveys and focus groups help you understand worker needs and their frustrations.

The value of metrics doesn't stop at determining employee needs. Once you identify their needs and implement your "people programs" to meet them you aren't finished. It is also essential that you continue to use measurement systems to ensure that the programs are actually meeting the goals you established. And since people programs are so underfunded, it's also important that you get it right the first time, because there won't be funds to try something else.

So even if you are a die-hard people advocate, I hope you can now see the value added by using metrics. The metrics don't really dehumanize and they can help you improve your efficiency and responsiveness. Remember in the end, if you don't agree with the metrics, you are still free to react emotionally if you so choose. The metrics just give you another option; they allow you, if you choose, to become a fact-based decision maker.

## Dooming People Programs to a Life of Underfunding

Funding issues have become one of the key drivers behind the use of metrics. In a world of extremely tight resources, the primary consideration for the funding of projects and programs is the quantifiable return on investment, ROI for short. It's not my fault, and yes, it wasn't always that way, but *it is now* and it will likely remain that way for the foreseeable future.

## Technology Forces Managers to Shift to Fact-Based Decisions

It's time to realize that failing to attempt to quantify the business impact of people program results essentially dooms people programs to a life of underfunding and under appreciation. Why? Because the world has changed. It started first with the proliferation of computers, databases, and ERP software allowing most decisions now to be fact based. Almost everything in business has been reduced to numbers. For example, product decisions that used to be made by humans have now frequently been turned into a metrics-driven operation at successful firms like Wal-Mart, GM, and Best Buy. The "human protectors" in HR don't want to admit that, in some cases, the limited knowledge, time, or experience that people have makes their decisions inferior to those decisions that can be made with the help of technology that uses metrics and sophisticated forecasting techniques. We might wish that it wasn't true but, in fact, it is true in more cases then we care to admit.

## Globalization and Mergers Also Force Managers to Shift to Fact-Based Decisions

In addition to technology, the globalization and consolidation of companies (through mergers) means that firms are now much larger and their workforces are spread over huge geographic areas. Once you lose the face-to-face contact that is possible in smaller firms, you are forced into the realization that you can't remotely assess performance without metrics and quantifiable goals. Global competition means you must make fast decisions and, in most cases, fast fact-based decisions are superior to fast "gut" decisions. Great fact-based decisions are decisions made by experienced humans using the data provided by measurement and metrics!

# Bringing Up the Rear—Supply Chain, JIT Inventory, CRM, and Six Sigma Are Forcing HR to Change

If you follow leading business publications you have more than likely noticed stories heralding the dramatic shift in business operations that have occurred during the last decade. Over the past 10 years many so-called "overhead functions" were called that because they made no direct impact on profitability. They were treated as second-class citizens because of that lack of impact. Functions like purchasing, shipping, and warehousing were even lower on the funding totem pole than HR. But something dramatic happened to the world of overhead functions during the late 1980s and early 1990s. They got tired of poor treatment because they were not "profit centers." What happened was a transformation almost unheard of in the world of business. Each of these functions began generating a demonstrateable profit through the use of measures and metrics. To this day, supply chain, just-in-time (JIT) inventory, lean manufacturing, customer relationship management (CRM), and similar programs are business heroes. What is their secret to successes? First, it was their courage to admit that numbers and metrics could drive decisions, and second, it was the adoption of comprehensive management systems (driven by metrics) to improve service, quality, and productivity. Where was HR during the transformation of these other overhead functions? The answer is, unfortunately, following well behind the pack.

## Improving People Productivity Has Huge Economic Consequences

What makes the overhead transformation even more startling is they became corporate heroes even though they only spend a single digit percentage of the total corporate budget. In direct contrast however, companies spend on average nearly 60 percent of all variable costs on their people. It doesn't take a vivid imagination to realize that if we move past our dehumanization problem and begin to improve the productivity of 60 percent of the budget, the overall economic result to a large company would be easily recognizable. The Watson Wyatt Human Capital Index™ study demonstrated that the potential impact of people programs on a firm's overall market value could be as high as 47 percent. The road is clear and the time is right. HR must now seize this unprecedented opportunity to adopt metrics and to become the next "corporate hero."

*Metrics and rewards take away all doubt about what you really want done! This is true because most people "can do a better job if they know precisely what is expected of them."*

—A management mantra often used at Hewlett-Packard

## The Benefits of Metrics—Why Do You Need to Use Them?

Metrics are the fastest and the cheapest way to change behavior in business. They work as motivators because they excite and occasionally embarrass performance-driven individuals. Although metrics might seem intimidating at first, once you grow accustomed to them you will not be able to live without them.

One of the major mistakes managers make when implementing any HR program is assuming that "having one" is sufficient. Nothing could be further from the truth. Merely "having one" doesn't mean that the program is meeting its goals, or that it is performing at its maximum potential. Common reasons to utilize metrics include:

- *Meeting your goals*—Rather than guessing or assuming you're doing good work, metrics help you determine precisely whether you are meeting each of your goals. Quantifying your goals also helps you more accurately assess your success.
- *Driving improvement*—In a fast changing world even historically strong performing programs must continually improve. Metrics are an excellent mechanism for assessing your strengths and weaknesses. Used effectively, they can help you determine where to refine your efforts over time. Metrics can also help you to determine how you should redistribute your resources (time and budget) from areas of low return to areas of higher return (ROI).
- *Obtain funding*—Any decision that must be approved by the CFO will be made primarily based on numbers and dollars. If you expect to convince management to fund or continue to support your people programs you will need to provide (at the very least) an ROI and a payback period. In addition, it's important to realize that the wide use of metrics demonstrates to top management that you are "results oriented." Metrics also forces you to shift your language away from terms like "happy," "running well," or "satisfied" and more towards terms used by CFOs including "margins," "productivity," and "decreased cost of service."

- *Early warning a.k.a "smoke detectors"*—Effectiveness metrics can provide you and your managers with early warning signs (or alerts) of potential failures or any decline in the performance of your key programs. Providing managers with an adequate "heads up" can minimize damage or, in some cases, even prevent people problems.
- *Understanding critical success factors*—In a fast changing world, running successful programs isn't enough. If you expect to improve them you'll need to understand the critical success factors that make them work. Metrics and analytics can help you understand why things work and what conditions and elements are necessary for success.
- *Shift to fact-based decisions*—HR has a long history of making decisions based on thinking and feeling. Since CFOs certainly don't "feel," if you want to increase funding it is important to shift decision making from "I think" to "I know." The one single factor that differentiates great HR departments from mediocre ones is fact- or data-based decision making.
- *Metrics change behavior*—If you distribute ranked results throughout the organization you will find that metrics, on their own, can drive change. Whether it stirs managers competitive juices or just causes a degree of "embarrassment," the fact is that distributed metrics will change behavior almost immediately.
- *Eliminate confusion*—Metrics send a clear message about what's important and what isn't. It gives managers and programs focus by telling them what to do more of and less of based on what you measure. If you add rewards to the mix, you can further strengthen the focus and the speed of change.
- *Builds coordination/cooperation*—Most metrics are internal to a project or department. However, if you develop metrics that assess performance across and between departmental lines you can encourage the breaking down of silos. If you add rewards to those cross-departmental metrics, you can further transform dissimilar HR or business units into an integrated process.

As you can see, metrics can have a variety of positive uses and impacts. If you're going to be a champion, you can use metric comparisons to give yourself legitimate bragging rights. They also ensure that you are meeting your customer's needs and eventually they will lead to giving your firm a distinct competitive advantage over others in your industry.

**A Fictitious Want Ad to Illustrate a Point:**
*Wanted: More HR funding that will make my life as an HR professional easy.*

However, it cannot require any

- Changes on my part
- The use of statistics, ratios, or financial information
- Proof that the money will have any business impact

## The Consequences of Not Using Metrics

Failing to utilize metrics can have a number of negative consequences. In addition to the obvious (you will lose a lot of budget battles), there are other consequences. For example, it's difficult to attract and retain top talent when you don't keep score because top performers love to keep score. They want to win and you can't tell who's winning without metrics.

There are also some personal consequences as an individual if you fail to use metrics. First your personal pride will suffer because you won't know precisely whether you actually met your personal, professional, or departmental goals. Is also true in the highly competitive world of HR that failing to use metrics will negatively impact your opportunities for pay increases, bonuses, promotions, and yes, even your job security. It turns out that merely working hard in HR is no longer sufficient, there are negative consequences if you can't prove you're doing great job.

## How to Begin—Steps in Developing Metrics

The following section outlines the eight basic steps in developing HR metrics. Consider it a "metrics toolkit" and from it you can select the best metrics for your organization. Whatever individual metrics you select be sure that you first check with the HRIS or the CIO's office to ensure that the data needed for each is easily available for each of them. Next, run them by your CFO's office to ensure that they mesh with other existing financial and performance metrics.

Once you're convinced of the need to utilize metrics the next steps include:

Step 1. Select a metric for each program goal
Step 2. Choosing between soft and hard metrics
Step 3. Understanding the different categories of business impact
Step 4. Selecting simple but attention-getting metrics
Step 5. Understanding the characteristics of great measures
Step 6. Selecting from standard HR metrics
Step 7. Selecting from advanced HR metrics
Step 8. Building the business case for increased HR funding

## Step 1. Select a Metric for Each Program Goal

Before you begin to determine which metrics to use, it's important to recognize this basic rule: "Select at least one metric for each of your program goals and what ever else you do, keep it simple."

Although metrics can make a significant contribution toward improving your performance, it is equally important not to overdo them. It's best to start simple and then to expand them into other areas when it's necessary. There is no standardized rule of thumb because every company has different goals and values as to what is important. The best approach is to build metrics that fit your needs and culture. Start with a few and then expand only if you see added value.

## Step 2. Choosing from Soft and Hard Metrics

CFOs break metrics into two different degrees of believability. Those that relate to items not counted in the budget are known as soft metrics, and those that relate to items that are included in the budget are known as hard metrics. In case of doubt, realize that CFOs are biased and in favor of hard metrics.

Perhaps some examples will illustrate the difference:

### Soft Results Metrics (Be careful of these because they get little credibility in the financial community.)

- *No impact measures*—I think my training program works, managers like me, no one complains, we are all working really hard, etc.
- *HR time savings*—Shifting HR work so that employees and managers (on paid time) do the same work on their own time. Although it saves on your budget, there are no net savings to the firm. In a similar light, shifting employee costs to consultants, outsource vendors, contractors, or temps may result in headcount savings but real costs may actually go up.
- *Time and cost savings from HR process re-engineering*—Streamlined processes and less paperwork, for example, are considered soft metrics because HR generally offers no proof that HR headcount will be reduced or that it will add value with the extra time and money it saves. If employee or manager time is saved (fewer calls, reports, or approvals required) it is still a soft metric unless you can first prove the time saving actually occurs and second that the saved time is actually shifted to more on the job productivity.
- *Employee satisfaction and less stress*—Although it may seem valuable on the surface, many CFOs wonder if the higher satisfaction or the reduced stress are a result of lower standards and less "pressure" to perform.

### Hard Results Metrics (Clint Eastwood–like metrics)

- *Increased on the job performance*—Demonstrating that individual performance increases as a result of a new program. For example, our new recruiting program produces hires with 25 percent higher on the job performance during their first year (compared to those hired under the old hiring system) and an industry low 1 percent termination rate in the first year.
- *Return on investment*—Showing that invested dollars bring a high rate of return. For example, our new incentive program spends $1,000 more per salesperson per month, but the sales revenue increases by an average of $100,000 for every salesperson under the new incentive program. It returns $100 for every 1 dollar invested (the firm average ROI is 2 to 1 and the next best in the firm is 8 to 1).
- *Program impact*—Where a single program has an immediate demonstrated impact. For example, revenue increased 17 percent within two months of the sales team completing the new XYZ sales training program. Other sales non-trained teams had no increase in revenue.
- *Correlation with performance*—When the productivity or performance increases proportionately as program usage increases. For example, productivity increases by 10 percent in departments that increase training expenditures by 1 percent (and vice-versa).
- *Revenue per people cost dollar*—Measures the margin performance of the organization as it relates to spending on people programs. For example, our revenue per dollar spent on employee costs went up 32 percent after our performance management system identified and released the bottom 5 percent of our employees in a business unit.
- *Decreased costs*—Where actual labor costs are reduced. For example, our new scheduling system in the factory resulted in a 10 percent decrease in people costs per unit of output within a week after implementation.

## Step 3. Understanding the Five Different Categories of Business Impact

When you attempt to measure the results of any particular business or HR program there are generally five different categories of business impacts that you can measure. A single HR program may have a measure in each of the five areas. These five distinct business impact categories include:

1. *Quality*—Error rate, quality of the features, usability, "Did it work?"
2. *Quantity or volume*—Capability, capacity, the number completed
3. *Time*—On time, response time, time to complete

4. *Money*—Cost, revenue
5. *Satisfaction*—Degree to which the user liked the process or result

The most overused metric category is cost. Often the costs of HR programs are miniscule compared to their relative impact. Tracking costs without also looking at quality is a common error. In contrast, the most underused metric category is quality. All too frequently HR omits this crucial category of measure. For example, recruiters quite often measure the cost-per-hire by recruiting source, but seldom measure the quality of the hire as expressed by performance on the job. Cutting costs makes no sense if the new hires have decreased on the job performance.

## Step 4. Selecting Some Simple but Attention-Getting Metrics

Metrics don't have to be complicated or extensive in order to have a dramatic impact. Here are some examples of simple but dramatic metrics just to demonstrate how simple metrics may provide all the "power" you need to get your manager's attention:

- *Retention rate of top performers*—How are those bulls doing without Michael Jordan? (four losing seasons after three championships)
- *Customer satisfaction to turnover rate correlation*—The turnover rate at our retail stores that scored in the bottom 10 percent of employee satisfaction is 148 percent. In contrast the turnover rate at our retail stores that scored in the top 10 percent on employee satisfaction equaling 49 percent. There is a nearly 100 percent difference in turnover rates. (A manager estimated that was worth $45 million each year.)
- *HR program impact on market value*—Watson Wyatt, a well-known consulting organization, found that great people practices can increase shareholder (stock) value by as much as 47 percent, while inferior ones can decrease shareholder value by as much as 33 percent.
- *Management practices and their impact on employee productivity*—McKinsey, a well-known consulting organization that focuses on strategy, found that American manufacturing firms operating in Britain are *90 percent more productive* than British firms (operating in their own country). The 90 percent difference in productivity resulted from failure on the part of British managers to identify and attract high-potential employees, set clear goals, use metrics and incentives, and failure to use lean manufacturing and other productivity tools.
- *Performance management*—Weak performance management systems that managed (or failed to manage) the performance of two employees caused a billion-dollar loss in stock value to a major health care chain.

Other Simple Measures:

- We beat yesterday . . . every day for 176 days.
- Your HR program is mentioned in the annual report.
- The program is so effective that line managers are willing to fund it.
- We stopped doing it and no one complained (a negative metrics).

## Step 5. Understanding the Characteristics of Great Measures

If you only use a few metrics it's critical that they be of the highest quality. Great metrics meet most of the following characteristics:

1. The CFO's office approves them in advance (I call this the CFO "B-S filter").
2. They are simple, credible, and easy to understand.
3. When possible, they use existing data or information.
4. They measure quality whenever looking at cost or quantity.
5. They are combined with no more than nine other metrics to assess any particular program.
6. They enable comparison against a pre-determined standard (last year, best in the industry, the average, etc.).
7. Instead of "counting" everyone or every item, it uses sampling (1 out of every 10) to reduce costs.
8. They are not easily manipulatable or "gameable."
9. They measure outputs or results, not process or effort.
10. Every crucial metric has a reward closely tied to it.
11. For every major program goal there is at least one measure.
12. The ranked results metrics are distributed to all concerned (to build competitive pressure because all can see how they did compared to others).
13. Some metrics extend between functions in order to encourage cooperation and team behavior. They measure the performance of an activity from beginning to end, across functions, and at major milestones along the way.
14. Some of the metrics are forward-looking to get managers of "heads up" about upcoming problems. They are designed in such a way that they enable forecasting.
15. Metrics are continuously refined and improved as time and experience yield proof of their effectiveness and impact.

# Step 6. Selecting Some Standard HR Functional Metrics

Standard HR metrics are "single issue" measures that are traditionally used within HR to improve effectiveness and efficiency. The following are some recommended metrics to select from:

## Sample Retention Metrics

- Turnover rate of top performers and key positions compared to our competitors
- Separation rate of bottom performers and bad managers
- Percent of employees rated as "needs improvement" that have improved or left
- Percent of voluntary turnover that go to direct competitors
- The cost of losing a key employee to a competitor
- The cost of retaining poor performers
- Percentage of voluntary turnover that participated in regular or post-exit interviews

## Sample Employee Relations Metrics

- Percent of employees that feel challenged, growing, and recognized by their manager
- Percent of agreement between a manager and their employees' self-rating on performance
- Post-exit interview scores are positive (The reasons top performers left the firm are beyond our control, they would highly recommend it to their friends, and a majority would like to return someday.)
- Percent of managers rated as weak in pulse surveys and 360-degree assessments
- The number and dollar cost of grievances, lawsuits, and employee relations complaints

## Sample Compensation Metrics

- Ratio of revenue per dollar of compensation and benefits paid out
- Percent of employees overall pay that is at risk (tied to performance and stock price)
- Percent of all managers' bonuses that is tied to great people management
- Percent of new hires that rate our total compensation approach as one of the top five reasons for accepting their job

- Percent of employees that cite a weak compensation approach as one of the top five reasons for leaving
- Percent of managers that cite compensation/benefits as a roadblock to hiring, time to market, retention, innovation, and productivity
- Benefits costs as a percentage of payroll

### Sample Development/Training Metrics
- Percent of Employees citing they are on the leading edge of knowledge
- Percentage of training available online
- Speed of best practice learning, copying between business units
- Percent of new hires that give training excellence as one of the top five reasons for accepting their job
- Percent of employees that cite a lack of training one of the top five reasons for leaving or as an inhibitor to their productivity
- Percent of managers that cite training and development (T&D) as a roadblock to time to market, hiring, retention, innovation, and productivity

### Sample HR Customer Satisfaction Metrics
- Manager and employee satisfaction with the speed of HR services
- Manager and employee satisfaction with the quality of HR services
- Applicant and new hire satisfaction with the hiring process

### Sample HRIS Metrics
- Percent of all HR services available online (self-service)
- Percent of HR services that are paperless
- Percent of HR services that are available worldwide
- Manager/employee satisfaction with service
- Response-time to service calls/questions
- Cost per hour of service

## Step 7. Selecting from Advanced Metrics

Once you master standard metrics like cost and quality of hire, trainee satisfaction, and ROI you might want to consider some more advanced metrics. Some types or categories of advanced metrics include:

- *An HR dashboard*—Similar to a car's dashboard it provides managers with a wide range of program efficiency metrics in order to ensure that operations are within standards.
- *An index*—Very much like the Dow Jones or the Standard & Poor's indices. An HR index is a single number that reflects the overall performance of the

function. Such an index might include at least one metric from each of the major categories (quantity, quality, time, and customer satisfaction). An index gives the manager a simple, quick but accurate snapshot of what's happening. An index also makes comparisons between distinct departments easier.

- *Alerts/ smoke detectors*—Alerts are leading indicators that warn managers of upcoming problems. While most metrics tell the manager about what happened last year, alerts provide valuable information to allow the manager to prevent problems prior to their occurrence.
- *Analytics*—Analytics are metrics that analyze trends to help you understand why things are happening and what the future pattern is likely to be.
- *Heuristics*—heuristics is the search for patterns in data in order to identify similar or related events. Once you identify a problem they help (generally using software) you find similar ones. (Heuristics are used in anti-virus programs to find new variations.)
- *A balanced scorecard*—A series of metrics that attempts to strike a balance between hard financial measures and soft HR measures. (Be forewarned, most CFO's are not "balanced.")

Each of these advanced metrics has both benefits and problems. If you want to have a great people management function you must move beyond the standard measures, especially in the areas of forecasting and alerts. Some examples of indexes and dashboards are found in the next section.

## Some Sample Advanced Metrics

An Example of a Recruiting Index

| Weight* | Performance Factor |
|---------|--------------------|
| 25% | Performance of hires |
| 20% | Percent of hires from referrals |
| 15% | Time to fill key positions |
| 15% | Time from referral to manager to interview |
| 15% | Manager satisfaction with employment |
| 10% | Diversity hiring ratios in exempt jobs |

*The weight shows the relative importance of the item in the overall index score. Many indexes are "normalized" so that the targeted overall number is easy to remember (ie.,100).

### An Example of an Overall HR Department Index

| | |
|---|---|
| 20% | Revenue per dollar spent on people costs |
| 15% | Turnover rate of the top 10 percent (top performers) |
| 15% | Performance of recent hires |
| 15% | Percent of key employees pay that is at risk (based on performance) |
| 10% | Percent of employees that feel they are challenged and growing in their current job |
| 10% | Turnover rate of poor managers |
| 5% | Manager satisfaction with HR services |
| 5% | Time to fill key jobs |
| 5% | Diversity ratios of the workforce |

### An Example of a Recruiting Dashboard

A dashboard has no weighted items. Each factor is treated individually. All are checked on a regular basis (weekly or monthly).

Performance of hires (6 to12 months after they are hired)

Time to fill in key positions

Time to minimum productivity (after hire)

Number of vacancies (in key positions)

Percent of bad hires (new hires that are released after 6-12 months)

Turnover of new hires (new hires that quit within the first 6 months)

Time to refer résumés to managers, time to interview, and interview to offer time

Reveal take away ratio (the number of employees we "take away from" and "lose to" a competitor)

Percent of diversity hires

Percent of hires from referrals

Percent of hires from the Web

A list of the top reasons why candidates excepted a job

Cost per source (per qualified applicant)

Cost per hire

*Satisfaction with the hiring process (applicants and managers)*

## Step 8. Building the Business Case for Increased HR Funding

As stated earlier, the predominate use for metrics is to build the business case for increased program funding. However, metrics by themselves do not comprise a business case, they are just the first step in a much more involved process. The remaining steps in the business case building process focus on making sure that your business case addresses each of the 11 most common decision factors used to evaluate program spending.

## The Top Decision Factors for Approving HR Projects

If you look at numerous projects that are approved or rejected by senior executives, you soon learn that there are certain standard decision factors that are used to determine whether a project should be funded or not. These 11 decision factors include:

1. A low initial investment (upfront money)
2. The project has a high return on investment (ROI or cost/benefit ratio)
3. Similar projects implemented elsewhere have a high success rate or a low risk of failure
4. The project starts right away without a long delay
5. There is a short payback period (the time required to payback the initial expense)
6. The project has a complete set of accurate results metrics and a method for collecting metric information
7. No new headcount is required
8. The project has negative consequences for failure built in (individual accountability)
9. The program gives us a competitive advantage over other firms
10. The program can demonstrate that it increases worker productivity (revenue per dollar spent on people costs)
11. A project team is credible and has a high success rate on previous projects

## Testing to Provide "Dead Bang Proof" of Business Impact

Implementing new HR programs and then measuring the results represents the traditional way that most HR professionals determine whether a new program is successful. However, simply noting that productivity or output increased following the introduction of a new program does not automatically convince most executives, because most understand that performance can be influenced by numerous factors that occur simultaneously. Without accounting for all of the factors that could have impacted productivity, the increase in performance cannot be directly tied to the introduction of the HR program.

For example, a new training program might seem to produce a productivity improvement, but if a new incentive program was simultaneously implemented, it would be hard to determine which one created the impact, or what percentage of the impact belonged to each. One way to provide what I call "dead bang proof" that a program works is to run a test; similar to the way a new drug gets tested prior to approval. If HR people began to think and act like scientists, they would have more credible proof regarding the effectiveness of new programs. Some of the "testing" approaches I recommend include:

- *Utilize a split sample*—Rather than implementing the program throughout the entire company, instead implement it in some teams or locations and not in others. If there is a significant difference in performance between the two samples you are home free.
- *Correlation*—Demonstrate that there is a direct connection or correlation between the increased usage of a particular service and business results. If you can show that when usage increases dramatically that productivity also improves, you are on the right track.
- *Put it in and take it out*—If you implement a program and it works, most HR people are satisfied. But if you really want to know if the program really works remove it to see if the productivity returns to the initial level.
- *Run a pilot*—Running a small pilot and then demonstrating that it immediately impacts the business provides you with some direct evidence. Pilots also put less "upfront" money at risk (as compared to a company-wide rollout) in the event of a failure. Pilots also give you time to revise and improve your program before you implement it company wide (thus reducing the risk of a highly visible company wide failure).
- *The top competitor has it*—Occasionally managers are fanatical about becoming more like an admired competitor. Occasionally, if you can demonstrate that the new program produced results at the benchmark firm that your senior leaders want to be like, you can get away with using the benchmark firm's data to justify your own program.

## Business Case Steps—Do Your Pre-Work

When the time comes to actually present your case for increased funding to senior management it is important to realize that the chances of receiving funding increases dramatically if you do your "pre-work." The steps that I recommend you undertake before you present your business case to senior management include:

*Step 1. Identify burning or crucial issues facing the business*—Make every attempt to show how your program contributes to solving one or more of the firm's major problems.

*Step 2. Identify supporters/blockers*—Identify the individuals in senior management that have supported or blocked similar programs in order to determine who is likely to be the enemy and who is likely to support you.

*Step  3. Identify past decision criteria*—Examine past funding decisions to determine what criteria that senior executives use when they approve or reject projects. Quite often there is a discernible pattern that changes very little over time.

*Step  4. Prove that you are an expert*—Senior executives feel more comfortable supporting programs when it is clear that the leader is a true expert in the subject area. You can often demonstrate your expertise through extensive benchmarking and your ability to answer any question without hesitation.

*Step  5. Forecast trends and patterns*—We don't live in an unchanging world, so projects that don't forecast changes in the economic and business environment are unlikely to be funded. You might also include information about the accuracy of your previous forecasts in your proposal.

*Step  6. Demonstrate your success rate*—Everyone supports a consistent winner so it is important that you demonstrate your track record in successfully completing projects. Compare your success rate to the average success rate at the firm.

*Step  7. Demonstrate that the solution fits our culture*—It is important to demonstrate that you understand our processes, technology, and culture and that any solution you propose will mesh with each of them.

*Step  8. Prove how often these types of solutions work*—Never assume that good people working hard automatically produce results. It is important to demonstrate to the decision makers that this type of project has a high success rate. First, calculate the likelihood of success and then highlight the possible risks and how you calculated them.

*Step  9. List the critical success failure factors*—It's not enough just to know that the program works, it is also important that you know why it works. Highlight the critical success factors of the project to demonstrate that you know what is essential for the project to succeed.

*Step 10. Demonstrate that we have the talent and skills*—Great ideas only work with great people. Demonstrate that our firm or your team has the necessary skills, technology, and talent to "pull it off." If we don't have the talent, demonstrate that we know how to recruit it.

*Step 11. Show the expected results*—Quantify the expected financial results (revenue, income, profit, ROI, margins, customer value, and payback period) and show your understanding of these financial measures.

*Step 12. List the program metrics*—Outline your program monitoring and measurement systems to show that project success will be closely watched and that problems won't get out of hand.

*Step 13. Calculate its impact on our products and services*—Although many HR programs are independent, demonstrate how your HR program will positively impact our products, product development, and customers.

*Step 14. Provide best-/worst-case scenarios*—Prove that you strategically planned ahead by demonstrating each of the possible best- and worst-case scenarios and your plan for each scenario.

*Step 15. List common problems*—Demonstrate that you are aware of the problems that normally occur during the implementation of these types of programs. Show that you are not naïve and that you know how others have handled each potential problem.

*Step 16. Show personal benefit to top managers*—Show how each key decision maker will either directly benefit or at least not suffer as a result of the new HR program. Personalize the results and impacts for powerful decision makers.

*Step 17. Show how you will learn and continually improve*—Provide information about the systems you have developed to ensure that the program continually improves over time. No project plan is perfect, just demonstrate that you will "learn fast" from your errors and you will be fine.

# CONCLUSION

Throughout this chapter I have attempted to demonstrate the importance of using metrics. I of course realize that there is a great deal of resistance within the HR community to utilizing metrics. I also understand the traditional reasons for that resistance. However, it is equally important that HR professionals understand that the world of business has recently lost its tolerance for decisions made without facts and for programs that don't produce measurable results. As technology spreads to every part of the business, that reliance on numbers will begin to increase at an even faster rate.

In a similar vein, as firms become more global, HR will be forced to rely even more heavily on metrics. In the "old days" you could personally connect with and assess your subordinates on a face-to-face basis. Now however, with so many employees working remotely, at home, on flexible schedules, or around the globe, the only option available for assessing their performance on a regular basis will be the use of pre-defined performance metrics. In addition, as companies increase the use of outside contractors and vendors, the need for effective metrics will again increase because you can't trust or control a vendor the same as you can an employee. No matter which way you slice it, metrics are becoming mandatory.

Looking at it from another perspective, consider the sports analogy as a way of understanding where we are headed: It would not be possible to win an Olympic gold medal without continually measuring your results and comparing them to the very best in the world. World-class athletes measure performance almost daily because they are striving to push their performance beyond all others. Metrics can provide you with the opportunity to be a superior performer by letting you know unambiguously where you are and how far you have to go. Your future path is clear; you can't become a champion . . . without measuring your results.

# ABOUT THE CONTRIBUTORS

## FOREWORD

**Dr. W. Warner Burke** is widely known as one of the founders of the field of organization development. He has authored more than 14 books including Managing Organizational Change and Behavioral Science and the Manager 's Role. He has consulted with a variety of organizations in business, education, government, religious, medical systems, and professional services firms about leadership development; including British Airways, NASA and SmithKline Beecham.

## CO-EDITORS

**David Ulrich** has been ranked by Business Week as #1 management educator. He has also been listed in Forbes as one of the "world's top five" business coaches." And he received the George Petitpas Memorial Award from World Federation of Personnel Management for lifetime contributions to human resource profession. David has published over 90 articles and book chapters. His books include: Organizational Capability: Competing from the Inside/Out (with Dale Lake) (published by Wiley); The Boundaryless Organization: Breaking the Chains of Organization Structure (with Ron Ashkenas, Steve Kerr, Todd Jick) (Jossey Bass); Human Resource Champions: The Next Agenda for Adding Value and Delivering Results (Harvard Business Press); Tomorrow's (HR) Management (with Gerry Lake and Mike Losey) (Wiley); Learning Capability: Generating * Generalizing Ideas with Impact (with Arthur Yeung, Mary Ann Von Glinow, Steve Nason) (Oxford); Results Based Leadership: How Leaders Build the Business and Improve the Bottom Line (with Norm Smallwood and Jack Zenger) (Harvard Business Press); HR

Scorecard: Linking People, Strategy, and Performance (with Brian Becker and Mark Huselid) (Harvard Business Press); GE Workout (with Steve Kerr and Ron Ashkenas) (McGraw Hill)

**Louis Carter** is president of Best Practice Publications, a best practice research, consulting, and publishing firm. Carter's work in leadership & organization development has been featured in Investors Business Daily and The Supervisors Guide to Quality and Excellence. He has spoken to international and U.S. audiences on the field of best practices. His books have been featured in AESC, SHRM, ASTD, and NEHRA as well as business and government courses around the world. Carter co-edited and authored; Best Practices in Organization Development and Change, Jossey Bass/John Wiley & Sons, 2001 with Marshall Goldsmith and other thought leaders including Richard Beckhard and Warner Burke; Linkage, Inc.'s Best Practices in Leadership Development Handbook with Warren Bennis, Marshall Goldsmith, Linkage, Inc. (Jossey Bass: 2000); Linkage Inc.'s Best Practices in Knowledge Management & Organizational Learning Handbook (Linkage Press:2000); and The Linkage Toolkit for Developing Leaders (Linkage Press: 2001) with Jay Conger.

**Norm Smallwood** is co-founder and President of Results-Based Leadership Inc. Results-Based Leadership provides education, tools and consulting services that increase organization and leadership capability to deliver the right results the right way. He has also authored Why The Bottom Line Isn't: How to Build Value through People and Organizations Wiley, April 2003. Dave and Norm also co-authored, Results-Based Leadership (with Jack Zenger). Norm is co-author of Real Time Strategy: Improvising Team-Based Planning for a Fast Changing World, Wiley & Sons, 1993 (which was part of their portable MBA series) and of Results-Based Leadership: How Leaders Build the Business and Improve the Bottom Line, Harvard Business School Press, 1999 (which was named book of the year by SHRM). His current book with Dave Ulrich, Why the Bottom Line ISN'T!: How to Build Value through People and Organizations will be published in April 2003 by Wiley. He has published more than 50 articles in leading journals and newspapers and has contributed chapters to multiple books.

**Jim Bolt** is Chairman and founder of Executive Development Associates (EDA). Jim was recently selected by the Financial Times as one of the top experts in executive leadership development. He is CEO of the Alliance for Strategic Leadership (A4SL). Jim is the author of the book Executive Development: A Strategy for Corporate Competitiveness .He has authored more than 20 articles, including "Tailor Executive Development to Strategy" published in the Harvard Business Review.

**Marshall Goldsmith** is widely recognized as one of the world 's foremost authorities in helping leaders achieve positive, measurable change in behavior: for themselves, their people and their teams. In 2000, Forbes listed Marshall as one of top five executive coaches and Human Resources rated Marshall as one of the world 's leading HR consultants. He has also been ranked by the Wall Street Journal as one of the "Top 10" executive educators. He has written and co-edited over 15 books on leadership development. Marshall's twelve recent books include: *The Leader of the Future* (a Business Week "Top 15" best-seller), *Learning Journeys* and *Coaching for Leadership*. *The Leadership Investment* won the American Library Association's *Choice* award as an "Outstanding Academic Business Book" of 2001. Amazon.com has ranked five of his books as the #1 best sellers in their field.

# PART I

## *Chapter 1*

**Kathleen Dannemiller** is the founding partner in Dannemiller Tyson Associates and co-inventor of Real Time Strategic Change and Real-Time Work Design™ (now called Whole-Scale™). She is co-author of Whole Scale Change: Unleashing the Magic in Organizations. She has been a passionate advocate of empowerment, systems theory and whole system change for more than 30 years. Kathie has been a consultant, coach and mentor to countless leaders, consultants and organizations as they build a better future. She has been a political organizer at the national, state and local levels as well as a community organizer. Kathie is recognized worldwide for her ability to move entire organizations forward with speed, depth and spirit. Kathie is a member of the National Training Laboratory and the National Organization Development Network.

**Mary Eggers** is a Partner in Dannemiller Tyson Associates. Mary has worked since 1985 helping tap the wisdom, heart and energy of individuals, organizations and communities to achieve their desired results. Mary has experience in healthcare, education, government, information technology, not for profits and manufacturing. She has an MS in Organization Development from the American University/National Training Laboratories. She is a member of the National Organization Development Network and the Chesapeake Bay Organization Development Network. Mary is co-author of: Unleashing the Magic in Healthcare, OD Practitioner, Vol. 32, No. 4, 2000.

**Lorri Johnson** is a Partner with Dannemiller Tyson Associates. Her consulting practice is devoted to helping people shape the organizations where they work and the communities in which they live through the use of whole system processes. Her experience in the application of Whole-Scale™ includes strategic planning, work redesign, culture change, and training. Lorri has consulted in many diverse settings ranging from information technology and manufacturing to the public sector and non-profit organizations. Lorri is a member of the National Organization Development Network. Her background includes 14 years experience with Xerox Corporation and Bell & Howell in the areas of human resources, sales and marketing.

Kathie, Mary and Lorri are co-authors of Whole-Scale Change: Unleashing the Magic in Organizations, and Whole-Scale Change Toolkit, Berrett-Koehler Publishing, Inc.

## *Chapter 2*

**Marshall Goldsmith** is widely recognized as one of the world 's foremost authorities in helping leaders achieve positive, measurable change in behavior: for themselves, their people and their teams. In 2000, Forbes listed Marshall as one of top five executive coaches and Human Resources rated Marshall as one of the world 's leading HR consultants. He has also been ranked by the Wall Street Journal as one of the "Top 10" executive educators. He has written and co-edited over 15 books on leadership development including The Many Facets of Leadership and Coaching for Leadership.

**Howard Morgan** is a Director of Leadership Research Institute. Since joining the firm in 1988, he has led a variety of international organizational change initiatives on behalf of his clients in the Financial Services, Manufacturing, Management Consulting, Communications, Media and High Tech. Industries. Howard specializes in executive coaching as a strategic change management tool leading to improved customer /employee satisfaction and overall corporate performance. His recent achievements include the development of an internal coaching model for a large international organization and coaching executives on the art of managing managers. He has worked with many executive committees of the world's largest organizations on improving corporate and executive performance. Howard brings over 17 years' experience as a line executive, most recently as an Executive Vice-President of a Canadian-held food and beverage company and currently serves on four Boards of Directors, located in Europe and the US.

**Marc Effron** is the Global Practice Leader for Hewitt Associates Leadership Practice. His leadership work centers on helping organizations attract, develop and retain top leadership talent. Some of his consulting clients have included Abbott Laboratories, American Standard Companies, Citigroup, JP Morgan Chase, Philips Electronics, Royal Dutch Shell and RR Donnelley. Marc has spoken to business groups and conferences throughout the world. He is widely quoted on leadership issues including in recent articles in the New York Times, Asian Wall Street Journal, Europe Wall Street Journal, HR Executive and others.

## Chapter 3

**Jerry Sternin** is widely known as the founder of applied positive deviance, with 24 years overseas experience in developing countries including 8 years with the Peace Corps in the Philippines, Nepal, Mauritania and Rwanda, and 16 years as a Save the Children Director in Viet Nam, Bangladesh, Egypt, Phillippines and most recently, Myanmar. Sternin has his MA degree in Asian Studies from Harvard University where he has also served as an Assistant Dean and Advisor to Students at the Business School. Jerry was the recipient of a writing grant from the Rockefeller Foundation at Bellagio, Italy, and is currently the recipient of a Ford Foundation grant to "amplify Positive Deviance." Jerry is currently a Visiting scholar at Tufts University, and an international consultant. He is currently involved in PD projects for the World Bank in Argentina, for USAID funded Development Organizations in Indonesia, and has recently presented the PD approach to Corporate and social Entrepreneurs a the Wold Econmic Forum in Geneva. In January 2000 Jerry published an article on "The Power of Positive Deviance" in the Harvard Business Review, In December, 2000 Jerry was featured in an article on Positive Deviance in Fast Company Magazine. The articles brought many queries from the corporate world on the use of PD and have helped to further broaden the PD audience.

## Chapter 4

**Ralph Jacobson** is the Principal of Synthesis Consulting, Minneapolis, Minnesota. The firm builds companies of leaders who effectively work together to ensure their organizations thrive during times of change. Jacobson's book, Leading for a Change: How to Master the Five Challenges Faced by Every Leader was nominated by www.mgeneral.com as one of the top business books for the year 2000. Jacobson received the American Express Quality Award for his consulting work with the company. He was appointed an examiner for the Minnesota Quality Award and was an adjunct faculty member at the University of St. Thomas, Executive MBA program. He holds advanced degrees in city planning, psychology, and human resources from The Ohio State University and the University of Minnesota.

## Chapter 5

**Jim Bolt** is Chairman and founder of Executive Development Associates (EDA). Jim was recently selected by the Financial Times as one of the top experts in executive leadership development. He is CEO of the Alliance for Strategic Leadership

(A4SL). Jim is the author of the book Executive Development: A Strategy for Corporate Competitiveness. He has authored more than 20 articles, including "Tailor Executive Development to Strategy " published in the Harvard Business Review.

**L. Ronald Meeks** is Principal at CDR International. He is formerly the President of EDA's Consulting Practice, where he was responsible for EDA's custom-designed executive and leadership development strategies and programs. Ron's interest in leadership development and change management comes from his experience in varied line management and staff roles in Hoechst, one of the world's largest pharmaceutical and chemical companies. During his 18-years with various companies of The Hoechst Group, Ron held positions with extensive responsibility in driving change in organizations to achieve and maintain competitive leadership positions. His recent clients include Aventis Pharmaceuticals, Mitsubishi, Sun Microsystems, and Johnson& Johnson.

**R. Steven Terrell** is president of Aspire Consulting, Inc. Steve was the Executive Director of Consulting Services for EDA where he was responsible for the custom-design of executive development strategies, systems and programs that improve leadership effectiveness and business performance. Steve has been also been the Director of the Leadership Practice at Dove Consulting, Senior Manager in the Change Management Practice at Andersen Consulting, and Senior VP, Leadership Development at NationsBank (now Bank of America). He has 20 years of executive and leadership development experience with companies such as American Express, AT&T, Australia Mutual Provident Society, Bank of America, Bankers Trust, Forest Laboratories, JP Morgan, and Motorola. He has presented at conferences sponsored by the American Society for Training and Development, and the Association for Psychological Type.

## *Chapter 6*

**David Cooperrider** is widely known as the founder of Appreciative Inquiry and the co-founder of the consulting firm Appreciative Inquiry. David is Professor of Organizational Behavior at the Weatherhead School of Management at Case Western Reserve University. He has received many awards for his work and has facilitated a series of dialogues among many of the world 's top religious leaders, led by His Holiness the Dalai Lama. David's books include Appreciative Inquiry (with Peter Sorenson, Diana Whitney and Therese Yeager); The Organizational Dimensions of Global Change (with Jane Dutton); Organizational Wisdom and Executive Courage and Appreciative Management and Leadership (both with Suresh Srivastva).

**David Bright** is a Doctoral Candidate in Organizational Behavior at the Weatherhead School of Management at Case Western Reserve University, located in Cleveland, Ohio. He previously attended Brigham Young University where he received the degrees of B.S. in Accounting (1996), M.A. in International Area Studies (1999), and Master of Organizational Behavior (1999). He has conducted research and consulting with organizations such as the U.S. Navy and Roadway International, one of the largest freight transportation companies in North America. His primary research interest explores factors and processes that promote "positive" relations in team and organizational environments. For example, his dissertation topic focuses on the conditions that promote forgiving stances between traditionally adversarial stakeholder groups.

# PART II

## *Chapter 7*

**George Land Ph.D.**, Chairman of the Farsight Group, is a General Systems scientist. His seminal book *Grow or Die* created a revolution in thinking about how organizational growth really works. The revolution continued with *Breakpoint and Beyond: Mastering the Future–Today*. where he charts the course for renewal, innovation and success in the new millenium. The Farsight Group provides innovation systems to a wide variety of organizations and governments, world wide. George Land's work on creativity has earned him the Lifetime Achievement Award from the Creative Education Foundation and the Innovation Network named their national award the **George Land World Class Innovation Award** in honor of his contributions to the field. Dr. Land has been elected a Fellow of the New York Academy of Sciences, the World Business Academy and a Senior Fellow of The University of Minnesota. His inventions include the first computer-assisted collaborative decision-support and creativity systems. Dr. Land's listings include Who's Who in America and Who's Who in the World.

**Greg Zlevor** is the president of Westwood International and founder of the Leadership Project. He works in the area of executive development, change management, teamwork creation, and organizational improvement. He consults to Fortune 100 companies as well as non-profits. Mr. Zlevor spent twelve years working with M. Scott Peck doing group dynamics and community building, seven years on staff at Boston College as a chaplain, and three years leading Arthur Andersen's National Team on Leadership Development (1997-2000). His unique experience and skills make him a sought after designer and implementer of organizational change and improvement. Past and present clients include Honeywell, GE, GE Capital, Sabre, Singapore Police Force, Intel, and United Airlines.

## Chapter 8

**Larry Susskind** is a professor at MIT and Harvard on negotiation and consensus building. He is the Director of the MIT-Harvard Public Disputes Program at Harvard Law School. Professor Susskind is one of the country's most experienced public and environmental dispute mediators and a leading figure in the dispute resolution field. He has served as court-appointed special master, trainer, and a mediator for neighborhood, municipal, state, and national agencies and organizations in North America, Europe, and the Far East. Professor Susskind is President of the Consensus Building Institute, a not-for-profit organization that provides mediation and dispute system design services to public and private clients worldwide. CBI facilitated the Policy Dialogue on Trade and the Environment that brought senior GATT/WTO officials together with international leaders of environmental organizations. Professor Susskind was the founder and Senior Editor of Environmental Impact Assessment Review, a peer-reviewed journal published in New York and the Netherlands from 1981-1996. He is also the publisher of Consensus, a quarterly newspaper distributed by the Public Disputes Network. Professor Susskind is the author or co-author of fifteen books, including Dealing With An Angry Public: The Mutual Gains Approach to Resolving Disputes, Reinventing Congress for the 21st Century: A Blueprint for Bringing Participation and Excellence to American Politics, Environmental Diplomacy: Negotiating More Effective Global Agreements, Breaking the Impasse: Consensual Approaches to Resolving Public Disputes, Negotiating Environmental Agreements: How to Avoid Escalating Confrontation, Needless Costs, and Unnecessary Litigation, Negotiating on Behalf of Others, The Consensus Building Handbook: A Comprehensive Guide to Reaching Agreement, Better Environmental Policy Studies: How to Design and Conduct More Effective Analyses and Transboundary Environmental Negotiation: New Approaches to Global Cooperation. In addition, Professor Susskind has published more than 85 book chapters, articles, working papers, and consulting reports.

## Chapter 9

**Judith H. Katz, Ed.D.,** is Executive Vice President of The Kaleel Jamison Consulting Group. Drawing on more than twenty years of experience in strategic culture change work, Judith helps clients achieve long-term, sustainable change by connecting business strategies (including initiatives for quality, leadership, empowerment, and teamwork) to efforts that leverage diversity and create cultures of inclusion. She serves on the Boards of Directors for Social Venture Network and The Group for Cultural Documentation. She is also a member of the Diversity Collegium, a think tank of renowned diversity professionals in the United States. Judith has published over forty articles on issues related to change management, the development of high performing organizations, and issues of oppression and diversity. She is the author of White Awareness: Handbook for Anti-Racism Training (University of Oklahoma Press, 1978) and co-author, with Frederick A. Miller, of The Inclusion Breakthrough: Unleashing the Real Power of Diversity (Berrett-Koehler, 2002).

## Chapter 10

**Steve Barnett** (Ph.D. in Anthropology from the University of Chicago) has an international reputation for his expertise in consumer research and scenario planning-based market strategy (especially in the financial, automobile, consumer/package goods, pharmaceutical, and energy sectors). Steve created the field of business anthropology when he founded The Cultural Analysis Group. He has held senior executive positions with Citibank, Ogilvy & Mather, Nissan North America, GBN (Global Business Network) and is now EVP at SmartRevenue, a consumer research and strategy consultancy. Steve's insights and accomplishments have been published in business books (including "The Nissan Report") and periodicals (including Advertising Age, American Demographics, and European Management Journal). He is currently Adjunct Professor at The Wharton School and has also taught at Princeton, Brown, and MIT. Steve is on numerous corporate advisory boards and thought Leadership groups for major companies, and has been an advisor to the U.S. Congress, the OECD, and Steven Spielberg.

## Chapter 11

**Scott Ventrella** is adjunct professor at Fordham University's Graduate School of Business where he teaches a full-credit course on applying quality management principles to balancing one's life. He is a visiting professor at Columbia University, and has been a guest lecturer at a number of schools and universities including the University of Connecticut, Dartmouth, and NYU's Stern School. Most recently, he was a featured speaker and panelist at Harvard Business School's "Dean's Conference on Leadership, Values, and Spirituality." In May 2001, he published his first book, "The Power of Positive Thinking in Business: 10 Traits for Maximum Results" (Simon & Schuster/Free Press) which has been translated in over 14 languages. He has completed his second book, "The Business of Living–Redefining the Meaning of Success," for expected publication in 2003. Scott recently appeared on CNNfn and ABC News World This Morning to discuss the topics of leadership and integrity in business. He has an MS in Psychology and a BBA in Marketing, both from Western Connecticut State University. Scott is a dynamic speaker who gives frequent keynotes to professional associations and societies.

## Chapter 12

**Bill Hawkins** is an independent consultant specializing in leadership development, performance management, and organizational change. In association with The Alliance for Strategic Leadership and Innovative Resources Consultant Group he as worked with and conducted leadership training in over twenty Fortune 500 companies in 17 countries. Listed in Who's Who in International Business, Bill was a contributing author in The Peter Drucker Foundation book The Organization of the Future, 1997. He also contributed in the book coaching for Leadership, 2000.

**Lori Riordan** has over ten years of hands on experience managing high growth organizations through the transition from small entrepreneurial companies to midsize high growth corporations. She was responsible for the start up of the Human Resources function for both Martha Stewart Living Omnimedia and Bloomberg Financial in New York. An H R council member of The Conference Board, Lori is currently an independent consultant advising Fortune 500 organizations.

## Chapter 13

**Dr. Jodi Knox** is president of Action Dialogue Associates, specializing in the creation and application of dialogue approaches that lead to shared understanding and committed action. Jodi was formerly a consultant with Metaplan, an international training and moderation firm. Jodi maintains alliances with Executive Development Associates (EDA), Metaplan, and the Alliance for Strategic Leadership (A4SL). She has extensive experience and training in strategic leadership development specializing in behaviorally-focused executive coaching for leaders. Bringing significant industry experience to her consulting work, Jodi has designed and implemented new communications and dialogue approaches for action and developed talent strategies and tactics to meet demands for business required talent. With a strong bias towards results, Dr. Knox has conducted practical research with Fortune 50 companies on leadership development programs to evaluate and leverage the outcomes and business impact of such initiatives. Jodi collaborated with worldrenowned authors demonstrating the power of storytelling to convey leadership and learning in *Learning Journeys: Top Management Experts Share Hard-Earned Lessons on Becoming Great mentors and Leaders (Davies-Black)*. Other publications include: *Global Leadership Development, Action Learning & 360 feedback:*

*A Case Study. Action Dialogue: Developing Leadership Effectiveness at the Individual and Organization Levels Through Action Learning.*

## Chapter 14

**Ryan Mathews** is the co-author of the best-selling The Myth of Excellence (Crown Business, 2001) and The Deviant's Advantage (Crown Business, 2002). An internationally renowned futurist and business observer, Mathews is a popular business speaker and consultant with clients in industries as diverse as advertising, consulting and consumer products.

## Chapter 15

**Stu Noble, MEd,** is President of 3D Learning LLC and Noble & Associates Consulting, having 18 years experience in various aspects of Human Resources and Organizaitonal Development and Learning. Prior to forming his own enterprises, Stu spent five years as a Senior Consultant with Block Petrella Weisbord, where he specialized in high involvement Strategic Planning and Work Redesign, as well as Leadership and Team Development. His specialties have since expanded to include simulation-based learning (including his own Vortex and Tall Ships) and Virtual Team Development. Among Stu's list of clients include United Airlines, Motorola, Conectiv, Ocean Spray, Rohm & Haas, Canon, Americredit, Natural Lands Trust, St. Vincent Hospital, Corning-Scicor, Textron. Aventis, and Schneider Electric. Stu has also been a Presenter/Facilitator at several professional conferences, including Linkage's 'Best of OD', ASTD, OD Network, ISPI and AQP. He has been published in the OD Practitioner ("Using Simulations to Accelerate Organizational Learning and Change" )and The Handbook of Best Practices for Teams (Site Visit Resource Guide) and has authored several other articles, among them 'Starting Up Your Virtual Team' and 'The Emergent Team'. Stu is an Adjunct Professor in the HRD Department at Villanova University.

## Chapter 16

**William J. Rothwell** is Professor of Human Resource Development, Department of Adult Education, Instructional Systems and Workforce Education and Development, Pennsylvania State University and is also Director of Penn State's Institute for Research in Training and Development. He has authored, coauthored, edited or co-edited over 50 books. Among his best-known works are Rothwell, W. Effective Succession Planning: Ensuring Leadership Continuity and Building Talent from Within, 2nd ed. (New York: Amacom, 2000); Dubois, D. and Rothwell, W. The Competency Toolkit. 2 vols. (Amherst, MA: Human Resource Development

Press); Rothwell, W. The Action Learning Guidebook: A Real-Time Strategy for Problem-Solving, Training Design, and Employee Development (San Francisco: Jossey-Bass/Pfeiffer); and Rothwell, W. and Kazanas, H. Building In-House Leadership and Management Development

# PART III

## *Chapter 17*

**David Ulrich** has been ranked by Business Week as #1 management educator. He has also been listed in Forbes as one of the "world's top five" business coaches." And he received the George Petitpas Memorial Award from World Federation of Personnel Management for lifetime contributions to human resource profession. David has published over 90 articles and book chapters. His books include: Organizational Capability: Competing from the Inside/Out (with Dale Lake) (published by Wiley); The Boundaryless Organization: Breaking the Chains of Organization Structure (with Ron Ashkenas, Steve Kerr, Todd Jick) (Jossey Bass); Human Resource Champions: The Next Agenda for Adding Value and Delivering Results (Harvard Business Press); Tomorrow's (HR) Management (with Gerry Lake and Mike Losey) (Wiley); Learning Capability: Generating * Generalizing Ideas with Impact (with Arthur Yeung, Mary Ann Von Glinow, Steve Nason) (Oxford); Results Based Leadership: How Leaders Build the Business and Improve the Bottom Line (with Norm Smallwood and Jack Zenger) (Harvard Business Press); HR Scorecard: Linking People, Strategy, and Performance (with Brian Becker and Mark Huselid) (Harvard Business Press); GE Workout (with Steve Kerr and Ron Ashkenas) (McGraw Hill)

**Norm Smallwood** is co-founder and President of Results-Based Leadership Inc. Results-Based Leadership provides education, tools and consulting services that increase organization and leadership capability to deliver the right results the right way. He has also authored Why The Bottom Line Isn't: How to Build Value through People and Organizations Wiley, April 2003. Dave and Norm also co-authored, Results-Based Leadership (with Jack Zenger). Norm worked in-house, at Procter & Gamble and at Exxon. At P&G he participated in the start-up of a successful cellulose plant in Georgia, implementing self-managed work teams to make the liners for Pampers diapers. It was too humid in Georgia, so he moved to Esso Resources Canada Ltd. in Calgary, Alberta and worked in R&D and Exploration as an organization effectiveness consultant. Norm is co-author of Real Time Strategy: Improvising Team-Based Planning for a Fast Changing World, Wiley & Sons, 1993 (which was part of their portable MBA series) and of Results-Based Leadership: How Leaders Build the Business and Improve the Bottom Line, Harvard Business School Press, 1999 (which was named book of the year by SHRM). His current book with Dave Ulrich, Why the Bottom Line ISN'T!: How to Build Value through People and Organizations will be published in April 2003 by Wiley. He has published more than 50 articles in leading journals and newspapers and has contributed chapters to multiple books.

## Chapter 18

**Jim Dowling** has built a series of careers in product engineering, quality improvement, information technology management, business development, and consulting and leadership development. A unique blend of systems thinking (engineering and IT), business management (three startups and large corporation), teaching (writer and lecturer), leadership (CIO, consultant and coach) and international experience delivering result through others has equipped Jim to see patterns and make valuable connections in many fields and industries. Now a Partner at Results-Based Leadership, Jim has been a popular speaker at IQPC, DCI, SIM, CIO and other conferences and seminars. He has also led "Thought Provoking" workshops at Boston University, London School of Economics and Political Science, The Technikum Winterthur and Babson College. Jim's current project Capable Company: building capabilities that make companies work (Blackwell, April 2003) provides business leaders with a method for taking their strategy to action through organization and business capabilities.

**Rich Lynch** is a partner at Results-Based Leadership. He has written three books, including his best seller: Measure Up! Rich's is also the co-author of Capable Company: Building Capabilities that make strategy work (Blackwell, April 2003). Prior to joining Results-Based Leadership, Rich was co-founder and partner at Corporate Renaissance, Inc., a firm focused on business process design and improvement and the balanced scorecard. His clients included GE Capital (where he was part of the six sigma team), The Prudential, Dialogic, State Street Corporation and US West. Rich has been a popular speaker at IQPC, IIR, AME, and other conferences and seminars. He was also a top ranked trainer at GE Capital's Six Sigma program. He has also authored dozens of articles in journals such as National Productivity Review, Quality Progress, and Executive Excellence and has contributed to several other books on leadership best practices. Rich received his MBA from the University of Massachusetts and a BS in Finance from Boston College.

## Chapter 19

**Ivy Ross** is Senior Vice President of Design and Development Girls Division of Mattel Inc. She oversees the design and development of all products and packaging for girls including Barbie dolls, accessories, Diva Stars, What's her Face, Ello,

Polly Pocket as well as six other unique brands, a total of approximately two billion dollars. In addition, Ross is in charge of the model shop, sound lab, and chem. Lab and sculpting functions for all of Mattel products. Ross' education was in design and psychology and included time at The Harvard Business School. Ross' high level background in fashion and design spans more than two decades. She came to Mattel from Calvin Klein, where she led a turnaround in men's accessories. Prior to Calvin Klein, Ross served as Vice President of product design and development for Coach, the maker of high–end leather goods and accessories. She also held positions at Liz Claiborne, Bausch & Lomb and Swatch Watch. In addition, Ross was a founding partner of two independent design firms and a retail store. She has a proven ability as a design leader and also possesses a strong sense of business management. A world renowned artist, Ross' innovative metal work in jewelry is in the permanent collection of 12 international museums, including the Smithsonian in Washington D.C., the Victorian Albert Museum in London and the Cooper Hewitt Museum in New York City, among others. A winner of the prestigious National Endowment for the Arts grant, Ross has also received the Women in Design Award and Diamond International award for her creative designs. She has served as a juror, teacher, and critic in a wide range of product categories.

**David Kuehler** is the Director of Project Platypus, an innovative product development initiative within the Girls Division of Mattel Inc. Kuehler's background encompasses over fifteen years in the design and entertainment fields. His education is in design, engineering and theater. Before joining Mattel, Kuehler was Director, Creative Development and Programming for Robert Redford's Sundance Film Centers. At the Walt Disney Company, Kuehler was instrumental in the design development and rollout of Club Disney, a location based entertainment concept. He produced initiatives for Walt Disney Imagineering, R&D, Disney Online and ESPN Zone. As an Instructor and Speaker at Art Center College of Design, he taught Spatial Graphics and successfully led students in a project sponsored by Intel Corporation, creating user interfaces and products for the next generation of wireless, personal computers. Kuehler, a versatile thinker with a unique ability to both conceive and implement innovative ideas, co-founded an entertainment design and production company. He has developed shows for Nelvana Communications and The Sundance Channel. He is currently co-creating children's programming with Britt Allcroft, best known for her popular Thomas the Tank Engine series.

## Chapter 20

**Lawrence Peters** is Professor of Management at the Neeley School of Business at Texas Christian University. He has published over 50 articles in leading journals and books, has written two casebooks, and is senior editor of the Encyclopedic Dictionary of Human Resource Management. He has been the recipient of college and university teaching awards, and specializes in the area of leadership, where he currently teaches leadership courses at the undergraduate, MBA and Executive MBA levels. He also has a consulting practice, called Leadership Solutions, and consults with private and public organizations in a variety of areas associated with change efforts. His recent client list includes Bell Helicopter, Chubb Insurance, Ford Motor Company, The Hartford Insurance Company, Lockheed Martin, Sprint PCS, Shared Medical Services, Verizon Communications, and Whole Foods Market.

**Joseph Grenny** is a founding partner in VitalSmarts, Inc., a management consulting and training company located in Orem, Utah. Prior to starting his own company, Joseph spent six years as an executive with the Covey Leadership Center. In over fifteen years of organization development consulting, he has worked with senior leaders in Fortune 100 and government organizations to bring about clear and measurable culture change. Joseph has authored or co-authored numerous articles in the areas of personal and organizational effectiveness, and co-authored The Balancing Act: Mastering the Competing Demands of Leadership and Crucial Conversations: Tools for Talking When Stakes are High. The latter book is a NY Times and WSJ best-seller. Joseph has designed and delivered major culture-change initiatives for AT&T, Coregis Insurance, IBM, the State of California, and Lockheed Martin, among others.

## *Chapter 21*

**Dr. Deborah Rozman** is a businesswoman, psychologist and author. As Executive Vice President, HeartMath LLC, she has been instrumental in the development of training programs based on innovative research showing the heart as an information processing system and a central source of intelligence within the human system. As Chief Strategy Officer she oversees HeartMath's strategic alliances in training and technology. She is the author of 5 books and editor of many of the HeartMath books, including Cut-Thru, How to Care Without Becoming a Victim , and Women Lead With Their Hearts, Intui-Technology® - The New Paradigm and New Solution For The 21st Century. Dr. Deborah Rozman studied attitude change theory and psychology at the University of Chicago. Her research includes the fields of stress management and awareness development in both children and adults. Dr. Rozman's research resulted in the publication of five books that have gained her worldwide recognition. Her books have been translated into several languages. In 1979, she founded a unique alternative school which specialized in innovative approaches in educational psychology, emphasizing the development of the whole child, whole brain learning, and creative and intuitive development. She has In 1991 she helped Doc Childre found the Institute of HeartMath and served as Executive Director from 1991 to 1998. Prior to that appointment she was Executive Vice President of Biogenics, Inc. and directed their research programs with Harvard University. She has been interviewed by such major networks as ABC news on stress reduction and new heart intelligence in the workplace for high performance results.

**Doc Childre** spent over thirty years researching the relationship between stress and human performance and developing best practices for stress relief and performance enhancement for individuals and workplaces to address the emotional issues. Doc founded the non-profit Institute of HeartMath (IHM) to research the effects of mental and emotional stress on the heart, brain, and nervous system. He chairs the scientific advisory board of the Institute of HeartMath, is chairperson of HeartMath LLC, and chairperson and CEO of Quantum Intech. He has his own executive consulting company called Top Down Consulting and is a consultant to business leaders, scientists, educators, and the entertainment industry.

He is the author of seven books. In addition, his HeartMath System and proprietary technology for coherence building, called the Freeze-Framer, has been featured in *USA Today*, NBC's *Today Show*, *ABC Good Morning America*, *ABC World News Tonight*, *CNN Headline News*, *CNN.Com*, *Harvard Business Review*, *Business 2.0*, *Industry Week*, *Prevention* magazine, *Psychology Today*, *Golf* magazine, *Golf Illustrated*, *Cosmopolitan*, *Self*, *New Woman* magazine, *Muscle and Fitness*, *Men's Fitness*, *New York Newsday*, *Los Angeles Times*, *San Francisco Chronicle*, *San Jose Mercury News*, and numerous other publications and media outlets around the world.

# *Chapter 22*

**Dr. John Sullivan** is a well-known HR "guru," international speaker, author, and advisor to Fortune 500 and Global 1000 firms. Training magazine has called him a "visionary " and named him as one of its top thought leaders. FastCompany magazine called him "the Michael Jordan of hiring!" Industr y guru Gerr y Crispin called him "the Tom Peters of HR " because of his energetic presentation style. Tom Peters called his e-HR work "brilliant."

# ABOUT THE PUBLISHER AND SPONSORING ORGANIZATION

## PUBLISHER

## B.P.P.
## BEST PRACTICE PUBLICATIONS

Best Practice Publications (BPP) creates best practice studies and publications that provide you with the world's leading organizations and practitioners' most successful approaches, tools, strategies, initiatives and programs. All content is highly pragmatic and applicable back on-the-job. Many of its recent studies focus on what Fortune 500 organizations are doing to lead successful change. Such organizations as Intel, GE Capital, Hewlett Packard, and Motorola are among the many organizations that have been featured in its best practice handbooks. In addition, BPP works closely with the America's best hospitals capturing their highly successful, results-oriented, and patient-centered transformation and change practices. *Best Practice Publications, LLC* is proud to publish this fieldguide for leading change within organizations today. We have brought together the leading minds in organization development, change, and leadership development in an effort to help you enable and sustain positive change in all that you do. For more information on Best Practice Publications, visit: *www.bestpracticepublications.com* or *www.bestpracticeboard.com* .

## SPONSORING ORGANIZATION

Since 1974 the Institute for Management Studies has led the way in executive and management development. Over 400 major organizations in the U.S., Europe and Canada have made IMS a critical component of their overall developmental strategy. IMS constantly refines its model to provide maximum benefit to the over 25,000 managers a year who attend IMS programs. Throughout its history IMS has presented the leading-edge ideas of many outstanding business thinkers, many of whom are represented within the pages of this book. It is with this in mind that IMS is proud to sponsor, and be a part of, this publication. For more information on the IMS, visit: *http://www.ims-online.com/* .

# INDEX

Printed in the United States
72721LV00004B/69-82